critique
influence
change

critique confronts the world. Without dogma, without new principles, it refuses to conform and instead demands insurrection of thought. It must be ruthless, unafraid of both its results and the powers it may come into conflict with. Critique takes the world, our world, as its object, so that we may develop new ways of making it.

influence is a step from critique toward the future, when effects begin to be felt, when the ground becomes unstable, when a movement ignites. These critiques of the state of our world have influenced a generation. They are crucial guides to change.

change is when the structures shift. The books in this series take critique as their starting point and as such have influenced both their respective disciplines and thought the world over. This series is born out of our conviction that change lies not in the novelty of the future but in the realization of the thoughts of the past.

These texts are not mere interpretations or reflections, but scientific, critical, and impassioned analyses of our world. After all, the point is to change it.

ABOUT THE AUTHORS

Maria Mies is a Marxist feminist scholar who is renowned for her theory of capitalist-patriarchy, one which recognizes third world women and difference. She is a professor of sociology at Cologne University of Applied Sciences, but retired from teaching in 1993. Since the late 1960s she has been involved with feminist activism. In 1979, at the Institute of Social Studies in The Hague, she founded the Women and Development programme. Mies has written books and articles that deal with topics relating to feminism, third world issues and the environment. Her other titles published by Zed Books include *The Lace Makers of Narsapur* (1982), *Women: The Last Colony* (1988), *Patriarchy and Accumulation on a World Scale* (1999) and *The Subsistence Perspective* (1999).

Vandana Shiva, a world-renowned environmental leader and thinker, is director of the Research Foundation on Science, Technology, and Ecology. In 1993, Shiva won the Alternative Nobel Peace Prize and in 2010 was awarded the Sydney Peace Prize for her commitment to social justice. She is the author of over twenty books. Her other titles published by Zed Books are *Staying Alive* (1989), *The Violence of the Green Revolution* (1991), *Biodiversity* (1992), *Monocultures of the Mind* (1993), *Biopolitics* (1995), *Stolen Harvest* (2001), *Protect or Plunder* (2001), *Earth Democracy* (2005) and *Soil Not Oil* (2009).

ECOFEMINISM
MARIA MIES
AND VANDANA
SHIVA
WITH A FOREWORD BY
ARIEL SALLEH

BLOOMSBURY ACADEMIC
LONDON · NEW YORK · OXFORD · NEW DELHI · SYDNEY

BLOOMSBURY ACADEMIC
Bloomsbury Publishing Plc
50 Bedford Square, London, WC1B 3DP, UK
1385 Broadway, New York, NY 10018, USA
29 Earlsfort Terrace, Dublin 2, Ireland

BLOOMSBURY, BLOOMSBURY ACADEMIC and the Diana logo are
trademarks of Bloomsbury Publishing Plc

First published in Great Britain, 1993
Previous edition published in 2014
Reprinted 2021 (twice)
This edition published by Bloomsbury Academic, 2022

A catalogue record for this book is available from the British Library.

A catalogue record for this book is available from the Library of Congress.

ISBN: HB: 978-1-8564-9155-6
PB: 978-1-3503-7988-6
ePDF: 978-1-7803-2978-9
ePub: 978-1-7803-2979-6

Typeset by Kali for Women
Printed and bound in Great Britain

To find out more about our authors and books visit www.bloomsbury.com and
sign up for our newsletters.

Contents

Foreword

Ariel Salleh

The word 'ecofeminism' might be new, but the pulse behind it has always driven women's efforts to save their livelihood and make their communities safe. From the Chipko forest dwellers of North India some 300 years ago to the mothers of coalmining Appalachia right now, the struggle to create life-affirming societies goes on. It intensifies today as corporate globalization expands and contracts, leaving no stone unturned, no body unused. The partnership of Maria Mies and Vandana Shiva symbolizes this common ground among women; it speaks of a grassroots energy that is found in a movement across all continents. Ecological feminists are both street-fighters and philosophers.

'Only connect' – this sums up what the perspective is about. Ecofeminism is the only political framework I know of that can spell out the historical links between neoliberal capital, militarism, corporate science, worker alienation, domestic violence, reproductive technologies, sex tourism, child molestation, neocolonialism, Islamophobia, extractivism, nuclear weapons, industrial toxics, land and water grabs, deforestation, genetic engineering, climate change and the myth of modern progress. Ecofeminist solutions are also synergistic; the organization of daily life around subsistence fosters food sovereignty, participatory democracy and reciprocity with natural ecosystems.

It was inevitable that Mies and Shiva would join together – with their strong postcolonial insights, exposé of the twentieth century ideology of 'catch-up' development and emphasis on women's skills in protecting sustainable local economies.

Maria trained as a sociologist. Her doctoral thesis, published in English in 1980 as *Indian Women and Patriarchy: Conflicts and Dilemmas of Students and Working Women*, focused on the role conflicts of women in India, where she also investigated the capitalist exploitation of lacemaker housewives. At home she joined the feminist movement and was active in a number of social movements, including the anti-nuclear power and ecology movements. Experiences such as these shaped her teaching of women's studies at the Institute of Social Sciences in the Hague. She mapped out a feminist research methodology, and went on to apply this in a critique of Marxism, with Veronika Bennholdt-Thomsen and Claudia von Werlhof. The book *Patriarchy and Accumulation on a World Scale* was brought out by Zed Books in 1986; in 1999 she co-authored *The Subsistence Perspective*; an autobiography, *The Village and the World*, was published in 2010.

Vandana gained a Canadian Ph.D. in theoretical physics. But as a young mother concerned by the nuclear threat to life on Earth, she left her job and set up a Research Foundation for Science, Technology, and Natural Resource Policy in her hometown, Dehradun. Her first book, *Staying Alive: Women, Ecology, and Development*, was published by Zed Books in 1989. It is an empirical account of India's so-called Green Revolution, and its ultimate devastation of food crops, soils and farmers' lives. *Ecofeminism*, co-authored with Mies, appeared in 1993. Others include *Biopiracy*, a co-edited reader on biotech in 1995; *Water Wars* in 2002; and *Earth Democracy* in 2005. A recipient of many awards, Shiva lectures widely, and has been cited as one of the world's most influential women.

Mies and Shiva are the leading ecofeminist thinkers; however, from the 1970s, women everywhere were formulating ecological feminist responses to the health and environmental impacts of 'modernization' – a euphemism for the conversion of World War II technologies into profitable consumer items like nuclear energy or garden pesticides. An international literature of ecological feminism today runs to many books and articles, and it is taught as a university major, as well as in courses on ecological ethics, social and political thought, gender studies, human geography, environmental humanities and, most recently, political ecology.

That said, the public is not always clear on the relation between ecofeminism and feminism per se. The mainstream of 'feminism' has many tributaries, with different objectives and strategies. The most fundamental form of feminism is expressed when radical feminists highlight the contradictions of women's everyday experience under masculine domination. On the other hand, cultural/spiritual feminists celebrate the liberatory potential of 'feminine values', even as they acknowledge that many such attitudes are historically imposed upon women. Socialist feminists examine the unique form of women's economic exploitation as unpaid domestic labour in the global market. Liberal feminists simply seek equal opportunities for women, leaving this same capitalist society intact. Poststructural feminists look at how women are socially constructed and positioned by language in the popular media, literature, religion, law, and so on.

With ecofeminism, the political focus turns outwards. Its first premiss is that the 'material' resourcing of women and of nature are structurally interconnected in the capitalist patriarchal system. Ecofeminists may draw on other strands of feminism at times, but liberal and postmodern approaches are generally unhelpful for building global political alliances with workers, peasants, indigenous peoples, and other victims of the Western drive to accumulation. A critically important facet of ecofeminism is that it offers an alternative to the relativism that takes over as capitalist commodification homogenizes cultures. Mies and Shiva paint a sharp contrast between the social decay of passive consumerism and the social vitality of skilful, self-sufficient and autonomous livelihood economies: subsistence.

In the twenty years since *Ecofeminism* was first published, every key socio-economic and cultural–psychological problem discussed is still current – and many situations have even worsened under the stranglehold of global neoliberalism. The methodology of power is 'divide and rule'. So, as Mies points out, affluent countries promote a public fear of terrorism in order to justify self-interested foreign interventions. Shiva observes that, in her own country, the imposition of free-trade-related structural adjustments lead to so much disorganization and stress that some communities report an 800 per cent increase in attacks on women. But the authors' most powerful deconstructive lens is applied to the 'reductionism' of contemporary science, a dogma that is deeply informed by old patriarchal motivations.

Had the message of this book been assimilated twenty years ago, it might well have forestalled many unhappy outcomes. For example, *Ecofeminism* explains how both financial and environmental crises are sex-gendered. Moreover, the book anticipates why each crisis has now energized new kinds of political resistance – youth, precarious workers, refugees from the geographical periphery. Today, labour is joined, if not led, by alter-globalization activists from the World Social Forum, Via Campesina, the Indigenous Environmental Network, World March of Women, Occupy and Animal Liberation. The call is for degrowth, commoning and *buen vivir.* And I can think of no better primer than this book, for people wanting an inclusive diagnosis of our troubled times.

'Only connect'. No other political perspective – liberalism, socialism, feminism, environmentalism – can integrate what ecofeminism does: why the Roma people are still treated like animals; why women do 65 per cent of the world's work for 10 per cent of its wages; why internet images of sexually abused children generate millions of dollars; why chickens are bred only for livers and wings; or why the Earth itself is manipulated as a weapon of war. Species loss is endemic; peak water is on the way; soils are losing organic integrity; the atmosphere is riven by angry storms. As Vandana says: 'We are in the midst of an epic contest ... between the rights of Mother Earth and the rights of corporations and militarized states using obsolete world-views.' This is the challenge of our generation.

Ariel Salleh,
The University of Sydney,
November 2013

Preface
to the critique influence change edition

Vandana Shiva

When Maria Mies and I wrote *Ecofeminism* two decades ago, we were addressing the emerging challenges of our times. Every threat we identified has grown deeper. And with it has grown the relevance of an alternative to capitalist patriarchy if humanity and the diverse species with which we share the planet are to survive.

Ecofeminism was first published one year after the Earth Summit, where two important treaties were signed by the governments of the world: the Convention on Biological Diversity and the UN Framework Convention on Climate Change. There was no World Trade Organization. However, two years after *Ecofeminism*, the WTO was established, privileging corporate rights, commerce and profits, and further undermining the rights of the Earth, the rights of women and the rights of future generations. We wrote about what globalization implied for nature and women. Every crisis we mentioned is deeper; every expression of violence more brutal. Diverse Women for Diversity was created to respond to a corporate globalization that was reducing the world to monocultures controlled by global corporations. We were in Seattle, and collectively stopped the WTO Ministerial in 1999. Yet new 'free trade' arrangements, like the EU–India Free Trade Agreement, the US–India Agriculture Agreement, designed to put India's food and agriculture in the hands of Monsanto, Cargill and Walmart, the Trans-Pacific Partnership and the US–Europe Partnership, are being pushed undemocratically to expand corporate rule even as we see the ruins it has left: ravaged farms, displaced people, devastated ecosystems, disappearing diversity, climate chaos, divided societies, and an intensification of violence against women.

The intensification of violence against women

Violence against women is as old as patriarchy. Traditional patriarchy has structured our world-views and mindsets, our social and cultural worlds on the basis of domination over women, and the denial of their full humanity and right to equality. But it has intensified and become more pervasive in the recent past. It has taken on more brutal forms, like the murder of the Delhi gang-rape victim and the suicide of the 17-year-old rape victim in Chandigarh.

Rape cases and cases of violence against women have increased over the years. The National Crime Records Bureau (NCRB) reported 10,068 rape cases in 1990, which increased to 16,496 in 2000. With 24,206 cases in 2011, rape cases increased an incredible 873 per cent compared to 1971, when NCRB first started to record rape statistics. Delhi has emerged as the rape capital of India, accounting for 25 per cent of cases.

The movement to stop this violence must be sustained until justice is done for every one of our daughters and sisters who has been violated. And while we intensify our struggle for justice for women, we need to also ask why rape cases have increased 240 per cent since the 1990s when the new economic policies were introduced.

Could there be a connection between the growth of violent, undemocratically imposed, unjust and unfair economic policies and the intensification in brutality of crimes against women? I believe there is. I am not suggesting that violence against women begins with neoliberal economics. I am deeply aware of the gender biases in our traditional cultures and social organizations. I stand empowered today because people before me fought against the exclusions and prejudices against women and children – my grandfather sacrificed his life for women's equality, and my mother was a feminist before the word existed.

Violence against women has taken on new and more vicious forms as traditional patriarchal structures have hybridized with the structures of capitalist patriarchy. We need to examine the connections between the violence of unjust, non-sustainable economic systems and the growing frequency and brutality of violence against women. We need to see how the structures of traditional patriarchy merge with the emerging structures of capitalist patriarchy to intensify violence against women.

Cyclones and hurricanes have always occurred. But as the Orissa supercyclone, Cyclone Nargis, Cyclone Aila, Hurricane Katrina and Hurricane Sandy show, the intensity and frequency of cyclones has increased with climate change.

Our society has traditionally had a bias against the girl child. But the epidemic of female feticide and the disappearance of 30 million unborn girls has taken that bias to new proportions and levels of violence. And it is to this context of the dynamics of more brutal and more vicious violence against women and multiple, interconnected forms of violence that the processes unleashed by neoliberalism are contributory factors.

First, the economic model focusing myopically on 'growth' begins with violence against women by discounting their contribution to the economy. The more the government talks *ad nauseam* about 'inclusive growth' and 'financial inclusion', the more it excludes the contributions of women to the economy and society. According to patriarchal economic models, production for sustenance is counted as 'non-production'. The transformation of value into disvalue, labour into non-labour and knowledge into non-knowledge is achieved by the most powerful number that rules our lives: the patriarchal construct of GDP, gross domestic product, which commentators have started to call the 'gross domestic problem'.

The national accounting systems which are used for calculating growth in terms of GDP are based on the assumption that if producers consume what they produce, they do not in fact produce at all, because they fall outside the production boundary. The production boundary is a political creation that, in its workings, excludes regenerative and renewable production cycles from the area of production. Hence all women who produce for their families, children, community and society are treated as 'non-productive' and 'economically inactive'. When economies are confined to the marketplace, economic self-sufficiency is perceived as economic deficiency. The devaluation of women's work, and of work done in subsistence economies of the South, is the natural outcome of a production boundary constructed by capitalist patriarchy.

By restricting itself to the values of the market economy, as defined by capitalist patriarchy, the production boundary ignores economic value in the two vital economies which are necessary to ecological and human survival: nature's economy and the sustenance economy. In these economies, economic value is a measure of how the Earth's life and human life are protected. The currency is life-giving processes, not cash or the market price.

Second, a model of capitalist patriarchy which excludes women's work and wealth creation in the mind deepens the violence by displacing women from their livelihoods and alienating them from the natural resources on which their livelihoods depend – their land, their forests, their water, their seeds and biodiversity.

Economic reforms based on the idea of limitless growth in a limited world can only be maintained if the powerful grab the resources of the vulnerable. The resource-grab that is essential for 'growth' creates a culture of rape – rape of the Earth, of local self-reliant economies, of women. The only way in which this 'growth' is 'inclusive' is by its inclusion of ever larger numbers in its circle of violence.

I have repeatedly stressed that the rape of the Earth and rape of women are intimately linked – both metaphorically, in shaping world-views, and materially, in shaping women's everyday lives. The deepening economic vulnerability of women makes them more vulnerable to all forms of violence, including sexual assault, as we found out during a series of public hearings on the impact of economic reforms on women organized by the National Commission on Women and the Research Foundation for Science, Technology and Ecology.

Third, economic reforms lead to the subversion of democracy and privatization of government. Economic systems influence political systems; governments talk of economic reforms as if they have nothing to do with politics and power. They talk of keeping politics out of economics, even while they impose an economic model shaped by the politics of a particular gender and class. Neoliberal reforms work against democracy. We have seen this recently in the Indian government pushing through 'reforms' to bring in Walmart through FDI in retail. Corporate-driven reforms create a convergence of economic and political power, a deepening of inequalities, and a growing separation of the political class from the will of the people they are supposed to represent. This is at the root of the disconnect between politicians and the public, which we experienced during the protests that have grown since the Delhi gang rape.

Worse, an alienated political class is afraid of its own citizens. This explains the increasing use of police to crush nonviolent citizen protests, as we have witnessed in Delhi; the torture of Soni Sori in Bastar; the arrest of Dayamani Barla in Jharkhand; the thousands of cases against the communities struggling against the nuclear power plant in Kudankulam. A privatized corporate state must rapidly become a police state. This is why politicians surround themselves with ever-increasing security, diverting the police from their important duties to protect women and ordinary citizens.

Fourth, the economic model shaped by capitalist patriarchy is based on the commodification of everything, including women.

When we stopped the WTO Ministerial in Seattle, our slogan was 'Our World is Not for Sale'.

An economics of the deregulation of commerce and of the privatization and commodification of seeds and food, land and water, and women and children degrades social values, deepens patriarchy and intensifies violence against women. Economic systems influence culture and social values. An economics of commodification creates a culture of commodification, where everything has a price and nothing has value.

The growing culture of rape is a social externality of economic reforms. We need to institutionalize social audits of the neoliberal policies which are a central instrument of patriarchy in our times. If there was a social audit of corporatizing our seed sector, 28,400 farmers would not have been pushed to suicide in India since the new economic policies were introduced. If there was a social audit of the corporatization of our food and agriculture, we would not have every fourth Indian hungry, every third woman malnourished, and every second child wasted and stunted due to severe malnutrition. India today would not be the Republic of Hunger that Utsa Patnaik has written about.

We must see the continuum of different forms of violence against women: from female feticide to economic exclusion and sexual assault. We need to continue the movement for social reforms required to guarantee safety, security and equality for women, building on the foundations laid during our independence movement and continued by the feminist movement over the last half-century. The agenda for social reforms, social justice and equality has been derailed by the agenda of 'economic reforms' set by capitalist patriarchy.

And while we do all this we need to change the ruling paradigm that reduces society to the economy, reduces the economy to the market, and is imposed on us in the name of 'growth', fuelling the intensity of crimes against women while deepening social and economic inequality. Society and economy are not insulated from each other; the processes of social reforms and economic reforms can no longer be separated. We need economic reforms based on the foundation of social reforms that correct the gender inequality in society, rather than aggravating all forms of injustice, inequality and violence. Ending violence against women needs to also include moving beyond the violent economy shaped by capitalist patriarchy to nonviolent, sustainable, peaceful economies that give respect to women and the Earth.

The Anthropocene age: humanity's choice
to be destructive or creative

When we wrote *Ecofeminism* we raised the issue of reductionist, mechanistic science and the attitude of mastery over and conquest of nature as an expression of capitalist patriarchy. Today the contest between an ecological and feminist world-view and a world-view shaped by capitalist patriarchy is more intense than ever.

This contest is particularly intense in the area of food. GMOs embody the vision of capitalist patriarchy. They perpetuate the idea of 'master molecules' and mechanistic reductionism long after the life sciences have gone beyond reductionism, and patents on life reflect the capitalist patriarchal illusion of creation. There is no science in viewing DNA as a 'master molecule' and genetic engineering as a game of Lego, in which genes are moved around without any impact on the organism or the environment. This is a new pseudo-science that has taken on the status of a religion.

Science cannot justify patents on life and seed. Shuffling genes is not making life; living organisms make themselves. Patents on seed mean denying the contributions of millions of years of evolution and thousands of years of farmers' breeding. One could say that a new religion, a new cosmology, a new creation myth is being put in place, where biotechnology corporations like Monsanto replace Creation as 'creators'. GMO means 'God move over'. Stewart Brand has actually said 'We are as gods and we had better get used to it.'

Scientists are now saying we have entered a new age, the Anthropocene age, the age in which our species, the human, is becoming the most significant force on the planet. Current climate change and species extinction are driven by human activities and the very large ecological footprint of our species.

Climate catastrophes and extreme climate events are already taking lives – the floods in Thailand in 2011 and in Pakistan and Ladakh in 2010, the forest fires in Russia, more frequent and intense cyclones and hurricanes, and severe droughts are examples of how humans have destabilized the climate system of our self-regulated planet, which has given us a stable climate for the past 10,000 years. Humans have pushed 75 per cent of agricultural biodiversity to extinction because of industrial farming. Between 3 and 300 species are being pushed to extinction every day.

How the planet and human beings evolve into the future will depend on how we understand the human impact on the planet. If we continue to understand our role as rooted in the old paradigm of capitalist patriarchy – based on a mechanistic world-view, an industrial, capital-centred competitive economy, and a culture of dominance, violence, war and ecological and human irresponsibility – we will witness the rapid unfolding of increasing climate catastrophe, species extinction, economic collapse, and human injustice and inequality.

This is the destructive Anthropocene of human arrogance and hubris. It is displayed in the attempt of scientists to do geo-engineering, genetic engineering and synthetic biology as technological fixes to climate crisis, the food crisis and the energy crisis. However, they will only aggravate old problems and create new ones. We have already seen this with genetic engineering: it was supposed to increase food production but has failed to increase crop yields; it was supposed to reduce chemical use but has increased the use of pesticides and herbicides; it was supposed to control weeds and pests but has instead created superweeds and superpests.

We are in the midst of an epic contest – the contest between the rights of Mother Earth and the rights of corporations and militarized states using obsolete world-views and paradigms to accelerate the war against the planet and people. This contest is between the laws of Gaia and the laws of the market and warfare. It is a contest between war against Planet Earth and peace with it. Planetary war is taking place with geo-engineering – creating artificial volcanoes, fertilizing the oceans with iron filings, putting reflectors in the sky to stop the sun from shining on the Earth, displacing the real problem of man's violence against the Earth, and the arrogant ignorance in dealing with it.

In 1997, Edward Teller co-authored a white paper 'Prospects for Physics-based Modulation of Global Change', where he advocated the large-scale introduction of metal particulates into the upper atmosphere to apply an effective 'sunscreen'.

The Pentagon is looking to breed immortal synthetic organisms with the goal of eliminating 'the randomness of natural evolutionary advancement'. What is being done with the climate is being done with the evolutionary code of the universe, with total indifference to the consequences.

Synthetic biology is an industry that creates 'designer organisms to act as living factories'. 'With synthetic biology, hopes are that by building biological systems from the ground up, they can create biological systems that will function like computers or factories.' The goal is to make biology easier to engineer using 'bio bricks':

> Use of standardized parts, following a formalized design process, the engineers approach to biology makes biology an engineering discipline, requiring the reduction of biological complexity. An engineering approach to biology based on the principles of standardization, decompiling and abstraction and heavy reliance on information technologies.

However, 'engineering' plants and ecosystems has undesired and unpredictable ecological impacts. For example, the Green Revolution destroyed biodiversity, water resources, soil fertility and even the atmosphere, with 40 per cent of greenhouse gases coming from industrialized, globalized agriculture. The second Green Revolution has led to the emergence of superpests and superweeds and to the increased use of herbicides and pesticides.

Synthetic biology, as the third Green Revolution, will appropriate the biomass of the poor, even while selling 'artificial life'. There is an intense scramble for the Earth's resources and ownership of nature. Big oil, pharmaceutical, food and seed companies are joining hands to appropriate biodiversity and biomass – the living carbon – to extend the age of fossil fuel and dead carbon. Corporations view the 75 per cent biomass used by nature and local communities as 'wasted'. They would like to appropriate the living wealth of the planet for making biofuels, chemicals and plastics. This will dispossess the poor of the very sources of their lives and livelihoods. The instruments for the new dispossession are technological tools of genetic engineering and synthetic biology and intellectual property rights.

Turning the living wealth of the planet into the property of corporations through patents is a recipe for deepening poverty and ecological crisis. Biodiversity is our living commons – the basis of life. We are part of nature, not her masters and owners. Bestowing intellectual property rights on life forms, living resources and living processes is an ethical, ecological and economic perversion. We need to recognize the rights of Mother Earth and therefore the intrinsic value of all her species and living processes.

The destructive Anthropocene is not the only future. We can undergo a paradigm shift. A change in consciousness is already taking place across the world. We can look at the destructive impact our species has had on the planet's biodiversity, ecosystems and climate systems and prevent it. The ecological shift involves not seeing ourselves as outside the ecological web of life, as masters, conquerors and owners of the Earth's resources. It means seeing ourselves as members of the Earth family, with responsibility to care for other species and life on Earth in all its diversity, from the tiniest microbe to the largest mammal. It creates the imperative to live, produce and consume within ecological limits and within our share of ecological space, without encroaching on the rights of other species and other people. It is a shift that recognizes that science has already made a change in paradigm from separation to non-separability and interconnectedness, from the mechanistic and reductionist to the relational and holistic.

At the economic level it involves going beyond the artificial and even false categories of perpetual economic growth, so-called free trade, consumerism and competitiveness. It means shifting to a focus on planetary and human well-being, to living economies, to living well, to not having more, to valuing cooperation rather than competitiveness. These are the shifts being made by indigenous communities, peasants, women and young people in new movements such as the Indignants in Europe and Occupy Wall Street in the USA.

This involves working as co-creators and co-producers with the Earth. This demands using our intelligence to conserve and heal, not conquer and wound. This is the creative and constructive Anthropocene of Earth Democracy, based on ecological humility in place of arrogance, and ecological responsibility in place of careless and blind exercise of power, control and violence. For humans to protect life on Earth and their own future we need to become deeply conscious of the rights of Mother Earth, our duties towards her and our compassion for all her beings. Our world has been structured by capitalist patriarchy around fictions and abstractions like 'capital', 'corporations' and 'growth', which have allowed the unleashing of the negative forces of the destructive Anthropocene. We need to get grounded again – in the Earth, her diversity, and her living processes – and unleash the positive forces of a creative Anthropocene.

We will either make peace with the Earth or face extinction as humans, even as we push millions of other species to extinction. Continuing the war against the Earth is not an intelligent option.

Maria Mies

When I read the Introduction to the 1993 edition of *Ecofeminism* again, I find that today – twenty years later – hardly anything needs to change. All our concerns about the oppression of women and the exploitation of nature, all our anger and critique of the ruthless killing of our common Mother Earth are still the same.

Yet, I ask myself: Is everything just still the *same*? Or have things changed in a way that makes a new edition of *Ecofeminism* necessary? What are these new issues? Or is there a continuity between then and now? And is there an answer to the burning question: What is the alternative? In this preface, I'll try to answer these questions.

What is still the same today?

Violence against nature and women

One of the problems that remains the same is the further construction of nuclear power plants all over the world. Around 1993 there were broad movements against atomic industries in the United States as well as in Europe. Thousands of people from all strata of society took to the streets. People in Germany understood immediately that nuclear power plants were not constructed primarily to produce energy for peaceful purposes but clearly to fight the Great Enemy in the East, the Soviet Union, whose realm began behind the Berlin Wall. People were afraid that a new world war would be fought from Germany.

Feminists joined this movement right from the beginning. We not only joined the demonstrations, the protest camps and sit-ins, but organized our own anti-atomic actions. During the demonstrations we organized special 'feminist blocs'. One of our slogans was: 'In Peace War against Women Continues'. The men did not like this slogan. It was clear that the damage done by nuclear fallout could not practically be removed from the Earth. We therefore saw a connection between violence against women and children and violence against nature. We also understood that the invention of nuclear power was not just the same as any other modern technology. The men who worked on the Manhattan Project in Los Alamos did not just want to understand nature. They knew what they were doing. Brian Easley found out that they understood themselves as 'fathers'. The bomb was their 'baby', their son. Before the bomb was dropped on Hiroshima, these men had codewords for the success of their invention. If there was a big explosion, the codeword was 'Fat Man'. If there was only a small explosion, the codeword was 'Little Boy'. After the 'success' of the bomb over Hiroshima they congratulated each other about the birth of their 'Little Boy'. After Nagasaki, it was a 'Fat Man'. Congratulations! Easley therefore called the inventors of the atom bomb the 'fathers of destruction'.[1]

We understood for the first time that modern science was indeed a 'brainchild' of such modern 'fathers of destruction'. To construct new machines they do not need human women as mothers. This insight led us to a fundamental critique of modern science, a science which knows neither feelings, nor morals, nor responsibility: in order to produce this technology, in all its avatars, they need violence. We also understood that women all over the world, since the beginning of patriarchy, were also treated like 'nature', devoid of rationality, their bodies functioning in the same instinctive way as other mammals. Like nature they could be oppressed, exploited and dominated by man. The tools for this are science, technology and violence.

The destruction of nature, the new weapons, genetic engineering, modern agriculture and other modern inventions are all 'brainchildren' of this supposedly value-free, reductionist science. We did not gain these insights sitting in the British Library, where Marx had studied capitalism. We learned our lesson in the 'University of the Streets', as I call it. We were activist scholars. We did not rely on book knowledge in the first place, but on experience, struggle and practice. Through a worldwide network of like-minded women we learned about their methods of protest, their successes and their failures. Like the women of Greenham Common in England we blockaded American missile bases in Germany. We joined hands with our American sisters to encircle the Pentagon with a chain of women. After this Pentagon Action a new global network was created: Women and Life On Earth. WLOE still exists today.

But the 'fathers of destruction' are incapable of learning, and they have short memories. They have not learned anything after Hiroshima and Nagasaki. They have not learned anything after the explosion of the nuclear plant in Chernobyl – an accident which according to them could never have happened. They continued to construct more nuclear plants in more countries and they promised these were absolutely safe and more efficient. Even Japan did not learn from Hiroshima and Nagasaki – or Chernobyl. The nuclear plant in Fukushima was also supposed to have the safest technology. When it exploded in 2011 the damage done to the people and to the environment was unbelievable and cannot be 'repaired'. Yet, the new government in Japan promises again that it will build more and safer nuclear plants. Hiroshima, Nagasaki, Chernobyl and Fukushima are just names for a system which promises a better life for all but ends in killing life itself.

Violence against women and biotechnology

Before we understood the deep connection between women and nature we began to fight against the violence of men against women in our own house, our city, our country and the world. In this sphere we also started with action from which we gained our theoretical insights. Violence against women was indeed the first issue which mobilized women in the whole world.

In the 1970s we wanted to stop this violence in its various forms: rape, wife beating, mobbing, laws against abortion, the discrimination of women and sexist behaviour in all its manifestations. In Cologne, where I live, my students and I started a campaign for a shelter for women who were beaten by their husbands. We started it in spring 1976, and by the end of the year we had our *Frauenhaus*. In Part I of our book the reader finds an extensive description of this struggle. For me, the lessons learned during this struggle were fundamental. I first learned how widespread and how inhumane violence against women was in Germany, a so-called civilized country. But the most important lesson was: you cannot understand an unbearable social situation unless you try to change it. We did not use the usual methodological tools to 'study' the issue of domestic violence, namely to collect statistics to quantify that there was a 'need' for social intervention. We did not first read books about domestic violence in Germany. We started with street action and we demanded a house for battered women. The response to our action for a *Frauenhaus* was enormous, and we got it within seven months. This struggle taught me the most important lesson for my further life: experience and struggle come before theoretical study.

When I look back at this learning by social action, I often think about the famous Thesis 11 in Marx and Engels' *Theses on*

Feuerbach: 'The philosophers have interpreted the world in different ways. The point, however, is to change it.' We tried to change the world before we began to philosophize on it. Yet we were not always successful in our efforts.

In spite of many feminist struggles against male violence, it has not disappeared. On the contrary, it has increased. It is still part and parcel of all institutions in our patriarchal societies. It is part of the economy, the family, religion, politics, the media, culture. It exists in so-called 'civilized' countries as well as in 'backward' countries. The forms of this violence may differ but the core is the same.

In the new wars which began as a consequence of 9/11, violence against women and children is a 'normal' side-effect, 'collateral damage'. What is different today is the training young boys get through violent computer games. These games teach 'boys' of all ages how to fix on a target and kill an enemy. Boys grow up with this computer technology to fight against virtual enemies in virtual wars. No wonder they then practice this violence in real life. The computer games industry is one of the fastest growing in the world. The promoters argue that children can differentiate between 'virtual' reality and 'real' reality. Today, the new wars are largely fought by such 'boys' who sit behind a computer, click a button and send a rocket or a drone to kill 'terrorists' in Afghanistan or Pakistan. They attack and kill without feeling anything and without being attacked themselves. These new wars are as virtual for them as their computer games. But they are part of the military training which produces men who do not know what a loving relationship to real women and real nature is.

Therefore the 'real' violence against real women and minorities, such as migrants of racialized backgrounds, has increased and is more brutal than before. Yet more people consider male violence against women as genetically programmed.

Internet violence and Internet wars are new developments by the 'fathers of destruction'. A further one is genetic and reproductive technology. Both have totally changed our world-view and anthropology. According to this development, most geneticists view human behaviour as mainly determined by our genes. Hence male violence is seen as consequence of their genetic make-up. The same is true for wars. Men are considered to be 'warriors' by nature. If they are not warriors, they are not true men. But violence of men against women and other 'enemies' is not determined by our genes. Men are not rapists by nature, nor are they genetically programmed to be killers of our Mother Nature, the origin of all life. This violence is a consequence of a social paradigm which began some 8,000 years ago. Its name is patriarchy. Although we did deal with patriarchy in our book of 1993, we did not talk about it specifically. It only emerged when the question came up why patriarchy did not disappear with the arrival of capitalism, or when we had to find a name for the paradigm that destroyed women and nature. Following Claudia von Werlhof we called this paradigm capitalist patriarchy.[2]

Patriarchal civilization is the effort to solve one problem of the male gender, namely the fact that men cannot produce human life on their own. They are not the beginning. They cannot produce children, particularly sons, without women. Mothers are the beginning. This was still evident to the old Greeks. Mothers are *arche,* the beginning of human life. Therefore men invented a technology for which mothers are not necessary. Technologies like the atom bomb or reproductive and genetic technology or the Internet are such 'motherless children'.

Another form of violence against women is still the same as in 1993; the invention of reproductive and genetic technology. With the artificial fabrication of the first test-tube baby, Louise Brown, it was clear women had lost their age-old monopoly on birth. From then onwards, male reproductive engineers could produce a baby without women. Now genetic engineering could control all the genetic and biological processes by which human and animal life could be produced, reproduced and manipulated. It seems that man has at last become the creator of life. A human relation between a man and a woman is no longer necessary to create new human life.

We understood the far-reaching consequences of these inventions. At that time ecofeminists from all over the world started an international campaign against these new technologies. In 1985 we founded the Feminist International Network of Resistance to Reproductive and Genetic Engineering (FINRRAGE). It was clear to us that the invention of reproductive and genetic engineering was not just the result of man's innocent curiosity to understand nature, but, as with nuclear energy, biotechnology was invented to overcome the limits which nature had set to humans. And through the liberalization of the laws on patents, privatization and commercialization became a new market. These new patented commodities had been common property; now they could be bought and sold. Without gene technology Monsanto could not have become the giant which today controls agriculture and the global food industry.

But violence against women is not only a 'side effect of modern science and war' (which are interconnected); it is still a normal feature of modern, civilized society. Many people were shocked by the latest brutal gang rapes in India, but they were not shocked when test-tube babies were produced, from technology invented by men. They were not shocked when genetically manipulated rice was introduced in the course of the Green Revolution in India and other poor countries. Vandana Shiva was the first to show that the Green Revolution in India was not only destroying the vast diversity of varieties of rice preserved over centuries by women; it led also to a new wave of direct violence against women.

Another example of violence against nature, people and future generations is the restructuring of the whole world economy according to the principles of neoliberalism: globalization, liberalization, privatization and universal competition. Since the opening up of all countries to free trade, transnational corporations (TNCs) have shifted part of their production to 'cheap labour countries'. Bangladesh is one of these countries. As we know, the cheapest of cheap labourers everywhere are young women. About 90 per cent of the workers in the textile factories in Bangladesh are young women. Their wages are the lowest in the world. The work conditions are inhuman: fires break out regularly and hundreds of women have died. There are no labour contracts, there is no work security. The factory buildings are not safe and the women often have to work more than twelve hours a day. The recent collapse of the Rana Plaza in Dhaka, in which more than 1,100 people were killed and many more wounded, most of them women, is an example of the brutal violence against women which this New Economy has caused. Without such violence capitalism could not continue its growth mania.

These are only some of the most dramatic cases of why we wrote *Ecofeminism* twenty years ago and which are still the same today. In fact they are even worse and have reached more threatening and gigantic dimensions. Therefore we have now to see what has changed since 1993.

What is different today?

The first thing that comes to mind when I ask this question is the collapse of the World Trade Center in New York on 11

September 2001, the event which has since been referred to only as 9/11. For the first time in its history, the United States realized it was vulnerable. President George W. Bush immediately coined a name for these criminals who destroyed the WTC, the symbol of global capitalism. They were *terrorists*. And terrorism became the new enemy of the entire 'free world'. Bush also named the ideological background which had inspired those terrorists, namely Islam. After 9/11 all Islamic countries became suspect as possible breeding grounds for terrorists and terrorism. Thus, the old enemy of the free world, Communism, was replaced by a new one: Terrorism and Islam. It is breathtaking to see how fast this new enemy changed public and private life in the USA and later in the whole world. Immediately a new law was passed, the Homeland Security Act, through which citizens and the country would be protected from the threat of terrorism. NATO states in Europe followed the USA and adopted similar security laws immediately and without great opposition from their parliaments. They introduced the same airport security checks as those in the USA. In the course of time this system of control became more refined and generalized, until eventually the security systems of the United States as well as those of other NATO states could spy on each citizen. At the same time new wars were started against countries with a Muslim majority. The first of these was the invasion of Afghanistan by American troops. Iraq was the next target.

At first I thought the true goal of these new wars was to gain control of the oil reserves in these countries. But what struck me immediately, particularly with regard to Afghanistan, was that part of the legitimation of this war, apart from eliminating Al Qaeda, was to liberate women from their backward, Islamic traditions, such as wearing a headscarf or the hijab. Not only the USA, but also its European NATO partners, Germany, France, the Netherlands and others, appeared on the new war scene as the great liberators of women! Whenever and wherever have wars been fought to 'emancipate' the women of the enemy? Everybody knows that the women of the enemy are the first victims of the victors. They are raped, brutalized and humiliated. Now foreign men are supposed to emancipate them by 'deveiling' them? This is the most ridiculous justification of modern war ever heard.

What is also different today is the new crisis in the rich countries of the West, first in the USA and now in Europe. Nobody knows when and how it will end. Politicians are at their wits' end, as are economists and managers of the big corporations.

All of a sudden poverty has returned to the West. Countries in southern Europe are more affected by the crisis than those in the north. In fact, the new crisis has split the eurozone into two parts: the richer North and the poorer South. Greece, Spain, Italy and Cyprus are so indebted to mighty banks like the Deutsche Bank that they have virtually become beggars, dependent on loans from Germany and the other richer countries.

What makes today's crisis different from earlier ones is the exhaustion of the resources which could earlier be used for the recovery of the economy. Oil, gas and raw materials such as coal, iron and other metals have become scarce. But what is more dangerous is the exhaustion, poisoning or destruction of the vital elements on which all life on Earth depends: water, soil, air, forests and, last but not least, the climate. When these vital elements are no longer there or when they are substantially damaged, life on our planet Earth is no longer possible.

What is the alternative?

More and more people, particularly young people, feel that they have no future in this scenario. They begin to rebel against this murderous system, against the dominance of money over all life, and they demand a fundamental change. Occupy Wall Street inspired a similar 'Blockupy' protest in front of the Deutsche Bank in Frankfurt. Large demonstrations against austerity politics in Greece, Spain, Portugal and Italy show that people want a change. In North Africa people are also demanding change. When their rebellion started it was first called the Arab Spring by the Western media. People's anger was directed against corrupt and dictatorial regimes. They demanded democracy and jobs. But what change do they mean? Do they just want to remove a dictator and corruption or do they want a totally new system based on a new vision of the world?

When we wrote *Ecofeminism* we asked the same questions from a woman's point of view. What could be an alternative? What would a new paradigm, a new vision be? We called this new vision the 'subsistence perspective'. Even today I do not know how better to conceptualize what a new world could be. Yet one thing is clear to me: this 'new world' will not come about with a Big Bang, or a Great Revolution. It will come when people begin to sow new seeds of this 'new world' while we are still living in the old one. It will take time for these seeds to grow and bear fruit;

but many people have already started sowing such seeds. Farida Akhter from Bangladesh talks about this process in her book, *Seeds of Movements: Women's Issues in Bangladesh.*[3] She shows that mainly women will be the sowers of these seeds because they and their children have suffered most in the old world of the 'Fathers of Destruction.'

Several years ago I was invited by the Association of Catholic Rural Women to a conference in Trier. I was supposed to give a talk about subsistence. I was at a bit of a loss. What should I say? How should I explain subsistence to rural women in the town where Marx was born? But when I entered the hall I saw a big banner, fixed to the platform, with the inscription, 'The World is Our Household'. It was October and the women had brought the fruits of their work during spring, summer and autumn: cabbages, beans, carrots, potatoes, apples, pears, plums, beetroots, and flowers too. They had put everything on the platform before me. What else could I say about subsistence than: *The World is Our Household! Let's Take Care of It.*

We consider the new edition of this book also as a contribution to this care-taking. And we thank Zed Books for including it in its new series.

July 2013

Notes

1. Brian Easley, *Fathering the Unthinkable. Masculinity, Scientists and the New Arms Race*, Pluto Press, London, 1986.
2. Claudia von Werlhof, 'The Failure of Modern Civilization and the Struggle for a "Deep" Alternative: A Critical Theory of Patriarchy as a New Paradigm', in *Beiträge zur Dissidenz* 26, Peter Lang Verlag, Frankfurt, 2011.
3. Farida Akhter, *Seeds of Movements: On Womens's Issues in Bangladesh*, Narigrantha Prabartana, Dhaka, 2007.

1. Introduction: Why We Wrote this Book Together

Maria Mies and Vandana Shiva

A jointly-authored book usually suggests that the writers have long been involved in an on-going dialogue arising out of common reading and discussions. When the two of us began thinking about writing this book we had to face the fact that no such collaboration was possible. We live and work thousands of miles apart: one in the so-called South — India; the other in the North — Germany: divided yet also united by the world market system, that affords privileges to peoples in the North at the expense of those in the South, and, too, by history, language and culture. Our training and background also differ: Vandana a theoretical physicist, from the ecology movement; Maria, a social scientist, from the feminist movement. One had looked at the capitalist world system from the perspective of the exploited people and nature of the South, the other had studied the same processes as they affect women from the viewpoint of someone who lives 'in the heart of the beast'. Could all these differences be overcome by good-will and effort? Moreover, was it appropriate at the present juncture even to try to write a book together, when all around people seem to be engaged in trying to discover their own particular identity, *vis-a-vis* sexual, ethnic, national, racial, cultural and religious difference as the basis for autonomy? Would we be accused of trying to create a new internationalism, under the banner of feminism and ecologism, when the old isms, particularly socialist internationalism, were collapsing? And too, in the South many women's movements see feminism as a Western/Northern import and accuse white (European and North American) feminists of sharing in men's privileges in their countries. Perhaps it was wiser to accept these differences, instead of trying to contain them within such a universalistic term as 'ecofeminism' — and instead, each of us should concentrate on our own work within our own countries and their cultural, ethnic, political and economic contexts and try to effect changes locally.

Nevertheless, these differences aside, we share common concerns that emerge from an invisible global politics in which women worldwide are enmeshed in their everyday life; and a convergence of thinking arising from our participation in the efforts of women to keep alive the processes that sustain us. These shared thoughts and concerns aim not to demonstrate uniformity and homogeneity but rather a creative transcendence of our differences. There are many reasons for our collaboration in this book. One is to make visible the 'other' global processes that are becoming increasingly invisible as a new world order emerges based on the control of people and resources worldwide for the sake of capital accumulation. Another is the optimistic belief that a search for identity and difference will become more significant as a platform for resistance against the dominant global forces of capitalist patriarchy, which simultaneously homogenizes and fragments.

This capitalist-patriarchal perspective interprets difference as hierarchical and uniformity as a prerequisite for equality. Our aim is to go beyond this narrow perspective and to express our diversity and, in different ways, address the inherent inequalities in world structures which permit the North to dominate the South, men to dominate women, and the frenetic plunder of ever more resources for ever more unequally distributed economic gain to dominate nature.

Probably we arrived at these common concerns because our experiences and insights, and the analyses we have formulated, grew out of participation in the women's and ecology movements rather than from within the cocoon of academic research institutions. In recent years we had increasingly been confronted by the same fundamental issues concerning survival and the preservation of life on this planet, not only of women, children and humanity in general, but also of the vast diversity of fauna and flora. In analysing the causes which have led to the destructive tendencies that threaten life on earth we became aware — quite independently — of what we call the capitalist patriarchal world system.

This system emerged, is built upon and maintains itself through the colonization of women, of 'foreign' peoples and their lands; and of nature, which it is gradually destroying. As feminists actively seeking women's liberation from male domination, we could not, however, ignore the fact that 'modernization' and 'development' processes and 'progress' were responsible for the degradation of the natural world. We saw that the impact on women of ecological disasters and deterioration was harder than on men, and also, that everywhere, women were the first to protest against environmental destruction. As activists in the ecology movements, it became clear to us that science and technology were not gender neutral; and in common with many other women, we began to see that the relationship of exploitative dominance between man and nature, (shaped by reductionist modern science since the 16th century) and the exploitative and oppressive relationship between men and women that prevails in most patriarchal societies, even modern industrial ones, were closely connected.

We discovered that our own active involvement in the women's and the ecology movements had coincidentally led us to a shared analysis and perspective. The search for answers had led us to similar theories, to similar authors for clarification and eventually to one another. Re-reading papers we had presented on various occasions and to different audiences revealed a spontaneous convergence of thought arising out of objective conditions to which we had each responded as women.

If the final outcome of the present world system is a general threat to life on planet earth, then it is crucial to resuscitate and nurture the impulse and determination to survive, inherent in all living things. A closer examination of the numerous local struggles against ecological destruction and deterioration, for example: against atomic power plants in Germany,[1] against chalk mining and logging in the Himalayas;[2] the activities of the Green Belt Movement in Kenya;[3] and of Japanese women against food pollution by chemically-stimulated, commercial agriculture and for self-reliant producer-consumer networks;[4] poor women's efforts in Ecuador to save the mangrove forests as breeding-grounds for fish and shrimp;[5] the battle of thousands of women in the South for better water management, soil conservation, land use, and maintenance of their survival base (forests, fuel, fodder) against the industrial interests, confirmed that many women, worldwide, felt the same anger and anxiety, and the same sense of responsibility to preserve the bases of life, and to end its destruction. Irrespective of different racial, ethnic, cultural or class backgrounds, this common concern brought women together to forge links in solidarity with other women, people and even nations. In these processes of action and reflection similar analyses, concepts and visions also sometimes emerged.

In South-West Germany, peasant women in the Whyl Movement were the most active in one of the first anti-nuclear power movements in that country. They established cross-border links with similar movements in Switzerland and France as well as with other movements in Germany, to intellectuals, students and to city-dwelling feminists. In this process they became conscious of the patriarchal men-women relationship; for many women this was the first step towards their own liberation.[6] When, some years later, two of the movement's leading women were interviewed they clearly articulated their vision of an alternative society, based not on the model of growth-oriented industrialism and consumerism but close to what we call the subsistence perspective.[7] Other examples of women's endeavours to overcome social fragmentation and create solidarity are Lois Gibbs' opposition to the dumping of toxic waste and Medha Patkar's to the construction of the Narmada dams. Women activists in the USA have led the campaign against toxic waste dumping, and Lois Gibbs' strenuous and persistent efforts in opposing toxic waste dumping in the now notorious Love Canal outrage are well-known. As Murray Levine wrote,[8] 'If Love Canal has taught Lois Gibbs — and the rest of us — anything, it is that ordinary people become very smart, very quickly when their lives are threatened. They become adept at detecting absurdity, even when it is concealed in bureaucratic and scientific jargon.'

In the 1980s toxic dumps began to be sited in areas inhabited by poor and coloured people; today, the strongest resistance against this practice is to be found in these areas. For women fighting against toxic dumping, the issue is not just NIMBY (not in my backyard) but 'everyone's backyard' (the title of a newsletter on citizen's action). Joan Sharp, who worked at the Schlage Lock Company in North Carolina USA until the factory was closed to be set up as a maquiladora in Tecate, Mexico, exemplifies this solidarity. In March 1992, then unemployed, she went to Mexico as a representative of Black Workers for Justice in order to give the Mexican workers information on the Company and hazardous chemicals which she and others believe caused 30 of her co-workers to die of cancer. The 200 pages of documents she had brought described Schlage's use of toxic chemicals, its contamination of the groundwater, and its failure to provide promised severance pay for production workers. None of the Tecate workers had been aware that Schlage had closed operations in San Francisco in order to take advantage of low wages in the Black Belt South, and then in Mexico.[9] In Narmada Valley, Medha Patkar is leading India's most vital environmental campaign against the construction of mega dams on the Narmada river. As she said in an interview: 'The concept of womanhood, of *mata*, [mother] has automatically got connected with this whole movement, although the concept of Narmada as *mata* is very much part of [it]. So if the feminine tone is given, both to the leadership and the participants — then [it all] comes together'.[10]

These examples show how the shared concern of countless women worldwide override their differences, and evokes a sense of solidarity that perceives such differences as enriching their experiences and struggles rather than as marking boundaries.

Why is it so difficult to see this common ground?

Some women, however, particularly urban, middle-class women, find it difficult to perceive commonality both between their own liberation and the liberation of nature, and between themselves and 'different' women in the world. This is because capitalist patriarchy or 'modern' civilization is based on a cosmology and anthropology that structurally dichotomizes reality, and hierarchically opposes the two parts to each other: the one always considered superior, always thriving, and progressing at the expense of the other. Thus, nature is subordinated to man; woman to man; consumption to production; and the local to the global, and so on. Feminists have long criticized this dichotomy, particularly the structural division of man and nature, which is seen as analogous to that of man and woman.[11]

Rather than attempting to overcome this hierarchical dichotomy many women have simply up-ended it, and thus women are seen as superior to men, nature to culture, and so on. But the basic structure of the world-view remains as also does the basically antagonistic relationship that, at the surface, exists between the two divided and hierarchically ordered parts. Because this world-view sees the 'other', the 'object', not just as different, but as the 'enemy'; as Sartre put it in *Huis Clos*: Hell is other people! In the resultant struggle one part will eventually survive by subordinating, and appropriating the 'other'. This is also the core of Hegelian and Marxian dialectics, of their concept of history and progress. Evolutionary theory too, is based on the concept of a constant struggle for survival, on an antagonistic principle of life. These concepts are integral to what, since the Enlightenment, constitutes the European project of so-called modernity or progress.

Since Hobbes' writings, society has been conceptualized as an assembly of social atoms, activated by antagonistic interests.

Modern economic theory sees self-interest as the impulse of all economic activity. Later, Darwin 'discovered' a similar principle in nature. Accordingly, the symbioses, the interconnections that nurture and sustain life are ignored, and both natural evolution and social dynamics are perceived as impelled by a constant struggle of the stronger against the weaker, by constant warfare. Such a world-view militates against an appreciation of the enriching potential of the diversity of life and cultures, which instead are experienced as divisive and threatening. Attempts to rejoin the atomized parts lead only to standardization and to homogenization by eliminating diversity and qualitative differences.

An ecofeminist perspective propounds the need for a new cosmology and a new anthropology which recognizes that life in nature (which includes human beings) is maintained by means of co-operation, and mutual care and love. Only in this way can we be enabled to respect and preserve the diversity of all life forms, including their cultural expressions, as true sources of our well-being and happiness. To this end ecofeminists use metaphors like 'reweaving the world', 'healing the wounds', and re-connecting and interconnecting the 'web'.[12] This effort to create a holistic, all-life embracing cosmology and anthropology, must necessarily imply a concept of freedom different from that used since the Enlightenment.

Freedom versus emancipation

This involves rejecting the notion that Man's freedom and happiness depend *on an ongoing process of emancipation from nature,* on independence from, and dominance over natural processes by the power of reason and rationality. Socialist utopias were also informed by a concept of freedom that saw man's destiny in his historic march from the 'realm of necessity' (the realm of nature), to the 'realm of freedom' — the 'real' human realm — which entailed transforming nature and natural forces into what was called a 'second nature', or culture. According to scientific socialism, the limits of both nature and society are dialectically transcended in this process.

Most feminists also shared this concept of freedom and emancipation, until the beginning of the ecology movement. But the more people began to reflect upon and question why the application of modern science and technology, which has been celebrated as humanity's great liberators, had succeeded only in procuring increasing ecological degradation, the more acutely aware they became of the contradiction between the enlightenment logic of emancipation and the eco-logic of preserving and nurturing natural cycles of regeneration. In 1987, at the congress 'Women and Ecology' in Cologne (Germany), Angelika Birk and Irene Stoehr spelt out this contradiction, particularly as it applied to the women's movement which, like many other movements inspired by the Enlightenment ideas, had fastened its hopes on the progress of science and technology, particularly in the area of reproduction, but also of house- and other work. Irene Stoehr pointed out that this concept of emancipation necessarily implied dominance over nature, including human, female nature; and, that ultimately, this dominance relationship was responsible for the ecological destruction we now face. How, then, could women hope to reach both their own and nature's 'emancipation' by way of the same logic?[13]

To 'catch-up' with the men in their society, as many women still see as the main goal of the feminist movement, particularly those who promote a policy of equalization, implies a demand for a greater, or equal share of what, in the existing paradigm, men take from nature. This, indeed, has to a large extent happened in Western society: modern chemistry, household technology, and pharmacy were proclaimed as women's saviours, because they would 'emancipate' them from household drudgery. Today we realize that much environmental pollution and destruction is causally linked to modern household technology. Therefore, can the concept of emancipation be compatible with a concept of preserving the earth as our life base?

This contradiction will be further explored in the following chapters, particularly those dealing with biotechnology. But our critique of the Enlightenment emancipation-logic was impelled not only by an insight into its consequences for women, but also a concern for those victims, who, since the White Man's march towards 'the realm of freedom' had paid for this freedom by the denial of their own subjectivity, freedom and, often, their survival base. As well as women, these include nature and other peoples — the colonized and 'naturized' — 'opened up' for free exploitation and subordination, transformed into the 'others', the 'objects', in the process of European (male) 'subject's' emancipation from the 'realm of necessity'.

From the perspective of these victims, the illusory character of this project becomes clear. Because, for them, this means not only, as noted above, the destruction of their survival base and so on but also that ever to attain (through so-called catching-up development) the same material level as those who benefited from this process is impossible. Within a limited planet, there can be no escape from necessity. To find freedom does not involve subjugating or transcending the 'realm of necessity', but rather focusing on developing a vision of freedom, happiness, the 'good life' within the limits of necessity, of nature. We call this vision the subsistence perspective, because to 'transcend' nature can no longer be justified, instead, nature's subsistence potential in all its dimensions and manifestations must be nurtured and conserved. Freedom *within* the realm of necessity can be universalized to all; freedom *from* necessity can be available to only a few.

False strategies

These dichotomies, which result in false perceptions of reality are criticized especially because they have led and lead to false strategies, mainly *vis-a-vis* the issue of equality, that is, of helping the oppressed and exploited to emerge from their parlous situation. So far the only remedy has been the strategy of 'catching-up development', at both macro and micro levels. This strategy, which has been tried out, and failed, in the colonized 'Third World', was also applied in the socialist, and now, by ex-socialist, countries. Large sections of the women's movement pursued the same strategy — of 'catching-up' with the men — through a policy of equalization, positive discrimination and special quotas for women in work, politics and education; in short, emulating the male model and sharing the privileges of the 'victors'. In the USA, this equalization policy goes so far as to hail women's participation in the actual combat forces of the US Army or Navy as a step towards their emancipation; a step 'achieved' during the Gulf War. Many feminists have rejected this equalization policy, refusing to share men's privileges in our capitalist-patriarchal society. By and large, however, this policy is still regarded by many as mainly one that will ultimately procure the liberation of women as well as of other oppressed groups.

The global versus the local

The 'global' versus the 'local' now figures widely in many ecological and development discourses. A closer examination of these reveals that the interest groups that seek free access to all natural resources as well as to human labour and markets, often present themselves as guardians of the 'world community', 'global peace', 'global ecology' or of universal human rights and the free world market. The implicit promise of this globalism is that a 'free world market' will lead to world peace and justice. In the name of common or global goals, which de facto acknowledge the fact that we all are dependent on the same planet, they nevertheless claim the right to exploit local ecology, communities, cultures and so on. The victims are always local, for example, as is manifest in the aftermath of the Gulf War — a war justified by the apparently universal or global principle of justice, in the name of the 'world community', represented by the United Nations. The world was called upon to feel responsibility for liberating Kuwait from Iraqi occupation. But, it is clear that the victims of this 'liberation' are local: Iraqi and Kuwaiti women and children, the Kurds, and the Gulf region's environment.

The new 'globalism' which emerged after the Gulf War — the 'New World Order' — was propagated by US President George Bush. With the end of the old superpower confrontation this New World Order is projected as a harbinger of world peace and harmony. But it is simply the Old World Order in a different garb.

As many of our book's subsequent chapters will emphasize, the 'global' in the global order means simply the global domination of local and particular interests, by means of subsuming the multiple diversities of economies, cultures and of nature under the control of a few multinational corporations (MNCs), and the superpowers that assist them in their global reach through 'free' trade, structural adjustment programmes and, increasingly, conflicts, military and otherwise. In unified Germany, there are now racist attacks on immigran ts, there are civil wars in the erstwhile Soviet Union and Eastern European countries recently 'integrated' in the world market, and ethnic conflicts in Sri Lanka, India and Africa — all of which point to new divisions and closed borders for the people, whereas for TNCs' investments and markets all borders are erased, in order to facilitate the grand design of a 'New World Order', of 'global integration'.

In the dominant discourse the 'global' is the political space in which the dominant local seeks global control, and frees itself of any local and national control. But, contrary to what it suggests, the global does not represent universal human interest but a particular local and parochial interest which has been globalized through its reach and control. The G-7, the group of the world's seven most powerful countries, dictate global affairs, but the interests that guide them remain parochial. The World Bank does not really serve the interests of all the world's communities, but is an institution in which decisions are based on voting, weighted by the economic and political power of the donors. In this decision-making, the communities who pay the real price, the real donors (such as the tribals of Narmada Valley), have no voice.

The independence movements against colonialism had revealed the poverty and deprivation caused by economic drain from the colonies to the centres of economic power. The post-war world order which saw the emergence of independent political states in the South, also saw the emergence of the Bretton Woods institutions like the World Bank and the IMF which, in the name of underdevelopment and poverty, created a new colonialism based on development financing and debt burdens. The environment movement revealed the environmental and social costs generated by maldevelopment, conceived of and financed by these institutions. Protection of the environment now figures in the rhetoric and is cited as the reason for strengthening 'global' institutions like the World Bank and extending their reach accordingly.

In addition to the legitimacy derived from co-opting the language of dissent is the legitimacy that derives from a false notion that the globalized 'local' is some form of hierarchy that represents geographical and democratic spread, and lower order (local) hierarchies should somehow be subservient to the higher (global). Operationalizing undemocratic development projects was based on a similar false notion of the 'national interest', and every local interest felt morally compelled to make sacrifices for what seemed the larger interest. This is the attitude with which each community made way for large dams in post-independent India. It was only during the 1980s when the different 'local' interests met each other nationwide, they realized that what was being projected as the 'national interest' were the electoral and economic interests of a handful of politicians financed by a handful of contractors and industrialists who benefit from the construction of all dams such as Tehri and the Narmada Valley project. Against the narrow and selfish interest that had been elevated to the status of the 'national' interest, the collective struggle of communities engaged in the resistance against large dams started to emerge as the real though subjugated common interest.

The breakdown of universalist (Western) ideologies and the emergence of cultural relativism

There are a number of people who interpret the end of the East-

West confrontation as not only signalling the end of all socialist dreams and utopias but also of all universal ideologies based on a universal concept of human beings and their relation to nature and other human beings. These ideologies have been 'deconstructed' as being eurocentric, egocentric and — according to some feminists — androcentric, and materialist.

The end of these ideologies is being proclaimed by post-modernist thinkers, who hold that the universalization of modernization — the European project of the Enlightenment — has failed. And there are environmentalists and developmentalists who argue that the emphasis on material or economic development and on emulation of the West's model of the industrial society has failed to appreciate that in most non-European societies culture plays a significant role. Moreover, they assert that the dualistic separation of economy and culture (or in Marxian terms of bases and superstructure) finds no resonance in most non-modern societies. They further criticize the Western development paradigm on the grounds that the modernization strategy has resulted in the destruction of cultural as well as biological diversity, to a homogenization of cultures on the US coca-cola and fast-food model, on the one hand and of life forms according to the demands of profit-oriented industries, on the other. We share much of the criticism directed to the West's paradigm of development; we reject the homogenization processes resulting from the world market and of capitalist production processes. We also criticize the dualistic division between superstructure or culture and the economy or base. In our view, the preservation of the earth's diversity of life forms and of human societies' cultures is a precondition for the maintenance of life on this planet.

But it is essential to beware of simply up-ending the dualistic structure by discounting the economy altogether and considering only culture or cultures. Furthermore, not all cultural traditions can be seen as of equal value; such a stance would simply replace eurocentric and androcentric and dogmatic ideological and ethical universalism with cultural relativism. This cultural relativism implies that we must accept even violence, and such patriarchal and exploitative institutions and customs as dowry, female genital mutilation, India's caste system and so on, because they are the cultural expressions and creations of particular people. For cultural relativists, traditions, expressed in language, religion, custom, food habits, man-woman relations are always considered as particular, and beyond criticism. Taken to extremes the emphasis on 'difference' could lead to losing sight of all commonalities, making even communication impossible. Obviously, cultural relativism, amounting to a suspension of value judgement, can be neither the solution nor the alternative to totalitarian and dogmatic ideological universalism. It is, in fact, the old coin reversed. It takes a liberal stance, but it should be remembered that European liberalism and individualism are rooted in colonialism, destruction of the commons, on wholesale privatization and on commodity production for profit. What must also be realized is that this new emphasis on the cultural, the local, and the difference, this cultural relativism, accords with MNCs' interests.

While intellectuals may concentrate on culture and on differences, international capital continues with its expansion of production and markets, insisting on free access to all natural resources and life forms and to localized cultures and traditions and their commodification. Local cultures are deemed to have 'value' only when they have been fragmented and these fragments transformed into saleable goods for a world market. Only when food becomes 'ethnic food', music 'ethnic music', and traditional tales 'folklore' and when skills are harnessed to the production of 'ethnic' objects for the tourist industry, can the capital accumulation process benefit from these local cultures.

While local cultures are thus dissected and their fragments commodified, these atomized parts are then 're-unified' in the global supermarket, thereby procuring a standardization and homogenization of all cultural diversity. Cultural relativism is not only unaware of these processes but rather legitimizes them; and the feminist theory of difference ignores the working of the capitalist world system and its power to transform life into saleable commodities and cash.

To find a way out of cultural relativism, it is necessary to look not only for differences but for diversities and interconnectedness among women, among men and women, among human beings and other life forms, worldwide. The common ground for women's liberation and the preservation of life on earth is to be found in the activities of those women who have become the victims of the development process and who struggle to conserve their subsistence base: for example, the Chipko women in India, women and men who actively oppose mega dam construction, women who fight against nuclear power plants and against the irresponsible dumping of toxic wastes around the world, and many more worldwide.

In the dialogues with such grassroots women activists cultural relativism does not enter. These women spell out clearly what unites women worldwide, and what unites men and women with the multiplicity of life forms in nature. The universalism that stems from their efforts to preserve their subsistence — their life base — is different from the eurocentric universalism developed via the Enlightenment and the rise of capitalist patriarchy.

This universalism does not deal in abstract universal human 'rights' but rather in common human needs which can be satisfied only if the life-sustaining networks and processes are kept intact and alive. These 'symbioses or living interconnectedness' both in nature and in human society are the only guarantee that life in its fullest sense can continue on this planet. These fundamental needs: for food, shelter, clothing; for affection, care and love; for dignity and identity, for knowledge and freedom, leisure and joy, are common to all people, irrespective of culture, ideology, race, political and economic system and class.

In the usual development discourse these needs are divided into so-called 'basic needs' (food, shelter, clothing et al) and so-called 'higher needs' such as freedom and knowledge and so on. The ecofeminist perspective, as expressed by women activists recognizes no such division. Culture is very much part of their struggle for subsistence and life. They identify freedom with their loving interaction and productive work in co-operation with Mother Earth;[14] knowledge is the subsistence knowledge essential for their survival. For women in the affluent North or in the affluent classes of the South, such a concept of universalism or commonality is not easy to grasp. Survival is seen not as the ultimate goal of life but a banality — a fact that can be taken for granted. It is precisely the value of the everyday work for survival, for life, which has been eroded in the name of the so-called 'higher' values.

Ecofeminism

Ecofeminism, 'a new term for an ancient wisdom'[15] grew out of various social movements — the feminist, peace and the ecology movements — in the late 1970s and early 1980s. Though the term was first used by Francoise D'Eaubonne[16] it became popular only in the context of numerous protests and activities against environmental destruction , sparked-off initially by recurring ecological disasters. The meltdown at Three Mile Island prompted large numbers of women in the USA to come together in the first ecofeminist conference — 'Women and Life on Earth: A Conference on Eco-Feminism in the Eighties' — in March 1980, at Amherst. At this conference the connections between feminism, militarization, healing and ecology were explored. As Ynestra King, one of the Conference organizers, wrote:

Ecofeminism is about connectedness and wholeness of theory and practice. It asserts the special strength and integrity of every living thing. For us the snail darter is to be considered side by side with a community's need for water, the porpoise side by side with appetite for tuna, and the creatures it may fall on with Skylab. We are a woman-identified movement and we believe we have a special work to do in these imperilled times. We see the devastation of the earth and her beings by the corporate warriors, and the threat of nuclear annihilation by the military warriors, as feminist concerns. It is the same masculinist mentality which would deny us our right to our own bodies and our own sexuality, and which depends on multiple systems of dominance and state power to have its way.[17]

Wherever women acted against ecological destruction or/and the threat of atomic annihilation, they immediately became aware of the connection between patriarchal violence against women, other people and nature, and that: In defying this patriarchy we are loyal to future generations and to life and this planet itself. We have a deep and particular understanding of this both through our natures and our experience as women.[18]

The 'corporate and military warriors' aggression against the environment was perceived almost physically as an aggression against our female body. This is expressed by many women who participated in these movements. Thus, women in Switzerland who demonstrated against the Seveso poisoning wrote: We should think of controlling our bodies in a more global way, as it is not only men and doctors who behave aggressively towards our bodies, but also the multinationals! What more aggression against the body of women, against the children than that of La Roche-Givaudan at Seveso? From 10 July 1976, their entire lives have been taken over by the 'accident' and the effects are going to last for a long time.[19]

On the night of 2-3 December 1984, 40 tons of toxic gas were released from a Union Carbide pesticides plant in Bhopal, India; 3,000 people died during the disaster and of the 400,000 others who were exposed, many have since died, and the suffering continues. Women have been those most severely affected but also the most persistent in their demand for justice. The Bhopal Gas Peedit Mahila Udyog Sangathan, has continued to remind the Government of India, Union Carbide and the world that they still suffer, and that no amount of money can restore the lives and health of the victims. As Hamidabi, a Muslim woman from one of the poor *bastis* which were worst hit in the disaster said, 'We will not stop our fight till the fire in our hearts goes quiet — this fire started with 3,000 funeral pyres — and it will not die till we have justice.' Or, as the women of Sicily who protested against the stationing of nuclear missiles in their country stated:

'Our "no" to war coincides with our struggle for liberation. Never have we seen so clearly the connection between nuclear escalation and the culture of the musclemen; between the violence of war and the violence of rape. Such in fact is the historical memory that women have of war . . . But it is also our daily experience in "peacetime" and in this respect women are perpetually at war . . . It is no coincidence that the gruesome game of war — in which the greater part of the male sex seems to delight — passes through the same stages as the traditional sexual relationship: aggression, conquest, possession, control. Of a woman or a land, it makes little difference.'[20]

The women who were a driving force in movements against the construction of nuclear power plants in Germany, were not all committed feminists, but to them also the connection between technology, war against nature, against women and future generations was clear. The peasant women who actively protested against the proposed construction of the nuclear power plant at Whyl in South-West Germany also saw the connection between technology, the profit-oriented growth mania of the industrial system and the exploitation of the 'Third World'.[21] This connection was also most clearly spelt out by a Russian woman after the Chernobyl catastrophe in 1986: 'Men never think of life. They only want to conquer nature and the enemy.'

The Chernobyl disaster in particular provoked a spontaneous expression of women's outrage and resistance against this war technology and the general industrial warrior system. The illusion that atomic technology was malevolent when used in bombs but benevolent when used to generate electricity for the North's domestic appliances was dispelled. Many women too, also understood that their consumerist lifestyle was also very much part of this system of war against nature, women, foreign peoples and future generations.

The new developments in biotechnology, genetic engineering and reproductive technology have made women acutely conscious of the gender bias of science and technology and that science's whole paradigm is characteristically patriarchal, anti-nature and colonial and aims to dispossess women of their generative capacity as it does the productive capacities of nature. The founding of the Feminist International Network of Resistance to Genetic and Reproductive Engineering (fiNRRAGE) in 1984, was followed by a number of important congresses: 1985 in Sweden and in Bonn, 1988 in Bangladesh, and 1991 in Brazil. This movement reached far beyond the narrowly defined women's or feminist movement. In Germany women from trade unions, churches and universities, rural and urban women, workers and housewives mobilized against these technologies; their ethical, economic, and health implications continue to be hotly debated issues. This movement was instrumental in preventing the establishment of a 'surrogate motherhood' agency in Frankfurt. The ecofeminist principle of looking for connections where capitalist patriarchy and its warrior science are engaged in disconnecting and dissecting what forms a living whole also informs this movement. Thus those involved look not only at the implications of these technologies for women, but also for animals, plants, for agriculture in the Third World as well as in the industrialized North. They understand that the liberation of women cannot be achieved in isolation, but only as part of a larger struggle for the preservation of life on this planet.

This movement also facilitates the creation of new connections and networks. An African woman at the Bangladesh congress, on hearing of these technologies exclaimed: 'If that is progress, we do not want it. Keep it!'

'Spiritual' or 'political' ecofeminism?

As women in various movements — ecology, peace, feminist and especially health — rediscovered the interdependence and connectedness of everything, they also rediscovered what was called the spiritual dimension of life — the realization of this interconnectedness was itself sometimes called spirituality. Capitalist and Marxist materialism, both of which saw the achievement of human happiness as basically conditional on the expansion of material goods' production, denied or denigrated this dimension. Feminists also began to realize the significance of the 'witch hunts' at the beginning of our modern era in so far as patriachal science and technology was developed only after these women (the witches) had been murdered and, concomitantly, their knowledge, wisdom and close relationship with nature had been destroyed.[22] The desire to recover, to regenerate this wisdom as a means to liberate women and nature from patriarchal destruction also motivated this turning towards spirituality. The term 'spiritual' is ambiguous, it means different things to different people. For some it means a kind of religion, but not one based upon the continuation of the patriarchal, monotheistic religions of Christianity, Judaism or Islam, all of which are arguably hostile to women and to nature *vis-a-vis* their basic warrior traditions. Hence, some tried to revive or recreate a goddess-based religion; spirituality was defined as the Goddess.

Some call it the female principle, inhabiting and permeating all things — this spirituality is understood in a less 'spiritual' , that is, less idealistic way. Although the spirit was female, it was not apart from the material world, but seen as the life-force in everything and in every human being: it was indeed the connecting principle. Spirituality in these more material terms was akin to magic rather than to religion as it is commonly understood.[23] This interpretation of spirituality is also spelt out in the writings of Starhawk,[24] for whom spirituality is largely identical to women's sensuality, their sexual energy, their most precious life force, which links them to each other, to other life forms and the elements. It is the energy that enables women to love and to celebrate life. This sensual or sexual spirituality, rather than 'other-worldly' is centred on and thus abolishes the opposition between spirit and matter, transcendence and immanence. There is only immanence, but this immanence is not inert, passive matter devoid of subjectivity, life and spirit. The spirit is inherent in everything and particularly our sensuous experience, because we ourselves with our bodies cannot separate the material from the spiritual. The spiritual is the love without which no life can blossom, it is this magic which is contained within everything. The rediscovered ancient wisdom consisted of the old magic insight into the existence of these all-embracing connections and that through these, powerless women could therefore influence powerful men. This at least informed the thinking of the women who, in 1980, surrounded the Pentagon with their rituals and who formulated the first ecofeminist manifesto.[25]

The ecological relevance of this emphasis on 'spirituality' lies in the rediscovery of the sacredness of life, according to which life on earth can be preserved only if people again begin to perceive all life forms as sacred and respect them as such. This quality is not located in an other-worldly deity, in a transcendence, but in every-day life, in our work, the things that surround us, in our imman-ence. And from time to time there should be celebrations of this sacredness in rituals, in dance and song.

This celebration of our dependence to Mother Earth is quite contrary to the attitude promoted by Francis Bacon and his fol-lowers, the fathers of modern science and technology. For them this dependence was an outrage, a mockery of man's right to freedom on his own terms and therefore had forcefully and vio-lently to be abolished. Western rationality, the West's paradigm of science and concept of freedom are all based on overcoming and transcending this dependence, on the subordination of nature to the (male) will, and the disenchantment of all her forces. Spiritual-ity in this context endeavours to 'heal Mother Earth' and to re-en-chant the world. This means to undo the process of disenchantment, which Max Weber saw as the inevitable outcome of the European rationalization process.

Ecofeminists in the USA seemingly put greater emphasis on the 'spiritual' than do those in Europe. For example, in Germany, particularly since the early 1980s this tendency has often been criticized as escapism, as signifying a withdrawal from the politi-cal sphere into some kind of dream world, divorced from reality and thus leaving power in the hands of men. But the 'spiritual' feminists argue that theirs is the politics of everyday life, the transformation of fundamental relationships, even if that takes place only in small communities. They consider that this politics is much more effective than countering the power games of men with similar games. In Germany, too this debate has to be seen against the background of the emergence of the Greens, who participated in parliamentary politics since 1978. Many feminists joined the Green Party, less out of ecological, than feminist con-cerns. The Greens, however, were keen to integrate these concerns too into their progammes and politics. The critique of the 'spiritual' stand within the ecofeminist movement is voiced mainly by men and women from the left. Many women, particu-larly those who combine their critique of capitalism with a critique of patriarchy and still cling to some kind of 'materialist' concept of history, do not easily accept spiritual ecofeminism, because it is obvious that capitalism can also co-opt the 'spiritual' feminists' critique of 'materialism'.

This, indeed, is already happening. The New Age and esoteric movement have created a new market for esoterica, meditation, yoga, magic, alternative health practices, most of which are fragments taken out of the context of oriental, particularly Chinese and Indian, cultures. Now, after the material resources of the colonies have been looted, their spiritual and cultural resources are being transformed into commodities for the world market.

This interest in things spiritual is a manifestation of Western patriarchal capitalist civilization's deep crisis. While in the West the spiritual aspects of life (always segregated from the 'material' world), have more and more been eroded, people now look towards the 'East', towards pre-industrial traditions in the search for what has been destroyed in their own culture.

This search obviously stems from a deep human need for wholeness, but the fragmented and commodified way in which it takes place is to be criticized. Those interested in oriental spiritualism rarely know, or care to know, how people in , for example India, live or even the socio-economic and political contexts from these which fragments — such as yoga or tai-chi — have been taken. It is a kind of luxury spirituality. It is as Saral Sarkar put it,[26] the idealist icing on top of the material cake of the West's standard of living. Such luxury spiritualism cannot overcome the dichotomies between spirit and matter, economics and culture, because as long as it fails to integrate this search for wholeness into a critique of the existing exploitative world system and a search for a better society it can easily be co-opted and neutralized.

For Third World women who fight for the conservation of their survival base this spiritual icing-on-the-cake, the divorce of the spiritual from the material is incomprehensible for them, the term Mother Earth does not need to be qualified by inverted commas, because they regard the earth as a living being which guarantees their own and all their fellow creatures survival. They respect and celebrate Earth's sacredness and resist its transformation into dead, raw material for industrialism and commodity production. It follows, therefore, that they also respect both the diversity and the limits of nature which cannot be violated if they want to survive. It is this kind of materialism, this kind of immanence rooted in the everyday subsistence production of most of the world's women which is the basis of our ecofeminist position. This materialism is neither commodified capitalist nor mechanical Marxist materialism, both of which are based on the same concept of humanity's relationship to nature. But the ecofeminist spirituality as we understand it is not to be confused with a kind of other-worldly spirituality, that simply wants 'food without sweat', not caring where it comes from or whose sweat it involves.

The following chapters are informed by our basic understanding of ecofeminism as a perspective which starts from the fundamental necessities of life; we call this the subsistence perspective. Our opinion is that women are nearer to this perspective than men — women in the South working and living, fighting for their immediate survival are nearer to it than urban, middle-class women and men in the North. Yet all women and all men have a body which is directly affected by the destructions of the industrial system. Therefore, all women and finally also all men have a 'material base' from which to analyse and change these processes. In the following chapters we discuss several questions which cropped up in the course of our struggles and reflections. Although these questions were not planned before, they nevertheless cover a large part of the issues and problems we are faced with if we want to preserve life on this planet: the issue of our concept of knowledge, the issue of poverty and development, the issue of industrialization of all life forms, the search for cultural identity and rootedness, the search for freedom and self-determination within a limited globe. And finally we attempt to spell out our vision of a society benevolent towards nature, women, children and men. We have not tried to iron out all differences of opinion and analysis in our respective contributions. At the present juncture and under the prevailing conditions as they actually exist, such differences are inevitable and we feel they should not be avoided, as they present a realistic picture of what an ecofeminist discourse at the global level can be.

Notes

1. Gladitz. N.,*Lieber heute aktiv als morgen radioaktiv*, Wagenbach, Berlin 1976.
2. Shiva, V. *Staying Alive: Women, Ecology and Survival*, Kali for Women, New Delhi and Zed Books, London 1988. Shiva, V., *Fight for Survival* (Interview with Chamun Devi and Itwari Devi) in: *Illustrated Weekly of India*, November 15 1987.
3. Dankelman, I. & J. Davidson, *Women and Environment in the Third World: Alliance for the Future*. Earthscan Publications Ltd., London 1988.
4. Ekins, Paul *A New World Order: Grassroots Movements for Global Change*. Routledge, London & New York 1992.

5. Bravo, E. Accion Ecologica, *Un Ecosistema en peligro: Los bosques de maglar en la costa ecuatoriana.* Quito, n.d.
6. This is based on an interview with Annemarie Sacher and Lore Haag, two of the women leaders of the anti-atomic movement, at Whyl, Kaiserstuhl, S.W. Germany. This was the first of these movements in Germany; it lasted from 1974 to about 1976 when the construction of the nuclear reactor was stopped. For more details see: Saral Sarkar: *Green Alternative Politics in West Germany,* Vol. I, The New Social Movements, Promilla Publishers, New Delhi 1992.
7. Dankelman & Davidson, op. cit.
8. Levine, Murray, *Love Canal: My Story,* SUNY, Albany NY 1982, p. xv.
9. *Voices Unidas,* Vol. I, No. 2, 1992.
10. Interview with Medha Patkar in: Indigenous Vision, Peoples of India, Attitudes to the Environment, *India International Centre Quarterly,* Spring-Summer 1992, p. 294.
11. Ortner, S., 'Is Female to Male as Nature to Culture?' In: Rosaldo, M. Z. & L. Lamphere, *Women, Culture and Society,* Stanford University Press, Stanford 1974.
12. Diamond, I. & G. F. Orenstein, *Reweaving the World: The Emergence of Ecofeminism.* Sierra Club Books, San Francisco, 1990. Plant, J. *Healing the Wounds: The Promise of Ecofeminism,* New Society Publishers, Philadelphia, Pa., Santa Cruz, Ca 1989. King, Y. 'The Ecology of Feminism and the Feminism of Ecology,' in: Plant, op. cit. pp. 18-28.
13. Birk, A. & I. Stoehr, Der Fortschritt entläßt seine Tochter, in: Frauen und Ökologie. Gegen den Machbarkeitswahn, Volksblattverlag, Köln 1987.
14. This is based on an interview by Vandana Shiva, see Shiva 1987, op. cit.
15. Diamond and Orenstein, 1990, op. cit.
16. D'Eaubonne, F., 'Feminism or Death,' in: Elaine Marks and Isabelle de Courtivron (eds), *New French Feminisms, an Anthology,* Amherst University Press, Amherst 1980.
17. King, Y., 'The Eco-Feminist Perspective,' in: Caldecott, L. & S. Leland (eds), *Reclaiming the Earth: Women Speak out for Life on Earth.* The Women's Press, London 1983, p. 10.
18. Ibid, p. 11.
19. Howard-Gorden, F., 'Seveso is Everywhere,' in: Caldecott & Leland, op. cit., pp. 36-45.
20. Statement of Sicilian Women, quoted in Caldecott & Leland, op. cit., p. 126.
21. See Gladitz, op. cit. This was also stated in the interview Maria Mies took in 1990 (see note 6).
22. Merchant, C., *The Death of Nature. Women, Ecology and the Scientific Revolution,* Harper & Row, San Francisco 1983.
23. Mies, M., TANTRA, Magie oder Spiritualität? in: beitraege zur .
24. Starhawk, 1982.
25. Caldecott & Leland, op. cit., p. 15.
26. Sarkar, S., Die Bewegung und ihre Strategie. Ein Beitrag zum notwendigen Klärungsprozeß, in: *Kommune,* Nr. Frankfurt 1987.
27. Diamond, I., 'Resisting the Logic of Control: Feminism, Fertility and the Living Earth,' paper (unpublished) 1990.

2. Reductionism and Regeneration: A Crisis in Science

Vandana Shiva

Knowledge and ignorance

Modern science is projected as a universal, value-free system of knowledge, which by the logic of its method claims to arrive at objective conclusions about life, the universe and almost everything. This dominant stream of modern science, the reductionist or mechanical paradigm, is a specific projection of Western man that originated during the fifteenth and seventeenth centuries as the much acclaimed Scientific Revolution. Recently, however, Third World and feminist scholarship[1] has begun to recognize that this dominant system emerged as a liberating force not for humanity as a whole (though it legitimized itself in terms of universal benefit for all), but as a Western, male-oriented and patriarchal projection which necessarily entailed the subjugation of both nature and women.[2]

Central to this domination and subjugation is an arbitrary barrier between 'knowledge' (the specialist) and 'ignorance' (the non-specialist). This barrier operates effectively to exclude from the scientific domain consideration of certain vital questions relating to the subject matter of science, or certain forms of non-specialist knowledge.

Two personal experiences exemplify this exclusion inherent in dominant knowledge. In the 1970s, while studying to be a nuclear physicist, I came home rejoicing in a summer training course, feeling 'high' at being part of a privileged minority: the atomic energy establishment. But my sister, a doctor, brought me down to earth by revealing my ignorance of the risks of nuclear hazards. As nuclear experts we knew how nuclear reactions occur, but not how radiation affects living systems. The radiation badges and overalls were merely the ritual garb signifying membership of an exclusive club. This sudden exposure to my own ignorance as a budding nuclear physicist left me feeling shocked and cheated and led to my shifting to a study of theoretical physics.

A decade later, when I was pregnant and already in labour, I again encountered this arbitrary boundary between expertise and ignorance. The doctor insisted that I needed to be delivered by Caesarean section because, she said, it would be a difficult birth. I had experienced no problems, had prepared myself for a natural childbirth and informed myself about the potential problems, including medical malpractices. As a mother, however, I was denied the status of 'expert' in child-bearing; that status was restricted to the doctor. I was the unknowing body; the doctor was the knowing mind. When I asked what were the indications for a Caesarean I was hesitantly told that I was too old, that is, I was 30 and apparently that was sufficient indication of the need for a Caesarean section. But I preferred to listen to my own good sense and walked out of the delivery room. My father drove me to a more modest hospital where they were willing to give my baby and me a chance to be natural. As expected, I had a smooth, untraumatic delivery.

There seems to be a deception inherent in divided and fragmented knowledge, which treats non-specialist knowledge as ignorance and through the artificial divide, is able to conceal its own ignorance. I characterize modern, Western patriarchy's special epistemological tradition of the 'scientific revolution' as 'reductionist' because: 1) it reduced the capacity of humans to know nature both by excluding other knowers and other ways of knowing; and 2) by manipulating it as inert and fragmented matter, nature's capacity for creative regeneration and renewal was reduced. Reductionism has a set of distinctive characteristics which demarcates it from all other non-reductionist knowledge systems which it has subjugated and replaced. Primarily, the ontological and epistemological assumptions of reductionism are based on uniformity, perceiving all systems as comprising the same basic constituents, discrete, and atomistic, and assuming all basic processes to be mechanical. The mechanistic metaphors of reductionism have socially reconstituted nature and society. In contrast to the organic metaphors, in which concepts of order and power were based on interdependence and reciprocity, the metaphor of nature as a machine was based on the assumption of divisibility and manipulability. As Carolyn Merchant has remarked:

In investigating the roots of our current environmental

dilemma and its connections to science, technology and the economy, we must re-examine the formation of a world-view and a science that, reconceptualising reality as a machine, rather than a living organism, sanctioned the domination of both nature and women.[3]

This domination is inherently violent, understood here as the violation of integrity. Reductionist science is a source of violence against nature and women, in so far as it subjugates and dispossesses them of their full productivity, power and potential. The epistemological assumptions of reductionism are related to its ontological assumptions: uniformity permits knowledge of parts of a system to stand for knowledge of the whole. Divisibility permits context-free abstraction of knowledge, and creates criteria of validity based on alienation and non-participation, which is then projected as 'objectivity'. 'Experts' and 'specialists' are thus projected as the only legitimate seekers after and producers of knowledge.

Value and non-value

Reductionism is protected not merely by its own mythology, but is also protected by the interests it serves. Far from being an epistemological accident, reductionism is a response to the needs of a particular form of economic and political organization. The reductionist world-view, the industrial revolution and the capitalist economy are the philosophical, technological and economic components of the same process. Individual firms and the fragmented sectors of the economy, whether privately or state owned, are concerned only with their own efficiency and profits; and every firm and sector measures its efficiency by the extent to which it maximizes its profits, regardless of the maximization of social and ecological costs. Reductionism has provided the logic of this efficiency. Only those properties of a resource system which generate profits through exploitation and extraction are taken into account; properties which stabilize ecological processes but are commercially non-profit generating are ignored and eventually destroyed.

Commercial capitalism is based on specialized commodity production and therefore demands uniformity in production, and the uni-functional use of natural resources. Reductionism thus reduces complex ecosystems to a single component, and a single component to a single function. Further, it allows for the manipulation of the ecosystem in a way that maximizes the single-function, single-component exploitation. In the reductionist paradigm, a forest is reduced to commercial wood, and wood is reduced to cellulose fibre for the pulp and paper industry. Forests, land and genetic resources are then manipulated to increase the production of pulpwood. This distortion is legitimized scientifically as overall productivity increase, regardless of whether it might decrease the output of water from the forest, or destroy the diversity of life forms that constitute a forest community. 'Scientific' forestry and forestry 'development' thus violate and destroy the living and diverse ecosystem. In this way, reductionist science is at the root of the growing ecological crisis, because it entails a transformation of nature that destroys its organic processes and rhythms and regenerative capacities.

The arbitrary boundaries between knowledge and ignorance are paralleled by arbitrary boundaries between value and non-value. The reductionist, mechanistic metaphor simultaneously creates the measure of value and the instruments for the annihilation of that which it considers non-value. It creates the possibility of colonizing and controlling that which is free and self-generative. Technological development proceeds from what it has already transformed and used up towards that which still remains untouched.

It is in this sense that the seed and women's bodies as sites of regenerative power are, in the eyes of capitalist patriarchy, among the last colonies.[4] These sites of creative regeneration are transformed into 'passive' sites where the expert 'produces' and adds value. Nature, women and non-white people merely provide 'raw' material. The devaluation of contributions from women and nature goes hand-in-hand with the value assigned to acts of colonization as acts of development and improvement. Separation, which signifies alienation, becomes a means of ownership and control. Locke's second treatise on government states that: 'Whatsoever then he moves out of the state that Nature hath provided and left it in he hath mixed his labour with and thereby makes it his property.'[5] The act of 'moving out' thus becomes the act of owning, and it is for the facilitation of the ability to 'move out', separate and fragment that capital depends on science and technology. Ownership procured through removal and 'mixing with labour', however, denies that prior to this, labour had been involved. There is no clear line between nature and human labour expended on the cultivated seed and nature and the human offspring. What the industrializing vision sees as nature is other people's social labour that it wants to denigrate by defining it as non-labour, as biology and nature, and defining both nature and women's work as passive.

From the dominant standpoint, as Claudia von Werlhof[6] has pointed out, 'nature' is everything that should be available free, and/or as cheaply as possible. This includes products of social labour. 'The labour of these people is therefore pronounced to be non-labour, to be biology; their labour power — their ability to work — appears as a natural resource, and their products as akin to a natural deposit.'

A number of artificial shifts are thus achieved through fragmenting knowledge. The sources of regeneration and renewal of life are transformed into inert and fragmented matter, mere 'raw material' to be processed into a finished product. The transformation of creativity into passivity relocates productivity in disruptive, coercive and exploitative acts, and defines it as a source of value; and simultaneously defines all other values as non-value. Through this relocation of production and value, external control over sites of regeneration becomes not just desirable but *necessary* for human survival and well-being. The destructive, ironically, emerges as the saviour.

The many shifts of value into non-value, labour into non-labour, creativity into passivity, destruction into production are exemplified in the takeover of biological reproduction by capital and technology.

The reduction of human reproduction

The medicalization of childbirth has been linked to the mechanization of the female body into a set of fragmented, fetishized and replaceable parts, to be managed by professional experts.

Pregnant women are viewed not so much as sources of human regeneration, as the 'raw material' from which the 'product' —the baby — is extracted. In these circumstances, the physician rather than the mother comes to be seen as having produced the baby. What seems significant is that the Caesarean section, which requires the most medical 'management' and the least 'labour' by the uterus and the woman, is often considered to provide the best products. In the case of in vitro fertilization (IVF), an expert committee saw doctors not only as 'enablers', but as 'taking part in the formation of the embryo itself'.[7]

Formerly, the focus was on the mother, and the organic unity of mother and baby, now it is centred on the 'foetal outcome' controlled by doctors. Women's wombs have been reduced to inert containers,[8] and their passivity has been constructed along with their ignorance. A woman's direct organic bond with the foetus is replaced by knowledge mediated by men and machines which claims the monolopy of expertise to educate women to be good mothers. As Ann Oakley, quoting from a medical textbook, writes:

> When a mother undergoes ultrasound scanning of the fetus, this seems a great opportunity for her to meet her child socially and in this way, one hopes, to view him as a companion aboard rather than as a parasite . . . Doctors and technicians scanning mothers have a great opportunity to enable mothers to form an early affectionate bond to their child by demonstrating the child to the mother. This should help mothers to behave concernedly towards the fetus.[9]

Not only has women's labour and knowledge been negated, but even their intimate link with and love for the child which emerges from their own body has to be demonstrated by doctors and technicians.

The new reproductive technologies accentuate the shift in power from the mother to the doctor, from women to men,[10] suggest that the production of sperm is of greater value than the production of eggs. They conclude that sperm-vending places a greater strain on the man than does egg 'donation' on the woman, in spite of the chemical and mechanical invasion into her body necessarily associated with this process. Furthermore, IVF and other technologies are currently offered for 'abnormal' cases of infertility, but the boundary between normal and abnormal is as ambiguous as is the boundary between nature and non-nature. When pregnancy was first transformed into a medical condition, professional management was limited to abnormal cases, while normal cases continued to be cared for by the original professionals: the midwife. While in the 1930s, 70 per cent of childbirths were thought sufficiently normal for the woman to be delivered at home, in the 1950s 70 per cent were identified as sufficiently abnormal to warrant delivery in hospital. To quote Anne Oakley again:

> The wombs of women are containers to be captured by the ideologies and practises of those who do not believe that women are able to take care of themselves. The

capturing of women's wombs is the domination of the physicalist and masculinist scientific paradigm, the ultimate logic, not merely of the medicalization of life, but of a Cartesian world-view, in which the behaviour of bodies can be explained and controlled independently of minds.[11]

A *Time* magazine article[12] — 'A Revolution in Making Babies' — describes techniques to cross the 'barrier' posed to pregnancy by menopause. The body's rhythms have been systematically interpreted as technological barriers — and crossing the barrier has involved fragmenting the organism, in the mind and materiality. Thus the *Time's* article states that 'new findings suggest that these women may be infertile not because their uteruses are too old but because their ovaries are'.

Reducing organic wholes to fragmented, separable and substitutable parts has been the reductionist method of going beyond nature's limits.

The reduction of plant reproduction

Since the scientific and industrial revolution, technology and economics have mutually reinforced the assumption that nature's limits must be overridden in order to create abundance and freedom. Agriculture and food production illustrate how overriding these limits has led to a breakdown of ecological and social systems. For centuries, agricultural societies operated in accordance with nature's limits in order to ensure the renewability of plant life and soil fertility. But natural processes for this renewal became perceived of as a constraint which had to be overcome. Industrially produced seed and fertilizer were considered superior substitutes for nature's seeds and fertility; yet these substitutes rapidly transformed soil fertility and plant life into a non-renewable resource. Soil and seeds used as raw material and inputs for Green Revolution and industrial agriculture, created diseased soils, water-logged or salinized wastelands, and pest- and disease-infested crops. The ultimate step in converting nature into a resource is the conversion of 'seed' — the source from which plant life rises again — into a 'genetic resource' to be engineered, patented and owned for corporate profit. Nature's ways of renewing plants are dismissed as too slow and 'primitive'. Natural limits on reproduction of life — 'species barriers' — are now to be crossed by engineering transgenic life-forms, whose impact on life can be neither known nor imagined.

The scientific revolution was to have rolled back the boundaries of ignorance. Instead, a tradition of knowledge that has viewed nature and women only as a resource, and nature's limits as constraints, has created unprecedented man-made ignorance — an ignorance which is becoming a new source of threat to life on this planet. Colonization of the seed, reflects the patterns of colonization of women's bodies. Profits and power become intimately linked to invasion into all biological organisms.

Hybridization was an invasion into the seed; it fractured the unity of seed as grain (food) and as means of production. In doing so, it opened the space for capital accumulation needed by private industry in order to become firmly established in plant breeding and commercial seed production. As in the case of women's regenerative process, the first step in colonization of the seed is its reduction by means of a mechanistic metaphor. A book on high yielding crop varieties states:

> Plants are the primary factory of agriculture where seeds are like the 'machine', fertilizers and water are like the fuel; herbicides, pesticides, equipments, credits and technical know-how are accelerators, to increase the output of this industry. The output in the plant industry is directly correlated with the genetic potential of the seeds to make use of the cash and non-cash inputs.[13]

Modern plant-breeding is primarily an attempt to eliminate the biological obstacle to the market in seed: its inherent ability to regenerate and multiply. Seed that reproduces itself stays free, a common resource and under the farmers' control. Corporate seed has a cost and is under the control of the corporate sector or agricultural research institutions. The transformation of a common source into a commodity, of a self-regenerative resource into a mere 'input' changes the nature of the seed and of agriculture itself. Peasants and farmers are thus robbed of their means of livelihood by the new technology which becomes an instrument of poverty and underdevelopment.

Divorcing seed as a source from grain (food) also changes the seed's status. From being complete, self-regenerating products seeds become mere raw material for the production of a commodity. The cycle of regeneration, of biodiversity, is therefore supplanted by a linear flow of free germ plasm from farms and forests into laboratories and research stations, and of modified uniform products as cost-bearing commodities from corporations to farmers. Potential diversity is nullified by transforming it into mere raw material for industrial production based on uniformity, and this also necessarily displaces the diversity of local agricultural practise. To quote Claude Alvares: 'For the first time the human race has produced seed that cannot cope on its own, but needs to be placed within an artificial environment for growth and output.'[14]

This change in the nature of seed is justified by creating a value and meaning system that treats self-regenerative seed as 'primitive', as 'raw' germ plasm, and the seed that, without inputs, is inert and nonreproducible as 'advanced' or 'improved'. The whole is rendered partial, the partial is rendered whole. The commoditized seed is ecologically crippled on two levels.

(1) It does not *reproduce* itself while, by definition, seed is a regenerative resource. Genetic resources thus, through technological manipulation, transform a renewable source into a non-renewable source.

(2) It cannot *produce* by itself, to do so it needs the help of artificial, manufactured inputs. As seed and chemical companies merge, dependence on inputs will increase. A chemical, whether externally or internally applied, remains an external input in the ecological cycle of the reproduction of seed.

This shift from the ecological processes of reproduction to the technological processes of production underlies two crucial problems. 1) Dispossession of farmers, because their seeds are rendered incomplete and valueless by the process that makes corporate seeds the basis of wealth creation; 2) genetic erosion because the indigenous varieties or land races, evolved both through natural and human selection, and produced and used by Third World farmers worldwide are called 'primitive cultivars', while those varieties created by modern plant-breeders in international research centres or by transnational seed corporations are called 'advanced' or 'elite'. The implicit hierarchy in the words 'primitive' and 'advanced' or 'elite' becomes explicit. Thus, the North has always treated the South's germ plasm as a freely available resource of no value. The advanced capitalist countries are determined to retain free access to the South's genetic storehouse; the South would like to have the proprietory varieties of the North's genetic industry similarly declared a freely available resource. The North, however, resists this reciprocity. Dr J. T. Williams, Executive Secretary of the International Board for Plant

Genetic Resources (IBPGR) has argued that, *'It is not the original material which produces cash returns.'*[15] A 1983 forum on plant breeding, sponsored by Pioneer Hi-Bred stated that:

> Some insist that since germ-plasm is a resource belonging to the public, such improved varieties would be supplied to farmers in the source country at either low or no cost. This overlooks the fact that *'raw' germ-plasm only becomes valuable after considerable investment of time and money*, both in adapting exotic germ-plasm for use by applied plant breeders in incorporating the germ-plasm into varieties useful to farmers.[16] [Emphasis added.]

In the corporate perspective, only that which makes profit is of value. However, all material processes also serve ecological needs and social needs, and these needs are undermined by the monopolizing tendency of corporations.

Patents have become a major means of establishing profits as a measure of value. To patent an object/material excludes others from creating/inventing a novel and useful variation of the patented object/material, usually for a specific period of time. In the area of industrial design and artifacts, patenting, 'owning' the 'products of the mind', is less problematic[17] than in the area of biological processes, where organisms are self-generating and often shaped, modified or augmented by techniques of breeding, selection and so on. Thus, to assess intellectual property claims in these processes is far more difficult, if not impossible.

Until the advent of biotechnologies, which changed concepts of ownership of life, animals and plants were excluded from the patent system. But now, with these technologies, life can be owned. The potential for gene separation and manipulation reduces the organism to its genetic constituents. Monopoly rights on life forms are conferred on those who use new technology to manipulate genes, while the contributions of generations of farmers and agriculturalists, in the Third World and elsewhere, in the areas of conservation, breeding, domestication and development of plant and animal genetic resources are devalued and dismissed. As Pat Mooney has observed, 'the argument that intellectual property is only recognizable when performed in laboratories with white lab coats is fundamentally a racist view of scientific development.'[18]

The clear inferences of this argument are: 1) that Third World farmers' labour has no value, while Western scientists' labour adds value; and 2) that value is measured only in terms of the market: profitability. It is, however, recognized that, 'the total genetic change achieved by farmers over the millennia was far greater than that achieved by the last hundred or two years of more systematic science based efforts'. Plant scientists are not the sole producers of utility in seed.

Invasion and justice

When labour is defined as non-labour, values becomes non-value, rights non-rights, and invasion becomes defined as improvement. 'Improved seeds' and 'improved foetuses' are, in reality, 'captured' seeds and foetuses. To define social labour as a state of nature is an essential element of this 'improvement'. This achieves three things simultaneously: 1) it denies any contribution by those whose products are appropriated, and by converting their activity in passivity transforms used and developed resources into 'unused', 'undeveloped' and 'wasted' resources; 2) by construing appropriation to mean 'development' and 'improvement', it transforms robbery into a right with the claim to ownership based on a claim of improving; and 3) and relatedly, by defining previous social labour as nature, and thus not conferring any rights, it transforms people's assertion of their customary, collective usufructory rights into 'piracy', and 'theft'.

According to Sir Thomas More, when 'any people holdeth a piece of ground void and vacant to no good or profitable use' its confiscation is justified, an argument he applied to the confiscation of the Americas from its indigenous inhabitants. In 1889, Theodore Roosevelt said that 'the settler and pioneer have at bottom had justice on their side; this great continent could not have been kept as nothing but a game preserve for squalid savages'.[19]

Native use was non-use, native lands were empty and 'void', and could be defined as valueless, free, 'nature', to be 'justly' appropriated. New colonies are now being created, carved out by reductionist thought, capital and profit, controlled by patriarchal might. The new technologies are making their greatest 'progress' in plant biotechnology and reproductive technologies — the boundaries between what is, and what is not nature, what is and what is not a right are being redrawn.

The 'seed wars', the trade wars, patent 'protection' and intellectual property rights designed by GATT[20] are modern versions of claim to ownership through separation. The US international trade commission estimates that US industry is losing between US\$ 100 and 300 million due to the absence of 'intellectual property rights'. If this regime of 'rights' being demanded by the US takes shape, the transfer of these extra funds from poor to rich countries would exacerbate the Third World debt crisis ten times over.[21]

Violence, power and ecological disruption are intimately linked as life-processes are rendered 'valueless' and their sundering becomes the source of the creation of value and wealth — when invasion into the space within (seeds and wombs) becomes a new space for capital accumulation and a new source of power and control which destroys the very source of control.

Regeneration, production and consumption

The colonization of regenerative sources of the renewal of life is the ultimate ecological crisis: patriarchal science and technology, in the service of patriarchal capitalism, have torn apart cycles of regeneration, and forced them into linear flows of raw materials and commodities. The self-provisioning, self-regenerative systems have been reduced into 'raw' material, and consuming systems have been elevated into 'production' systems which supply commodities to consumers. The disruption of natural growth cycles becomes the source of capital growth because, as Marilyn Waring has pointed out, the principle underlying collection of data for the national accounts is to exclude data relating to production where the producer is also the consumer. The destruction of regeneration is not revealed as destruction, instead the multiplication of 'producers' and 'consumers' and commodities signals growth.

Mainstream environmentalists, as manifested at the 1992 Earth Summit, divorced from feminism, continue to use the model of the world designed by capitalist patriarchy. Instead of rebuilding ecological cycles, it focuses on technological fixes. Instead of relocating human activity in regeneration, it maintains the categories of production and consumption, and offers 'green consumerism' as an environmental panacea.

The feminist perspective is able to go *beyond* the categories of patriarchy that structure power and meaning in nature and society. It is broader and deeper because it locates production and consumption within the context of regeneration. Not only does this relate issues that have so far been treated as separate, such as linking production with reproduction, but more significantly, by making these links, ecological feminism creates the possibility of viewing the world as an active subject, not merely as a resource to be manipulated and appropriated. It problematizes 'production' by exposing the destruction inherent in much of what capitalistic patriarchy has defined as productive and creates new spaces for the perception and experience of the creative act.

The 'activation' of what has been, or is being construed as 'passive' according to patriarchal perception, becomes then the most significant step in the renewal of life. Overcoming estrangement from nature's rhythms and cycles of renewal and becoming a conscious participant in them becomes a major source of this activation. Women everywhere are indicating this. Whether it is Barbara McLintock[23] referring to a 'feeling for the organism', Rachel Carson[24] talking of participating in nature's perennial rhythms, or Itwari Devi[25] describing how *shakti* (power) comes from forests and grasslands.

That search and experience of interdependence and integrity is the basis for creating a science and knowledge that nurtures, rather than violates, nature's sustainable systems.

Notes

1. Alvares, Claude, *Decolonising History*. The Other India Book Store, Goa, 1992.
2. Harding, Sandra, *The Science Question in Feminism*. Cornell University Press, Ithaca, 1986.
3. Merchant, Carolyn, *The Death of Nature*. Harper & Row, New York, 1980.
4. Mies, M. et al., *Women, the Last Colony*. Zed Books, London, 1988.
5. Locke, John *Two Treatises of Government*. J. M. Dent & Sons, London, 1991.
6. Claudia von Werlhof, 'On the Concept of Nature and Society in Capitalism', in Maria Mies et al, op. cit.
7. Martin, Emily, *The Woman in the Body*. Beacon Press, Boston.
8. UNICEF, *Children and the Environment*. 1990.
9. Oakley, Ann, *The Captured Womb*, Blackwell, London, 1989.
10. Singer and Wells, *The Reproduction Revolution, New Ways of Making Babies*. Oxford University Press, Oxford, 1984.
11. Ann Oakley, op. cit.
12. *Time* magazine, 6 November 1990.
13. Ram, Mahabal, *High Yielding Varieties of Crops*. Oxford University Press, New Delhi, 1980.
14. Alvares, Claude, 'The Great Gene Robbery', *The Illustrated Weekly of India*. 23 March 1986.
15. Quoted in Jack Kloppenburg 'First the Seed', *The Political Economy of Plant Biotechnology* 1492-2000. Cambridge University Press, 1988.

16. Ibid.
17. Sheewood, Robert, *Intellectual Property and Economic Development.* Westview, Colorado, 1990.
18. Mooney, Pat *From Cabbages to Kings, Intellectual Property vs Intellectual Integrity.* ICDA report, 1990.
19. Roosevelt, Theodore, *The Winning of the West.* New York.
20. Draft Final Agreement, General Agreement for Trade and Tariffs, GATT Secretariat, December 1991.
21. Hobbelink, Henk *Biotechnology and the Future of World Agriculture.* Zed Books, London, 1991.
22. Waring, Marilyn *If Women Counted.* Harper & Row, 1989.
23. Keller, Evelyn Fox, *A Feeling for the Organism: The Life and Work of Barbara McLintock.* W. M. Freeman, New York, 1983.
24. Hynes, Patricia, *The Recurring Silent Spring.* Athene Series, Pergamon Press, New York, 1989.
25. Quoted in Vandana Shiva, op. cit.

3. Feminist Research: Science, Violence and Responsibility*

Maria Mies

One of the astonishing experiences of the new Women's Liberation Movement was the realization that in the nineteenth and
early twentieth centuries there had been a Women's Movement of
which we, when we started the new Women's Liberation Movement in 1968/69, were completely unaware. The prevailing
historiography and teaching of history had totally suppressed it.
This was similar to our surprise when we rediscovered the persecution and murder of millions of our sisters, the witches, which
went on for at least three centuries. Even this holocaust has been
largely neglected by mainstream historiography. The documenta-
tion and assimilation of our history, therefore became an important requirement of the new Women's Movement.

This also holds true for Women's Studies which, it is already
necessary to remind ourselves, grew out of this movement. It was
not the result of academic efforts, it did *not* arise in research institutes, it was *not* invented by a few gifted women scholars, but
arose on the street, in countless women's groups, in which housewives, secretaries, students, and a few social scientists came together, who jointly, *as women,* wanted to fight against patriarchal
exploitation and oppression. In other worlds, it was feminists who
had a *political* goal — in broad terms, the liberation of women from
domination by men, violence, and exploitation — who created
Women's Studies.

This political objective was in the foreground when, in West
Germany, between 1973 and 1980, women students and feminist
lecturers began to use the universities as a battleground for the
liberation of women by organizing women's seminars, by opening the Berlin Summer University for Women, later by organizing

* This is an extensively revised version of a lecture at the University of Innsbruck,
1986, and earlier published in German in Hildegard Fassler, (ed) *Das Tabu der
Gewalt, Vol. I,* (1985-87). Innsbruck: Universitätsverlag.

the Women's Weeks in Hamburg, Bremen and other cities, and finally by setting up some feminist organizations, such as the Association of Social Science Research and Praxis for Women (1978) and the Women's Research Section in the German Sociological Society (1979). Similar feminist organizations were also set up in other disciplines.

At that time, it was clear to us that feminist research, in view of its roots in the Women's Liberation Movement, 'would have to cut across all the disciplines' (as it was formulated at the Bielefeld Sociologists Congress in 1976), that Women's Studies could not just be added on to the existing disciplines as a new hyphen sociology, psychology, and so on. As feminist research, it was of necessity a *criticism of the prevailing paradigm of science* and social science, which had not only made women and their contribution *invisible*, but was most profoundly imbued with androcentric, that is, male-centred prejudices, both in its general assumptions and conceptualizations and in its theories and methods. In fact, we discovered that this science had provided the most important instruments for the oppression and exploitation of women: biologism and its regard to the relations between the sexes in the social sciences, in psychology, in behavioural sciences, in education, and so on.

When we gathered for the first Congress on Women's Studies in Frankfurt in 1978, we tried to work out for ourselves a theoretical and methodological foundation for a different, feminist understanding of social science, which would not exclude our experience and involvement as women in the study of the oppression of women and our political goal of abolishing that oppression, but would integrate it in the research process. At that time I presented my ideas on a methodology for Women's Studies, which were subsequently widely circulated and accepted by many as the theoretical-methodological basis for Women's Studies. These methodological postulates or guidelines were introduced by the remark that:

> . . . *there is a contradiction between the prevalent theories of social science and methodology and the political aims of the women's movement.* If Women's Studies is to be made into an instrument of Women's Liberation we cannot uncritically use the positivist, quantitative research methodology . . . Women's Studies means more than the fact that women have now been discovered as a 'target group' for

research or that an increasing number of women scholars
and students are taking up women's issues. (Mies, 1983,
p. 120)

What follows is a brief summary of my methodological postulates for Women's Studies, demonstrating its commitment to the
goal of Women's Liberation. (Mies, 1983, pp. 117-37)

Methodological guidelines for feminist research

(1) The postulate of *value free research,* of neutrality and indifference towards the research objects, has to be replaced by *conscious
partiality,* which is achieved through partial identification with the
research objects.

For women who deliberately and actively integrate their dou-
ble-consciousness into the research process, this partial identification will not be difficult. It is the opposite of the so-called
'Spectator-Knowledge' *(Maslow, 1966:50)* which is achieved by
showing an indifferent, disinterested, alienated attitude towards
the 'research objects'. Conscious partiality, however, not only con-
ceives of the research objects as parts of a bigger social whole but
also of the research subjects, that is, the researchers themselves.
Conscious partiality is different from mere subjectivism or simple
empathy. On the basis of a limited identification it creates a critical
distance between the researcher and his 'objects'. It enables the
correction of distortions of perception on both sides and widens
the consciousness of both: the researcher and the 'researched'.

(2) The vertical relationship between researcher and 'research
objects', the *view from above,* must be replaced by the view *from
below.* This is the necessary consequence of the demands of conscious partiality and reciprocity. Research, which so far has been
largely an instrument of dominance and legitimation of power
elites, must be brought to serve the interests of dominated, exploited and oppressed groups, particularly women. Women scholars, committed to the cause of women's liberation, cannot have an
objective interest in a 'view from above'. This would mean that
they would consent to their own oppression as women, because
the man-woman relationship represents one of the oldest examples of the view from above and may be the paradigm of all
vertical, hierarchical relationships.

The demand for a systematic 'view from below' has both a
scientific and an ethical-political dimension. The scientific significance is related to the fact that despite the sophistication of the

quantitative research tools, many data gathered by these methods are irrelevant or even invalid because the hierarchical research situation as such defeats the very purpose of research: it creates an acute distrust in the 'research objects' who feel that they are being interrogated. This distrust can be found when women and other underprivileged groups are being interviewed by members of a socially higher stratum. It has been observed that the data thus gathered often reflect 'expected behaviour' rather than real behaviour (Berger, 1974).

Women who are committed to the cause of women's liberation, cannot stop at this result. They cannot be satisfied with giving the social sciences better, more authentic and more relevant data. The ethical-political significance of the view from below cannot be separated from the scientific one: this separation would again transform all methodological innovations in Women's Studies into instruments of dominance. Only if Women's Studies is deliberately made part of the struggle against women's oppression and exploitation can women prevent the misuse of their theoretical and methodological innovations for the stabilization of the status quo and for crisis management. This implies that committed women scholars must fight, not only for the integration of women's issues into the academic establishment and research policies but also for a new orientation regarding areas and objectives of research. The needs and interests of the majority of women must become the yardstick for the research policy of Women's Studies. This presupposes that women in the academic world know these needs and interests. The 'view from below', therefore, leads to another postulate.

(3) The contemplative, uninvolved 'spectator knowledge' must be replaced by *active participation in actions, movements and struggles* for women's emancipation. Research must become an integral part of such struggles.

Because Women's Studies grew out of the women's movement, it would be a betrayal of the aims of the movement if academic women, who were never involved in any struggle or were never concerned about women's oppression and exploitation, should try to reduce Women's Studies to a purely academic concern, restricted to the ivory tower of research institutes and universities, thus blunting the edge of all this discontent.[3] To avert this danger, Women's Studies must remain closely linked to the struggles and actions of the movement.

Max Weber's famous principle of separating science and politics (praxis) is not in the interests of women's liberation. Women scholars who want to do more than a mere paternalistic 'something for their poorer sisters' (because they feel that, as a privileged group, they are already liberated) but who struggle against patriarchy as a system, must take their studies into the streets and take part in the social actions and struggles of the movement.

If they do so, their contribution will be not to give abstract analyses and prescriptions but to help those involved in these struggles to discover and develop their own theoretical and methodological potentials. The elitist attitude of women social scientists will be overcome if they are able to look at all who participate in a social action or struggle as 'sister-or-brother-sociologists' (adapting Gouldner). The integration of research into social and political action for the liberation of women, the dialectics of doing and knowing, will lead to more than better and more realistic theories. According to the approach, the object of research is not something static and homogeneous but an historical, dynamic and contradictory entity. Research, therefore, will have to follow closely the dynamics of this process.

(4) Participation in social actions and struggles, and the integration of research into these processes, further implies that the *change of the status quo* becomes the starting point for a scientific quest. The motto for this approach could be: 'If you want to know a thing, you must change it.'

('If you want to know the taste of a pear, you must change it, that is, you must chew it in your mouth', Mao Zedong, 1968.) If we apply this principle to the study of women, it means that we have to start fighting against women's exploitation and oppression in order to be able to understand the extent, dimensions, and forms and causes of this patriarchal system. Most empirical research on women has concentrated so far on the study of superficial or surface phenomena such as women's attitudes towards housework, career, part-time work, etc. Such attitudes or opinion surveys give very little information about women's true consciousness. Only when there is a rupture in the 'normal' life of a woman, that is, a crisis such as divorce, the end of a relationship, etc., is there a chance for her to become conscious of her true condition. In the 'experience of crises'[4](Kramert, 1977) and rupture with normalcy, women are confronted with the real social relationships in which they had unconsciously been submerged as objects without being able to distance themselves from them. As long as normalcy is not disrupted they are not able to admit, even to themselves, that these relationships are oppressive or exploitative.

This is why in attitude surveys women so often are found to subscribe to the dominant sexist ideology of the submissive, self-sacrificing woman. When a rupture with this normalcy occurs, however, the mystification surrounding the natural and harmonious character of these patriarchal relations cannot be maintained.

Changing a situation in order to be able to understand it applies not only to the individual woman and her life crises, but also to social processes. The very fact that today we are talking about a methodology for research in Women's Studies is the result of a change in the status quo that was brought about by the women's movement and not by intellectual endeavours in universities.

If women scholars begin to understand their studies as an integral part of a liberating struggle and if they focus their research on the processes of individual and social change, then they cannot but change themselves also in this process, both as human beings and as scholars. They will have to give up the elitist narrow-mindedness, abstract thinking, political and ethical impotence and arrogance of the established academician. They must learn that scientific work and a scientific outlook is not the privilege of professional scientists, but that the creativity of science depends on it being rooted in living social processes. Methodologically, this implies the search for techniques with which to document and analyse historical processes of change.

(5) *The research process must become a process of 'conscientization'*, both for the so-called 'research subjects' (social scientists) and for the 'research objects' (women as target groups).

The methodology of 'conscientizaao' (conscientization) was first developed and applied by Paulo Freire in his problem-formulating method.[4] The decisive characteristic of the approach is that the study of an oppressive reality is carried out not by experts but by the objects of the oppression. People who were previously objects of research become subjects of their own research and action. This implies that scientists who participate in this study of the conditions of oppression must give their research tools to the people. They must inspire them to formulate the problems with which they struggle in order that they may plan their action. The women's movement so far has understood the process of conscientization largely as that of becoming conscious of one's individual suffering as a woman. The emphasis in consciousness-raising groups was on group dynamics, role-specific behaviour and relationship problems, rather than the social relations that govern the capitalist patriarchal societies.

The problem-formulating method, however, sees individual problems as an expression and manifestation of oppressive social relations. Whereas consciousness-raising groups often tend to psychologize all relations of dominance, the problem-formulating method considers conscientization as the subjective precondition for liberating action. If processes of conscientization do not lead subsequently to processes of change and action, they may lead to dangerous illusions and even to regression.

(6) I would like to go a step further than Paulo Freire, however. The collective conscientization of women through a problem-formulating methodology *must be accompanied by the study of women's individual and social history.*

Women have so far not been able to appropriate, that is, make their own, the social changes to which they have been subjected passively in the course of history. Women do make history, but in the past they have not *appropriated* (made it their own) it as subjects. Such a subjective appropriation of their history, their past struggles, sufferings and dreams would lead to something like a collective women's consciousness without which no struggle for emancipation can be successful.

The appropriation of women's history can be promoted by feminist scholars who can inspire and help other women document their campaigns and struggles. They can help them to analyse these struggles, so that they can learn from past mistakes and successes and, in the long run, may become able to move from mere spontaneous activism to long-term strategies. This presupposes, however, that women engaged in Women's Studies remain in close contact with the movement and maintain a continuous dialogue with other women. This in turn implies that they can no longer treat their research results as their private property, but that they must learn to collectivize and share them. This leads to the next postulate.

(7) Women cannot appropriate their own history unless they *begin to collectivize their own experiences.* Women's Studies, therefore, must strive to overcome the individualism, the competitiveness, the careerism, prevalent among male scholars. This has relevance both for the individual woman scholar engaged in research and for her methodology.

It is important today to recall these beginnings and foundations because what I criticized in the opening remark to these postulates has occurred: Women's Studies is understood to the extent that the topic of woman has entered the research area, that female — and male — scholars are working on this topic, but the political goal of linking up Women's Studies with the Women's Liberation Movement has largely been abandoned, and Max Weber's old separation of science and politics is again accepted as proof of the scientific quality of Women's Studies. In other words, in a number of countries, in tandem with the institutionalization of Women's Studies in the universities, *an academization of Women's Studies has occurred*. It seems that Women's Studies became socially acceptable only when women scholars were prepared to give up its original political goal, or when people began pursuing Women's Studies who have never shared this goal and never taken part in the Women's Movement.

In my view, the renewed separation of politics and science, life and knowledge, in short, the academization of Women's Studies not only betrays the feminist movement and its goals, but will also eventually kill the spirit of Women's Studies and turn it into some sterile and irrelevant feminology, much in the same way as the academization of Marxism led to Marxology. The same could also happen to ecofeminism if it restricts itself to an academic discourse.

The feminist critique of science was initially directed against mainstream social sciences because many of us were *social scientists*. This criticism has also reached the *natural sciences* and its central paradigm, its underlying world view, its anthropology, its methods, and its application. This critique did not initially arise in research institutes and universities either, but in connection with the ecological, peace, and women's movements particularly with the movement against reproductive and gene technology. The more women and feminists became involved in these movements, the clearer the link became to many of us between 'medium-range rockets and love affairs', as Helke Sander (1980, pp. 4-7) put it — that is, the man-woman relationship between militarism and patriarchy, between technical destruction and domination of nature and violence against women, and between the exploitation of nature and the exploitation of 'foreign' peoples. Women, nature, and foreign peoples and countries are the *colonies of White Man*. Without their colonization, that is, subordination for the purpose of predatory appropriation (exploitation), the famous Western civilization would not exist, nor its paradigm of progress and, above all, not its *natural science and technology* either (see Werlhof, Mies, and Bennholdt-Thomsen, 1983).

This thesis is corroborated by a series of feminist works on the history of modern science which have exploded the patriarchal myth of this allegedly sexless, value-free, impartial, pure science and of the innocence of its mainly male practitioners (see Griffin, 1978; Merchant, 1983; Fox Keller, 1985).

Carolyn Merchant in particular convincingly demonstrated in her book, *The Death of Nature* (1983), that modern natural science, particularly mechanics and physics, are based above all on the destruction and subordination of nature as a living organism — and indeed an organism understood as female — and that at the end of this process nature is considered only as dead raw material, which is dissected into its smallest elements and then recombined by the great (white) engineer into new machines which totally obey his will. Merchant shows that this new domination over Mother Earth of necessity went hand in hand with violence. Natural discovery and knowledge of nature was linked in particular by Francis Bacon — a new father of this natural science — with *power*. And it was he who called for the subordination, suppression, and even torture of nature, to wrest her secrets from her, analogous to the witch-hunts which also took place in the sixteenth and seventeenth centuries. What is more, Bacon was not only the inventor of the new empirical method based on experimentation, he also advised the new heroes of natural science to brush aside all the old taboos without a qualm and to expose them as superstitions with which people had hitherto surrounded Mother Earth, for example, the taboo against driving mines into the womb of Mother Nature in order to get sought-after metals. Bacon said that nature must be forced by torture to yield her secrets, like a bad woman who keeps her treasures avariciously to herself and withholds them from her children (sons).[1]

What Merchant does not mention, but what we must surely see behind Bacon's witch-hunt against Mother Nature, is the fact that these taboos were first, and probably with the least scruple, violated in the countries which the White Man had colonized — South America and the Caribbean. In plundering the gold and silver mines in America, the conquerors no longer needed to worry about those old taboos. Their superiority in weaponry gave them the power to ignore the old fears that Mother Nature would take her revenge. If we enquire into this source of the power that has, since Bacon, entered into a monogamous, chaste marriage with natural science, we cannot then ignore the violent destruction of the witches and the conquest and pillage of the colonies. Not only can the new relation between Man (= White Man) and Nature be seen as the first experiment, but from it also sprang wonderful new riches (that is, not based on one's own labour), which the popes, kings, princes, adventurers, and finally the rising bourgeoisie appropriated as the basis on which the new natural sciences could finally be erected. Bacon was not only a scientist, he was also a well-paid counsellor of King James of England.

Evelyn Fox Keller (1985) unfurls the history of this new patriarchal science from another perspective, the psychological side, which mainly expresses itself in the sexist linguistic symbolism of the fathers of natural science. For these men, nature is by no means an asexual being; it is a woman, an evil, dangerous woman who must be dominated. Man can best maintain dominion over this whore through his mind, his intellect. Of course, only if he has the material military power behind him, as otherwise *mind is as impotent as a withered stick*. Only in combination with material force can Bacon promise his son 'that his chaste marriage with science' would be fruitful, that is, would produce *many works* — today we would say machinery and commodities. For that is what the new fathers of natural science are after: ultimately they want to bring the art of production, the power of creation, which hitherto lay with women and with nature, under their control, the control of the 'pure' male spirit. They want to be creators themselves. But for that they must first rob women and nature of their subjectiveness, that is, of their own dignity, their spirituality, and turn them into lifeless, controllable matter. Living organisms became raw material for the fathers of the future machinery and goods.

Evelyn Fox Keller shows that these new men have also waged this battle against Mother Nature in themselves. The organ in which their new potency is localized is not the phallus, but the *head*, the *brain*. What lies below is considered inferior, is mere animal nature and indeed, is nature already subjected, disciplined, forced into service. For this reason, the new men are no longer capable of Eros, of Love, which for Plato still belonged inalienably to knowledge: Eros, in Plato's case of course, as love of the older wise man for the younger man. Of course in Plato, too, we already find the devaluation of women and matter, but he was still in love with the bodies of young, impressionable men and still saw spirit incorporated in them. According to Fox Keller, modern natural scientists are mostly people incapable of relationships and love. The passion with which they pursue science is the 'chaste' passion mentioned by Bacon, but which in fact can only be sparked off by competitive pressure within the male confederacy and by a mania for omnipotence (see Easlea, 1986). The feminist critique of the natural sciences and natural scientists has disclosed this mania as the patriarchal core of the whole progress model of the White Man.

We could simply sit back with this new knowledge and say: there you go, even science is patriarchal . . . (not male, as many say, even Fox Keller), if the works of these new men were not threatening the foundations of our very life on this Mother Earth, and not thanks to their brain, but thanks to the fatal marriage between brain and violence, which they, mostly euphemistically, call power.

They can only propagate the slogan 'Knowledge is power' with impunity — and people believe in this phrase — because scientists since Bacon, Descartes and Max Weber have constantly concealed the impure relationship between knowledge and violence or force (in the form of state and military power, for example) by defining science as the sphere of a pure search for truth. Thus, they lifted it out of the sphere of politics, that is, the sphere of force and power. The separation of politics (power) and science which we feminists attack is based on a lie. It does not exist and it has never existed, that value-free, disinterested pure science, devoted only to the infinite search for truth, which is legally protected as scientific freedom in our constitutions. Even those scientists who only want to satisfy their presumably irresistible urge for pure knowledge and research cannot do so unless such basic research is funded. And it is not difficult to identify militaristic, political, and economic interests behind this funding of fundamental research (Easlea, 1986; Butte, 1985).

As Carolyn Merchant has shown (1983), the new epistemological principle upon which, since Bacon, the scientific method is based is violence and power. Without violently disrupting the organic whole called Mother Nature, without separating the research objects by force from their symbiotic context and isolating them in the laboratory, without dissecting them — analysing them — into ever smaller bits and pieces in order to discover the secret of matter (atomic research) or the secret of life (biotechnology), the new scientists cannot gain knowledge. They cannot, it seems, understand nature and natural phenomena if they leave them intact within their given environment. Violence and force are therefore intrinsic methodological principles of the modern concept of science and knowledge. They are not, as is often assumed, ethical questions which arise only on the *application of the results* of this science. They belong to the epistemological and methodological foundations of modern science. But in order to be able to do violence to Mother Nature and other sister beings on earth, *homo scientificus* had to set himself apart from, or rather above, nature. A concept of the human being had to be developed in which his own symbiosis with nature and with the woman who gave birth to him, and with women in general, had to be negated. The modern scientist is the man who presumably creates nature as well as himself out of his brain power. He is the new god, the culture hero of European civilization. In the centuries following Bacon, this disruption of the symbiosis between the human being, Mother Nature, and the human mother became synonymous with the processes of emancipation and processes of liberation. This, in my view, is the link between the new scientific method, the new capitalist economy, and the new democratic politics. Without turning a reciprocal, symbiotic relationship between humans and nature into a one-sided, master-and-servant relationship, the bourgeois revolutions would not have been possible. Without turning foreign peoples and their lands into colonies for the White Man, the capitalist economy could not have evolved. Without violently destroying the symbiosis between man and woman, without calling woman mere animal nature, the new man could not have risen as master and lord over nature and women.

For the new scientific subject, this violent separation from and the subjection of nature and women meant that a concept of knowledge had to be created which was completely purified of all traces of the fact that we are born of women and that we shall die, that we are carnal, mortal beings. The brothers Bohme have shown how Immanuel Kant, another father of the modern concept of science, developed a concept of knowledge, of rationality, from which all other sources of knowing, linked to the carnal existence of human beings, are eliminated: our sensuous knowledge, our experience, all feelings and empathy, all power of imagination and intuition. Pure reason has no trace of all these, it is but abstract and

cold, calculating and quantifying — in short, disinterested rationality. To reach this concept of knowledge or reason, a clear cut
between subject and object is necessary (Bohme & Bohme, 1985).

If violence towards nature and human beings, including oneself, is necessary in order to gain knowledge, then the ethical
question immediately arises: *Where do you draw the line?* Where do
you make the break between the subject and the object? Are only
humans subjects and all non-humans objects? Meanwhile, we also
know that humans are used as objects for experimentation. And
women, slaves, and other colonized people are not considered as
subjects, neither are mentally handicapped people.

Today reproductive and gene technology are breaking down
even the last boundary that so far had protected the human person, the individual, from violent invasions and from becoming a
mere object for research. This is particularly true for women who
are in the main the object of research in reproductive technology.
The question of where to draw the line between subject and object,
human and non-human cannot be answered from within science
itself. Because the scientific paradigm is based on the dogma that
there are *no limits* for the scientific urge, the quest arises for ever
more abstract knowledge. No moral interventions are allowed
within the research process. Therefore, scientists cannot themselves answer the questions of ethics. But as scientists are also
ordinary citizens, husbands, fathers, and so on, they also cannot
avoid being confronted more and more with ethical questions
about what they are doing in their laboratories. They usually solve
this problem according to the scientific method, namely by draw-
ing the line between what is allowed and what is not somewhere
new. This means, *they offer new definitions* of what is subject and
what is object, what is human and what is non-human, what is
allowed and what should not be. An example of this method is the
way the new bioethicists deal with the tricky question of embryo
research. For many people — not only the Right-to-Life Movement — embryo research is morally unacceptable. They demand a
ban on embryo research. In Britain, the Warnock Committee and
the Voluntary Licensing Authority (a self-appointed watchdog for
reproductive technology) found a way out of the problem. They
deemed the beginning of life as two weeks after conception. Before the age of two weeks, an embryo is no longer defined as an
embryo, but as a pre-embryo. Therefore, research can be done on
this pre-embryo. Obviously, it is just a question of definition!
Meanwhile, this definition has been accepted by a number of

countries who want to regulate reproductive technology. From the point of view of the scientists and the medical establishment, the case is clear: if reproductive technology, particularly IVF technology, is to be successful, then more embryo research is needed. The success rates at present are simply too low (Klein, 1989). Helga Kuhse and Peter Singer, two bioethicists from Monash University (Australia), go even further in their power of definition. For them the embryo of two weeks is just 'a lettuce'. They make a distinction, or draw the line, between a member of the species *homo sapiens* and a human person:

> What about the human embryo, then? Quite clearly, it is a member of the species *homo sapiens*, but it does not have any of the qualities distinctive of a person: it is not a self-aware, autonomous rational being: it has no nervous system, no brain — it cannot experience anything at all. In lacking any capacity for experience, it is much more like a lettuce than a person or even a laboratory mouse or rat. (Kuhse & Singer, 1986, p. 15)

It is clear that for Kuhse and Singer an embryo of two weeks is not 'a subject that needs to be taken into account' (Kuhse & Singer, 1986, p. 19); therefore not only should research be allowed, but spare embryos could be thrown away or artificially aborted. They want to draw the line even nearer the human person and choose for their definition the time when an embryo would be able to feel pain, that is, after the development of the central nervous system, which they think may be as late as 18 or 20 weeks. They therefore advocate extending the time limit well beyond the 14 days currently set by the Warnock Committee and by the Waller Committee in Australia (Kuhse and Singer, 1986, p. 21). They nowhere mention that an embryo is part and parcel of a woman, that it cannot live outside its symbiosis with the woman. The first division, therefore, is that of embryo and woman.

For the bioethicists, the problem arising with gene and reproductive technology is *just* a question of definitions. The violence of the scientist is mainly the power of definition. It has been transformed from direct violence to structural violence, which appears as clean and pure. We should remember that it is precisely this power of definition of what is human and what is non-human that broke down the moral barriers for those scientists who did their research on people in Nazi concentration camps, particularly on mentally handicapped people. The scientists who did their fundamental research on such people accepted that they were non- or sub-human. The definitions of personhood given by Kuhse and Singer (rational, self-aware, autonomous) are totally open to the manipulations of power because it is a question of power who is defined as human or non-human. Here we may remember that for a long time women also were not considered as rational, self-aware, or autonomous.

The same arbitrary divide-and-rule logic is applied with regard to the distinction between basic and applied research, or the application of research results. Fundamental or basic research is, morally speaking, no better or purer than applied research; if in basic research all taboos may be violated, all moral principles be cast aside, which otherwise hold in society, then this will also occur in the application of research results. There is no other way, according to the paradigm of the new patriarchs — what *can* be done *will* be done. This becomes quite clear not only in the case of animal and human experimentation, but also in gene and reproductive technology. Experiments first carried out on cows and pigs are now being carried out on women (Corea, 1985). However, the natural scientists do not cut themselves and us off from Mother Nature with impunity. This becomes increasingly evident through the catastrophes which have arisen from the works of these basic researchers.

Finally, there is the connection, or rather, contradiction, *between science and responsibility,* as indicated in the title of this chapter. It should be clear that the science we have been discussing so far — and that is what is called science in our society — *does not recognize any responsibility.* Even more, natural science and responsibility are concepts which, according to the self-concept of scientists, are mutually exclusive. Anyone who doubts this should have another look at Max Weber's work on science as a profession. Because if scientists *as scientists,* not as husbands or citizens, bore responsibility for life on this earth, in their environment, in their daily life, they could not follow the abstract ideal of accumulation of knowledge *at any price.* They would have to give up, for example, basic and applied research in gene and reproductive technology.

What I as a feminist criticize is this hypocritical and schizophrenic segregation of scientists into allegedly impartial researchers who follow a different moral code in the laboratory from that which they follow outside. The reduction of ethics, morals, and responsibility to the problem of application or non-application of the results of science is bankruptcy of all ethics. This *reactive ethics* will always chase helplessly behind the inventions and fabrications of the natural scientists and attempt to regulate their most damaging effects, as, for example, ethics committees try to do with regard to gene and reproductive technology. But even in these committees' value-free science, with its claim to impartiality, prevails unassailed. Not only are they predominantly composed of scientists and doctors, but ethics is also understood as science and thus follows the same paradigm. The taboo never touched in these ethics committees is the profoundly *immoral* marriage between science and force, science and militarism, science and patriarchy.

Brian Easlea has proved that from the outset, nuclear physicists, even when they were still allegedly engaged in pure research, already had the military application of these gigantic forces at the back of their minds and that some of them even drew the attention of the war ministries to their research. He also describes very convincingly the phallic birth fantasies of these fathers of atom bombs and rockets (Easlea, 1986).

The feminist critique of science — particularly after Chernobyl — has made it eminently clear that all current science and technology is quite fundamentally *military science and technology*, and not just when it is applied in bombs and rockets (Mies, 1986). Since Bacon and Descartes, modern natural scientists have been 'fathers of destruction' (Easlea, 1986). If we take our responsibility towards life, women, children, the future, Mother Earth and our own human dignity seriously, we must first clearly state that *this* science is *irresponsible*, amoral, immoral, and second, that we no longer want to go along with this game of a double moral standard — one set for the laboratory, another for private or political life. What the scientist would not do to *himself*, neither should he do to any other being.

There is no abstract gain of knowledge which justifies the drastic destruction of vital links between self-sustaining living systems on earth, of the inherent worth of plants, animals, and humans in their living environment. The *marriage between knowledge and force must be dissolved*. It is imperative to alter *this* science. Another paradigm of science cannot start, however, with the famous male urge for limitless knowledge, omniscience and omnipotence. Therefore, it cannot start within science itself but has to come from a different world-view, a different view of the relationship between human beings and our natural environment, of the relationship between woman and man, of the relationship between different people, races, and cultures. These relationships can no longer be defined according to the militaristic model of White Man, who, by force, defined himself as human and the rest as non-human.

Ideas about a different science should be based on different *ethical and methodological principles.* I think that a lot of my criticisms with regard to the feminist critique of social sciences as mentioned earlier should also apply to the natural sciences. Central to a new science would be the principle of *subject-subject reciprocity.* This presupposes that the research object is again regarded as living and endowed with its own dignity/soul/subjectivity. A new science should never lose sight of the fact that we ourselves are part of Nature, that we have a body, that we are dependent on Mother Earth, that we are born by women, and that we die. It should never lead to the abdication *of our senses as a source of knowledge,* as modern natural science does, particularly since Kant. It should proceed in such a way that our senses can still be our guide through reality and not just organs rendered obsolete because they have been replaced by machines. Our sensuality is not only a source of knowledge, but above all also a source of all human happiness.

A new science should also reject the moral double standard which prevails today. It should finally prove itself responsible to society at large both in its methods and theories as well as in the application of its results. This new responsibility would in my view be based on the fact that the *earth and its resources are limited,* that our life is limited, that time is limited. In a limited universe, therefore, there can be no infinite progress, no infinite search for truth, no infinite growth unless others are exploited. It is a hopeful sign that the radical critique of science, which came from feminists and is still carried out by them, has meanwhile led a few men to think about themselves, too, as well as about the patriarchal image of White Man, the cultural hero of Western civilization, especially of the natural scientist, who in collaboration with the male confederacy in the military, in politics, and in economics has dealt us all these wars and catastrophes (cf. Bohme and Bohme, 1985; Easlea, 1986; Butte, 1985; Theweleit, 1977).

Chernobyl showed us more clearly than anything before that the modern techno-patriarchs destroy life, living systems, and symbioses. Afterwards they can even measure the destruction perpetrated. *But they cannot restore life.* For that, they still need — as we all do — Gaia, Mother Earth, and woman.

Notes

1. Carolyn Merchant (1983) quotes the following passages from Bacon's Works (Vol. 4) to prove that Bacon suggested applying inquisition methods in the witch trials to nature (Bacon, 1623/1870, pp. 96, 298; italics by Merchant):

   For you have but to follow and as it were hound out nature in her wanderings, and you will be able when you like to lead and drive her afterward to the same place again. Neither am I of the opinion in this history of marvels that superstitious narratives of sorceries, witchcrafts, charms, dreams, divinations and the like, where there is an assurance and clear evidence of the fact, should all be altogether excluded ... howsoever the use and practice of such arts is to be condemned, yet from the speculation and consideration of the ... useful light may be gained, not only for the true judgement of the offenses of persons charged with such practices, *but likewise for the further disclosing of the secrets of nature. Neither ought a man make scruple of entering and penetrating into these holes and corners, when the inquisition of truth is his whole object* — as your majesty has shown in your own example.

   For like as a man's disposition is never well known or proved till he be crossed, nor Proteus never changed shapes till he was *straitened* and *held fast*, so nature exhibits herself more clearly under the trials and vexations of art (mechanical devices) than when left to herself.

   The new natural scientist is thus called upon to treat nature like a slave who must be pressed into service and who must be remodelled by mechanical inventions.

2. A large proportion of present-day basic research in the industrialized countries is paid for from the military budget; worldwide, over half the natural scientists are working on military technology, in the United States as many as 60% (Butte, 1985).

References

Bacon, Francis. (1623/1870) *De Dignitate et augmentis Scientarium.* In James Spedding, Robert Leslie Ellis, and Douglas Devon Heath (eds.), *Francis Bacon: Works,* Vol. 4. London: Longman's Green.

Bohme, Gernot, and Bohme, Hartmut (1985) *Das andere der Vernunft: Zur Entwicklung der Rationalitätsstrukturen am Beispiel Kants.* Frankfurt: Suhrkamp Verlag.

Butte, Werner (ed.) (1985) *Militarisierte Wissenschaft.* Reinbek: Rororo aktuell, Technologie und Politik 22: Rowohlt Verlag.

Corea, Gena (1985) *The Mother Machine.* New York: Harper & Row.

Easlea, Brian (1986) *Fathering the Unthinkable: Masculinity, Scientists and the Nuclear Arms Race.* London: Pluto Press.

Fox Keller, Evelyn (1985) *Reflections on Gender and Science.* New Haven, CT: Yale University Press.

Griffin, Susan (1978) *Woman and Nature: the Roaring Inside Her.* New York: Harper Colophon Books.

Klein, Renate (ed.) (1989) *Infertility: Women Speak out About Their Experiences of Reproductive Medicine*. London: Pandora.

Kuhse, Helga, and Singer, Peter (1986) *Ethical Issues in Reproductive Alternatives for Genetic Indications*. Paper presented at 7th International Congress of Human Genetics, Berlin.

Merchant, Carolyn (1983) *The Death of Nature: Women, Ecology and the Scientific Revolution*. New York: Harper & Row.

Mies, Maria (1983) 'Towards a Methodology for Feminist Research.' In G. Bowles and Renate D. Klein (eds.), *Theories of Women's Studies* (pp. 117-139). London: Routledge and Kegan Paul.

—(1984) Frauenforschung oder feministische Forschung. *Beiträge zur feministichen Theorie und Praxis*, 11, 40-60.

— (1985) 'Why do we need all this?' A call against genetic and reproductive technology. *Women's Studies International Forum*, 8, 553-560.

— (1986) Wer machte uns die Natur zur Feindin? In: Marina Gambaroff, Maria Mies, Annegret Stopczyk and Claudia v. Werlhof, (eds.) *Tschernobyl hat unser Leben verändert. Vom Ausstieg der Frauen*. Reinbek, Rororo Aktuell, No. 5922: Rowohlt Verlag.

Sander, Helke (1980) *Über die Beziehungen von Liebesverhältnissen und Mittelstreckenraketen*. Courage, Nr. 4: 4-7. Berlin: Courage Verlag.

Theweleit, Klaus (1977) *Männerphantasien*. Frankfurt: Roter Stern Verlag.

Werlhof, Claudia v., Mies, Maria, and Bennholdt Thomsen, Veronika. (1983). *Frauen, die letzte Kolonie*. Reinbek, Rororo technik und Politik, No. 20: Rowohlt Verlag [English version: *Women, The Last Colony* (1988) London: Zed Books.]

4. The Myth of Catching-up Development

Maria Mies

Virtually all development strategies are based on the explicit or implicit assumption that the model of 'the good life' is that prevailing in the affluent societies of the North: the USA, Europe and Japan. The question of how the poor in the North, those in the countries of the South, and peasants and women worldwide may attain this 'good life' is usually answered in terms of what, since Rostow, can be called the 'catching-up development' path. This means that by following the same path of industrialization, technological progress and capital accumulation taken by Europe and the USA and Japan the same goal can be reached. These affluent countries and classes, the dominant sex — the men — the dominant urban centres and lifestyles are then perceived as the realized utopia of liberalism, a utopia still to be attained by those who apparently still lag behind. Undoubtedly the industrialized countries' affluence is the source of great fascination to all who are unable to share in it. The so-called 'socialist' countries' explicit aim was to catch up, and even to overtake capitalism. After the breakdown of socialism in Eastern Europe, particularly East Germany, the aim is now to quickly catch up with the lifestyle of the so-called market economies, the prototype of which is seen in the USA or West Germany.

A brief look at the history of the underdeveloped countries and regions of the South but also at present day East Europe and East Germany can teach us that this catching-up development path is a myth: nowhere has it led to the desired goal.

This myth is based on an evolutionary, linear understanding of history. In this concept of history the peak of the evolution has already been reached by some, namely, men generally, white men in particular, industrial countries, urbanites. The 'others' — women, brown and black people, 'underdeveloped' countries, peasants — will also reach this peak with a little more effort, more education, more 'development'. Technological progress is seen as the driving force of this evolutionary process. It is usually ignored that, even in the early 1970s, the catching-up development theory was criticized by a number of writers. Andre Gunder Frank,[1] Samir Amin,[2] Johan Galtung,[3] and many others have shown that the poverty of the underdeveloped nations is not as a result of 'natural' lagging behind but the direct consequence of the overdevelopment of the rich industrial countries who exploit the so-called periphery in Africa, South America and Asia. In the course of this colonial history, which continues today, these areas were progressively underdeveloped and made dependent on the so-called metropolis. The relationship between these overdeveloped centres or metropoles and the underdeveloped peripheries is a colonial one. Today, a similar colonial relationship exists between Man and Nature, between men and women, between urban and rural areas. We have called these the colonies of White Man. In order to maintain such relationships force and violence are always essential.[4]

But the emotional and cognitive acceptance of the colonized is also necessary to stabilize such relationships. This means that not only the colonizers but also the colonized must accept the lifestyle of 'those on top' as the only model of the good life. This process of acceptance of the values, lifestyle and standard of living of 'those on top' is invariably accompanied by a devaluation of one's own: one's own culture, work, technology, lifestyle and often also philosophy of life and social institutions. In the beginning this devaluation is often violently enforced by the colonizers and then reinforced by propaganda, educational programmes, a change of laws, and economic dependency, for example, through the debt trap. Finally, this devaluation is often accepted and internalized by the colonized as the 'natural' state of affairs. One of the most difficult problems for the colonized (countries, women, peasants) is to develop their own identity after a process of formal decolonization — identity no longer based on the model of the colonizer as the image of the true human being; a problem addressed by Fanon,[5] Memmi,[6] Freire,[7] and Blaise.[8] To survive, wrote Memmi, the colonized must oppress the colonization. But to become a true human being he/she, him/herself, must oppress the colonized which, within themselves, they have become.[9] This means that he/she must overcome the fascination exerted by the colonizer and his lifestyle and re-evaluate what he/she is and does.

To promote the elimination of the colonizers from within the colonized, it is useful to look more closely at the catching-up development myth.

It may be argued that those who have so far paid the price for development also look up to those at the top as their model of the future, as their concrete utopia; that this is a kind of universal law. But if we also consider the price nature had to pay for this model, a price that now increasingly affects people in the affluent societies too, it may be asked why do not these people question this myth? Because even in the North, the paradigm of unlimited growth of science and technology, goods and services — of capital — and GNP have led to an increasing deterioration in the environment, and subsequently the quality of life.

Divide and rule: modern industrial society's secret

Most people in the affluent societies live in a kind of schizophrenic or 'double-think' state. They are aware of the disasters of Bhopal and Chernobyl, of the 'greenhouse' effect, the destruction of the ozone layer, the gradual poisoning of ground-water, rivers and seas by fertilizers, pesticides, herbicides, as well as industrial waste, and that they themselves increasingly suffer the effects of air pollution, allergies, stress and noise, and the health risks due to industrially produced food. They also know that responsibility for these negative impacts on their quality of life lies in their own lifestyles and an economic system based on constant growth. And yet (except for very few) they fail to act on this knowledge by modifying their lifestyles.

One reason for this collective schizophrenia is the North's stubborn hope, even belief, that they can have their cake and eat it: ever more products from the chemical industry *and* clean air and water; more and more cars and no 'greenhouse' effect; an ever increasing output of commodities, more fast- and processed-foods, more fancy packaging, more exotic, imported food *and* enjoy good health and solve the waste problem.

Most people expect science and technology to provide a solution to these dilemmas, rather than taking steps to limit their own consumption and production patterns. It is not yet fully realized that a high material living standard militates against a genuinely good quality of life, especially if problems of ecological destruction are clearly understood.

The belief, however, that a high material living standard is tantamount to a good or high quality of life is the ideological support essential to uphold and legitimize the constant growth and accumulation model of modern industrial society. Unless the masses of people accept this the system cannot last and function. This equation is the real ideological-political hegemony that over-lies everyday life. No political party in the industrialized countries of the North dares question this schizophrenic equation, because they fear it would affect their election prospects.

We have already shown that this double-think is based on assumptions that there are no limits to our planet's resources, no limits to technological progress, no limits to space, to growth. But as, in fact, we inhabit a limited world, this limitlessness is mythical and can be upheld only by colonial divisions: between centres and peripheries, men and women, urban and rural areas, modern industrial societies of the North and 'backward', 'traditional', 'underdeveloped' societies of the South. The relationship between these parts is hierarchical not egalitarian, and characterized by exploitation, oppression and dominance.

The economic reason for these colonial structures is, above all, the *externalization of costs*[10] from the space and time horizon of those who profit from these divisions. The economic, social and ecological costs of constant growth in the industrialized countries have been and are shifted to the colonized countries of the South, to those countries' environment and their peoples. Only by dividing the international workforce into workers in the colonized peripheries and workers in the industrialized centres and by maintaining these relations of dominance even after formal decol-onization, is it possible for industrial countries' workers to be paid wages ten times and more higher than those paid to workers in the South.

Much of the social costs of the reproduction of the labour force within industrial societies is externalized *within* those societies themselves. This is facilitated through the patriarchal-capitalist sexual division of labour whereby women's household labour is defined as non-productive or as non-work and hence not remu-nerated. Women are defined as housewives and their work is omitted from GNP calculations. Women can therefore be called the internal colony of this system.

The ecological costs of the industrial production of chemical fertilizers, pesticides, atomic energy, and of cars and other com-modities, and the waste and damage for which they are responsi-ble during both the production and the consumption process, are being inflicted on nature. They manifest themselves as air-, water-, soil-pollution and poisoning that will not only affect the present, but all future generations. This applies particularly to the long-term effects of modern high technology: atomic industry, genetic engineering, computer technology and their synergic effects which nobody can either predict or control. Thus, both nature and the future have been colonized for the short-term profit motives of affluent societies and classes.

The relationship between colonized and colonizer is based not on any measure of partnership but rather on the latter's coercion and violence in its dealings with the former. This relationship is in fact the secret of unlimited growth in the centres of accumulation. If externalization of all the costs of industrial production were not possible, if they had to be borne by the industrialized countries themselves, that is if they were internalized, an immediate end to unlimited growth would be inevitable.

Catching-up impossible and undesirable

The logic of this accumulation model, based on exploitation and colonizing divisions, implies that anything like 'catching-up development' is impossible for the colonies, for all colonies. This is because just as one colony may, after much effort, attain what was considered the ultimate in 'development', the industrial centres themselves have already 'progressed' to a yet more 'modern' stage of development; 'development' here meaning technological progress. What today was the TV is tomorrow the colour TV, the day after the computer, then the ever more modern version of the 'computer generation' and even later artificial intelligence machines and so forth.[11] This catching-up policy of the colonies is therefore always a lost game. Because the very progress of the colonizers is based on the existence and the exploitation of those colonies.

These implications are usually ignored when development strategies are discussed. The aim, it is usually stated, is not a reduction in the industrialized societies' living standards but rather that all the 'underdeveloped' should be enabled to attain the same level of affluence as in those societies. This sounds fine and corresponds to the values of the bourgeois revolutions: equality for all! But that such a demand is not only a logical, but also a material impossibility is ignored. The impossibility of this demand is obvious if one considers the ecological consequences of the universalization of the prevailing production system and life-style in the North's affluent industrial societies to everyone now living and for some further 30 years on this planet. If, for example, we note that the six per cent of the world's population who live in the USA annually consume 30 per cent of all the fossil energy produced, then, obviously, it is impossible for the rest of the world's population, of which about 80 per cent live in the poor countries of the South, to consume energy on the same scale.[12]

According to Trainer, those living in the USA, Europe and Japan, consume three-quarters of the world's energy production. 'If present world energy production were to be shared equally, Americans would have to get by on only one-fifth of the per capita amount they presently consume'.[13] Or, put differently, world population may be estimated at eleven billion people after the year 2050; if of these eleven billion people the per capita energy consumption was similar to that of Americans in the mid-1970s, conventional oil resources would be exhausted in 34-74 years;[14] similar estimations are made for other resources.

But even if the world's resource base was unlimited it can be estimated that it would be around 500 years before the poor countries reached the living standard prevailing in the industrialized North; and then only if these countries abandoned the model of permanent economic growth, which constitutes the core of their economic philosophy. It is impossible for the South to 'catch-up' with this model, not only because of the limits and inequitable consumption of the resource base, but above all, because this growth model is based on a colonial world order in which the gap between the two poles is increasing, especially as far as economic development is concerned.

These examples show that catching-up development is not possible for all. In my opinion, the powers that dominate today's world economy are aware of this, the managers of the transnational corporations, the World Bank, the IMF, the banks and governments of the club of the rich countries; and in fact they do not really want this universalization, because it would end *their* growth model. Tacitly, they accept that the colonial structure of the so-called market economy is maintained worldwide. This structure, however, is masked by such euphemisms as 'North-South relations', 'sustainable development', 'threshold-countries' and so on which suggest that all poor countries can and will reach the same living standard as that of the affluent countries.

Yet, if one tries to disregard considerations of equity and of ecological concerns it may be asked if this model of the good life, pursued by the societies in the North, this paradigm of 'catching-up development' has at least made people in the North happy. Has it fulfilled its promises there? Has it at least made women and children there more equal, more free, more happy? Has their quality of life improved while the GDP grew?

We read daily about an increase of homelessness and of poverty, particularly of women and children,[15] of rising criminality in the big cities, of growing drug, and other addictions, including the addiction to shopping. Depression and suicides are on the increase in many of the affluent societies, and direct violence against women and children seems to be growing — both public and domestic violence as well as sexual abuse; the media are full of reports of all forms of violence. Additionally, the urban centres are suffocating from motor vehicle exhaust emissions; there is barely any open space left in which to walk and breathe, the cities and highways are choked with cars. Whenever possible people try to escape from these urban centres to seek relief in the countryside or in the poor South. If, as is commonly asserted, city-dwellers' quality of life is so high, why do they not spend their vacations in the cities?

It has been found that in the USA today the quality of life is lower than it was ten years ago. There seems to be an inverse relationship between GDP and the quality of life: the more GDP grows, the more the quality of life deteriorates.[16] For example: growing market forces have led to the fact that food, which so far was still prepared in the home is now increasingly bought from fast-food restaurants; preparing food has become a service, a commodity. If more and more people buy this commodity the GDP grows. But what also grows at the same time is the erosion of community, the isolation and loneliness of individuals, the indifference and atomization of the society. As Polanyi remarked, market forces destroy communities.[17] Here, too, the processes are characterized by polarizations: the higher the GDP the lower the quality of life.

But 'catching-up development' not only entails immaterial psychic and social costs and risks, which beset even the privileged in the rich countries and classes. With the growing number of ecological catastrophes — some man-made like the Gulf War or Chernobyl — material life also deteriorates in the rich centres of the world. The affluent society is one society which in the midst of plenty of commodities lacks the fundamental necessities of life: clean air, pure water, healthy food, space, time and quiet. What was experienced by mothers of small children after Chernobyl is now experienced by mothers in Kuwait. All the money of oil-rich Kuwait cannot buy people sunlight, fresh air, or pure water. This scarcity of basic common necessities for survival affects the poor and the rich, but with greater impact on the poor.

In short, the prevailing world market system, oriented towards unending growth and profit, cannot be maintained unless it can exploit external and internal colonies: nature, women and other people, but it also needs people as consumers who never say: 'IT IS ENOUGH'. The consumer model of the rich countries is not generalizable worldwide, neither is it desirable for the minority of the world's population who live in the affluent societies. Moreover, it will lead increasingly to wars to secure ever-scarcer resources; the Gulf War was in large part about the control of oil resources in that region. If we want to avoid such wars in future the only alternative is a deliberate and drastic change of lifestyle, a reduction of consumption and a radical change in the North's consumer patterns and a decisive and broad-based movement towards energy conservation (see chapter 16).

These fact are widely known, but the myth of catching-up development is still largely the basis of development policies of the governments of the North and the South, as well as the ex-socialist countries. A TV discussion[18] in which three heads of state participated — Robert Mugabe of Zimbabwe, Vaclav Havel of the CSFR, and Richard von Weizsacker, President of the then FRG — is a clear illustration of this. The discussion took place after a showing of the film *The March*, which depicted millions of starving Africans trying to enter rich Europe. The President of the FRG said quite clearly that the consumption patterns of the 20 per cent of the world's population who live in the affluent societies of the industrialized North are using 80 per cent of the world's resources, and that these consumption patterns would, in the long run, destroy the natural foundations of life — worldwide. When, however, he was asked, if it was not then correct to criticize and relinquish the North's consumption patterns and to warn the South against imitating the North he replied that it would be wrong to preach to people about reducing consumption. Moreover, people in the South had the right to the same living standard as those in the North. The only solution was to distribute more of 'our' wealth, through development aid, to the poor in the South, to enable them to 'catch-up'. He did not mention that this wealth originated as a result of the North's plundering of the colonies, as has been noted.

The President of socialist Zimbabwe was even more explicit. He said that people in the South wanted as many cars, refrigerators, TV sets, computers, videos and the same standard of living as the people in the North; that this was the aim of his politics of development. Neither he nor von Weizsacker asked whether this policy of universalizing the North's consumption patterns through a catching-up strategy was materially feasible. They also failed to question the ecological consequences of such a policy. As elected heads of state they dared not tell the truth, namely that the lifestyle of the rich in the North cannot be universalized, and that it should be ended in these countries in order to uphold the values of an egalitarian world.

Despite these insights, however, the catching-up development myth remains intact in the erstwhile socialist countries of the East. Development in East Germany, Poland and the ex-Soviet Union clearly demonstrate the resilience of this myth; but also the disaster that follows when the true nature of the 'free' market economy becomes apparent. People in East Germany, the erstwhile GDR, were anxious to participate in the consumer model of capitalist FRG and, by voting for the destruction of their own state and the unification of Germany, hoped to become 'equal'. Political democracy, they were told, was the key to affluence. But they now realize, that in spite of political democracy and that they live in the same nation state as the West Germans, they are *de facto* treated as a cheap labour pool or a colony for West German capital, which is interested in expanding its market to the East but hesitates to invest there because the unification of Germany means that the East German workers will demand the same wages as their counterparts in West Germany. Where, then, is the incentive to go East? Less than a year after the unification, people in East Germany were already disappointed and depressed: unemployment had risen rapidly; the economy had virtually broken down; but no benefits had accrued from the new market system. According to the politicians, however, a period of common effort will be rewarded by catching-up with the West Germans. And, inevitably, the women in East Germany are worst affected by these processes. They who formerly had a participation rate of 90 per cent in the labour force are the first to lose their jobs, and more rapidly than men; they form the bulk of the unemployed. Simultaneously, they are losing whatever benefits the socialist state had provided for them: creches, a liberal abortion law, job security as mothers, time off for child-care, and so on.

But due to their disappointment with the socialist system people do not, yet, understand that this is the normal functioning of capitalism; that it needs colonies for its expansionism, that even democracy and formal equality do not result automatically in an equal standard of living or equal economic rewards.

In East Germany, the anger and the disappointment about what people call their betrayal by West German politicians, particularly Chancellor Kohl, has been converted into hostility towards other minorities, ethnic and racial minorities, foreign workers, other East Europeans, all of whom wanted to enter the 'European House' and sit at the table of the rich.

In other parts of the world the collapse of the catching-up development myth leads to waves of fundamentalism and nationalism directed against religious, ethnic, racial, 'others' within and outside their own territory. The main target of both nationalism and fundamentalism, and communalism, is women, because religious, ethnic and cultural identity are always based on a patriarchy, a patriarchal image of women, or rather control over 'our' women, which, as we know from many examples, almost always amounts to more violence against women, more inequality for women.[19] Moreover, the collapse of the myth of catching-up development results in a further militarization of men. Practically all the new nationalisms and fundamentalisms have led to virtual civil war in which young, militarized men play the key role. As unacceptable as equals by the rich men's club and unable to share their lifestyle they can only show their manhood — as it is understood in a patriarchal world — by shouldering a machine-gun.

The myth of catching-up development, therefore, eventually leads to further destruction of the environment, further exploitation of the 'Third World', further violence against women and further militarization of men.

Does catching-up development liberate women?

So far we have looked at the ecological cost effects of the catching-up strategy for the countries of the South. This strategy has been pursued, virtually since the Enlightenment and the bourgeois revolutions, as well as in the various movements for emancipation from oppression and exploitation: the working-class movement, the national liberation movements, and the women's movement. For women living in the industrialized countries catching-up development meant and continues to mean the hope that the patriarchal man-woman relationship will be abolished by a policy of equal rights for women. This policy is at present pursued by demands for positive discrimination for women, special quotas or reservations for women in political bodies, and in the labour market. Several state governments in Germany have issued special promotion programmes for women. Efforts are made to draw women into those sectors of the economy that formerly were exclusively men's domains, such as the new high-tech industries. Women's resistance to these technologies is seen as a handicap for their liberation, because technology as such is considered as men's area of power and therefore one that women must invade if they are to be 'equal'. All these efforts and initiatives at the political level add up to the strategy of women catching-up with men. This equalization policy is usually promulgated by the political parties in power or formally in opposition; it is shared by many in the women's movement, conversely, it is also opposed by many women. They see that there is a wide gap between the rhetoric and the actual performance of the political and economic system, which continues to marginalize women. What is more important, this strategy of catching-up with the men means that men generally, and white men in influential positions, are seen as the model to which women must aspire. The implications of this strategy are that the structure of the world economy remains stable, that nature and external colonies continue to be exploited, and that to maintain this structure militarism is necessary as a final resort.

For affluent societies' middle-class women this catching-up policy presupposes that they will get a share of the White Man's loot. Since the Age of Enlightenment and the colonization of the world the White Man's concept of emancipation, of freedom and equality is based on dominance over nature, and other peoples and territories. The division between nature and culture, or civilization, is integral to this understanding. From the early women's movement up to the present, a large section of women have accepted the strategy of catching-up with men as the main path to emancipation. This implied that women must overcome within themselves what had been defined as 'nature', because, in this discourse, women were put on the side of nature, whereas men were seen as the representatives of culture. Theoreticians of the women's movement, such as Simone de Beauvoir[20] and Shulamith Firestone,[21] made this culture-nature divide the core of their theory of emancipation. Today this dichotomy again turns up in the discourse on reproductive engineering and gene technology (see chapter 19).

But more specifically let us ask why, for women, the catching-up development path even in the affluent societies of the industrialized North, is and will remain an illusion.

1. The promises of freedom, equality, self-determination of the individual, the great values of the French Revolution, proclaimed as universal rights and hence also meant for women, are betrayed for many women because all these rights depend on the possession of property, and of money. Freedom is the freedom of those who possess money. Equality is the equality of money. Self-determination is the freedom of choice in the supermarket. This freedom, equality, self-determination is always dependent on those who control the money/property. And in the industrialized societies and nations they are mostly the husbands or the capitalists' state. This at least is the relationship between men and women that is protected by law; the man as breadwinner, the woman as housewife.[22]

Self-determination and freedom are *de facto* limited for women, not only because they themselves are treated as commodities but also because, even if they possess money, they have no say in what is to be offered as commodities on the market. Their own desires and needs are constantly manipulated by those whose aim is to sell more and more goods. Ultimately, women are also persuaded that they want what the market offers.

2. This freedom, equality and self-determination, which depend on the possession of money, on purchasing power, cannot be extended to all women in the world. In Europe or the USA the system may be able to fulfil some of women's demand for equity with men, as far as income and jobs are concerned (or wages for housework, or a guaranteed minimum income), but only as long as it can continue the unrestricted exploitation of women as producers and consumers in the colonies. It cannot guarantee to *all* women worldwide the same standard of living as that of middle-class women in the USA or Europe. Only while women in Asia, Africa or Latin America can be forced to work for much lower wages than those in the affluent societies — and this is made possible through the debt trap — can enough capital be accumulated in the rich countries so that even unemployed woman are guaranteed a minimum income; but all unemployed women in the world cannot expect this. Within a world system based on exploitation 'some are more equal than others'.

3. This, however, also means that with such a structure there is no real material base for international women's solidarity. Because the core of individual freedom, equality, self-determination,

linked to money and property, is the *self-interest of the individual* and not altruism or solidarity; these interests will always compete with the self-interests of others. Within an exploitative structure interests will necessarily be antagonistic. It may be in the interest of Third World women, working in the garment industry for export, to get higher wages, or even wages equivalent to those paid in the industrialized countries; but if they actually received these wages then the working-class woman in the North could hardly afford to buy those garments, or buy as many of them as she does now. In her interest the price of these garments must remain low. Hence the interests of these two sets of women who are linked through the world market are antagonistic. If we do not want to abandon the aim of international solidarity and equality we must abandon the materialistic and self-centred approach to fighting only for our own interests. The interests' approach must be replaced by an ethical one.

4. To apply the principle of self-interest to the ecological problem leads to intensified ecological degradation and destruction in other parts of the world. This became evident after Chernobyl, when many women in Germany, desperate to know what to feed to their babies demanded the importation of unpolluted food from the Third World. One example of this is the poisoning of mothers' milk in the affluent countries by DDT and other toxic substances as a result of the heavy use of fertilizers, pesticides and insecticides in industrialized agriculture. Rachel Carson had already warned that poisoning the soil would eventually have its effect on people's food, particularly mothers' milk;[23] now this has happened many women in the North are alarmed. Some time ago a woman phoned me and said that in Germany it was no longer safe to breastfeed a baby for longer than three months; mothers' milk was poisoned. As a solution she suggested starting a project in South India for the production of safe and wholesome baby food. There, on the dry and arid Deccan Plateau, a special millet grows, called *ragi*. It needs little water and no fertilizer and is poor people's cheap subsistence food. This millet contains all the nutrients an infant needs. The woman suggested that ragi should be processed and canned as baby food and exported to Germany. This, she said, would solve the problem of desperate mothers whose breast milk is poisoned and give the poor in South India a new source of money income. It would contribute to their development!

I tried to explain that if ragi, the subsistence food of the poor, entered the world market and became an export commodity it would no longer be available for the poor; its price would soar and that, provided the project worked, pesticides and other chemicals would soon be used to produce more ragi for the market in the North. But ragi production, she answered, would have to be controlled by people who would guarantee it was not polluted. This amounts to a new version of eco-colonialism. When I asked her, why as an alternative, she would not rather campaign in Germany for a change in the industrialized agriculture, for a ban on the use of pesticides, she said that this would take too much time, that the poisoning of mothers' milk was an emergency situation. In her anxiety and concerned only with the interests of mothers in Germany she was willing to sacrifice the interests of poor women in South India. Or rather she thought that these conflicting interests could be made compatible by an exchange of money. She did not realize that this money would never suffice to buy the same healthy food for South Indian women's infants that they now had free of cost.

This example clearly shows that the myth of catching-up development, based on the belief of the miraculous workings of the market, particularly the world market, in fact leads to antagonistic interests even of mothers, who want only to give their infants unpolluted food.

Notes

1. Frank, A. G., *World Accumulation 1492-1789*. Macmillan, New York, 1978.
2. Amin, S., *Accumulation on a World Scale. A Critique of the Theory of Underdevelopment*. Monthly Review Press, New York, 1974.
3. Galtung, J., Eine Strukturelle Theorie des Imperialismus, in D. Senghaas (ed.) *Imperialismus und strukturelle Gewalt. Analysen über abhängige Reproduktion*. Suhrkamp, Frankfurt, 1972.
4. Mies, M., *Patriarchy and Accumulation on a World Scale, Women in the International Division of Labour*. Zed Books, London, 1989.
5. Fanon, F., *Peau Noire, Masques Blancs*. Edition du Seuil, Paris, 1952; English version: *Black Skin, White Masks*. Paladin, London, 1970.
6. Memmi, A., *Portrait du Colonise*. Edition Payot, Paris, 1973.
7. Freire, P., *Pedagogy of the Oppressed*. Penguin Books, Harmondsworth, 1970.
8. Blaise, S., *Le Rapt des Origines. ou: Le Meurtre de la Mere*. Maison des Femmes, Paris, 1988.
9. Memmi, op. cit., quoted in Blaise (1988) p. 74.
10. Kapp, W. K., *Social Costs of Business Enterprise*. Asia Publishing House, Bombay, 1963.

11. Ullrich, O., *Weltniveau. In der Sackgasse des Industriesystems.* Rotbuchverlag, Berlin, 1979, p. 108.
12. See *The Global 2000 Report to the President* US Foreign Ministry (ed.) Washington, Appendix, 1980, p. 59.
13. Trainer, F. E., *Developed to Death. Rethinking World Development.* Green Print, London, 1989.
14. Ibid., p. 61.
15. Sheldon, Danzinger and Stern.
16. Trainer, op. cit., p. 130.
17. Polanyi, K., *The Great Transformation.* Suhrkamp, Frankfurt, 1978.
18. This discussion took place under the title: 'Die Zukunft gemeinsam meistern' on 22 May 1990 in Norddeutscher Rundfunk (NDR). It was produced by Rolf Seelmann-Eggebert.
19. Chhachhi, A. 'Forced Identities: The State, Communalism, Fundamentalism and Women in India', in Kandiyoti, D. (ed.) *Women, Islam and the State.* University of California Press, 1991.
20. de Beauvoir, S., *The Other Sex.* Alfred A. Knopf Inc., New York, 1952.
21. Firestone, S., *The Dialectic of Sex.* William Morrow & Co., New York, 1970.
22. Mies, M., op. cit, 1989.
23. Carson, R. *Silent Spring.* Fawcett Publications, Greenwich,1962. Hynes, P. H. *The Recurring Silent Spring.* Pergamon Press, New York, 1989

5. The Impoverishment of the Environment: Women and Children Last*

Vandana Shiva

Ruth Sidel's book, *Women and Children Last*[1], opens with an account of the sinking of the unsinkable *Titanic.* Women and children were, indeed, the first to be saved on that dreadful night — that is, those in the first and second class. But the majority of women and children did not survive — they were in the third class.

The state of the global economy is in many ways comparable to the *Titanic:* glittering and affluent and considered unsinkable. But as Ruth Sidel observed, despite our side-walk cafes, our saunas, our luxury boutiques, we, too, lack lifeboats for everyone when disaster strikes. Like the *Titanic,* the global economy has too many locked gates, segregated decks and policies ensuring that women and children will be first — not to be saved, but to fall into the abyss of poverty.

Environmental degradation and poverty creation

Development was to have created well-being and affluence for all in the Third World. For some regions, and some people, it has delivered that promise, but for most regions and people, it has instead brought environmental degradation and poverty. Where did the development paradigm go wrong?

Firstly, it focused exclusively on a model of progress derived from Western industrialized economies, on the assumption that Western style progress was possible for all. Development, as the improved well-being of all, was thus equated with the Westernization of economic categories — of human needs, productivity, and growth. Concepts and categories relating to economic development and natural resource utilization that had emerged in the specific context of industrialization and capitalist growth in a

---

* This is an extensively revised version of a background paper presented for the UNCED Workshop 'Women and Children First', Geneva, May 1991

centre of colonial power, were raised to the level of universal assumptions and thought to be successfully applicable in the entirely different context of basic-needs satisfaction for the people of the erstwhile colonies — newly independent Third World countries. Yet, as Rosa Luxemburg[2] has pointed out, early industrial development in Western Europe necessitated permanent occupation of the colonies by the colonial powers, and the destruction of the local 'natural economy'. According to Luxemburg, colonialism is a constant, necessary condition for capitalist growth: without colonies, capital accumulation would grind to a halt. 'Development' as capital accumulation and the commercialization of the economy for the generation of 'surplus' and profits thus involved the reproduction of not only a particular form of wealth creation, but also of the associated creation of poverty and dispossession. A replication of economic development based on commercialization of resource-use for commodity production in the newly independent countries created internal colonies and perpetuated old colonial linkages. Development thus became a continuation of the colonization process; it became an extension of the project of wealth creation in modern, Western patriarchy's economic vision.

Secondly, development focused exclusively on such financial indicators as GNP (gross national product). What these indicators could not demonstrate was the environmental destruction and the creation of poverty associated with the development process. The problem with measuring economic growth in GNP is that it measures some costs as benefits (for example, pollution control) but fails to fully measure other costs. In GNP calculations clear-felling a natural forest adds to economic growth, even though it leaves behind impoverished ecosystems which can no longer produce biomass or water, and thus also leaves impoverished forest and farming communities.

Thirdly, such indicators as GNP can measure only those activities that take place through the market mechanism, regardless of whether or not such activities are productive, unproductive or destructive.

In the market economy, the organizing principle for natural resource use is maximization of profits and capital accumulation. Nature and human needs are managed through market mechanisms. Natural resources demands are restricted to those registering on the market; the ideology of development is largely based on a notion of bringing all natural resources into the

market economy for commodity production. When these resources are already being used by nature to maintain production
of renewable resources, and by women for sustenance and livelihood, their diversion to the market economy generates a scarcity
condition for ecological stability and creates new forms of poverty
for all, especially women and children.

Finally,the conventional paradigm of development perceives
poverty only in terms of an absence of Western consumption
patterns, or in terms of cash incomes and therefore is unable to
grapple with self-provisioning economies, or to include the poverty created by their destruction through development. In a book
entitled *Poverty: the Wealth of the People,* [3] an African writer draws a
distinction between poverty as subsistence, and poverty as deprivation. It is useful to separate a cultural conception of subsistence
living as poverty from the material experience of poverty resulting from dispossession and deprivation. Culturally perceived
poverty is not necessarily real material poverty: subsistence economies that satisfy basic needs through self-provisioning are not
poor in the sense of deprivation. Yet the ideology of development
declares them to be so because they neither participate over-
whelmingly in the market economy nor consume commodities
produced for and distributed through the market, even though
they might be satisfying those basic needs through self-provisioning mechanisms. People are perceived as poor if they eat millets
(grown by women) rather than commercially produced and distributed processed foods sold by global agribusiness. They are
seen as poor if they live in houses self-built with natural materials
like bamboo and mud rather than concrete. They are seen as poor
if they wear home-made garments of natural fibre rather than
synthetics. Subsistence, as culturally perceived poverty, does not
necessarily imply a low material quality of life. On the contrary,
millets, for example, are nutritionally superior to processed foods,
houses built with local materials rather than concrete are better
adapted to the local climate and ecology, natural fibres are generally preferable to synthetic ones — and often more affordable. The
cultural perception of prudent subsistence living as poverty has
provided legitimization for the development process as a 'pov-
erty-removal' project. 'Development', as a culturally biased process destroys wholesome and sustainable lifestyles and instead
creates real material poverty, or misery, by denying the means of
survival through the diversion of resources to resource-intensive
commodity production. Cash crop production and food process-

ing, by diverting land and water resources away from sustenance needs deprive increasingly large numbers of people from the means of satisfying their entitlements to food.

The resource base for survival is being increasingly eroded by the demand for resources by the market economy, dominated by global forces. The creation of inequality through ecologically disruptive economic activity arises in two ways: first, inequalities in the distribution of privileges and power make for unequal access to natural resources — these include privileges of both a political and economic nature. Second, government policy enables resource intensive production processes to gain access to the raw material that many people, especially from the less privileged economic groups, depend upon for their survival. Consumption of this raw material is determined solely by market forces, unimpeded by any consideration of the social or ecological impact. The costs of resource destruction are externalized and divided unequally among various economic groups in society, but these costs are borne largely by women and those who, lacking the purchasing power to register their demands on the modern production system's goods and services, provide for their basic material needs directly from nature.

The paradox and crisis of development results from mistakenly identifying culturally perceived poverty with real material poverty, and of mistaking the growth of commodity production as better satisfying basic needs. In fact, however water, soil fertility, and genetic wealth are considerably diminished as a result of the development process. The scarcity of these natural resources, which form the basis of nature's economy and especially women's survival economy, is impoverishing women, and all marginalized peoples to an unprecedented extent. The source of this impoverishment is the market economy, which has absorbed these resources in the pursuit of commodity production.

Impoverishment of women, children and the environment

The UN Decade for Women was based on the assumption that the improvement of women's economic position would automatically flow from an expansion and diffusion of the development process. By the end of the Decade, however, it was becoming clear that development itself was the problem. Women's increasing underdevelopment was not due to insufficient and inadequate 'participation' in 'development' rather, it was due to their enforced but asymmetric participation whereby they bore the costs but were excluded from the benefits. Development and dispossession augmented the colonial processes of ecological degradation and the loss of political control over nature's sustenance base. Economic growth was a new colonialism, draining resources away from those who most needed them. But now, it was not the old colonial powers but the new national elites that masterminded the exploitation on grounds of 'national interest' and growing GNPs, and it was accomplished by more powerful technologies of appropriation and destruction.

Ester Boserup[4] has documented how women's impoverishment increased during colonial rule; those rulers who had for centuries subjugated and reduced their own women to the status of de-skilled, de-intellectualized appendages, discriminated against the women of the colonies on access to land, technology and employment. The economic and political processes of colonial underdevelopment were clear manifestations of modern Western patriarchy, and while large numbers of men as well as women were impoverished by these processes, women tended to be the greater losers. The privatization of land for revenue generation affected women more seriously, eroding their traditional land-use rights. The expansion of cash crops undermined food production, and when men migrated or were conscripted into forced labour by the colonizers women were often left with meagre resources to feed and care for their families. As a collective document by women activists, organizers and researchers stated at the end of the UN Decade for Women:

> The almost uniform conclusion of the Decade's research is that with a few exceptions, women's relative access to economic resources, incomes and employment has worsened, their burden of work has increased, and their relative and even absolute health, nutritional and educational status has declined.[5]

Women's role in the regeneration of human life and the provisioning of sustenance has meant that the destructive impact on women and the environment extends into a negative impact on the status of children.

The exclusive focus on incomes and cash-flows as measured in GNP has meant that the web of life around women, children and the environment is excluded from central concern. The status of women and children and the state of the environment have never functioned as 'indicators' of development. This exclusion is achieved by rendering invisible two kinds of processes. Firstly, nature's, women's and children's contribution to the growth of the market economy is neglected and denied. Dominant economic theories assign no value to tasks carried out at subsistence and domestic levels. These theories are unable to encompass the majority in the world — women and children — who are statistically 'invisible'. Secondly the negative impact of economic development and growth on women, children and environment goes largely unrecognized and unrecorded. Both these factors lead to impoverishment.

Among the hidden costs generated by destructive development are the new burdens created by ecological devastation, costs that are invariably heavier for women, in both the North and South. It is hardly surprising, therefore, that a rising GNP does not necessarily mean that either wealth or welfare increase proportionately. I would argue that GNP is becoming increasingly a measure of how real wealth — the wealth of nature and the life sustaining wealth produced by women — is rapidly decreasing. When commodity production as the prime economic activity is introduced as development, it destroys the potential of nature and women to produce life and goods and services for basic needs. More commodities and more cash mean less life — in nature through ecological destruction and in society through denial of basic needs. Women are devalued, first, because their work co-operates with nature's processes, and second, because work that satisfies needs and ensures sustenance is devalued in general. More growth in what is maldevelopment has meant less nurturing of life and life support systems.

Nature's economy — through which environmental regeneration takes place — and the people's subsistence economy — within which women produce the sustenance for society through 'invisible' unpaid work called non-work — are being systematically destroyed to create growth in the market economy. Closely reflecting what I have called the three economies, of nature, people and the market in the Third World context, is Hilkka Pietila's[6] categorization of industrialized economies as: the free economy; the protected sector; and the fettered economy.

The free economy: the non-monetary core of the economy and society, unpaid work for one's own and family needs, community activities, mutual help and co-operation within the neighbourhood and so on.

The protected sector: production, protected and guided by official means for domestic markets; food, constructions, services, administration, health, schools and culture, and so on.

The fettered economy: large-scale production for export and to compete with imports. The terms dictated by the world market, dependency, vulnerability, compulsive competitiveness and so forth.

For example, in 1980, the proportions of time and money value that went into running each category of the Finnish economy were as follows!

Table 5.1

		Time	Money
A.	The free economy, informal economy	54%	35%
B.	Protected sector	36%	46%
C.	The fettered economy	10%	19%

In patriarchal economics, B and C are perceived as the primary economy, and A as the secondary economy. In fact as Marilyn Waring[7] has documented, national accounts and GNP actually exclude the free economy as lying outside the production boundary. What most economists and politicians call the 'free' or 'open' economy is seen by women as the 'fettered' economy. When the fettered economy becomes 'poor' — that is, runs into deficit — it is the free economy that pays to restore it to health. In times of structural adjustment and austerity programmes, cuts in public expenditure generally fall most heavily on the poor. In many cases reduction of the fiscal deficit has been effected by making substantial cuts in social and economic development expenditure, and real wages and consumption decrease considerably.

The poverty trap, created through the vicious cycle of 'development', debt, environmental destruction and structural adjustment is most significantly experienced by women and children. Capital flows North to South have been reversed. Ten years ago, a net $40 billion flowed from the Northern hemisphere to the countries of the South. Today in terms of loans, aid, repayment of interest and capital, the South transfers $20 billion a year to the North. If the effective transfer of resources implied in the reduced prices industrialized nations pay for the developing world's raw materials is taken into account, the annual flow from the poor to the rich countries could amount to $60 billion annually. This economic drain implies a deepening of the crisis of impoverishment of women, children and the environment.

According to UNICEF estimates, in 1988[8] half-a-million children died as a direct result of debt-related adjustment policies that sustain the North's economic growth. Poverty, of course, needs to be redefined in the emerging context of the feminization of poverty on the one hand, and the link to environmental impoverishment on the other.

Poverty is not confined to the so-called poor countries; it exists in the world's wealthiest society. Today, the vast majority of poor people in the US are women and children. According to the Census Bureau, in 1984, 14.4 per cent of all Americans (33.7 million) lived below the poverty line. From 1980 to 1984 the number of poor people increased by four-and-a-half million. For female-headed households in 1984, the poverty rate was 34.5 per cent — five times that for married couples. The poverty rate for white, female-headed families was 27.1 per cent; for black, woman-headed families, 51.7 per cent; and for woman-headed Hispanic families, 53.4 per cent. The impact of women's poverty on the economic status of children is even more shocking: in 1984, the poverty rate for children under six was 24 per cent, and in the same year, for children living in women-headed households it was 53.9 per cent. Among black children the poverty rate was 46.3 per cent; and for those living in female-headed families, 66.6 per cent. Among Hispanic children 39 per cent were poor, and for those living in female-headed families, the poverty rate was 70.5 per cent.[9]

Theresa Funiciello, a welfare rights organizer in the US, writes that 'By almost any honest measure, poverty is the number one killer of children in the U.S.' (Waring, 1988).

In New York City, 40 per cent of the children (700,000) are living in families that the government classifies deprived as 7,000 children are born addicted to drugs each year, and 12,000 removed to foster homes because of abuse or neglect (Waring 1988).

The first right mentioned in the Convention of the Rights of the Child is the inherent right to life. Denial of this right should be the point of departure for evolving a definition of poverty. It should be based on denial of access to food, water and shelter in the quality and quantity that makes a healthy life possible.

Pure income indicators often do not capture the poverty of life to which the future generations are being condemned, with threats to survival from environmental hazards even in conditions otherwise characterized by 'affluence'. Poverty has so far been culturally perceived in terms of life styles that do not fit into the categories of Western industrial society. We need to move away from these restricted and biased perceptions to grapple with poverty in terms of threats to a safe and healthy life either due to denial of access to food, water and shelter, or due to lack of protection from hazards in the form of toxic and nuclear threats.

Human scale development can be a beginning of an operational definition of poverty as a denial of vital human needs. At the highest level, the basic needs have been identified as subsistence, protection, affection, understanding, participation, leisure, creation, identity, freedom. These needs are most clearly manifest in a child, and the child can thus become our guide to a humane, just and sustainable social organization, and to a shift away from the destructiveness of what has been construed as 'development'.[10]

While producing higher cash flows, patriarchal development has led to deprivation at the level of real human needs. For the child, these deprivations can become life threatening, as the following illustrates.

The food and nutrition crisis

Both traditionally, and in the context of the new poverty, women and children have been treated as marginal to food systems. In terms of nutrition the girl-child is doubly discriminated against in such countries as India (see Table 5.2)[11].

The effects of inadequate nourishment of young girls continue into their adulthood and are passed on to the next generation. Complications during pregnancy, premature births and low birth weight babies with little chance of survival result when a mother is undernourished; and a high percentage of deaths during pregnancy and childbirth are directly due to anaemia, and childhood undernourishment is probably an underlying cause.[12] Denial of nutritional rights to women and children is the biggest threat to their lives.

Programmes of agricultural 'development' often become programmes of hunger generation because fertile land is diverted to grow export crops, small peasants are displaced, and the biological diversity, which provided much of the poor's food entitlements, is eliminated and replaced by cash crop monocultures, or land-use systems ill-suited to the ecology or to the provision of people's food entitlements. A permanent food crisis affects more than a 100 million people in Africa; famine is just the tip of a much bigger underlying crisis. Even when Ethiopia is not suffering from famine, 1,000 children are thought to die each day of malnutrition and related illnesses.[13]

Everywhere in the South, the economic crisis rooted in maldevelopment is leading to an impoverishment of the environment and a threat to the survival of children. It is even possible to quantify the debt mortality effect: over the decade of 1970 to 1980, each additional $10 a year interest payments per capita reflected 0.39 of a year less in life expectancy improvement. This is an average of 387 days of life foregone by every inhabitant of the 73 countries studied in Latin America.[14] Nutritional studies carried out in Peru show that in the poorest neighbourhoods of Ijma and surrounding shanty towns, the percentage of undernourished children increased from 24 per cent in 1972 to 28 per cent in 1978 and to 36 per cent in 1983.

Table 5.2

**Foods received by male and female children
3-4 and 7-9 years (India)**

Food items in grams				Age in years		
		3 - 4			7 - 9	
	RDA	Male	Female	RDA	Male	Female
Cereals	173	118	90	250	252	240
Pulses	55	22	18	70	49	25
Green leafy vegetables	62	3	0	75	0	0
Roots and tubers	40	15	13	50	42	0
Fruits	50	30	17	50	17	6
Milk	225	188	173	250	122	10
Sugar and jaggery	22	13	16	30	30	12
Fats and oils	30	5	2	50	23	8

Source: Devadas, R. and G. Kamalanathan, 'A Women's First Decade', Paper presented at the Women's NGO Consultation on Equality, Development and Peace, New Delhi, 1985.

In Argentina, according to official sources, in 1986 685,000 children in greater Buenos Aires and a further 385,000 in the province of Buenos Aires did not eat enough to stay alive; together constituting one-third of all children under 14.[15]

Starvation is endemic in the ultra-poor north-east of Brazil, where it is producing what IBASE (a public interest research group in Brazil) calls a 'sub-race' and nutritionists call an epidemic of dwarfism. The children in this area are 16 per cent shorter and weigh 20 per cent less than those of the same age elsewhere in Brazil — who, themselves, are not exactly well-nourished.

In Jamaica, too, food consumption has decreased as is shown:

Table 5.3

Item	No. of calories August 1984	No. of calories November 1985	Change %
Flour	2,232	1,443	-35
Cornmeal	3,669	2,013	-45
Rice	1,646	905	-45
Chicken	220	174	-20
Condensed milk	1,037	508	-51
Oil	1,003	823	-18
Dark sugar	1,727	1,253	-27

Source: Susan George, *A Fate Worse than Debt, 1988, p.188.*

As the price of food rose beyond people's ability to pay, children's health demonstratively declined. In 1978, fewer than two per cent of children admitted to the Bustamente Children's Hospital were suffering from malnutrition, and 1.6 per cent from malnutrition-related gastro-enteritis. By 1986, when the full effects of the adjustment policies were being felt, the figures for malnutrition-related admissions had doubled, to almost four per cent; gastro-enteritis admissions were almost five per cent.[16]

Numerical malnutrition is the most serious health hazard for children, particularly in the developing countries. Surveys in different regions of the world indicate that at any moment an estimated ten million children are suffering from severe malnutrition and a further 200 million are inadequately nourished.[17]

The increase in nutritional deprivation of children is one result of the same policies that lead to the nutritional deprivation of soils. Agriculture policies which extract surplus to meet export targets and enhance foreign exchange earnings generate that surplus by creating new levels of nutritional impoverishment for women, children and the environment. As Maria Mies has pointed out,[18] this concept of surplus has a patriarchal bias because, from the point of view of nature, women and children, it is based not on material surplus produced *over and above* the requirements of the environment or of the community, it is violently stolen and appropriated from nature (which needs a share of her produce to reproduce herself) and from women (who need a share of nature's produce to sustain and to ensure the survival of themselves and their children). Malnutrition and deficiency diseases are also caused by the destruction of biodiversity which forms the nutritional base in subsistence communities. For example, *bathua* is an important green leafy vegetable with very high nutritive value which grows in association with wheat, and when women weed the wheat field they not only contribute to the productivity of wheat but also harvest a rich nutritional source for their families. With the intensive use of chemical fertilizer, however, *bathua* becomes a major competitor of wheat and has been declared a 'weed' to be eliminated by herbicides. Thus, the food cycle is broken; women are deprived of work; children are deprived of a free source of nutrition.

The water crisis

The water crisis contributes to 34.6 per cent of all child deaths in the Third World. Each year, 5,000,000 children die of diarrhoeal diseases.[19] The declining availability of water resources, due to their diversion for industry and industrial agriculture and to complex factors related to deforestation, desertification and drought, is a severe threat to children's health and survival. As access to water decreases, polluted water sources and related health hazards, increase. 'Development' in the conventional paradigm implies a more intensive and wasteful use of water — dams and intensive irrigation for green revolution agriculture, water for air-conditioning mushrooming hotels and urban-industrial complexes, water for coolants, as well as pollution due to the dumping of industrial wastes. And as development creates more water demands, the survival needs of children — and adults — for pure and safe water are sacrificed.

Antonia Alcantara, a vendor from a slum outside Mexico City, complains that her tap water is 'yellow and full of worms'. Even dirty water is in short supply. The demands of Mexico City's 20 million people have caused the level of the main aquifer to drop as much as 3.4 metres annually.[20] Those with access to Mexico City's water system are usually the wealthy and middle classes. They are, in fact, almost encouraged to be wasteful by subsidies that allow consumers to pay as little as one-tenth the actual cost of water. The poor, on the other hand, are often forced to buy from *piperas*, entrepreneurs, who fix prices according to demand.

In Delhi, in 1988, 2,000 people (mainly children) died as a result of a cholera epidemic in slum colonies. These colonies had been 'resettled' when slums were removed from Delhi to beautify India's capital. This dispensable population was provided with neither safe drinking water, nor adequate sewage facilities; it was only the children of the poor communities who died of cholera. Across the Yamuna river, the swimming pools had enough chlorinated water to protect the tourists, the diplomats, the elite.[21]

Toxic hazards

In the late twentieth century it is becoming clear that our scientific systems are totally inadequate to counteract or eliminate the hazards — actual and potential — to which children, in particular, are subjected. Each disaster seems like an experiment, with children as guinea pigs, to teach us more about the effects of deadly substances that are brought into daily production and use. The patriarchal systems would like to maintain silence about these poisonous substances, but as mothers women cannot ignore the threats posed to their children. Children are the most highly sensitive to chemical contamination, the chemical pollution of the environment is therefore most clearly manifested in their ill-health.

In the Love Canal and the Bhopal disasters, children were the worst affected victims. And in both places it is the women who have continued to resist and have refused to be silenced as corporations and state agencies would wish.

Love Canal was a site where, for decades, Hooker Chemical Company had dumped their chemical wastes, over which houses were later built. By the 1970s it was a peaceful middle-class residential area but its residents were unaware of the toxic dumps beneath their houses. Headaches, dizziness, nausea and epilepsy were only a few of the problems afflicting those near the Canal. Liver, kidney, or recurrent urinary strictures abounded. There was also an alarmingly high rate of 56 per cent risk of birth defects, including childhood deafness, and children suffered an unusually high rate of leukemia and other cancers.[22] There was a 75 per cent above normal rate of miscarriage, and among 15 pregnancies of Love Canal women, only two resulted in healthy babies.

It was the mothers of children threatened by death and disease who first raised the alarm and who kept the issue alive.

In Japan, the dependence of Minamata Bay's fishermen and their families on a fish diet had disastrous results as the fish were heavily contaminated with methylmercury, which had been discharged into the Bay over a period of 30 years by the Chissio chemical factory.

In Bhopal, in 1984, the leak from Union Carbide's pesticide plant led to instant death for thousands. A host of ailments still afflicts many more thousands of those who escaped death. In addition women also suffer from gynaecological complications and menstrual disorders. Damage to the respiratory, reproductive, nervous, musculo-skeletal and immune systems of the gas victims has been documented in epidemiological studies carried out so far. The 1990 report of the Indian Council of Medical Research[23] states that the death rate among the affected population is more than double that of the unexposed population. Significantly higher incidences of spontaneous abortions, still-births and infant mortality among the gas victims have also been documented.

> A few months after the gas disaster, I had a son. He was alright. After that I had another child in the hospital. But it was not fully formed. It had no legs and no eyes and was born dead. Then another child was born but it died soon after. I had another child just one and a half months back. Its skin looked scalded and only half its head was formed. The other half was filled with water. It was born dead and was white all over. I had a lot of pain two months before I delivered. My legs hurt so much that I couldn't sit or walk around. I got rashes all over my body. The doctors said that I will be okay after the childbirth, but I still have these problems.[24]

Nuclear hazards

Hiroshima, Three Mile Island, the Pacific Islands, Chernobyl — each of these nuclear disasters reminds us that the nuclear threat is greater for future generations than for us.

Lijon Eknilang was seven years old at the time of the Bravo test on Bikini Island. She remembers her eyes itching, nausea and being covered by burns. Two days after the test, Lijon and her people were evacuated to the US base on Kwajalein Atoll. For three years they were kept away because Rongelap was too dangerous for life. Lijon's grandmother died in the 1960s due to thyroid and stomach cancer. Her father died during the nuclear test. Lijon reports that:

> I have had seven miscarriages and still-births. Altogether there are eight other women on the island who have given birth to babies that look like blobs of jelly. Some of these things we carry for eight months, nine months, there are no legs, no arms, no head, no nothing. Other children are born who will never recognise this world or their own parents. They just lie there with crooked arms and legs and never speak.[25]

Every aspect of environmental destruction translates into a severe threat to the life of future generations. Much has been written on the issue of sustainability, as 'intergenerational equity', but what is often overlooked is that the issue of justice between generations can only be realized through justice between sexes. Children cannot be put at the centre for concern if their mothers are meantime pushed beyond the margins of care and concern.

Over the past decades, women's coalitions have been developing survival strategies and fighting against the threat to their children that results from threats to the environment.

Survival strategies of women and children

As survival is more and more threatened by negative development trends, environmental degradation and poverty, women and children develop new ways to cope with the threat.

Today, more than one-third of the households in Africa, Latin America and the developed world are female headed; in Norway the figure is 38 per cent, and in Asia 14 per cent.[26] Even where women are not the sole family supporters they are primary supporters in terms of work and energy spent on providing sustenance to the family. For example, in rural areas women and children must walk further to collect the diminishing supplies of firewood and water, in urban areas they must take on more paid outside work. Usually, more time thus spent on working to sustain the family conflicts with the time and energy needed for child care. At times girl children take on part of the mother's burden: in

India, the percentage of female workers below 14 years increased from four to eight per cent. In the 15-19 year age group, the labour force participation rate increased by 17 per cent for females, but declined by eight per cent for males.[27] This suggests that more girls are being drawn into the labour force, and more boys are sent to school. This sizeable proportion perhaps explains high female school dropout rates, a conclusion that is supported by the higher levels of illiteracy among female workers, compared with 50 per cent for males. It has been projected that by the year 2001 work participation among 0-14 year old girls will increase by a further 20 per cent and among 15-19 year olds by 30 per cent.[28]

The International Labour Organization (ILO) has estimated that at the beginning of the 1980s the overall number of children under 15 who were 'economically active' was around 50 million; the World Health Organization (WHO) estimates put it at 100 million. There are another 100 million 'street' children, without families or homes. These are victims of poverty, underdevelopment, and poor environmental conditions — society's disposable people — surviving entirely on their own, without any rights, without any voice.

Chipko women of Himalaya have organized to resist the environmental destruction caused by logging.

The Love Canal home owner's association is another well-known example of young housewives' persistent action to ensure health security for their families; this has now resulted in the Citizens' Clearinghouse for Hazardous Waste.

The Bhopal Gas Peedit Mahila Udyog Sangathan, a group of women victims of the Bhopal disaster, has continued to struggle for seven years to obtain justice from Union Carbide Corporation.

Across different contexts, in the North and in the South, in ecologically eroded zones and polluted places, women identify with the interest of the earth and their children in finding solutions to the crisis of survival. Against all odds they attempt to reweave the web which connects their life to the life of their children and the life of the planet. From women's perspective, sustainability without environmental justice is impossible, and environmental justice is impossible without justice between sexes and generations.

To whom will the future belong? to the women and children who struggle for survival and for environmental security? or to those who treat women, children and the environment as dispensable and disposable? Gandhi proposed a simple test for making

decisions in a moment of doubt. 'Recall the face of the least privileged person you know', he said, 'and ask if your action will harm
or benefit him/her.'[29] This criterion of the 'last person' must be
extended to the 'last child' if we are serious about evolving a code
of environmental justice which protects future generations.

Dispensability of the last child: the dominant paradigm

From the viewpoint of governments, intergovernmental agencies,
and power elites, the 'last child' needs no lifeboat. This view has
been explicitly developed by Garrett Hardin in his 'life-boat
ethics'[30]: the poor, the weak are a 'surplus' population, putting an
unnecessary burden on the planet's resources. This view, and the
responses and strategies that emerge from it totally ignore the fact
that the greatest pressure on the earth's resources is not from large
numbers of poor people but from a small number of the world's
ever-consuming elite.

Ignoring these resource pressures of consumption and destructive technologies, 'conservation' plans increasingly push the last
child further to the margins of existence. Official strategies, reflecting elite interests, strongly imply that the world would be better
off if it could shed its 'non-productive' poor through the life-boat
strategy. Environmentalism is increasingly used in the rhetoric of
manager-technocrats, who see the ecological crises as an opportunity for new investments and profits. The World Bank's Tropical
Action Plan,the Climate Convention, the Montreal Protocol are
often viewed as new means of dispossessing the poor to 'save' the
forests and atmosphere and biological commons for exploitation
by the rich and powerful. The victims are transformed into villains
in these ecological plans — and women, who have struggled most
to protect their children in the face of ecological threats, become
the elements who have to be policed to protect the planet.[31]

'Population explosions' have always emerged as images created by modern patriarchy in periods of increasing social and
economic polarizations. Malthus[32] saw populations exploding
at the dawn of the industrial era; between World War I and II
certain groups were seen as threatening deterioration of the
human genetic stock; post World War II, countries where unrest
threatened US access to resources and markets, became known
as the 'population powderkegs'. Today, concern for the survival
of the planet has made pollution control appear acceptable and
even imperative, in the face of the popularized pictures of the
world's hungry hordes.

What this focus on numbers hides is people's unequal access to resources and the unequal environmental burden they put on the earth. In global terms, the impact of a drastic decrease of population in the poorest areas of Asia, Africa and Latin America would be immeasurably smaller than a decrease of only five per cent in the ten richest countries at present consumption levels.[33]

Through population control programmes, women's bodies are brutally invaded to protect the earth from the threat of over-population. Where women's fertility itself is threatened due to industrial pollution, their interest is put in opposition to the interests of their children. This divide and rule policy seems essential for managing the eco-crisis to the advantage of those who control power and privilege.

The emerging language of manager-technocrats describes women either as the passive 'environment' of the child, or the dangerous 'bomb' threatening a 'population explosion'. In either case, women whose lives are inextricably a part of children's lives have to be managed to protect children and the environment.

The mother's womb has been called the child's 'environment'. Even in the relatively sheltered environment of the mother's uterus the developing baby is far from completely protected. The mother's health, so intimately linked to the child's well-being is reduced to a 'factor within the foetus's environment'.

Similar decontextualized views of the womn-child relationship are presented as solutions to managing environmental hazards in the workplace. 'Foetal protection policies' are the means by which employers take the focus off their own hazardous production by offering to 'protect the unborn' by removing pregnant (or wanting-to-be pregnant) women from hazardous zones.[34] In extreme cases, women have consented to sterilization in order to keep their jobs and keep food on the table. More typically, practices include surveillance of women's menstrual cycles, of waiting for a woman to abort her pregnancy before employing her. As Lin Nelson has stated: 'It is all too easy to "assume pollution" and accept industrial relocation and obstetrical intervention, but they are responses to the symptoms, not the disease.'[35]

Grassroots response

Community groups, NGOs, ecology movements and women's movements begin the reversal of environmental degradation by reversing the trends that push women and children beyond the edge of survival. As mentioned earlier, the Chipko movement in

India has been one such response. In Kenya, the Green Belt movement has fostered 1,000 Community Green Belts. In Malaysia, the Sahabal Alain Malaysia (SAM) and Consumer Association of Penang have worked with tribal, peasant, and fishing communities to reverse environmental decline. Tribals' blockades against logging in Sarawak are another important action in which these organizations have been involved. In Brazil the Acao Democratica Feminina Gaucha (ADFG) has been working on sustainable agriculture, indigenous rights, debt and structural adjustment.

What is distinctive about these popular responses is that they put the last child at the centre of concern, and work out strategies that simultaneously empower women and protect nature. Emerging work on women, health and ecology, such as the dialogue organized by the Research Foundation of India and the Dag Hammarskjold Foundation of Sweden,[36] the Planeta Femea at the Global Forum in Rio 1992[37] are pointing to new directions in which children's, women's and nature's integrity are perceived in wholeness, not fragmentation.

Putting women and children first

In 1987, at the Wilderness Congress, Oren Lyons of the Onondaga Nation said: 'Take care how you place your moccasins upon the earth, step with care, for the faces of the future generations are looking up from the earth waiting for their turn for life.'[38]

In the achievements of growing GNPs, increasing capital accumulation, it was the faces of children and future generations that receded from the minds of policy makers in centres of international power. The child had been excluded from concern, and cultures which were child-centred have been destroyed and marginalized. The challenge to the world's policy makers is to learn from mothers, from tribals and other communities, how to focus decisions on the well-being of children.

Putting women and children first needs above all, a reversal of the logic which has treated women as subordinate because they create life, and men as superior because they destroy it. All past achievements of patriarchy have been based on alienation from life, and have led to the impoverishment of women, children and the environment. If we want to reverse that decline, the creation, not the destruction of life must be seen as the truly human task, and the essence of being human has to be seen in our capacity to recognize, respect and protect the right to life of all the world's multifarious species.

Notes

1. Sidel, Ruth, *Women and Children Last*. Penguin, New York, 1987.
2. Luxemburg, Rosa, *The Accumulation of Capital*. Routledge and Kegan Paul, London, 1951.
3. Quoted in R. Bahro, *From Red to Green*. Verso, London, 1984, p. 211.
4. Boserup, Ester, *Women's Role in Economic Development*. Allen and Unwin, London, 1960.
5. DAWN, 1985, *Development Crisis and Alternative Visions: Third World Women's Perspectives*. Christian Michelsen Institute, Bergen.
6. Pietila, Hilkka, *Tomorrow Begins Today*. ICDA/ISIS Workshop, Nairobi, 1985.
7. Waring, Marilyn *If Women Counted*. Harper & Row, San Francisco, 1988.
8. UNICEF, *State of the World's Children*, 1988.
9. Quoted in Marilyn Waring, op. cit. p. 180; and Ruth Sidel, op. cit.
10. Max-Neef, Manfred, *Human Scale Development, Development Dialogue*. Dag Hammarskjold Foundation, 1989.
11. Chatterjee, Meera, *A Report on Indian Women from Birth to Twenty*. National Institute of Public Cooperation and Child Development, New Delhi, 1990.
12. Timberlake, Lloyd, *Africa in Crisis*, Earthscan, London, 1987.
13. Susan George, *A Fate Worse than Debt*. Food First, San Francisco, 1988.
14. Ibid.
15. Ibid.
16. Ibid.
17. UNICEF, *Children and the Environment*, 1990.
18. Maria Mies, *Patriarchy and Accumulation on a World Scale*. Zed Books, London, 1987.
19. UNICEF, op. cit., 1990.
20. Moser, Caroline, Contribution on OECD Workshop on Women and Development. Paris, 1989.
21. Shiva, Mira 'Environmental Degradation and Subversion of Health' in Vandana Shiva (ed.) *Minding Our Lives: Women from the South and North Reconnect Ecology and Health* , Kali for Women, Delhi, 1993.
22. Gibbs, Lois, *Love Canal, My Story*. State University of New York, Albany, 1982.
23. Bhopal Information and Action Group, Voices of Bhopal. Bhopal, 1990.
24. Ibid.
25. *Pacific Women Speak*, Women Working for a Nuclear Free and Independent Pacific, 1987.
26. United Nations, *World's Women*, 1970-1990.
27. Chatterjee, Meera op. cit.
28. UNICEF, op. cit., 1990.
29. Kothari, Rajni, Vandana Shiva, 'The Last Child', Manuscript for United Nations University Programme on Peace and Global Transformation.
30. Hardin, Garrett, in *Bioscience*, Vol. 24, (1974) p. 561.
31. Shiva, Vandana 'Forestry Crisis and Forestry Myths: A Critical Review of Tropical Forests: A Call for Action,' World Rainforest Movement, Penang, 1987.
32. Malthus, in Barbara Duden, 'Population', in Wolfgang Sachs (ed) *Development Dictionary*. Zed Books, London, 1990.
33. UNICEF, op. cit., 1990.

34. Nelson, Lin, 'The Place of Women in Polluted Places' in *Reweaving the World: The Emergence of Ecofeminism*, Irene Diamond and Gloria Orenstein (eds). Sierra Club Books, 1990.
35. Ibid.
36. 'Women, Health and Ecology,' proceedings of a Seminar organized by Research Foundation for Science, Technology and Natural Resource Policy, and Dag Hammarskjold Foundation, in *Development Dialogue* 1992.
37. 'Planeta Femea' was the women's tent in the Global Forum during the UN Conference on Environment and Development, 1992.
38. Lyons, Oren 4th World Wilderness Conference, 11 September 1987, Eugene, Oregon.

6. Who Made Nature Our Enemy?

Maria Mies

When, what we have theoretically known would happen does happen what then is the use of writing about it? The ecology movement, large sections of the women's movement, and other groups and individuals repeatedly campaigned against the construction of nuclear power plants, because nuclear power is a source of energy so dangerous that it cannot be controlled by human beings; a fact confirmed by the Chernobyl disaster and its aftermath. What purpose can be served by writing about it now? Should we not rather emulate those feminists who say: 'We are not responsible for this destructive technology. We do not want it. Let those men, or those patriarchs who are so enthusiastic about their technological dominance over nature now clear up the mess. We are fed up with being the world's housewives.'

This reaction is understandable, but does it help us? Women don't live on an island; there is no longer any place to which we can flee. Some women may feel that it is better to forget what happened at Chernobyl and to enjoy life as long as it lasts since we must all die eventually. But women with small children cannot afford this nihilistic attitude. They try desperately to keep children off the grass, because the grass is contaminated; they wash their shoes after they have been outside; they follow the news about the latest measurements of nuclear contamination in vegetables, milk, fruit, and so on, and become experts in choosing relatively uncontaminated food for their children. Their daily life has drastically changed since the Chernobyl disaster. Therefore we must ask: how has this catastrophe changed women's lives and their psychic condition? And what have women to learn from all this?

Everything has changed — everything is the same

Spring at last! Everything is green, flowers everywhere, it is warmer! After a long and depressing winter people long to get out of their houses, to breathe freely and enjoy nature. But everywhere there are invisible signboards which warn: 'Don't touch me. I am contaminated!' We can enjoy the trees, the flowers, the grass only as voyeurs, as if nature was a TV show. We cannot touch nature, we cannot communicate with nature as living natural creatures; an invisible barrier separates us. Those within whom an empathy for nature is already dead, those who have become machine-men, may not even mind. Their sensuality has already been reduced to a mechanical stimulus-response reaction. But those in whom it is still alive — the children and many women — experience this sudden separation from nature as a deep, almost physical pain. They feel a sense of deprivation, of loss. This barrier between themselves and the rest of the natural world seems to undermine their own life energy.

I met many women in April 1986 who felt that the Chernobyl event had destroyed their *joie de vivre*, as if radioactivity had already penetrated and broken their bodies. They reported not only depressions but also feeling sick; to look at children and the glorious spring made their stomachs turn and ache. Why go on? I had similar feelings when I had to face the young women and men who were my students. What was their future? What was the use of teaching and preparing them for a future profession? The physical radioactive contamination had become augmented by psychic contamination.

And yet women continued to live, to shop, clean, cook, go to their workplace, water the flowers, as they had always done. After Chernobyl, this meant more work, more care, more worries, similar to life in times of war. While the propagators of atomic energy, the scientists, politicians and economists still maintain that atomic energy is necessary to maintain our standard of living, women must worry where to get uncontaminated food for their family, their children. It is women who began to realize that this 'standard of living' had already been swept away. Can they still buy lettuce? Milk is dangerous, so are yoghurt and cheese; meat is contaminated. What to cook and to eat? Women began to search for cereals or milkpowder from the years before Chernobyl, or to look for imported food, from the USA or the 'Third World', Sweden flew in fresh vegetables from Thailand every week. What would happen when the pre-Chernobyl reserves were used up and when imports from non-contaminated countries stopped?

It was women who had to keep small children indoors, to keep them occupied, to pacify them. Those advocates of nuclear technology — and responsible for the Chernobyl disaster — the scientists and the politicians, simply decreed: 'Don't allow children to play in the sand!'

And what of pregnant women? What were their fears, their anxieties? How did they cope? Many asked their doctors if it was 'safe' to continue their pregnancy. Many felt isolated with their fears of perhaps giving birth to a handicapped child. Many others miscarried, without clearly being able to connect this to Chernobyl.

Women, both in the then Soviet Union and in the West, felt responsible for life. Not the men in science, politics, and economics, who are usually seen as the 'responsible' ones. It is the women who are afraid of contaminating their families, not their men. Women, not the politicians or scientists, feel guilty if they are unable to get uncontaminated food. As a woman from Moscow put it in May 1986: 'Men do not think of life, they only want to conquer nature and the enemy, whatever the costs may be!' *(Die Tageszeitung,* 12.5.1986). Men seem to be experts for technology, women for life, men make war, women are supposed to restore life after the wars. Can this division of labour be upheld after Chernobyl?

Some lessons — not only for women

What happened in Chernobyl cannot soon be undone. This technology is irreversible. We already knew this. What can we do? I think we must first draw the correct lessons from this event and then act accordingly to prevent worse catastrophies. These lessons are not new, but after Chernobyl they developed a new urgency.

1. No one can save herself or himself individually; it is an illusion to think that 'I alone' can save my skin. Industrial catastrophies like Chernobyl may happen far away, but their effects do not recognize political borders. Therefore, geographical distance is no longer a guarantee for safety.

2. What modern machine-man does to the earth will eventually be felt by all; everything is connected. 'Unlimited Progress' is a dangerous myth because it suggests that we can rape and destroy living nature, of which we are an integral part, without ourselves suffering the effects. As White Man has for centuries treated nature like an enemy it seems that now nature is hostile to us.

3. To trust those who call themselves the 'responsible' ones is dangerous. Chernobyl has shown clearly that the main concern of those 'responsible ones' is to remain in power. Politicians' arbitrary manipulation of permissible limits of pollution is clear evidence that science bows to political opportunity. The politicians' promise compensations only where they must fear

election losses: traders and farmers. They would find the suggestion of compensating women for their extra work to protect their children absurd; such work does not appear as work and as labour costs. But all the work in the world cannot undo what Chernobyl has done to the environment.

4. Confidence in the ruling men in politics and science is dangerous, above all because their thinking is not based on principles of ethics. It is well-known that many scientists are prepared to do research which is morally questionable because it is paid for; in the US 60 per cent of scientists do research paid for by the Pentagon. Even scientists who warn of the dangers of nuclear energy and genetic engineering still distinguish between 'value-free' 'pure' research and applied research. At a public discussion on gene technology in Germany one of the leading researchers in genetic engineering, when asked where he saw the limits of scientific research said: 'I do not see such limits. In order to know whether certain technologies are dangerous we must first develop and apply them. Only then can the public decide, following democratic principles, whether these technologies should be used.' This means, in order to know the dangers of atomic energy, the atom bomb must be made and exploded. Similar arguments can be applied for gene technology. Many scientists' 'value-free' research is hindered by moral considerations, fears of the people, emotions, and particularly any financial restrictions by the politicians. Ethics and morality should have a say only after the research has been done, when the question arises whether or not it should be applied. Only then are ethics commissions created. But the final decision is left to the politicians. These, on the other hand, turn again to the scientists for guidance and expertise when they have to make difficult ethical decisions like fixing the permissible limits of contamination. In reality, both the scientists and the politicians are dependent on those who have the money to finance a certain technology and who want to promote it for the sake of profit.

5. It is dangerous to trust politicians and scientists not only because they have no ethics, but also because of their lack of imagination and emotion. To be able to do this type of research a scientist must kill in himself all feelings of empathy, all imagination that would lead to thinking about the consequences of this research. As Brian Easlea[1] and the two Böhme brothers[2] have shown, modern science, particularly nuclear physics, demands people who are emotionally crippled.

6. After Chernobyl the reactions of some of the leading 'responsible ones' in science and politics were extraordinary. Those who, for years, had assured us repeatedly that nuclear energy was safe, that the scientists had everything under their control, that their safety measurements were correct, in 1986 told the public that the figures shown on their Geiger-counter — 200, 500, or even 2,000 becquerel — were not dangerous, there was no need to panic. Both scientists and politicians minimized the danger, in spite of the high level of radioactivity measured by their accurate machines. Instead of 'believing' their apparatuses they told the housewives to 'wash the lettuce', to 'keep the children at home', to 'wash their shoes'. And the wife of Chancellor Kohl appeared on TV, buying and preparing lettuce, in order to show people that even the Chancellor's family did not believe the evidence of the high rates of radioactivity revealed by the Geiger-counters. Suddenly the old magic of science with its statistics and precise measurements is being replaced by an older imitative and picture magic.[3] The public relations managers try to pacify the people by showing public salad-eating performances on TV by some scientists and politicians. Scientific organizations publish full page advertisements in which they reassure the public that 'scientific analysis has shown' that radioactivity so far measured was so low that panic or fear for health risks were unnecessary. These advertisements were financed by the nuclear industry (*Frankfurt Rundschau,* 12.6.1986).

7. Chernobyl made clear there is no 'peaceful' use of atomic energy. Atomic energy, and, too, the other new 'future' technologies, such as reproductive and genetic engineering, are war technologies. Not only were they developed as a result of military research financed, originally at least, by defence departments, but their methodology is based on the destruction of living connections and symbioses. Modern science means, as Carolyn Merchant has shown, warfare against nature. Nature is the — female — enemy which must be forced into man's service.[4]

8. But all the frantic endeavours to pacify the people also showed that those in power were afraid of the people, they were afraid of the people's fear, they were less afraid, unlike the women, that life on this planet could be destroyed. But women were no longer ready to listen to them: they went into the streets, they demonstrated and demanded an immediate end to nuclear power plants. Women saw fear and anger as the most rational emotions, as the most powerful energies to be mobilized in the

months after Chernobyl. Everywhere spontaneous groups of 'Women Against Nuclear Power', 'Mothers Against Atomic Energy', 'Parents Against Atomic Energy' etc. sprang up demanding a halt to this war-technology against nature.

9. Chernobyl taught us the lesson that it is not those who demand an immediate opting out of nuclear energy who push us back 'into the Stone Age' but rather those who propagate this technology in the name of progress and civilization. They are, as became evident in the months after Chernobyl, the 'fathers of want' not those who have warned against this 'progress'. They are responsible for the fact that in the midst of abundant commodities there is a lack of the simple necessities of life: of green vegetables, of clean water or milk for children.

Atomic energy, but also gene- and computer-technology are often legitimized by the argument that it would take too long to change social relations and to develop an alternative to the prevailing scientific paradigm and its technology based on a different relationship of human beings to nature; women also use this argument and demand short term, 'pragmatic' solutions or technological fixes. Chernobyl, on the other hand, forced us to think in other time dimensions. We had no time to form a different relationship to nature. We now have to wait for 30 years till cesium 137 loses half of its radioactivity; the half life of plutonium is 24,000 years; that of strontium 90, 28 years.

The ruin of Chernobyl will contaminate the surrounding area for many years to come, causing disease, death and despair for many people. These time dimensions are the outcome of technical solutions propagated by the 'realists', the 'pragmatists', of those who favoured quick results. If we reflect on these time dimensions we should at last ask the really important questions now. And we should no longer leave the questions of survival to those experts in politics, science and the economy. It is time to demand an immediate end to nuclear power plants, an opting out of gene- and reproduction technology and to begin to establish a new, benevolent and reciprocal relationship with nature. It is time to end the warfare against nature, it is time that nature is no longer seen and treated as our enemy, but as a living entity, of which we are an integral part.

Notes

1. Easlea, Brian, *Fathering the Unthinkable, Masculinity, Scientists and the Nuclear Arms Race.* Pluto Press, London, 1986.
2. Böhme, Gerhard, Hartmut Böhme, Das Andre der Vernunft, 1987.
3. Neususs, Christel, Sie messen und dann essen sie es doch: Von der Wissenschaft zur Magie, in: Gambaroff et al: *Tschernobyl hat unser Leben verandert.* Vom Ausstieg der Frauen, rororo aktuell, Reinbek, 1986.
4. Merchant, Carolyn, *The Death of Nature: Women, Ecology and the Scientific Revolution.* Harper & Row, San Francisco, 1983.

7. Homeless in the 'Global Village'

Vandana Shiva

Global market integration and the creation of the 'level playing field' for transnational capital, creates conditions of homelessness in real and imaginary ways. The transnational corporation executive who finds a home in every Holiday Inn and Hilton, is homeless in terms of the deeper cultural sense of rootedness. But the culturally-rooted tribal is made physically homeless by being uprooted from the soil of her/his ancestors.

Two classes of the homeless seem to be emerging in this 'global village'. One group is mobile on a world scale, with no country as home, but the whole world as its property; the other has lost even the mobility within rootedness, and lives in refugee camps, resettlement colonies and reserves. The cumulative displacement caused by colonialism, development and the global marketplace has made homelessness a cultural characteristic of the late twentieth century.

Development as uprooting

Dams, mines, energy plants, military bases — these are the temples of the new religion called 'development', a religion that provides the rationale for the modernizing state, its bureaucracies and technocracies. What is sacrificed at the altar of this religion is nature's life and people's life. The sacraments of development are made of the ruins and desecration of other sacreds, especially sacred soils. They are based on the dismantling of society and community, on the uprooting of people and cultures. Since soil is the sacred mother, the womb of life in nature and society, its inviolability has been the organizing principle for societies which 'development' has declared backward and primitive. But these people are our contemporaries. They differ from us not in belonging to a bygone age but in having a different concept of what is sacred, what must be preserved. The sacred is the bond that connects the part to the whole. The sanctity of the soil must be sustained, limits must be set on human action. From the point of view of the managers of development, the high priests of the new religion, sacred bonds with the soil are impediments and hindrances to be shifted and sacrificed. Because people who hold the soil as sacred will not voluntarily allow themselves to be uprooted, 'development' requires a police state and terrorist tactics to wrench them away from their homes and homelands, and consign them as ecological and cultural refugees into the wasteland of industrial society. Bullets, as well as bulldozers, are often necessary to execute the development project.

In India, the magnitude of this sacrifice is only now becoming evident. Victims of progress have, of course, experienced their own uprooting and have resisted it. But both the victims and the state perceived each sacrifice as a small one for the larger 'national interest'. Over 40 years of planned development, the planned destruction of nature and society no longer appears negligible; and the larger 'national interest' turns out to be embodied in an elite minority without roots. Fifteen million people have been uprooted from their homelands in India during the past four development decades.1 They, and their links with the soil, have been sacrificed to accommodate mines, dams, factories, and wildlife parks.

One word echoes and reverberates in the songs and slogans of Indian people struggling against 'development': *'mati'* — soil. For these people soil is not simply a resource, it provides the very essence of their being. For large segments of Indian society the soil is still a sacred mother.

'Development' has meant the ecological and cultural rupture of bonds with nature, and within society, it has meant the transformation of organic communities into groups of uprooted and alienated individuals searching for abstract identities. What today are called ecology movements in the South are actually movements for rootedess, movements to resist uprooting before it begins. And what are generally perceived as ethnic struggles are also, in their own way, movements of uprooted people seeking social and cultural rootedness. These are the struggles of people taking place in the ruins wrought by development to regain a sense of selfhood and control over their destinies.

Soil as a sacred mother

Wherever development projects are introduced, they tear apart the soil and sever the bonds between people and the soil:

'*Mati Devata, Dharam Devata*' — The soil is our Goddess; it is our religion.' These are the words of adivasi women of the 'Save Gandmardhan'[2] movement, as they embraced the earth while being dragged away by the police from the blockade sites in the Gandmardhan hills in Orissa. Dhanmati, a 70-year-old woman of the movement had said, 'We will sacrifice our lives, but not Gandmardhan. We want to save this hill which gives us all we need.'

The forests of Gandmardhan are a source of rich plant diversity and water resources. They feed 22 perennial streams which in turn feed major rivers such as the Mahanadi. According to Indian mythology, Gandmardhan is the sacred hill where Hanuman gathered medicinal herbs to save Laxman's life in the epic Ramayana; the saviour has now to be destroyed for 'development'. It has to be desecrated by the Bharat Aluminium Company (BALCO) to mine for bauxite. BALCO had come to Gandmardhan after having destroyed the sanctity and ecology of another important mountain, Amarkantak — the source of the rivers Narmada, Sone, and Mahanadi. The destruction of Amarkantak was a high cost to pay for reserves which, in any case, turned out to be much smaller than originally estimated. To feed its 100,000 tonne aluminium plant at Korba in Madhya Pradesh, BALCO has now moved to Orissa to begin the rape of the Gandmardhan hills.

Since 1985 the tribals of the region have obstructed the work of the company and refused to be tempted by its offers of employment. Even police help has failed to stop the determined protest.

The conflict and destruction were unnecessary because India does not need so much aluminium, it already has a surplus. The mining activity however, is dictated not by the needs of the Indian people but by the demands of industrialized countries which are closing their own aluminium plants and encouraging imports from countries like India. Japan has reduced its aluminium smelting capacity from 1,200,000 tonnes to 140,000 tonnes and now imports 90 per cent of its aluminium requirements. The same Japanese companies have proposed setting up joint ventures in Indian export processing zones to manufacture aluminium products with buy-back arrangements.[3] The survival of the tribals of Gandmardhan is thus under threat because the rich countries want to preserve their environment, their economies and their luxurious lifestyle.

In Bihar, the homelands of tribals in the Chotanagpur plateau are being destroyed to mine coal and iron ore and to build dams on its rivers. The World Bank-financed Suvarnarekha dam is being built, with a US$127 million loan, primarily to provide industrial water for the expanding steel city of Jamshedpur. These dams will displace 80,000 tribals. In 1982, Ganga Ram Kalundia, the leader of the tribal anti-dam movement was shot dead by the police. Seven years later, his fellow tribals continue to resist the building of the dam because it will tear them away from the soil of their birth, the soil which has provided them sustenance and which links them to their ancestors. As Surendra Biruli of the movement against Suvarnarekha dam says:

> Our links with our ancestors are the basis of our society and of the reproduction of our society. Our children grow up playing around the stones which mark the burial sites of our ancestors. They learn the ways of our ancestors. Without relating to our ancestors, our lives lose all meaning. They talk of compensation. How can they compensate us for the loss of the very meaning of our lives if they bury these burial stones under the dam? They talk of rehabilitation. Can they ever rehabilitate the sacred sites they have violated?[4]

In coastal Orissa, the people of Balliapal are resisting the setting up of the national rocket test range which will displace 70,000 people from their fertile homeland. The protesters repeatedly assert their bonds with the soil as the basis of their resistance to the test range. 'The land and the sea is ours. We shall sacrifice our lives but not our mother earth.' They have rejected compensation offers because cash cannot compensate for the broken links with the soil which has nurtured and sustained generations of Balliapal farmers. As the Oriya poet Brajnath Rai writes:

> Miles of cocoa
> and cashew plantation,
> countless, luxuriant
> betel-vines
> draw green artistic designs
> on the carpet of brown sand.
> Sweet-potato, ground-nut

musk-melon vines
have adorned your dusty soil
ever green.
They have given the people
a high hope for
a long, prosperous life,
infused into hearts
of working people
an eternal hope to live.
But, today, suddenly,
covetous eyes of a power-mad hunter
has fallen on your green body
To cut it to pieces,
to drink to heart's content
fresh red blood.
A damned hunter
has indiscreetly taken aim
at your heart
To launch a fiery missile.

For communities who derive their sustenance from the soil it is not merely a physical property situated in Cartesian space; for them, the soil is the source of all meaning. As an Australian aborigine said, 'My land is my backbone. My land is my foundation.' Soil and society, the earth and its people are intimately interconnected. In tribal and peasant societies, cultural and religious identity derive from the soil, which is perceived not as a mere 'factor of production' but as the very soul of society. Soil has embodied the ecological and spiritual home for most cultures. It is the womb not only for the reproduction of biological life but also of cultural and spiritual life; it epitomizes all the sources of sustenance and is 'home' in the deepest sense.

The Hill Maris tribe in Bastar see *bhum*, or soil, as their home. *Shringar Bhum* is the universe of plants, animals, trees, and human beings. It is the cultural spiritual space which constitutes memory, myths, stories and songs that make the daily life of the community. *Jagha Bhum* is the name for the concrete location of social activities in a village. Savyasaachi reports a village elder as saying:

> The sun, the moon, the air, the trees are signs of my
> continuity. Social life will continue as long as these con-
> tinue to live. I was born as a part of the *bhum*. I will die

when this *bhum* dies. . . I was born with all others in this *bhum;* I go with them. He who has created us all will give us food. If there is so much variety and abundance in *bhum,* there is not reason for me to worry about food and continuity.[5]

The soil is thus the *condition* for the regeneration of nature's and society's life. The renewal of society therefore involves preserving the soil's integrity; it involves treating the soil as sacred.

Desacralization of the soil takes place through changes in the meaning of space. Sacred space, the universe of all meaning and living, the ecological source of all sustenance, is transformed into a mere site, a location in Cartesian space. When that site is identified for a development project, it is destroyed as a spiritual and ecological home. There is a story that elders tell to their children in central India to illustrate that the life of the tribe is deeply and intimately linked to the life of the soil and the forest.

The forest was ablaze. Pushed by the wind, the flames began to close in on a beautiful tree on which sat a bird. An old man escaping the fire, himself, saw the bird and said to it, 'Little bird, why don't you fly away? Have you forgotten you have wings?' And the bird answered, 'Old man, do you see this empty nest above? This is where I was born. And this small nest from which you hear the chirping is where I am bringing up my small child. I feed him with nectar from the flowers of this tree and I live by eating its ripe fruit. And do you see the dropping below on the forest floor? Many seedlings will emerge from them and thus do I help to spread greenery, as my parents before me did, as my children after me will. My life is linked to this tree. If it dies I will surely die with it. No, I have not forgotten my wings.' [6]

The fact that people did not move from their ancestral homelands, that they continued to reproduce life in nature and society in sustainable ways was not seen as the conservation of the earth and of the soil ethic. Instead, it was seen as evidence of stagnation, of an inability to move on — to 'progress'. The stimulation to move on and progress was provided by the development project, and the uprooting and destruction it involved was sanitized under the neo-Cartesian category of 'displacement'.

Peter Berger has described development as the 'spreading condition of homelessness'.[7] The creation of homelessness takes place both through the ecological destruction of the 'home' and the cultural and spiritual uprooting of peoples from their homes. The word 'ecology' was derived from oikos, the household — and ecological destruction in its essence is the destruction of the *bhum* as the spiritual and ecological household. By allocating a Cartesian category to space in substitution for the sacred category it becomes possible for development technocrats and agencies to expand their activities into the management of 'Involuntary Resettlement in Development Projects'. An irreversible process of genocide and ecocide is neutralized by the terms 'displacement' and 'resettlement'. It becomes possible for agencies such as the World Bank to speak of reconciling the 'positive' long-term 'national' interests served by development projects and the 'negative' impacts of displacement borne by 'local' communities through resettlement and rehabilitation projects.

For those who hold the soil as sacred, relocation is inconceivable. At the public hearing of the World Commission of Environmental Development, an elder of the Krenak tribe spoke of the impossibility of resettlement:

> When the government took our land in the valley of the Rio Doce, they wanted to give us another place somewhere else. But the state, the government, will never understand that we do not have another place to go.
>
> The only possible place for the Krenak people to live and to re-establish our existence, to speak to our Gods, to speak to our nature, to weave our lives is where God created us. It is useless for the government to put us in a very beautiful place, in a very good place with a lot of hunting and a lot of fish. The Krenak people, we continue dying and we die insisting that there is only one place for us to live.
>
> My heart does not become happy to see humanity's incapacity. I have no pleasure at all to come here and make these statements. *We can no longer see the planet that we live upon as if it were a chess board where people just move things around. We cannot consider the planet as something isolated from the cosmic.*[8] [Emphasis added.]

This approach to nature which sees the soil as the mother and people as her offspring, not her master, was and is universally shared even though it has everywhere been sacrificed as representing only a narrow, parochial viewpoint and approach.

In its place has been introduced the culture of the white man, universalized first through colonialism and then development, which sees the soil only in terms of territory to be conquered and owned.

Colonialism and capitalism transformed land and soil from being a source of life and a commons from which people draw sustenance, into private property to be bought and sold and conquered; development continued colonialism's unfinished task. It transformed man from the role of guest to predator. In a sacred space, one can only be a guest, one cannot own it. This attitude to the soil and earth as a sacralized home, not private property, is characteristic of most Third World societies. Chief Seattle's letter has become an ecological testament, telling us that

> The earth does not belong to man, man belongs to the earth. All things are connected like the blood which unites one family. Whatever befalls the earth befalls the sons of the earth. Man did not weave the web of life; he is merely a strand of it. Whatever he does to the web, he does to himself.[9]

In the indigenous world-views in Africa, the world in its entirety appears as consisting of a single tissue. Man cannot exercise domination over it by virtue of his spirit. What is more, this world is sacralized, and man must be prudent in the use he makes of it. Man must act in this world as a guest and not as an exploiting proprietor.[10]

When the rhythms and patterns of the universe are displaced the commons is displaced by private property. In indigenous communities, individuals have no private property rights, instead, the entire tribe is the trustee of the land it occupies, and the community or tribe includes not only the currently living members but also the ancestors and future generations. The absence of private property rights and of a territorial concept of space make for easy dispossession of indigenous communities' land.

In defining a sacred space, soil does not define cartographic space on a map, or a territorial unit. As Benedict Anderson[11] has shown, the creation of territorial space in large areas of the world was an instrument of colonization. Tracing the shift from cultural space to territorial space in Thailand, he shows how, between 1900 and 1915, the traditional words *brung* and *muang* largely disappeared because they imaged 'sovereignty' in terms of sacred sites and discrete population centres. In their place came *prathet*,

'country' which imaged it in the invisible terms of bounded ter-
ritori al space. Sovereignty thus shifted from the soil and
soil-linked communities to sovereignty of the nation state.
Laws of nature and their universality were replaced by the
laws of a police state which dispossessed peoples of their
original homelands, to clear the way for the logic of the
world market.

In this way organic communities give way to slum dwellers or
urban and industrial jungles. Development builds new 'temples'
by robbing nature and society of their integrity, and their soul.
Development has converted soil from sacred mother into disposable object — to be ravaged for minerals that lie below, or
drowned beneath gigantic reservoirs. The soil's children, too, have
been made disposable: mines and dams leave behind wastelands
and uprooted people. The desacralization of the soil as sacred
space was an essential part of colonialism then and of development now. As Rifkin[12] has so aptly stated, 'Desacralization serves
as a kind of psychic ritual by which human beings deaden their
prey, preparing it for consumption.'

The irony involved in the desacralization of space and uprooting of local communities is that the secular categories of space as
used in development, transform the original inhabitants into
strangers while intruders take over their homes as private property. A political redefinition of people and society is taking place
with shifts in the meaning of space. New sources of power and
control are being created in relationship to nature and to society.
As relationships between nature and society and between different communities are changed and replaced by abstract and rigid
boundaries between nature and people and between peoples,
power and meaning shift from roots in the soil to links with the
nation state and with global capital. These one-dimensional, homogenizing concepts of power create new dualities and new exclusions.

The new borders, evidently, are created for the people who
belong to that land. There are no borders for those who come in to
colonize and destroy the land. In the words of financial consultant
Kenichi Ohmae:

> On a political map, the boundaries between countries are as
> clear as ever. But on a competitive map, a map showing the
> real flows of financial activity, these boundaries have largely
> disappeared . . . Borderless economy . . . offers enormous

opportunities to those who can criss-cross the boundaries in search of better profits. We are finally living in a world where money, securities, services, options, futures, information and patents, software and hardware, companies and know-how, assets and memberships, paintings and brands are all traded without national sentiments across traditional borders.[13]

Notes

1. Fernandes, Walter and Enakshi Ganguly Thukral, *Development, Displacement and Rehabilitation.* Indian Social Institute, 1989, p. 80.
2. Bahuguna, Sunderlal in *Chipko News.* Mimeo, Navjeevan Ashram, Silyara, 1986.
3. Bandyopadhyay, J. 'Havoc.' *Illustrated Weekly of India,* 13 December 1987.
4. As told to the author during a field trip to Suvarnarekha submergence area in September 1989.
5. Savyasaachi, in Frederique Marglin and Tariq Banuri, *Dominating Knowledge.* Zed Books, forthcoming.
6. Rane, Ulhas 'The Zudpi Factor', *Sanctuary,* Vol. VII, No. 4, 1987.
7. Berger, Peter et. al. *The Homeless Mind.* London, Pelican Books, 1981.
8. Krenak, Ailton. Co-ordinator of Indian Nation's Union, WCED Public Hearing, Sao Paulo, 28-29th October, 1985. Quoted in *Our Common Future,* Oxford, Oxford University Press, p. 115.
9. Chief Seattle, Letter to the President of the USA, reproduced in 'If all the beasts were gone', London, Royal College of Art, 1977.
10. Mbiti, John S. *The Prayers of African Religion.* London, SPCK, 1975.
11. Benedict Anderson, 'Nationalism', Paper presented at WIDER Seminar on Systems of Knowledge as Systems of Power, Karachi, 1989.
12. Rifkin, Jeremy and Nicanor Peelas, *Algeny.* New York, The Viking Press, 1983.
13. Ohmae, Kenichi, *The Borderless World.* London, Collins, 1990, p.18.

8. Masculinization of the Motherland

Vandana Shiva

By 1992, that is in a short span of half a century, we in South Asia have had to become accustomed to three meanings and structures of 'motherland'. The feminine attribute, as a symbol of the land and its people has slowly disappeared.

During the colonial period, 'Mother India' was the symbol and inspiration for the struggle of independence against British colonialism. It was a decolonizing category.

During the four decades from 1947 to the end of the 1980s when 'development' was the major target of the nation state, the 'motherland' metaphor disappeared from the discourse of nation building. The state behaves as *parens patriae* — the patriarchal parent — dominating life, but also attempting to provide for basic needs by protecting the national economy and natural resources from predation by international interests.

The 1990s have seen a dramatic change in the state's role. At the economic level, the state has been totally subjugated to the superstate run by the transnational corporations (TNCs) and the Bretton Woods institutions — World Bank, International Monetary Fund (IMF) and the General Agreement on Tariffs and Trade (GATT). Liberalization through IMF conditionalities and the World Bank Structural Adjustment Programme is working hand-in-hand with 'free trade' for TNCs as demanded through GATT. Yet precisely when the state is disappearing as a patriarchal yet protective parent for the citizens of India in the global market place, 'Mother India' is emerging as Bharat Mata in fundamentalist discourse, not as a source of shakti (power) but as a battlefield for communal and ethnic conflicts.

The paradoxical process of the masculinization of the motherland has been that precisely when external borders disappear, new, internal borders and boundaries are being created. It seems that the deeper the global integration, the deeper the national disintegration. The further removed centres of governance become from people's lives, the deeper are the divisions that appear where there was diversity before. The collapse of global distances hides the creation of unbridgeable local distances between those who have previously shared homes, streets, villages, towns and countries. Markets that grow by forcibly depriving more and more people of their livelihoods provide the climate for militarized minds that seek freedom in the context of unfreedom through the use of guns and bombs.

The country as motherland has been replaced by a masculinized nation state, which exists only to serve TNCs on the one hand, and a militarized notion of nationalism on the other. Together, the state in the service of the market, and nationalism in the service of fundamentalism, obliterate the feminine symbolism of Mother India that had inspired and motivated our freedom struggle during the first half of the twentieth century.

Globalization and the rise of nationalism

One of the most pervasive paradoxes of our times is the simultaneous rise of narrow nationalisms and the globalization of the world economy. The 'level playing field' is supposedly intended to level all cultures, all differences. Yet the more violent the 'levelling', the more violent is the expression of ethnic and cultural identity as the basis for nationalism.

Globalism, as defined in the perspective of capitalist patriarchy, means only the global reach of capital to embrace all the world's resources and markets. The instruments for achieving freedom for capital are simultaneously instruments for creating unfreedom for local communities.

The formation of the nation state in South Asia at the time of independence was a departure from the earlier pattern of nations within a country perceived as motherland. Everyday life was locally determined and governed. With independence, however, the protective mother gave way to a dictatorial but protective father. The state had two roles: first, to provide the services and fulfil the needs that colonialism had destroyed or the state itself had abrogated from the people's economy; and second, to protect its citizens from domination by foreign interests.

After 40 years of international aid and development, international free trade has become the state's *raison d'etre*. The role of the state has been inverted. Its new role has become that of provider of natural resources, of basic and essential services, concessions, infrastructure and patent protection for TNCs, and to protect them from people's demands for labour rights, health, environmental, and human rights.

This involves withdrawal of services from citizens, the imposition of austerity, and a more aggressive use of the state's law and order enforcement machinery to protect TNC interests. The state may be said to have withered away except as a law and order force. It no longer performs the role of protector of the public interest, and by extension the national interest. Rather than acting as a regulator of TNCs, the state now acts as their protector.

Recent debates in India about patent protection highlight the inverted role of the state. The aim of India's patent act of 1970 is primarily to protect the public interest. The US however, is demanding that through Clause Special 301 of its trade act India adopt the US patent system which is aimed at protecting TNC profits and monopolies. When 250 parliamentarians published a statement[1] demanding a parliamentary debate on the issue of patents and intellectual property rights, the Minister of Commerce, who had been negotiating with the US trade representative, called the public debate the popular interest and said this need not accord with the 'considered national interest'. When public interest is divorced from national interest, and national interest is predicated on international interests, then sovereignty is in crisis, along with democracy.

The erosion of the state's sovereignty vis-a-vis external forces leads to those forces' increased use of the state as an instrument; and this tends to erode the sovereignty of citizens. The pseudo nationalism of the fundamentalists based on ethnic and religious identity steps in to fill the political vacuum that an inverted state has created.

The emergence of Hindutva, or Hindu fundamentalism as a nationalist ideology is an example of a political ideology blind to the economic processes of global integration and the disintegration this leads to. Fundamentalists fail to relate the current erosion of freedom and autonomy to the Indian state's subservience to global capitalism. Recolonization as an emergent trend is not addressed as a political issue. Instead of looking at the present and future, fundamentalism as a pseudo-nationalist ideology attempts to reconstruct the past on masculinized and militarized categories. While failing to create the type of nationalism needed to protect freedom in a period of recolonization, pseudo-nationalism's political culture creates internal divisions and incites violence. Rather than basing the recovery of national identity on economic and political non-cooperation in global markets, as in Gandhi's worldview, it is based on full economic and political participation in the global marketplace, and non-cooperation between neighbouring communities. Funding the 'enemy' within also goes hand in hand with the rise in the discourse on virility and violence.

As Paola Bacchetta[2] has shown, for two of India's important spiritual leaders, Rama Krishna and Aurobindo, the mother as a symbol of the country was charged with love for all her children, in all their diversity; she was the source of energy and protection; Hindutva's Bharat Mata needs to be protected by her 'virile sons'. From Mother India to Bharat Mata is a move from activity to passivity in feminine symbolism: Kali's feminine strength gives way to male virility. Masculinization of the motherland thus involves the elimination of all associations of strength with the feminine and with diversity. Strength and power is now defined in forms of the militarized masculine identity while tolerance of diversity is defined as effeminate and weak. A politics of exclusion and violence is thus built in the name of nationalism. Nationalism reconstructs the past to legitimize its ascendancy. 'Nationalism' in this mould emerges not as a resistance against transnational domination and Westernization of production, consumption patterns and cultural values, but as the local ideology that facilitates global takeover. Hindutva, it is being repeatedly stated, is the ideology of a modernizing India. Yet, as they are unfolding, liberalization and modernization are based on breaking all links with the motherland. Masculinization of the motherland results in the disappearance of the motherland from the hearts and minds of the people.

From plurality to duality

In effect, the process of development leads to turning away from the soil as a source of meaning and survival, and turning to the state and its resources for both. The destruction of organic links with the soil also leads to the destruction of organic links within society. Diverse communities, co-operating with each other and the land become different communities competing with each other for the conquest of the land. The homogenization processes of development do not fully eliminate differences. These persist, not in an integrating context of plurality, but in the fragmenting context of homogenization. Positive pluralities give way to negative dualities, each in competition with every 'other', contesting the scarce resources that define economic and political power. The project of development is propounded as a source of growth and abundance. Yet by destroying the abundance that comes from the soil and replacing it by resources of the state, new scarcities and new conflicts for scarce resources are created.[3] Scarcity, not abundance, characterizes situations where nothing is sacred but everything has a price. As meaning and identity shift from the soil to the state and from plural histories to a singular, linear history of movement from 'traditional' to 'modern' societies, as Rostow's model suggests,[4] ethnic, religious, and regional differences which persist are forced into the strait-jacket of 'narrow nationalism'. Instead of being rooted spiritually in the soil and the earth, uprooted communities attempt to reinsert themselves by fighting for fragmented statehood and narrow nationalism. Diversity is mutated into duality, into the experience of exclusion, of being 'in' or 'out.' Intolerance of diversity becomes a new social disease, leaving communities vulnerable to breakdown and violence, decay and destruction. The intolerance of diversity and the persistence of cultural differences sets one community against another in a context created by a homogenizing state, carrying out a homogenizing project of development. Difference, rather than being seen as a basis of the richness of diversity, becomes the basis of division and an ideology of separatism.

In the South Asian region, the most 'successful' experiments in economic growth and development (Punjab and Sri Lanka) have become, in less than two decades, crucibles of violence and civil war.[5] Culturally diverse societies, engineered to fit into models of development have lost their organic community identity. From their fractured, fragmented and false identities, they struggle to compete for a place in the only social space that remains — the social space defined by the modern state.

It is not improbable that the upsurge of ethnic religious and regional conflicts in the Third World today is connected with the ecological and cultural uprooting of people deprived of positive identities, pushed into a negative sense of self with respect to every 'other'. Punjab, the exemplar of the Green Revolution miracle, until recently one of the fastest growing agricultural regions of the world is today riddled with conflict and violence.[6] According to official estimates, at least 10,000 people have lost their lives in Punjab during the last ten years.[7] During 1986, 598 people were killed in violent conflicts; in 1987, the number was 1,544; and in 1988 it had escalated to 3,000. And 1992 showed no sign of peace. Punjab provides the most advanced example of technological changes based on the disruption of links between soil and society. The Green Revolution strategy integrated Third World farmers into the global markets of fertilizers, pesticides and seeds, and disintegrated their organic links with their soils and communities. One outcome of this was violent disruption to the soil resulting in water-logged or salinated deserts, diseases, and pest-infested monocultures.[8] Another outcome was violence in the community, especially towards women and children. Commercialization linked with cultural disintegration created new forms of addiction and of abuse and aggression.

The religious resurgence of the Sikhs in the early 1980s was an expression of a search for identity in the ethical and cultural vacuum that had been created by destroying all value except that which serves the market place. Women were the most active members of this movement. There was also a parallel movement of farmers, most of whom happened to be Sikh, protesting against the state's centralized and centralizing farm policies, which left the Punjab farmers disillusioned after a short lived prosperity. The struggles of Sikhs as farmers and as a religious community were, however, rapidly communalized and militarized. On the one hand, in June 1984 the people of Punjab became victims of state terrorism exemplified by the attack on the most sacred Sikh shrine — the Golden Temple — in a military operation — Operation Bluestar — which was aimed at the extremists hiding in the Temple, but which was responsible for killing 400 innocent pilgrims and badly damaging the holy shrine.9 On the other hand, they were victims of the terrorism of Sikh youth whose sense of justice was constrained by the political contours of a narrow state concept of the Sikh identity. Punjab, the land of the five rivers, was forgotten and redefined as Khalistan. The soil gave way to the state as the metaphor for organizing the life of society.

The conflicts were thus relocated in a communalized zone for the contest of statehood and state power. They moved away from their beginnings in tensions between a disillusioned, discontented, and disintegrating farming community and a centralizing state which controls agricultural policy, finance, credit, inputs and prices of agricultural commodities. And they also moved away from the cultural and ethical reappraisal of the social and economic impact of the Green Revolution.

The Green Revolution was to have been a strategy for peace and abundance. Today there is no peace in Punjab. There is also no peace with the soils of Punjab and without that peace, there can be no lasting abundance.

Sri Lanka was another miracle of development in the 1970s. It was projected as the Singapore of South Asia. Instead it has become its Lebanon. Free trade zones were set up to open Sri Lanka to global markets and gigantic development projects such as the Mahaweli Ganga Hydroelectric Irrigation Project,[10] which were designed to transform Sri Lanka overnight from a peasant society into an industrial power. Export liberalization created one level of uprooting through economic dislocation. Development projects uprooted in more direct ways. The plan of the Mahaweli project alone involved the shifting of one million people, one-sixteenth of the country's population.[11] Besides large-scale ecological disruption, the project created new imbalances between genders and ethnic groups. The project denied women rights to land which they had enjoyed traditionally. It resettled displaced peasants in parts of the North Central and Eastern provinces. This resettlement policy led to a dramatic change in the demographic pattern, particularly of the Eastern provinces, thereby altering the ethnic composition and aggravating ethnic conflict.[12] The 'open' economy created new costs for local economic and ecological security, fragmented and corrupted the social fabric. With the destruction of rootedness in the soil and local social structures, new insecurities and scarcities grew, new zones of contest between communities were created and the contest was carried out mimicking the militarized power of the nation state. Violence is now the social order in Sri Lanka. During 1989, 30,000 people were killed, and the killings continue unabated.

One of the recent victims of the violence in Sri Lanka was a friend, Rajini Thiranagama, who taught at Jaffna's Medical School. Early in 1989 we had spent ten days together at a dialogue of South Asian Feminists, where Rajini had repeatedly brought up the issue of violence and the culture of death. She urged us to find feminist ways to end the celebration of death by renewing the celebration of life.

Just nine days before being shot down, Rajini had written about 'the enormous brutalization and deterioration that has been brought about by guns — states that have militarized entire communities — narrow nationalist slogans that have sanctioned many killings' — and she had called on the women to come out and 'plead for life — for no guns'.

Yet, more and more young women in Sri Lanka have been taking to guns, emulating the men in a militarized and violent search for freedom as freedom becomes more elusive.

In May 1991, India's then Prime Minister Rajiv Gandhi was assassinated by a young woman supposedly from the Tamil Tigers who had used herself as a human bomb. A few years earlier, Rajiv's mother Indira Gandhi had been assassinated in connection with the Punjab problem. So rapidly, in less than a decade, militarism and the intolerance of diversity has infected this land of non-violence, of Buddha and Gandhi.

Notes

1. National Working Group on Patents, Statement of Parliamentarians.
2. Bacchetta, Paola 'The construction of male and female in RSS Discourse,' mimeo.
3. Shiva, V. *Violence of the Green Revolution.* Zed Books, London, 1991.
4. Rostow, W. E. *The Stages of Economic Growth,* Cambridge University Press, Cambridge, 1979, p. 4.
5. *Pressing Against the Boundaries,* Report of the Workshop on Feminist Theory in South Asia, Bangalore, 1990.
6. Shiva, V. op. cit.1991.
7. *Frontline;* 8th Anniversary of Operation Bluestar, 1 July, 1992.
8. Shiva, V. op cit.
9. Singh, Patwant and Malik, Harji, 'Punjab: The Fatal Miscalculation', Patwant Singh, New Delhi, 1985.
10. The United National Party (UNP) came to power in Sri Lanka in 1977 and the Mahaweli Project was central to their strategy. This project involved building five dams on Sri Lanka's longest river and richest agricultural valley at a cost of $1.25 billion.
11. Alexis, L. 'Sri Lanka's Mahaweli Ganga Project: The Damnation of Paradise' in E. Goldsmith and N. Hildyard (eds) *The Social and Environmental Effects of Large Dams,* Vol. II, Wadebridge Ecological Centre, U.K., 1984, p. 276.
12. Personal communication, Lalanath de Silva.

9. Women have no Fatherland

Maria Mies

In 1989 when, every week, the dissatisfied people of the erstwhile German Democratic Republic (GDR) gathered in Leipzig for their 'Monday-demonstrations' they shouted the slogan: *'Deutschland, einig Vaterland!'* (Germany, united Fatherland!) They expected that all their problems would be solved by the rapid (re) unification of the Federal Republic of Germany (FRG) and the German Democratic Republic (GDR). They hoped that with political unification they would not only enjoy the same freedom as the citizens of West Germany but also share the same living standard as those 'privileged' Germans in the capitalist West. In view of the euphoria surrounding this slogan it was pertinent to ask what this unification process meant for women in both East and West Germany. What could women expect from this German 'Fatherland'? Or for that matter, from any fatherland? Were the changes in the socialist states of the Eastern block not accompanied by rising nationalism? What does this new wave of nationalism mean for women? What role do they play in these processes? And finally, what role did women play historically in the rise of the modern nation state — because it is the nation state that is referred to as the fatherland par excellence? Should not at least feminists remember Virginia Woolf's words, that women have no land? Or, as I want to put it here: women have no fatherland? Moreover, from an ecofeminist perspective we have to ask whether these processes lead to further environmental degradation or not. Will the new nation-states protect nature better than the old ideological states? In the following pages I shall try to answer these and some related questions by postulating theses.

Women pay the price

As is now well-known women in both East and West Germany are paying the price for German unification.

In January 1990, in East Berlin, I attended one of the first congresses of the then GDR's newly-founded *Unabhangiger Frauenrerband* (UFV) (Independent Women's Association).[1] The women who had founded this new organization in protest against the state-ordained socialist *Demokratischer Frauenverband* (Democratic Women's Association) were full of energy and determined to participate fully and equally in the processes of political change that were taking place. They decided to take part in the spring 1990 elections — as a separate women's organization. They were resolutely confident that this would enable them to preserve some of the benefits — denied to their Western sisters — women had enjoyed in socialist Germany; and simultaneously they wanted to fight patriarchal structures, which had remained intact under socialism.

The fast set-back to these high hopes came in the elections in March 1990: the Independent Women's Association failed to win enough votes. It had formed an election alliance with the East German Green Party, but even the Greens were unwilling to give a seat to the women's organization because it did not get enough votes. The next disappointment came with the FRG-GDR unification on 3 October 1990. After the all-German Federal elections in December 1990, when the Christian Democrats (CDU) under Chancellor Kohl won a majority (particularly owing to the enthusiasm of the East Germans) it became clear that the women would be unable to protect and preserve those institutions, structures and laws which had been created under socialism to 'draw women into production on an equal footing' with men. Among others these were creches for small children, job security for working mothers, the right to send a child to a kindergarten, a year's paid maternity leave, the guarantee of a flat for single mothers, paid leave for mothers in the event of a child's illness.

In addition, the GDR's abortion law had been more liberal than in West Germany. East German women could have an abortion — on demand — up to the third month of pregnancy. It soon became evident that the fact that the East Germans had opted to 'join' West Germany, thereby accepting the West German Constitution as it stood, did not allow the women any room for negotiation: West German laws were simply extended to East Germany.

Meanwhile the euphoria in East Germany has given way to a deep sense of disappointment and depression. Women particularly suffer most from the rising unemployment in the East. They lost their creches, they became the first to be fired when factories were wound up, offices closed, or the universities were *abgewickelt* (de-developed) according to the laws of the market economy. East German women now experience the classic process of belonging to the capitalist reserve army of labour; they are being sent home to '*Kinder und Kuche*' (children and kitchen). In spring 1991, there were more than 1.2 million unemployed in East Germany, more than 50 per cent of whom were women.

The politicians kept assuring people in East Germany that their economic problems, particularly the high unemployment, were only temporary. They attributed the lack of growth to 40 years of socialism and to excessive wage demands of the trade unions. But even a year later, in February 1992, the economic and social situation in the so-called new federal states in East Germany was worse than the previous year, particularly for women.

In January 1992 the total figure for unemployed in united Germany was 3.2 million, an increase of 6.3 per cent for West Germany and 16.5 per cent for East Germany in comparison to the previous month. Of the 3.2 million unemployed 1.35 million live in East Germany, which has only 17 million inhabitants, whereas West Germany has 60 million; and, as expected, the greater impact of this rising unemployment falls on women. The proportion of women unemployed rose from 50 per cent in 1991 to 62 per cent in 1992. Among all women 21.8 per cent are jobless, whereas it is only 12.6 per cent among the men.[2]

For many of the women this means dependence on social welfare, particularly for those who have no 'earning husband': the divorced or unmarried, and those who are too old to find another job. One of the main points of the January 1990 UFV congress was that women wanted to maintain their economic existence independently of a male breadwinner. However, now, they are experiencing housewifization,[3] as is common to many women under capitalism.

Confrontation with the realities of capitalism, which had so far been known only through propaganda and TV, came as a shock to many women in East Germany. At a conference in Dresden on 'World Economy, Ecology and Solidarity' (17 January 1992)[4] I witnessed the bitterness, anger and depression of many women in East Germany. They were particularly bitter about the abrupt devaluation of their qualifications and education. Women who had been in professional positions and who had gained self-respect from their knowledge and experience are now unemployed and have to undergo a re-education programme for such flimsy occupations as, for example, a 'European Assistant'. Due to these experiences, most East German women present at this meeting — and many East German men too — immediately understood my

thesis, that capitalism always needs colonies, internal and external, and that as housewives, women everywhere constitute one
internal colony. East Germany is now again part of the political
German nation-state, but its actual economic, social and socio-
psychological status is that of a colony. This is how people at least
expressed their feelings at this meeting. West German 'development experts' are being sent to East Germany to help them to learn
the laws of a market economy and democracy. The East Germans
have coined the term for these Westerners: *'Besserwessi'*, literally:
'People from West Germany who know everything better'. The
dilemma for women and men in East Germany is that with the
disappearance of the socialist alternative, capitalism appears as
the only other possible solution. But they still have to realize that
capitalism has two sides: the winners and the losers.

I was surprised, however, that the women formulated their
rejection to the policy of 'catching-up development' (see Ch. 4).
They understood that this catching-up strategy was neither a solution for women, for the colonized in the Third World, nor for the
erstwhile socialist countries.

Women in West Germany too, have to pay for 'Germany, united
Fatherland.' Many of the projects and improvements for which
the women's movement had fought such as safe houses for battered women, creches for working women's children, for example,
are threatened because the cash to finance them is now either
diverted to accommodate refugees from the East or for the recon-
struction of East Germany. The united fatherland is proving to be
more costly than was expected in the first nationalistic euphoria
(including increased taxes), therefore, this extra money will be
obtained by denying it to those projects women wanted in order to
improve their situation.

As a feminist who has studied the functioning of capitalist
patriarchy for a long time, I am not surprised by the cold blooded
strategy which is used *vis-a-vis* women in East, as well as in West
Germany. I am rather surprised at the optimism of East German
women in hoping that the achievement of political unity in Germany would give them a greater opportunity to influence their
country's politics. But the history of the unification process is very
similar to that of other revolutions. Women had fought in the
forefront of the protest movement in East Germany, and played a
crucial role in the round-table negotiations in the GDR before
unification. But when political unity was achieved and when the
distribution of the new power was on the agenda of history the

women were again relocated to the place patriarchy had long since assigned to them.

Must we conclude from this that there is some unwritten law decreeing that men will always allow women to fight in the forefront of social movements and revolutions, but it is men who harvest the fruits of victory while women are relegated once more to their traditional position in patriarchal society? Is it, as Christina Thurmer-Rohr suggests, a kind of male 'monoculture' that always overrides the political will of women?[5] In order to understand better what the relationship is between women and these so-called fatherlands, we must look more closely at the history of the modern nation-state and ask what its emergence had to do with women's oppression and exploitation.

Colonization of women

Since the beginning of the modern nation-state (the fatherlands) women have been colonized. This means the modern nation-state necessarily controlled their sexuality, their fertility and their work capacity or labour power. Without this colonization neither capitalism nor the modern nation state could have been sustained. And it is this colonization that constitutes the foundation of what is now being called 'civil society'.

Social analysts have frequently concluded that the most important modern division of labour is that between the so-called public wage labour of mainly men and so-called private housework of women. In this division, wage labour is directly controlled by capital, or the economy. But the economy cannot directly control women's sexuality, fertility and work capacity; to do this, the state, with its family policy, is necessary. The state must also exercise control of women, because it needs soldiers to defend its territory, functionaries for its bureaucracy; and, too, the economy needs new labourers and consumers. Women are essential for this procreation of people. But neither the state nor the economy need women *qua* women, but only to fulfil a particular 'role'. In the erstwhile GDR women coined the slogan: 'Without women you can't make a state'. This is correct, but its precise meaning is rather contrary to what the GDR women had struggled for, that is: to be equal partners in running this state. In reality this phrase means that the women of a nation-state must be colonized as housewives in order to maintain this modern state.[6]

This housewifization is not the result of some inborn male sadism but is necessary for an economy which has as its goal unlimited growth. Within a limited world these goals can be achieved only by dividing up the world and exploiting and colonizing the separate parts. The task of the new state, of the nation-state, is to organize this external and internal colonization — and that means to legalize it. As Polanyi has convincingly demonstrated, the modern capitalist market economy did not emerge merely through the free play of the market forces, as liberalism would have us believe. This new market, particularly the market of labour power, and of land, had to be brought into existence, had to be created by direct state intervention and power.[7] This state intervention also aimed to manipulate the reproductive behaviour of women; nineteenth century family policy was, and remains, largely population policy.[8]

In addition, the nation-state's task is to mediate between what are universally declared human rights, according to which all people are equal and free, and the *de facto* unequal segments of the different external and internal colonies: between wage-workers and non-wage workers; between citizens and foreigners; between men and women; between ethnic and racial minorities and the majority. Here we encounter a structural contradiction of 'civil society'. All modern democratic nation-states have written into their constitution the fundamental human rights of equality, freedom and fraternity. But if these rights, particularly the right to equality, were implemented for all people not only politically, but economically as well, the economic system would collapse. Therefore, foreign workers, women, those demanding political asylum and so on, are denied economic and political status equal to that enjoyed by the 'normal' male citizen.[9]

A similar contradiction can be observed when we look at the external history of the modern nation-state, that is: the contradiction between global world-market orientation and national self-interest.[10]

Global orientation and national self-interest

The modern fatherlands, the nation-states, were constructed and can survive only on the foundation of a colonial, world economic order. Since from its outset capitalism functioned as a 'world system' (Wallerstein) which overran and conquered foreign motherlands, it was able to accumulate more wealth in the centre and there construct the modern nation-state. These new nation-states, these fatherlands, also integrated, that is, swallowed up, smaller countries and tribes and homogenized them within a new 'national culture'. In this process the competition of the modern nation-states about economic and political hegemony played a crucial role.

What appears as a contradiction in this thesis — global orientation on one hand and national self-interest on the other — is, at a closer look, a necessary precondition both for the nation-state and the market economy or capitalism. This economy needs borders open to the outside world, free access to foreign markets, environments, resources and labour power.[11] Economic liberalism therefore propagates the free world market and free trade. But this freedom is not meant to extend to the colonies; trade relations between the core states of this world system[12] and the peripheries or colonies are a one way street. The peripheries are denied equal access to the markets, the resources and the labour power of the core states. The relationship between the two, so-called 'trade partners' is not one of reciprocity, but the economically strong — the industrial nations — the USA, Europe, Japan, determine the price of the products imported from the peripheral countries. The GATT-negotiations are further evidence of the asymmetric and hierarchical relationship between the rich North and the poor South (see chapter 14) and of the contradictory policy of free-trade and open, world-market orientation, the rhetoric 'one world', and the pressure brought to bear on Third World countries (particularly by the USA), to eliminate all 'trade barriers' against the importation of goods produced in the USA. In particular the clauses related to the new patent rights and intellectual property are meant to open up Third World markets for new US-products, such as genetically engineered seeds, for example, and intended to facilitate control over these new markets (see chapter 11). The service sector, too, expects new markets in the South. This policy no longer respects the sovereignty of the South's nation-states, which might have opted for a policy of self-sufficiency and import control. This sovereignty has to retreat before the trade interests of the North's transnational corporations, above all their needs for new markets. Thus, the global orientation of the North's nation-states and their national self-interest are two sides of the same coin.

Violence and the state

In order to protect these contradictory relations from opposition either from within or outside, the modern nation-state needs to exercise violence and coercion. The nation-state, as Giddens shows, was constructed by means of direct violence,[13]but it cannot be upheld without state monopoly over direct violence and means of coercion in the form of the military and the police. This monopoly of direct violence implies the militarization of men, with the army as the new school of manhood. Militarization of men, on the other hand, always implies violence against, and the degradation of women.[14]

Susan Brownmiller was one of the first feminists to show the close connection between warfare against foreign peoples and warfare against women in the form of rape. The discussion on rape and warfare or militarism for long centred on the question of whether men are inherently more aggressive than women. The root cause was thus sought in the psychological and physiological differences between men and women, while the economic and political context was often ignored. Similarly, Cynthia Enloe's analysis of the construction of the new Rambo-image as the model for modern maleness, and its counterpart the weak, feminine, passive woman, describes correctly what is happening at present. But she explains these new strategies merely by the role-theory and suggests a change of role-images of men and women.[15]

Such analyses are useful for an assessment of the situation, but by ignoring the fact that the capitalist-patriarchal nation state, the fatherland, needs exactly such images of maleness as Rambo personifies in order to pursue its economic and political goals, they fail to explain why, in modern nation-states, men are being militarized and why this militarization always hits women. Not only the women of the 'enemy', but also the women of their own nation.

The Gulf War clearly illustrated this combination of Ramboism and political economic interest on both sides. Neither George Bush nor Saddam Hussein were prepared to relinquish their position of 'the strong man'; both interpreted withdrawal as a sign of weakness, that is, femaleness. Mitterand, the French President, even talked of a quasi natural 'logic of war' which had to take its course, irrespective of all warnings of the consequences of such a war, when two brutally armed Rambos confront each other. Neither he nor any one of the men involved in this war were willing to admit that this so-called war-logic is nothing but Rambo-logic, patriarchal male logic which is simply betting on the survival of the strongest. The victors are always right. But this Ramboism was/is closely linked to the economic and political interests of the USA, and the other rich industrial countries of the North, to control access to the oil reserves in the Middle East. The industrialized North's living standards depend to a very high degree on their free access to cheap oil, most of which comes from the Gulf countries. As is well known, these oil reserves will be exhausted in the foreseeable future. The Gulf War can also be seen as the first of the new colonial wars about the distribution of scarce resources between countries of the North and the South; wars of distribution that will need more Ramboized men and also a strengthening of the concept of the nation-state.[16] The main victims in these wars are not only women and children, but also nature.

Today we experience the dissolution not only of the big hegemonic military blocks but also of states like Yugoslavia and Czechoslovakia. But this does not lead, as was expected, to an era of global peace. Instead, the external enemy is replaced by internal enemies, particularly in the former Soviet block. New nationalisms are emerging in the Soviet Union, in Yugoslavia, in Rumania, for example. All these nationalities, which supposedly were integrated in the big socialist fatherland, now demand and fight for autonomy *and* against each other. Moreover, most want not only autonomy, but a separate nation-state, a separate fatherland. In these new civil wars young men play the main role. The militarization of these young men goes beyond the immediate aim of these wars, it determines the concept of their role-identity for a whole generation.

As Cynthia Enloe has shown, this also applies for the young men who fight in the guerrilla forces of liberation movements, as, for example, in the Philippines. The circumstances of militarization have formulated an identity of manhood as manifest in one who carries a gun and can shoot and kill.[17] All they have learned is to be a soldier, as can be observed today in Lebanon, Sri Lanka, South Africa, Israel, for example; and particularly in ex-Yugoslavia; eventually these young men are unable to distinguish friend from foe. Warfare has become a way of life. *He who is able to kill determines who may live, not he who is born of a woman.*

Mother nation and father state

To legitimize this militarization of men and the 'logic of warfare' and to bring about their identification with a fatherland, it is essential that the yearning for the destroyed and lost 'motherlands' (homelands) be mobilized and projected on to the nation-state. Nationalism, as well as religious fundamentalism, thrive on the social-psychological plane, on these yearnings and projections.

In spite of all wars that took place historically to create the nation-state, in spite of colonial expansion and the material benefits this brought to the citizens of the North's nation-states, and in spite of the competition between different nation-states and all internal pacification by the bureaucracy and police, the modern capitalist nation-state would have been unable to procure the loyalty of its citizens, to mobilize people in order to create their emotional identification with this new state, without taking recourse to the older category of the nation. Father State had to be married to Mother Nation.

What is the meaning of the term 'nation'?

The Romans used the word *natio* for the tribes they had conquered. They themselves called the people living in the Roman Empire *'populus romanus'*, the Roman people. *Natio* is obviously derived from *natus*, that is 'born'. *Natio* is a person's place of birth, his/her tribe, territory, homeland. We could therefore also call these 'nations' the motherland. An individual was identified by the motherland where he/she was born, the place where his/her mother lived. This terminology, ultimately, has its roots in the mother-right traditions, where the clan and tribal organization was based on matrilocality, matrilinearity and where all were equally children of the tribe or clan.[18] This organization, as we know, was destroyed through warfare and conquest. But even the fatherlands, whose patriarchal systems were built upon the ruins of these tribal motherlands, following a different logic, had to legitimize themselves by rooting the sentiments of the people in the old category of the nation, the home- and motherland. First the feudal aristocracy claimed this term 'nation' for the construction of the new absolutist state, later the bourgeoisie, after it became strong through colonialism, organized itself in nation-states. In this process it integrated a number of nations — former tribes — into a new nationhood.

The sentiments connected with the term 'nation', however, differ from those connected with the term 'state'. The former are characterized by such qualities as warmth, community, personal, informal relations, freedom, closeness, homeliness, closeness to nature, in short, memories connected with childhood. These emotions also include the community created by a common language, culture and history, but not necessarily a state history. An Indian friend who was born in the Punjab which is now part of North Pakistan expressed these feelings in the following way: 'I can never hate this country, because it is my *'janma bhumi'*, the land where he was born, the motherland. *Bhumi* means Mother Earth in Hindi, sometimes *Bhumi-Devi* is also referred to as Goddess Earth.

When politicians and journalists talk of the 'arch-enmity' between India and Pakistan, such feelings are ignored.

During the Indian Independence movement this shifting of sentiments from 'mother nation' to 'father state' was a deliberate tactic by such writers and propagandists as Bankim Chandra, who wrote the text of the national song *Bande Mataram* (I praise thee, Mother). In the beginning, this 'mother' was Bengal, the home-land of the poet, later it meant all India, the mother who had been 'raped' by colonialism. Against the 'rape' every man who still felt some manhood in himself had to stand up. India is a land, how-ever, of many nations (tribes) and identities. In order to build a modern nation-state these particular identities and the sentiments connected with them had to be projected onto the nation-state of modern India. As we know, this was a painful process. The Muslim-majority parts of the country were separated and formed into Pakistan. And today other parts of India want to form their own independent nation-states. This movement demonstrates the desire to return to what they consider to be their original mother-land, their original regional, cultural and religious identity.

The Japanese feminist writer, Yayoi Aoki,[19] described another example of this process. She explains how, during the Meiji re-forms, the sentiments of the young men — still rooted in partly mother-right traditions like the *wakomonoyado*, the youth houses of rural Northern Japan — were devalued and destroyed and then projected on to the new modern Japanese state and the emperor. According to Yayoi Aoki rural Japan, before the Meiji reforms, was less patriarchal than it is now. In the *wakomonoyado*, relations be-tween the sexes were quite liberal: young people had common bathing places and toilets, they had free zones where they could learn self-management. All who had shared the same *wakomonoyado* were united by a bond of loyalty even stronger than family ties. They were obliged to practice mutual help and solidar-ity. During the Meiji reforms all these traditions were regarded with contempt, and devalued as backward and barbaric. The new values were derived both from the West and from patriarchal Confucianism. 'Civilization and Enlightenment' became the slo-gan of the time and the desire to emulate the West was combined with the Confucian family ideal, thus wedding the two patriarchal traditions. The young men's loyalty was separated from the now b ackward-looking *wakomonoyado* and geared towards the modern Japanese nation-state. In this process the patriarchal traditions and values of the warrior class, the Samurai, who were the first to accept Western values and Confucian morality, played an important role. Now the young peasant men also began to identify with the morality of this modern warrior class and with the Japanese state. The former Youth Houses and Clubs became a spy system for the new government.

> When these were turned into Seinendan (youth groups) and Shobodan (fire-fighting groups) the lifeblood of resistance was, in effect, drained away. And now the village network was turned into a spy system, in order to ensure co-operation with government policies. This may even help to explain why it was the farming people who co-operated most whole heartedly in the militarization of Japan from the time of the Sino-Japanese War in 1895-6.[20]

National identity or catching-up development?

The rise of the new nationalisms which we witness today is inspired not only by the modern values of 'civilization and enlightenment', by the desire for ethnic and cultural identity but perhaps even more by the myth of 'catching-up development', that is, by the hope of sharing as soon as possible the material wealth and living standards of the rich nations of the North. They want to join the club of the rich EC. The slogan: 'Germany, united Fatherland ', also meant: 'Germany, united land of equal consumption'.

As we saw, the goal of catching-up development, the emulation of the European industrial-colonial-patriarchal nations already played an important role in the nineteenth century reforms in Japan. Also, as is shown elsewhere in this volume (chapter 4), it plays an important role in the development strategies imposed upon the poor nations in the South; but for them this goal turns out to be a myth, a mirage.

A similar hope or myth also seems to underlie many of the tendencies towards greater ethnic, cultural or national autonomy and identity, which can be observed particularly in those nation-states which had been held together by a universalistic socialist ideology: the Soviet Union, Yugoslavia, Czechoslovakia and other countries of the erstwhile Socialist bloc. But these tendencies can also be seen in other parts of the world. This search for national identity, based on historical, cultural, racial, ethnic or religious difference is motivated usually by a strong rebellion against centralism and the totalitarian rule of a dominant political, economic or ethnic group. This rebellion goes hand in hand with the demand for regional self-determination or autonomy. From the outside and from an ecofeminist perspective this development might be welcomed, because the huge economic and political power blocs are strongly criticized by both ecology movements and feminists who demand small economic regions for the maintenance of ecologically sustainable systems. But a closer look at the processes taking place today reveals a less optimistic picture. Yugoslavia may serve as an illustrative case.

The emotions aroused by appeals to nationalism and a sense of ethnicity do not reflect the real aims of so-called nationalist struggles, but rather, in Yugoslavia, for example, these passions are harnessed as a driving force in the struggle for a fairer distribution of ever-shrinking shares of the economic cake. It is economic and political power that are the real stakes in these new civil wars.

The regions in erstwhile Yugoslavia which demanded autonomy and secession from the Yugoslav state are those which had benefited most from the tourist industry and their closeness to the EC: Slovenia and Croatia. As the EC is about to establish itself as the new regional economic power, these regions want to join the club of the rich Europeans before they close their doors to 'outsiders'. Basically, they are unwilling to share their relative wealth with the poorer areas of Yugoslavia.

Therefore, their demand for self-determination in the name of religion, language, culture and so on, does not mean that Slovenia and Croatia want to establish themselves as economically self-sufficient, self-reliant regions. They reject the centralism of the socialist nation-state but are keen to join the new superstate of the rich EC: Slovenia, and particularly Croatia, are seeking recognition as sovereign states by the EC or the UN.

This brings us to the next point. The search for national identity is almost always understood as the search for separate statehood. And that means that these regions or provinces want to establish themselves as nation-states according to the model of the big nation-states. This implies the need to have their own army, border security force, and bureaucracy and government. Necessarily, these movements towards self-determination thus lead to increased militarism and violence.

Moreover, this demand for self-determination by one province or region inevitably leads to antagonistic relations with other provinces and regions, with which these secessionist provinces had lived in peace for many years. As the struggle is *de facto* about economic and political power within a given territory, cultural

and historical differences are mobilized to prove why, for example, the Croatians can no longer live together with the Serbians in
the same state. Once these differences can no longer be settled by
negotiations but by arms, old memories of injustice and atrocity
are being revived. Thus the Serbians accuse the Croatians of fascism, because they collaborated with the Nazis, and the Croatians
accuse the Serbians of imperialist tendencies in that they want to
create a new Serbian empire.

The result of the breakdown of the universalist ideology of
socialism, which still holds that all people are equal irrespective of
sex, ethnicity, religion, culture, language is not, therefore, the
blossoming of cultural diversity, but universal civil war. These
new civil wars are not fought in the name of ecological and cultural regionalism but to establish ever more new fatherlands. The
legitimate desire for cultural and ethnic roots and self-determination is again transformed into machoistic and racist wars of a
genocidal nature. The sexist and racist character of these new civil
wars becomes evident when one hears of the atrocities committed
against the respective 'enemies' by the fighting warriors. Thus one
reads that the Serbian Cetniks who massacred Croatian militia
men, cut off their dead enemies' penises and put them into their
mouths; or sees TV pictures in which the enemy's genitalia were
shot off.

Women cannot support these wars, not only because the victims are mainly women and children, but because all victims are
children of women, even the massacred soldiers. Moreover, this
search for national identity even if it is subconsciously inspired by
the desire to return to one's 'motherland', leads everywhere to
increased machoism and further militarization and brutalization
of men. It is always men, young men, whom we see in these
pictures fighting, supposedly, for their own nation-state, their fatherland. And within the framework of capitalist patriarchy this
means they are fighting for control over territory and women.[21]

In the ongoing and potential civil wars about new fatherlands
and self-determination, however, women and children alone will
not pay the price, but Mother Earth, the environment too, as has
already been noted, these wars are also about bigger shares of the
economic cake, therefore there will be further contamination and
destruction of the still remaining commons: air, water, the soil,
forests, fields. Although all 'civilized nations' recognize nations'
right to self-determination it seems that this right is also based on
exploitation and destruction of some 'others', as may be observed

in the case of the individual (see Ch 12). These new civil wars could be avoided only if those who struggle for ethnic and national identity would accept an economic policy of self-sufficiency and restraint.

It would, however, be wrong to see women as only the victims in these new wars about fatherlands; there are many examples of women's support for patriotic wars. The First World War was supported by patriotic women's organizations, in Germany and elsewhere; Hitler's national socialism as well as the Second World War were also supported by women, some of whom were enthusiastic admirers of Hitler's system. In Yugoslavia, too, as elsewhere, we also find women who support these civil wars and even volunteer to fight against the 'enemy'. In the erstwhile USSR, one of the movements for a new, independent nation-state — Tatarstan — is even led by a woman, Fauzia Bairamova. Even more surprisingly Fauzia Bairamova is a Muslim woman who fights for a Muslim fatherland. It would be naive, therefore, to conclude that all women, because they pay the price for the fatherlands, together with Mother Earth, would reject these suicidal and fratricidal wars.

On the other hand, there are organizations and groups of women who still hold on to some degree of feminist internationalism, an internationalism that has not lost sight of the fact that we are all born of women, and depend on the same Mother Earth.

Without a recognition of this ecological, feminist and international aspect, the search for national identity, within the framework of capitalist patriarchy with its consumerist incentive can lead only to ever more sexist civil wars, wars that will destroy all life, including human life, and ultimately the planet itself.

Notes

1. For the first UFV programme see Merkel, Ina, 'Ohne Frauen ist kein Staat zu machen'. Unpublished paper, Berlin, 1989.
2. *Die Tageszeitung*, 6 February 1992.
3. Mies, Maria, *Patriarchy and Accumulation on a World Scale: Women in the International Division of Labour*. Zed Books, London, 1989.
4. This Conference was organized by the Heinrich Böll Stiftung in co-operation with the Green Party.
5. Thurmer-Rohr, Christina, 'Gedanken zur deutsch-deutschen Sturzgeburt', in *Die Tageszeitung*, 2 April 1990.

6. See, for example, Bock, Gisela, and Barbara Duden, 'Labor of Love, Love as Labor' in *Development*, Special Issue: Women. Protagonists of Change, No 4, 1984, pp. 6-14. v. Werlhof, Claudia, 'Women's Work, the Blind Spot in the Critique of Political Economy', in Mies, Maria et al *Women: the Last Colony*. Zed Books, London, 1988; and Mies, Maria (1989) op. cit.

7. Polanyi, Karl, *The Great Transformation*, Suhrkamp, Frankfurt, 1978.

8. Heinsohn, Gunnar, Rolf Knieper and Otto Steiger, *Manschenproduktion. Allgemeine Bevölkerungslehre der Neuzeit*. Suhrkamp, Frankfurt, 1979.

9. Mies, Maria and Saral Sarkar, 'Menschenrechte und Bildung für alle? in *Vorgänge*, No 5, October 1990, p. 85.

10. Thurmer-Rohr, Christina, op. cit.

11. Potts, Lydia, *The World Labour Market: A History of Migration*. Zed Books. London, 1990.

12. Wallerstein, Immanuel, *The Modern World System*. Vol I. Capitalist Agriculture and the Origin of the European World Economy in the Sixteenth Century. Academic Press, New York, 1974.

13. Giddens, Anthony, *The Nation State and Violence*. University of California Press, Berkeley and Los Angeles, 1987.

14. Brownmiller, Susan, *Against Our Will: Men, Women and Rape*. Simon and Schuster, New York, 1975.

15. Enloe, Cynthia, 'Beyond Rambo: The Gendered politics of Militarization' paper published in: *Sangharsh*, Vimochana No 3 (no date). Women's Book Shop, Bangalore, India; and Chapkis, Wendy, Sexualität und Militarismus, in *Antimilitarismus-informationen*, Vol. XVII, No 8, August 1987.

16. See Chomsky, Noam: Ol schmiert auch die Moral, in *Wochenzeitung*, No. 4, Zurich, 25 January 1991; see also: Chomsky, N. *The New World Order*. Open Magazine Pamphlet Series. Noam Chomsky was one of the few intellectuals in the USA who openly criticized the Gulf War as a neo-colonial war, carried out by the US Administration for the control of the oil-rich Gulf region. A year after the Gulf War, Chomsky clearly accuses the US Administration of corrupting the UN, so that the Security Council agreed to this war, and of lying to the world's public about this war of aggression, mainly against civilians, children, women and nature. (Interview with Noam Chomsky by Martin Völker in *Frankfurter Rundschau*, 30 January 1992).

17. Enloe, Cynthia, op. cit.

18. In the 1860s Bachofen had already pointed out that the original clan and tribal loyalties to a particular region or land were based on mother-right traditions. Bachofen J.J. (1975) *Das Mutterrecht*, Suhrkamp, Frankfurt. See also Eric Hobsbawm *Nation and Nationalism since 1780. Programme, Myth and Reality*. Cambridge University Press, Cambridge, 1990.

19. Yayoi, Aoki, 'In Search of the Roots of Sexual Discrimination. Thoughts on Japan's Modernization and Confucian Ideology.' Unpublished paper, undated.

20. Ibid., p. 19.

21. It should be mentioned here, however, that these two aspects were understood by thousands of women all over the world who protested against the Gulf War, who were in the forefront of the peace movement, and who now oppose the civil wars.

10. White Man's Dilemma: His Search for What He Has Destroyed

Maria Mies

In the urban centres of the industrialized North may be observed a curious mass behaviour from time to time. Those who apparently consider urban culture and lifestyle as the pinnacle of progress and modernity, for whom the cities are centres of 'Life', of freedom, of culture, rush away from these very cities whenever they can. A flight into 'Nature', the 'wilderness', 'underdeveloped' countries of the South, to areas where White Man, they hope, has not yet 'penetrated'. Originally the targets of this mass exodus were the sunny beaches of Spain, Italy, Greece, Tunisia, later of Turkey and — very occasionally — the 'unspoilt' villages of their own countryside. But with the advent of cheap, mass tourism we are increasingly urged by the media to undertake 'adventure' travels and tour. To see 'cave people', 'cannibals', 'wild head-hunters', 'stone-age people' in the Philippines, Malaysia, Papua New Guinea, the Amazon and so on. Like the fifteenth and sixteenth century adventurers and pirates, affluent, late twentieth century men are urged to experience the challenges of early 'discoverers' and to commune with Nature — and suddenly you feel like John Wayne! Man feels like a man again in his confrontation with 'wild Nature'.[1] They, too, want to 'penetrate' 'virgin' land and open it up for white civilization, which today means tourism and the money economy. In this, writes Klemens Ludurf,[2] 'they destroy what they look for while they find it'.

In what has been called 'integrated rural tourism' in, for example, Senegal, European tourists can live in villages in close contact with the 'natives' in African-style huts, with minimum comfort, African food, no running water and where European and African children play together. The 'real' Africa to be touched![3] The German Association for the Alps organizes trekking tours through Ladakh, where German tourists may not only get dysentery but can also again experience a sense of belonging to the 'master people' *(Herrenmenschen)* and look down upon the local people as

Drecksacke (dirty pigs).⁴ The contradictions inherent in this behaviour were typified by a woman in Cologne who spends almost all her holidays trekking in Nepal. But when it was suggested that, at home she should use public transport instead of a private car for ecological reasons, she indignantly refused: how could she be expected to sit by strangers with their different smells and behaviour? She would rather walk! Unable to tolerate the proximity of an unknown human body she nevertheless sought wild nature in the distant mountains of Nepal, nature to be smelt and touched and physically experienced.

Despair in the midst of plenty

What, then, is actually happening here? People who celebrate their own civilization and the subjection and control of Nature choose to spend their leisure time far away from these beautiful, modern cities. Why? Why this nostalgia, this seeking for untouched Nature? Can it be that white civilization, this apogee of modernity, has ultimately turned out to be 'a painted desert'? This urban civilization obviously does not make for happiness. Rather it engenders deep feelings of malaise, even of despair and poverty in the midst of plenty. And it seems that as more and more commodities are heaped on the supermarkets' shelves the deeper the despair and an inarticulate desire for some absent basic element essential for a sense of fulfilment. People are not happy. There is a second aspect. This yearning, this desire for nature is not directed to the nature that surrounds us, even in a city, or of which we are a part. It is rather fixated on the nature which has explicitly been externalized by White Man, which has been defined as colony, backward, exotic, distant and dangerous, the nature of Asia, Africa, South America. This nature is the 'Hinterland' of white civilization. It is an idealized, unreal nature — rather like D.H. Lawrence's 'sex in the head', it is 'nature in the head'.

The same can be said of the nostalgia for things rural. Since the eighteenth century nature, the rural areas around cities, the land of the peasants has been increasingly transformed into mere Hinterland for the cities, or perceived as an aesthetic experience: the romantic landscape. Like the external colonies, the land, where food for the urban population is grown, is not only ruthlessly exploited and destroyed by industrialized agriculture, it is also devalued as backward and unprofitable, like a colony. But paradoxically, this land is also the object of urban longing.

But no one wants to alleviate this feeling by helping with work on the fields as, up to some generations ago, was the urban workers' normal holiday. These families went 'home' to their villages and shared in the farm work. Now adults, some of them still look back on their family farm or village holidays with nostalgia. Today, however, tourists want only to experience nature and the landscape in a purely consumptionist manner, as voyeurs, not as actors, but like visitors to an art gallery or cinema. This has become possible because they have more money with which to buy this experience than did people in former times. Their relationship to the land, as to distant, exotic countries is not a productive one. Instead they use up and consume this wild nature or the land as a commodity, and having consumed it they leave only a heap of waste, as they do when they consume other goods. Therefore the result of this yearning, which they hope to satisfy through consumptionist tourism, is: *They destroy what they yearn for.*

Violence and desire

The third space for which modern people — modern men — yearn is woman, more precisely woman's body. Woman's body is the projection screen for most of men's desires.

A closer look at this 'third colony'[5] will probably enable us to better understand the interconnectedness between the destruction of Nature and this yearning. But before we analyse this connection let us first look at some examples.

As far as the *history* of this polarized relationship between Man and Nature and Man and Woman goes, we have to reconsider the holocaust of women in the course of the European witch hunt; an event that took place in those same centuries which are hailed as the beginning of the modern, enlightened era.[6]

After this orgy of violence against women which continued until the era of Enlightenment, the end of the eighteenth century,[7] came a new yearning for the 'feminine', the romantic and sentimental identification of women in eighteenth century literature and art.[8] It seems that real living, strong and independent women had first to be physically destroyed and subdued before the men of the new bourgeois class could create a new romantic ideal of womanhood. An ideal in which the frail, submissive sentimental woman, one dependent on the man as 'breadwinner and protector', woman as the epitome of the world of feelings rather than of reason, plays the main role. As Sheila Rowbotham remarks, throughout the nineteenth century and even until today this romantic ideal of womanhood has been the 'desired space' for men's longings and still largely determines the man-woman relationship. This ideal of womanhood was the necessary complement to the strong, enterprising, bourgeois white man who began to conquer and colonize the world for the sake of capital accumulation.[9]

Moreover, this cult of the frail, sentimental woman, who supposedly represents 'nature' *vis-a-vis* 'rational man', is largely based on fantasy, on symbolic constructions. And men began to project their desire on to these female fantasy figures, rather than on to real flesh and bone.

Pornography and prostitution tourism

Today, a clear example of the connection between violence and desire, yearnings and fantasy, is pornography. Pornography presents men with images of the female body, or rather selected areas — a dissected body. Their desire is centred on these pieces, not on a whole woman, let alone a real living woman. At the same time, these images reflect the violence that characterizes men's relationship to this body.[10] This pornographic gaze, which thrusts together desire and violence, is the basis for much commercial advertising, for the flood of magazines, videos, TV and other films etc. Economic growth, it seems, is increasingly dependent on this type of advertising, based on the pornographic gaze. Like the yearning for nature, the yearning for the dissected, naked female body is wholly consumerist. It cannot be satisfied by interaction with a living person but only by the response to lifeless pictures. Even the psychic activity, usually necessary to conjure up a fantasy, is reduced and replaced by a simple optic stimulus-response mechanism in which not even a relationship to one's own person exists. An automat reacts to an automat. A further point is that these one-dimensional images in no way threaten the male ego.

Prostitution tourism is another example of the connection between desire and violence. Here, the desire is projected on to an 'exotic' woman, a non-white woman, a woman of the colonized, who due to her poverty has to serve the white man. The desire for the subject and colonized woman is related to the desire for the 'noble savage'. In this case, too, the relationship is not active and loving but consumerist and passive, based on the purchasing power of the D-Mark, the dollar or the yen. This purchasing power also enables Western and Japanese working-class men, from time to time, to enjoy playing the colonial lord and master.[11]

It seems that for European, Japanese and American men the attraction of prostitution tourism lies largely in the power, the master-servant relationship between man and woman they are able to experience. The psychologist Berti Latza made a study of German men who visited Thailand as sex tourists. She found that they commanded their Thai 'lovers' to clean their cottage, feed them throughout the day and serve them as slaves. Sex often played a secondary role, but what the men enjoyed was their absolute power over these women.

Berti Latza also found another type of sex tourist: the regressive male who reverts to the phase of his early infancy. They demand that the Thai women bath and feed them like a baby, and oil and powder their buttocks. 'They even fall back into a kind of baby language and would like to be even carried to the toilet', writes Latza.[12]

It seems that with the little Thai women these adult males may safely abandon their self-image of 'big strong man', and afford to indulge in all that has been repressed, negated, eliminated from their image of manhood by white, Western, patriarchal civilization. Thus they must travel around half the globe to find an exotic, colonized woman with whom they feel free to satisfy these regressive needs.

It seems that many of those men who order a Filipina bride from a catalogue or go on a sex tour to Thailand, Kenya or the Dominican Republic are incapable of developing a real human, egalitarian, adult and loving relationship with a woman, but can deal only with women who are subordinated to them; women who are economically, politically weaker, do not know the men's language, are entirely dependent on them. Such men often have a communication problem in their own society.[13] Even those men who marry a Thai woman or a Filipino, are rarely capable of forging a human relationship with them.

Sexuality and nature

Most analyses dealing with sex-tourism and international trade in women focus on the problems in the women's own countries: Thailand, the Philippines, Kenya. Poverty, military bases, certain local traditions are usually identified as causes for this new phenomenon.[14]

But it is rarely asked what problem prompts European, American and Japanese men to travel to exotic places to satisfy their sexual needs. Moreover, why do these men want women whom they otherwise do not respect? What is the content of their desire? Why can they not satisfy their sexual needs and desires with their own women, or even with pornography, sex-shops, sex-machines etc? What, apart from the intoxication of power and dominance, do these men want from those poor, foreign, colonized women?

In order to identify the underlying reasons we must ask what eroticism and sexuality mean for men in industrialized societies, because sex tourism only manifests an extension of the relationship that men have to themselves, to women in their own society, to others and to nature.

On average men in industrialized societies have, for most of their lives, hardly any direct body-contact with plants, the earth, animals, the elements. Almost everywhere their relationship to nature is mediated through machines which function as a kind of 'distancing weapon', by which nature is dominated, manipulated, destroyed. The more technology progresses the greater this distance, the more abstract becomes the relationship between man and nature, and the more alienated man becomes from his own organic, mortal body, which, nevertheless remains the source of all happiness and enjoyment. The more modern man interposes machines between himself and nature, the more he dissects nature and women, the more he projects his desire only to these sections of the whole, the greater becomes his hunger for the original whole, wild, free, woman and nature: the more he destroys the greater his hunger.

The satisfaction of this hunger seems to be necessary for survival, irrespective of the fascination which machines have for men. This fascination obviously is not sufficient to make them 'happy'. I agree with Roger Garaudy who says that the sexual act has become virtually the only direct contact to nature available to civilized man. 'A break has occurred between the very rhythm of production, consumption and the sexual act, disconnected usually from all other dimensions of life, a sexual act which itself becomes entangled in the net of consumption and economic exploitation, or which becomes the sacred refuge, outside ordinary life.'[15] The growing sex obsession apparent in all industrial societies is, in my view, a direct consequence of alienation from nature, the absence of a sensual interaction with nature in people's work life. Sexuality is supposed to be the totally 'other' from work, sexuality should not interfere with work, should be strictly separated from the work life. Sexuality is the 'transcendence' of work, the 'heaven' after the 'valley of tears and sweat' of work, the real essence of leisure.

This seems to me the deeper reason for the combination of tourism, sex and sun. The tragedy is, however, that this 'heaven' is also a commodity, to be bought like any others. And like the acquisition of other consumer goods, ultimately, it disappoints. The envisioned fulfilment is never realized, is, at the moment of apparent consummation, finally elusive. Therefore, the constantly disappointed striving to attain this 'heaven' transforms need into an addiction.

Reproduction technology

Today, men and women who want a child, even if they are infertile, try to satisfy their desire by means of biotechnology. For women this yearning is located in their own body and its generative potency.

The generative potency, or 'wild fertility' of the female body has, since the beginning of this century, been identified as one of the most formidable handicaps for women's emancipation. In an effort to restrain this 'wild fertility' it has been fought with mechanical, chemical and biological 'devices' or weapons, from contraceptives to sterilizations. This struggle has gone on for decades. It now seems, in many cases, that the female body and its generative potency cannot be switched on again at will. As Renate Klein has shown in her study on women in IVF-programmes in Australia, their infertility was often as a result of their previous use of contraceptives.[16] Also, for men and women, sterility is frequently the result of continuous stress and ecological pollution.

Of the many reasons why women want their 'own' child, one is the desire to experience their own body's natural creativity and productivity, to experience that living power in their body which permeates nature. They not only desire the product of this creative process, the child, but the process itself. From time immemorial, women have dealt with pregnancy and childbirth in a creative way. But this creative process, this natural power, was not totally controlled by them, rather to a certain extent it remained 'wild'. And here, I think, lies precisely the core of this yearning. Because, to create a child is quite different from constructing a car or other machine. The woman does not have a blueprint in her head according to which she makes the child. She may have fantasies, wishes, but the child that forms in her body, in co-operation with nature, which she herself represents and is, is not determined by her will. Ultimately, neither the process nor the 'product' are at her disposal. I think it is precisely this unpredictability that constitutes the newness of each child and provides the fulfilment that is being sought. It answers the craving for the diversity, the unexpected, the manifold new possibilities that constitute life and living beings. Newness, spontaneity, surprise are what we admire in children. In the desire to bear a child of one's own body this seeking for the new, the natural, the spontaneous manifests itself with great power.

The irony is, however, that for those who use reproductive techniques this desire is satisfied by the same external, artificially controlled methods and techniques which formerly may not only have destroyed women's fertility but are also based on the same philosophy of science employed for the construction of machines. The medical-technical bio-engineers may be able to construct a child for the woman, after they have isolated through invasive methods the necessary 'reproductive component' — as this is revealingly called. They may even construct this child, with the help of genetic manipulations, according to the wishes of the parents, but they cannot satisfy this deep longing for the new, the spontaneous. On the contrary. Instead of experiencing pregnancy as a time of 'good hope', as it is called in German, most women who have enrolled in an IVF-programme experience this period as one of alternating anxiety and hope, and of fear and disappointment and basically one of total alien control over this creative process in their body. Reproductive technology alienates both men and women from their bodies and from this most intimate process in which they normally co-operate with their own nature, which they want to experience as creative, productive and spontaneous. As for men in the case of tourism, the woman experiences a longing for what has been lost and, in seeking, finds only that it is irrecoverable, namely that their wild, spontaneous, unalienated, organic, untamed generative potency has been destroyed. Renate Klein reports how a woman of whom, after many failed efforts to get a child through the IVF technology, the reproductive doctors had said was a hopeless case, totally humiliated and disappointed she finally gave up trying. Shortly afterwards she became naturally pregnant, without the intrusion of any technical devices.[17]

There are many similar examples of the connection between violent destruction of living symbioses by modern science and technology, the industrialization of all such processes and the deep longing for these very symbioses.

The source of these desires

It may be useful to look more closely at what these diverse desires *have in common*. Why are they increasingly in the industrialized countries? What are people seeking? It seems obvious that what is sought is exactly the opposite of what the myth of modernity has promised and sees as positive: the total control of nature and natural processes by science and technology, the 'civilizing', that is, taming of all 'wild' forces of nature for the benefit of man.

There is, for example, this nostalgia for 'wildness', for nature not yet dissected, manipulated, tamed for man's utilitarian purposes. In spite of any fears of nature's wild, chaotic, threatening and destructive aspects, to experience the potential risks, the uncertainty of this very wildness is the fundamental motivation for this longing. But simultaneously nature is sought as the good, the mother, our friend. In spite of all scientific knowledge and the control over nature there is a deep acknowledgement that, in the last analysis we are an inescapable part of this nature, that we are nature's children, that we are born of women and that eventually we shall die. And that this is acceptable and as it should be.

Integral to this searching is a *nostalgia for childhood*. That is, seeking for a simple, spontaneous, open and confidential relationship with our surroundings, with the natural world and with other human beings. This implies the experiencing of love, tenderness, care, warmth as gifts, without the need of prior achievement for reward. In almost all societies these expectations are directed to *the mother*. Woman as Mother is the social 'place' towards which all regressive desires and longings are directed. The psychoanalytical term 'regression', however, already has a negative connotation. It implies that healthy adults should not fall back into such infantile needs for 'a mother'.

The nostalgia for childhood also implies a searching for freedom and adventure. But freedom here means something other than what Western democracies mean when they talk of freedom or liberty, meaning the freedom of choice in the economic and political supermarket. The search for the freedom of childhood is mainly a reaction to the total structural regimentation and ordering of everyday life by the industrial and bureaucratic society. Whereas in former times nature may have been seen as an obstacle to free movement today civilized society itself is experienced as curbing our desire for freedom.

Also the search for adventure is a reaction to modern society with its many technical novelties. Obviously, people's basic curiosity is not satisfied with ever-newer technical inventions. On the contrary, industrial society, in spite of its affluence and its leisure and entertainment industry, is permeated by a deep sense of *boredom* and apathy. The modern lifestyle leaves little to people's own creativity and work, everything is preplanned and organized, there are no more adventures. We are entertained, animated, fed, stimulated by professional experts.

In this society shopping is the only adventure still allowed. But obviously, this adventure, the joy of acquiring something new, soon palls. In many cases the adventure consists only of the act of shopping. People have become shopaholics, because they want to experience this adventure of acquiring something new again and again.[18] It is a futile attempt to compensate for the lack of creativity, the sterility inherent in modern, urban lifestyles.

For men, as we have seen, this search for adventure is often combined with the desire to experience themselves again as 'real men'. In patriarchal civilization this means to experience themselves as the great hero who challenges wild nature, pushing the 'frontier' ever further.

The nostalgia for childhood and the search for motherliness are often combined with the search for *homeland* or *home,* for belonging, for one's own place. Strangely enough, this need is often satisfied by travelling away from the cities, to foreign lands, to 'underdeveloped' countries, to the countryside, to the village. But cities are rarely seen as *homelands* or *homes.* The feelings associated with such terms are centred around closeness, community, a rural habitat, while cities are places of anonymity, homelessness, loneliness, indifference, coldness, atomization.

It seems that the devaluation of rural work, life and production, and the attraction and fascination of urban life have as their counterpart homesickness, not necessarily for a particular village, house, or landscape, but for roots. The exodus from the cities to the countryside during vacation time is an expression of this rootlessness.

Part of this reaching out towards nature in all its manifestations is the search for beauty, for aesthetic pleasure. Obviously, the cities' consumer paradises, the abundance of man-made commodities fail to answer this desire. The aesthetic promises of the commodities are not fulfilled. They become obsolete, because new ones have appeared and the previous ones now seem ugly, so more and more objects are bought to renew the feelings of owning beauty. The current demand for handmade goods: clothes from natural fibres, real wood furniture, hand-thrown pottery, 'home grown' food and so on. *Plus* the 'nostalgia' business — for old things — Victoriana in UK (and US) even the art nouveau of the 1930s; reissues of old 'pop' songs et al are manifestations of this nostalgia for things lost. People tire of all these man-made goods and seek something that encapsulates the beauty of nature in all its variety, a symbol of its ever changing rhythms of seasons, of day and night, cold and warmth. Nature is always surprising. We always delight in looking at it, as we delight in looking at a child. Industrial civilization promised to create wealth for everybody, a life beyond mere subsistence, a rich life, not only free of material wants, but providing the means for a fuller life, satisfying the deeper, human, non-material needs. But it seems industrial civilization has failed to fulfil this promise, even for those who benefit from it. It seems that the affluence in goods and money in the industrialized countries has as its consequence not only the pauperization of others (nature, the Third World etc.) but also among the people a growing unappeased want, not only in a psychological but also in a material sense. In the glamorous urban centres today it is the *quality* of life that is absent, clean air, quiet, clean water, wholesome food; above all, urban life is characterized by a dearth of human warmth, of a sense of belonging to a human community and to the world of nature. Therefore we find slogans at city walls like: We want life! which are an expression of the need for living interconnectedness.

Dissection and the search for wholeness

Industrial civilization's promise was to enhance life by dissecting all symbioses, biological and social, as well as the symbiosis which the human individual as such represents. These symbioses are also called ecological systems: the interdependence of humans, animals, plants, but there is also the social ecology of people living together, of men and women, children and parents, older and younger generations.

Industrial civilization and its science and technology have disrupted these ecological and socio-ecological systems. The whole was dissected into its elementary parts, which then were recombined in the construction of new machines.[19] But life is not the sum of elements put together, life was excised in these processes of dissection, analysis and synthesis. The nostalgia and searching already noted, the goal of the ecology movement, the alternative health movement, and large parts of the women's movement is the restoration of such ecological and socio-ecological inter-connectedness. Within the existing industrial and patriarchal-capitalist society the satisfaction of these desires and needs for wholeness, interdependence, is not typically sought in a renaissance of earlier subsistence relations; instead people hope to satisfy them via the commodity market. Fulfilment of the desire for wild nature is satisfied not by working on the land but by adventure tourism; the search for sexuality and erotic relations is satisfied not by loving real live women but by pornographic magazines or sex-tourism. Satisfaction of the needs for rootedness and 'belonging', for warmth, motherliness, freedom and adventure is sought not by working in co-operation with nature but rather by consumerism, by purchasing images. These needs are a very effective motor which drives on the economic growth of commodity production and consumption. The capitalist commodity production system can transform any desire into a commodity.

This means that, although the search is for the 'real thing' the 'real life', the commodity-producing system can only provide this in a symbolic, sentimental and romanticized form of fulfilment. Thus people have only imagined relationships which they enjoy (if at all) as metaphors of real life, real nature, real women, real freedom, they enjoy them only as consumers not actors or creators. But people within industrial society have no wish to 'go back to nature', to reject the project of modernity, or the exploitation of nature and other peoples in the course of commodity production. They do not want to opt out of industrial society but hope to have both: the affluence and abundance of the supermarket *and* unpolluted nature; further growth of the GNP *and* a healthy environment; more cars *and* more quiet and clean air in the cities; more medicalization of pregnancy and childbirth *and* more self-determination of autonomy for women over reproductive processes.

Violence, progress and sentimentalism

Industrial capitalist-patriarchal society is based on fundamental dichotomies between Man and Nature, Man and Woman, City and Village, Metropoles and Colony, Work and Life, Nature and Culture and so on. I call these dichotomies colonizations. The desires analysed are all directed towards that part of these dichotomies which has been amputated, externalized, colonized, submerged, repressed and/or destroyed. This is one reason why the longing for these colonized parts can only be sentimentalized; they must be romanticized and added on to the existing modern paradigm. They are the icing on top of the cake, as S. Sarkar put it,[20] they do not replace the cake, which is made precisely out of the exploitation and colonization of these parts.

As modern industrial society is based on the ongoing conversion of Nature into cash and industrial products and since this process is the necessary condition for industrial society to survive, the modern relationship to Nature can only be a sentimental one, it cannot be 'real.'[21] This relationship to nature necessarily depends not only on an — imagined — division between Man and Nature but also on the very destruction of nature. This means the disruption of the various symbioses or living connections which constitute life on this planet Earth.

Therefore it is not enough to speak of ambivalences only, when referring to the changing waves of romanticism and rationalism, which have characterized European history since the Enlightenment. Eder has shown that this twin theme of the modern relationship to nature — fear of nature as the enemy and love of nature as Mother and Friend — has been the dominant one since the seventeenth century, particularly modern science and technology's domination and objectification of nature as the 'other', meaning the enemy. The theoretical curiosity went hand in hand with the 'lust for nature', the love, the romanticizing and sentimentalizing of nature. Eder even talks of a zero-sum-game,

> There is an increase, at the same time, both of the instrumental and of the non-instrumental way of dealing with Nature. The dealing with the organic, the bodily existence which humans share with animals becomes part of a history of social control. The utilization of the body finds its apotheosis in the medical, criminological, psychiatric instrumentalization of the human body. On the other hand this very corporality is being moralized: it is filled with psyche and sentiments. A new sensibility towards nature emerges.[22]

What is usually omitted from this discourse on nature is the direct and structural *violence* which has accompanied the process of modernization right from its beginning until today. This violence is not accidental, it is the structural necessity, the mechanism by which Nature, women and other colonized parts are separated from the 'whole', that is, the living interconnectedness or symbiosis, and made into an object, or the 'other'. As the existence of this violence does not appear in the discourse of modernity, it cannot be explained why the search for the 'other side of reason'[23] the sentimental yearning for the originality of nature, the spontaneity of LIFE, based at the same time on the instruments of modern industrial society and its methods, will inevitably lead only to further destruction. The European tourists who flee to the beaches of the Mediterranean at the same time destroy these beaches. The car drivers who flee from the overcrowded cities into the hills and the countryside destroy these landscapes, and forests where they want to find unpolluted nature are destroyed by the fumes from car exhausts. The sex-tourists who flee to Thailand destroy the women there, make them into prostitutes and possibly infect them with AIDS.[24] In conclusion therefore, we can say: Before yearning there was destruction, before romanticizing there was violence.

Before the idyll

Women: It is the merit of the New International Women's Movement that it has made public violence, structural as well as direct, the central mechanism that creates and maintains exploitative and oppressive man-woman relations. This did not develop by way of an academic discourse but through numerous initiatives, campaigns, projects against rape, women battering, pornography, sexism in the media, the public and the workplace and so on. For the first time in contemporary history it became manifest that unpinning this apparently progressive, peaceful, democratic and egalitarian 'civil society' — the industrial society — was violence and brutality, particularly against women and non-white people. It became evident that the 'civilizing process' which Norbert Elias described as a process of taming aggressive tendencies[25] had not only failed to eliminate this violence, but rather was founded on it. In the context of this feminist politics of resistance to male or patriarchal violence the question regarding the history of this violence became urgent.[26]

This led to a renewed study of the witch-hunt in Europe. This holocaust of women was not, as is usually assumed, an outcome of the dark, superstitious Middle Ages, but was contemporaneous with the beginning of the New Age, of modernity, the era of discoveries and inventions, of modern science and technology.

This mass killing of women has not been paralleled in any of the so-called uncivilized societies in Africa, Asia or South America. Its forms, causes, ideological justifications have been analysed by many feminist scholars, therefore I will not elaborate on them here. But it must be reiterated that this orgy of violence was the foundation upon which modern science, medicine, economy and the modern state were built up. It is the particular merit of Carolyn Merchant that she has demonstrated the direct link between the torture of the witches and the rise of the new empirical scientific method; the destruction of the integrity of both the female body and the body of Nature. Both were to become mere sources of raw material for the rising capitalist mode of production. A similarly violent relationship was established between the core states and the colonies in Asia, South America and Africa.[27] Only after the witches had been killed as 'bad women' could a new image of the 'good woman' emerge in the eighteenth and nineteenth centuries. This was, as already noted, the image of the vapid, sentimental, weak, oppressed woman, the woman dependent on a breadwinner and the state. This new ideal of womanhood, based on the women of the bourgeois class, was necessary for the new sexual and social division of labour, the division between production and reproduction, production and consumption, work and life, without which capitalism would not have got off the ground.[28]

And it is only at this point that the romanticizing of this 'good woman' begins. She is the weak woman who must be protected. But she is also the mother, the embodiment of feeling, caring, humane-ness. This image of womanhood was constructed as the counter-image to the new, modern rational man who had to compete with other such men in the world of economics and politics, which became the foundation of modern wealth. This subservient and romanticized woman of feelings became the central figure of the domestic idyll, an idyll that provided the social site to which the new man could withdraw, to relax and restore his humanness after the murderous competition for more profit, wealth, and progress.

This idyll, though longed for, was nevertheless devalued. In fact, it could and should not be included within the world of capitalist valuation, into the world of commodity production. If it had, it would have lost its charm. The veil hiding the reality behind the idyll would have been torn apart to expose the brutality of this new era of reason. Therefore, only after oppression and destruction and ghetto-ization into this domestic idyll could the new woman become the aim of all longing for unalienated and spontaneous, 'natural' life.

This new image of womanhood was not an unintended outcome of the social changes that took place in the eighteenth century. It was, as Leiselotte Steinbrugge has shown, a deliberate construction of the Enlightenment philosophers, who led an extensive discourse on the 'nature of woman'. Particularly Diderot, Rousseau, and others played a key role in constructing the new woman as 'the moral gender', the embodiment of emotionality, human caring, motherliness, a closeness to nature. This woman had to be excluded from the realm of politics and economics, from the public arena, governed by (male) reason. She had to be naturized and at the same time privatized in a society, which, according to Steinbrugge, had excluded certain feelings from its code of public social interaction, particularly consideration of mercy, pity, humaneness, even moral considerations. 'Woman becomes the "moral gender."' Femaleness is transformed into the *feminine principle*. The concern is to preserve at least some humaneness in a society where, after Hobbes, economic reproduction is based on the war of all against all.[29]

This search for the feminine or the 'feminine principle' (not the living woman) accompanies each wave of romanticism, as counter-movement against the Enlightenment, rationalism, industrialism and modernism. Even today it can be observed that some men who despair of the destructions brought about by White Man and his reason, see the only remedy in a renaissance of the 'feminine principle'.[30]

The 'Savages': We can observe the same mechanism of simultaneously doing violence to and romanticizing the victims of this violence in the case of the European attitude towards people living in the colonies, people who, in the seventeenth, eighteenth, nineteenth and even at the beginning of the twentieth century, were called 'the savages'. The discourse on the 'good or noble savage' is as old as White Man's penetration into these peoples' lands. That this penetration was a history of violence and brutal repression, of destruction of autonomous subsistence economies, of freedom, and that it led to coercion and dependence everywhere was not made public by the Enlightenment philosophers and their followers. Instead, even today the eurocentric myth is spread that the expansion of European industrial culture over the rest of the world was due to superior intelligence, rationality, science and hence productivity of labour. And yet, there are abundant studies which show the direct connection between the violence and brutality of the European colonizers against tribal people worldwide and the rise of these colonizers to dominant groups, classes and nations. I want to draw attention to the work of H. Bodley who traces the path of destruction of tribal people by industrial civilization which continues even today.[31]

In numerous accounts Bodley follows the blood-trace of White Man in the colonies. The white colonizers were convinced that tribal people were creatures in a lower evolutionary state than themselves and that the universal law of history demanded their surrender to 'progress'. It was plain social Darwinism that justified the brutalities against tribal people, and the right of the more 'advanced' civilization. In the 1830s tribal people in Africa and America were regarded as sub-humans, as not really members of the human species. In Canada, to kill an Indian was considered meritorious. The attitude towards the 'Indians' of white settlers in the USA is epitomized by Sheridan: 'the only good Indian is a dead Indian'. In South Africa the killing of the native people by the pious Dutch colonists was an everyday affair. One settler supposedly was proud to say that he personally killed 300 natives. In Australia arsenic was mixed with flour to kill the aborigines. Bodley quotes Price (1950:107-108) who reported that, 'It was well known that the black fellows were killed like crows and that nobody cared or took notice.' Things were not different in South America. 'In Sao Paulo a man reported in 1888 that he had killed 2,000 Kaingang Indians by mixing strychnine with their drinking water.[32]

But even today the killing of tribal people continues. Bodley tells us that in 1971 many Guayaki Indians were killed by white settlers, including many Germans, who wanted to decorate their houses with Guayaki trophies. Both from Brazil and Columbia are accounts of cattle farmers who used guns, poison and dynamite to annihilate the Indians who lived in areas which they wanted for their cattle.

Typically none of these criminals thought they were doing wrong. 'I was not aware of having done something wrong', said one of these murderers.[33] 'I killed these Indians because I knew that the government would not punish us or ask for compensation for the crime.'[34]

Indians, savages, natives may be killed by White Man because they are doomed anyhow to disappear from history, they cannot withstand the onslaught of progress and white civilization. The logic of the connection between annihilation and progress, brutality and civilization, barbarism and emancipation is the same as it was in the eighteenth century. Annihilation of tribal people is justified simply by the right of the stronger one. After the genocide of the Hereros by the Germans in South-West Africa, the head of the settlers' commission, Paul Rohrbach said in 1907:

> It is obvious . . .that the natives have to disappear from the land where they grazed their cattle till now so that the White Man can graze his cattle on the same land. If one asks for a moral justification of this standpoint the answer is that people who live on a cultural level similar to that of the South African natives must lose their free, national barbarism. They must be developed to a class of workers, getting wages and bread from the Whites, if they want a higher right of existence. This applies both for individuals and for nations, or tribes. Their existence is only justified in so far as they appear as useful for the general development. There is no argument in the world which can prove that the preservation and maintenance of any degree of national self-determination, national property and political organisation among the tribes of South Africa was a greater gain for humanity as a whole or the German people in particular than making them subservient, and to exploit their former territory by the white race.[35]

People like Rohrbach saw clearly that the rise of the proletarian masses in the 'culture nations' like Germany was possible only if and when the native people of Africa were treated not as human beings with equal rights, but subjected to the iron historical law of 'development of productive forces'. In 1909 he wrote:

> A right of the natives, which could only be realised at the expense of the development of the white race, does not exist. The idea is absurd that Bantus, Sudan negroes and Hottentots in Africa have the right to live and die as they please, even when by this, uncounted people among civilized nations of Europe were forced to remain tied to a miserable proletarian existence, instead of being able, by the full use of productive capacities of our colonial possessions to rise to a richer level of existence themselves and also to help construct the whole body of human and national welfare.[36]

The savages had to be driven away from their territory before

White Man could take possession and exploit it and its resources to generate profit.

The autarchic subsistence economy of the tribes had to be destroyed, because as long as people were able to survive on a subsistence base they could not easily be tempted by the promises of industrial, urban civilization. There are numerous tribes and nations which, till today, fight to preserve their autonomous subsistence.

Only after people have been forcefully separated from their territory, only after the privatization of the commons, after the destruction of clan and tribal structures and relations and culture can a colonial 'inferiority complex' arise: the self-devaluation of one's culture, way of life, one's own strength and roots. Only then can the new white industrial culture and way of life exert its power of fascination on the uprooted people.

Part of this uprooting process was the denial of political sovereignty to these nations. The territory they inhabited was declared 'empty land', 'virgin land', *'territorium nullus'*: land that belonged to nobody. It was essential for the new colonial masters to establish their political hegemony over these nations and their territory in order to use the colonies 'productively' for the development of industry in their own countries. The European working class supported this colonialism, because they also realized that the improvement of their lives was dependent on maintaining colonies.

Romanticizing the 'Savage'

Yet, along with this inhuman treatment of the 'savages' we find the same type of romanticizing and sentimentalizing that we have already observed in the case of women. 'Natives', native peoples' or 'Nature' peoples in contrast to 'civilized' or 'culture' peoples, were some of the concepts coined. The notion that such 'natives' were closer to nature, which civilization had destroyed and subdued, remains with us even today. Simultaneous with the beginnings of brutalities against the 'savages' was the start of the Enlightenment discourse about the 'noble savage' and his arcadia, the primeval paradise in which man still lived in harmony with nature. The encyclopedian Diderot considered that in the newly 'discovered' Tahiti, human nature could be studied in its innocent, primeval state, where neither property nor hierarchy existed, and sexual repression was unknown. Tahiti became the site of the Golden Age upon which were projected all dreams, desires and utopian hopes.

The connection between Tahiti and the desired Golden Age which modernity was supposed to bring about, means that human history becomes part of natural history, as Steinbrugge points out. It was above all Rousseau who 'historicized' nature while at the same time he 'naturized' women and 'savages'.[37] For Rousseau, women and 'savages', as part of 'nature', were therefore excluded from the realm of reason, competition, money-making and the rat-race of all against all. But they also represent those attributes such as emotionality, spontaneity, humane-ness, without which modern society with its principles of egotism, self-interest, private property and hierarchy would destroy itself. The 'savages' and women, therefore, must be constructed symbolically as *complementary* 'other' to rational modern Man. And they have to be fixed into a kind of state of nature, as representing the second stage of human and social development: the 'Golden Age'; this is where they are meant to remain so that modern rational, civilized Man maintains his nature base, without which he could not survive.[38]

However, neither Rousseau nor any Enlightenment thinkers refer to the violence that accompanies this process of 'naturization' of women and 'savages'. The relationship between violence and reason, progress and retrogression, self-determination and subordination, emancipation and enslavement is an unbroken thread that runs through modern, real history since the Enlightenment to the present. To clearly understand the character of this relationship we must go beyond such concepts as 'ambivalence', contradiction and even dialectics. Because even a dialectical view of this relationship implies that every respective 'servant' (the 'savages') will eventually overcome the 'masters' (Hegel) and thus arrive at a higher synthesis. The dialectical view of history accepts the creation of victims today as necessary for a better future for all tomorrow. But those who are sacrificed today will never be those who will eventually benefit from this betterment; not even their children will benefit. Because in many cases their sacrifice consists in the sacrifice of their life. The beneficiaries are others than the victims of this process of development and modernization. This is clearly understood by, for example, those tribal peoples who refuse to leave their ancestral lands because the World Bank and governments want to flood their land and forest to build giant dams to generate electricity for the big cities. They refuse this kind of development and want only to continue with their subsistence-oriented way of life.

For them 'development' means their destruction, physically, economically, ecologically and culturally, and thus, for them, development cannot be romanticized or idealized. They know that they will be the losers in this process, and that progress means only violence for them. The kind of historic teleology to which Rohrbacher — and many others even today — adheres, namely that white 'culture' nations' violent subordination of the 'savages' and their utilization and exploitation to generate surplus value for capitalist industrialism would eventually also lead to a 'richer', 'higher', more 'human', 'freer' life for these 'nature people' — is a promise that has nowhere been fulfilled. On the contrary, the gap between the 'culture nations' and the 'natives' has become an abyss. The utopia of 'catching-up development', of modernism and progress, the utopia of the Enlightenment has betrayed the 'savages.'

Romanticizing nature

The nostalgia for Nature is the most general expression of what is sought in the romanticizing and longing for women and the 'savages'. In fact, the modern concept of 'nature' since the Enlightenment is a result of this double-faced process of destruction and sentimentalization which has made up the modern era. This becomes obvious if we look at the modern aestheticism of nature and landscapes and at what then became the movement for the protection of nature.

Lucius Burckhard, in his 'Travel Map for the Journey to Tahiti' writes: 'Only where man has destroyed Nature the landscape can become really beautiful. Only where tanks have left their traces a biotope can come up. Tahiti is not a peaceful place because the lion grazes side by side with the lamb, but because in reality it has been a battlefield.'[39]

Claudia v. Werlhof points out that this new beauty of nature, the beauty that emerges on the battlefields of modernity, is always the creation of Man. Whatever is there, which has not been created by Man, is not considered beautiful. It may therefore be plundered, planned, ordered, made even and 'beautified' in the same way that a dead body is cosmeticized before the funeral. What is now called beautiful was before called ugly. Beautification is preceded and presupposed by destruction.[40]

There are many examples of this combination of destruction and beautification or protection. For instance, only after peasant farming has been largely destroyed in Germany do we find a campaign to: 'Make your village more beautiful'. The emergence of landscape planning and environmental protection is related to the destruction of the environment and nature by capitalist-industrial processes. Protection of the environment, landscape planning and so on serve as cosmetics to conceal the identity of those responsible for the destruction in the first place, while the victims of this destruction are themselves identified as perpetrators, the guilty.

This means that the culprits are not the chemical industry with its inbuilt growth mechanism, not the state with its capitalist agrarian policy and incentives for capitalist farming but the farmers and peasants who use chemical fertilizers and pesticides and who have industrialized farming in accordance with the accepted policy. Many urban people now see their task as 're-naturalizing' this landscape 'destroyed by the peasants'.

The same mechanism of 'blaming the victim' is applied in many cases of environmental destruction in the 'Third World'. Nomadic tribes in Africa are blamed for ecological degradation in the Sahel, because supposedly overgrazing by their herds has largely led to the desertification of this region. Poor women in Africa and Asia are blamed for the destruction of forest areas because they must now search for fuelwood higher and higher in forest-covered hills, cutting trees and shrubs, with no care for regeneration of the forests. Tribes which still practise slash and burn cultivation are blamed for the destruction of forests. In this search for the guilty the loggers, timber merchants, the furniture, sports and paper industries, the cattle farmers and the food export industry, are seldom mentioned. And the consumers of the end products of this ecological destruction are largely absolved from any share in the guilt. The blanket explanation is usually the neo-Malthusian argument that it is the poor who are destroying nature because they breed too many poor, that nature cannot support more people.

Meanwhile, environmentalists in the North demand that the 'protection' of nature should no longer be left to the 'natives', who they maintain are responsible for environmental destruction. Protection of rainforests, protection of animals, protection even of tribals should become the concern of northern environmental protection NGOs. The Debt-for-Nature-Swaps suggested to help solve the debt problem of many countries of the South, illustrate this.

This victimizing tactic is applied to women who either seek

abortion or who accept modern reproductive technologies. The efforts to, for example, frame an 'Embryo Protection Law' passed in Germany in 1991, are based on the assumption that women are their embryos' potential enemies; and that the state must protect the embryo against women's aggression. Patriarchal men-women relations, a social environment hostile to children, the incompatibility of gainful employment with motherhood, the crass utilitarianism and materialism of modern society, the obsession with growth in this society, are all absolved from responsibility. Women, who so far have been the only protectors of human life, are seen as the worst enemies of this life. The 'Embryo Protection Law' is also meant to protect embryos against arbitrary utilization for scientific experiments; the state becomes wary about the various uses and misuses of modern genetic and reproductive engineering. But instead of banning this technology — which is still considered as necessary and as contributing to 'progress' — the women are defined universally as the potential enemies of the foetuses. It is the same strategy employed in respect of protection of nature, of animals, of rain forests and so on. The state does not intervene in industrial capitalism's or modern technology processes of destruction of these living symbioses; the state accepts both the destructive technology and the capitalist utilization thereof. But it blames and punishes women — all women — for actual or potential misuse of supposedly progressive technologies.[41]

C. v. Werlhof rightly asks for whom all these Protection Laws are made. Against whom have nature, the animals, plants, children, embryos, life to be protected?

> How come that Nature, plants, animals, women and children and life are still there if they were not always protected? ... Why is this special Protection necessary all of a sudden? Protection of Nature begins in the 18th century, in the very Age of Enlightenment, of clarity, of the declaration of Universal Human Rights, of Equality and Freedom and Brotherhood ... Who had attacked Nature and human life all of a sudden so that they had to be protected?
> ... Protection of Nature deals with the results of an intervention of Man into Nature's processes. This protection necessarily presupposes an aggression. Real Protection of nature should indeed prevent such aggression,

remedy its consequences, or turn this aggression into its opposite, namely a kind of caress.[42]

But this is precisely what contemporary protection movements are *not* doing. The aggression, the interventions and invasions, the war against Nature, including our human nature, particularly female nature, is not to be finally ended. To do so would mean that White Man's project, his model of civilization, progress and modernity would be terminated. This project is based on warfare against Nature. The aim is not to create a new and peaceful and harmonious relationship with Nature, but to maintain the beautiful *image* of nature, a metaphorical nature, not nature as a subject. Man-Nature harmony intrinsic to this aim can only be achieved by an aesthetic voyeuristic simulation of Nature. But these simulations do not change the antagonistic relationship between Man and Nature characteristic of European modernity. Only in the 'dream of nature' can modern Man's independence *from Nature* — the central idea of modern science — and his imagined lust for Nature be celebrated simultaneously; and, of course, Nature can only be a beautiful illusion, an exhibit or reservation.[43] This connection between destruction and exhibition is exemplified by Chernobyl which, after the catastrophe, became inaccessible for the next 1000 years. According to plans of Soviet scientists it should now become an exhibit — a nature museum. Only in this way can nature be translated into an abstract idea, both for conservatives and progressives, neither of which are concerned to end the warfare between man and nature, man and woman, metropoles and colonies. They reach out for what they are destroying. And this reaching out, this searching for the beautiful illusion of nature protects those who organize this warfare in the name of profit from public criticism and conceals the ugly face of modernity: the war of all against all, the insensible machine-like and corpse-like character of the world of commodities. The beautiful illusion of Nature, the simulation of originality and spontaneity, the aesthetic and symbolic representation of Nature makes this world of machines more tolerable. The market opportunities for selling these symbolic representations of Nature grow in proportion to people's growing frustrations with the hollow benefits of modern civilization.

As we have noted, however, even these illusions cannot be bought unless the symbioses, the living relationships between humans and other natural beings, is disrupted. Progress, since the time of Enlightenment, means precisely this disruption and separation of the modern human ego, the modern subject, from all such symbioses. To begin with, progress means a *going away* from Nature.[44] Since the Enlightenment, this going away, this distancing from Nature has been considered a necessary precondition for emancipation, as a step from Nature to Culture, from the realm of necessity to the realm of freedom, from immanence to transcendence. This concept of emancipation, based on Man's domination over Nature, ignores the fact that even modern man is born of woman, that he must eat food that comes from the earth, and that he will die; and further that he can be alive, healthy and achieve fulfilment only as long as he retains an organic connection with Nature's symbioses. Such symbioses and living interconnectedness once ruptured, cannot be healed and restored by aesthetics, 'nature' museums or any kind of protected reservations. Only if Nature is again recognized as a living being with whom we must co-operate in a *loving* manner, and not regard as a source of raw material to be exploited for commodity production, can we hope to end the war against Nature and against ourselves.

How fascism uses these desires

Since the Enlightenment the discourse on Nature has played a dominant role in the ideological and political camps, dividing the so-called progressives from the so-called conservatives ('so-called' because this differentiation is rather superficial). Each camp uses a concept of nature which is apparently different from the other. The progressives — the leftists and liberals — who consider themselves to be the heirs of the seventeenth and eighteenth century rationalist movement, see Nature as the enemy to be subordinated and put at the service of Man by the new science and technology; in Marxian terms, by the development of productive forces.

Modern rationality is fighting an embittered fight against the old world, which it wants to subject to its training. The wilderness, non-domesticated Nature that stands at the opposite side of Reason, is the enemy which Reason has to conquer and subordinate.[45]

The conservatives, on the other hand see Nature as the friend, the good Mother to be protected against industrial capitalism's crass utilitaristic exploitation. As we saw, however, this protection is possible only in reservations, museums, in art and in romanticizing Nature, not in a fundamental opposition against capitalism. These two concepts of nature correspond to two different types of criticism of capitalism: left and conservative. According to

Sieferle, these two types of critique stem from two different social utopias: the left, projected into the future; and the conservative, projected into the past.[46]

Conservative criticism of modern civilization and capitalism, its romanticizing and idyllizing of pre-modern, pre-scientific times is considered as reactionary and irrational by liberals and leftists, as anti-progress, anti-technology and close to Ludditism.

In Germany, since the historic experience of Fascism, such critique is often denounced as potentially fascist. The left, particularly, clings to the Hegelian and Marxist philosophy of history, according to which the development of productive forces, Man's progressive domination over Nature constitutes the precondition for political and economic emancipation from obsolete relations of production. This progress, this development is regarded as a kind of natural law, a necessary process, which romantic criticism cannot stop. 'There is no going backward in history' can often be heard from this side. The sense of sadness for the destruction of Nature, the lost homeland, fear about ecological destruction, despair, hopelessness and alienation about the cold, indifferent world of machines and factories, recognition of the futility of the work people must do, panic about industrial and ecological catastrophes, mothers' despair about nuclear and chemical pollution — all these are characterized by the progressives as hysterical and irrational, as merely a continuation of the anti-rationalist, anti-revolutionary, conservative-romantic movement of the nineteenth century. By labelling these themes and the feelings they arouse as reactionary and irrational, the liberals and leftists, using a superficial left-right dichotomy, leave all these feelings to the rightists. But these feelings and longings are found not only among bored middle-class urban citizens, they are also shared by the proletarian masses. Christel Neusss has shown that the discourse on rationalism and rationalization, carried out by the Social Democrats (SPD) in the Weimar Republic in the late 1920s, was opposed by many factory workers. In this debate the SPD took the side of rationalism and propagated the necessity of technical rationalizations and innovations which replaced manual by mental labour and thus made labour 'more productive'. The workers' resistance to these rationalizations was not motivated by their desire to get a bigger share of the capitalist cake — this was the argument of the SPD — but a resistance to further alienation of work, of alienation from 'Mother Nature', from their own bodies. It was motivated by a sense of sorrow about the loss of a homeland, a village, about their separation from natural, organic rhythms. But both the Social Democrats and the Communists, unable to integrate this complex into their rationalist utopia, either ignored these feelings or labelled them irrational and fascist. In so doing they left this whole psycho-social reality unexplained and indeed, left it to the fascists to exploit for their propaganda.[47]

The fascists, however, 'occupied' these feelings of alienation and yearning and used them for their utopia of an organistic, new society. In my understanding the success of the German national socialists cannot be explained without understanding that they were able to mobilize feelings which were already prevalent among the people, also among the proletarian masses. Without the mobilization and integration of such feelings into their strategy they would have failed to come to power through elections. Of course, all these feelings were then projected onto the great patriarchal leader, who promised to be their saviour. Their policy specifically concentrated on such evocative 'areas' as 'our land' 'homeland' *(Heimat)*, the 'soil and the blood' *(Blut and Boden)*, mothers, nature, as the material and emotional base of the 'people' as a whole *(Volksgemeinschaft)*.

After the defeat of fascism, these 'symbolic sites' and the feelings associated with them have fallen under a moral taboo and subjected to censorship in Germany; this censorship is particularly strong within the German left. The Greens, for example, who did and do mobilize these feelings, were initially criticized — and sometimes still are today — as irrational and pro-fascist. Parts of the ecology movement, such as the ecological-democratic party, were regarded as rightist and excluded from the Green Party. This explicit or implicit accusation of fascism functions as a kind of thought-taboo which prevents people looking at the crucial issues of our time — the ecological crisis, the man-woman relationship, war and peace, the colonial question — from a different perspective. Whoever tries to focus public attention on the 'land', the 'homeland', peasants, mothers, children, nature is often accused of simply continuing and repeating the tradition of the nature and homeland-protection movements, the life-reform movement, the anti-urban and anti-industrial movements that preceded the Third Reich and were integrated in its strategy.[48]

In the women's movement in Germany this sterile left-right thinking is also employed to criticize women who focus on children, on ecological issues, on a concern for nature and rural life. The movement of mothers against nuclear energy, which emerged

spontaneously after the Chernobyl disaster, was especially criticized by parts of the feminist movement as being a falling back
into the mother-idolatory which the Nazis had propagated. There
was a new split in the movement when sections of the women in
the Green Party issued a 'Mother's Manifesto', stating that the
feminist movement was too much oriented towards the needs of
unmarried, childless 'career women' and that mothers of small
children had no place in this movement. In the passionate debate
that followed the publication of this Manifesto the women who
had issued it were accused of fascist tendencies.[49]

A similar critique was expressed in the context of the movement of women against the Gulf War. Women in Germany who
had issued a leaflet in which they explicitly said 'NO TO THE
WAR' because they were particularly worried as mothers, were
criticized as 'mother-pacifists' which, in this context also was interpreted as anti-semitic. It is this perception of interpreting every
new social movement in Germany in the context and against the
backdrop of our Nazi past, and within the dualistic framework of
rationalism-irrationalism, which makes it difficult to develop a
new perspective beyond these left-right schemas.

This kind of thought-taboo around issues like motherhood,
land, and so on, and the fear of being accused of fascist tendencies,
often leads to merely tactical statements. If women have to be
afraid to be put in the rightist corner if they try to think anew
about the fact that women can be mothers, they tend to stop
thinking publicly about such issues. This thought-taboo prevents
a real critique of fascism and its use of women for its motherhood
ideology, because those who profited most from fascism were not
'irrational' women but rather, in particular, those scientists who
were wedded to the rationalist paradigm and the industrialists
who used this rationalist science for their war preparations. The
more the 'irrational' women, peasants, and other such 'backward'
sections are accused of fascist collaboration, the easier it is for the
industrial-capitalist-militarist complex to wash its hands off its
complicity with fascism. The left critics of the new social movement, particularly their critique of possible fascist deja-vu
phenomena have so far been unable to develop a utopia, a perspective of a new society other than the rationalist one which
presupposes irrecoverable destructions of nature. Perhaps, because of this inability to step out of the dualistic rationalism and
irrationalism schema, many erstwhile progressives are now, after
the collapse of socialism in Eastern Europe, abandoning all search

for perspectives and utopias. They rather embrace total relativistic post-modernism, which does not want to project those feelings and hopes on to anything, because, according to this school of thought, all utopias have failed. Thus, all that remains is a kind of nihilistic hedonism and individualism, and a kind of critical criticism for its own sake. This position can always count upon being on the right side because it does not take sides at all.

In the English-speaking world, particularly in the US and Britain, ecofeminists are accused not of fascist tendencies, but of essentialism. This critique stems mainly from the left which considers that not only the social world but nature too is socially constructed, following the constructivist school of thought. They maintain an historical-materialist view of women and nature, and consider that much of what US ecofeminists write to be inspired by a reified naturalism, where socially determined relationships are seen as solely biological or natural, and where reason is being replaced by intuition and imagination. This controversy between 'essentialist' and historical-materialist-Marxist views on women and nature is, in my view, a continuation of the same dualistic paradigm of thinking that we criticize in this book. The Marxist or 'materialist' interpretation or — as the jargon goes today — construction of nature and women, is in our view not 'materialist' enough, in the sense that the reality of our finite globe and of our finite female organic body and that of other animals, is idealistically transcended. Femaleness is and was always a *human* relation to our organic body. Only under capitalist patriarchy did the division between spirit and matter, the natural and the social lead to the total devaluation of the so-called natural. I agree with Mary Mellor who tries to overcome the sterile controversy between ecofeminists and social ecologists by insisting on a necessary integration of both views; but such an integration would not be possible 'without reconstructing the whole socialist project'.[50]

The problem with the 'essentialism' *vs* 'historical materialism' discourse, as discussed by Mary Mellor, is also that it remains within the constraints of an academic, and that means idealistic discourse only; it seems to distance itself from the fact that women and men are confronted by urgent problems which need solutions. In view of the ongoing destruction of our ecological life-base, of increasing male violence against women, and of increasing aimless civil wars and Ramboism around the world, the constructivist 'essentialism' *vs* 'materialism' discourse seems out of place. It is time that we renounced this fruitless and destructive dualism of 'good and bad' nature, 'rationality *vs* irrationality' subject *vs* object, 'nature *vs* society or culture'. Nature is, as the American Indians say, our mother, not a mere source of raw material, she is a subject, animated matter, materializing spirit. We forget that what we do to her we do to ourselves. Women, due to their historic experience of patriarchal violence and, despite this, their knowledge of survival are less likely to forget this than are men. And it is women — and some men — who, in the fight against the destruction of their survival base, have begun to develop a new, realistic, vision of another relationship between humans and nature.

Notes

1. Gaserow, Vera, 'Plötzlich fühlst du dich wie John Wayne', in *Die Tageszeitung*, 13 May 1989.
2. Ludurf, K., 'Sie zerstoren was sie suchen', in *Frankfurter Rundschau*, 14 January 1989.
3. Meckel, W. 'Afrika zum Anfassen', in *Die Tageszeitung*, 13 May 1989.
4. Hildebrand, U. 'Alles nur Drecksäcke', in *Die Tageszeitung*, 17 September 1989.
5. Mies, M., V. Bennholdt-Thomsen, C. v. Werlhof, *Women, the Last Colony*, Zed Books, London, 1988.
6. Mies, M. *Patriarchy and Accumulation on a World Scale: Women in the International Division of Labour*, Zed Books, London, 1989.
7. Dross, A. *Die erste Walpurgisnacht. Hexenverfolgung in Deutschland*, Verlag Roter Stern, Frankfurt, 1988.
8. Rowbotham, S. *Women, Resistance and Revolution. A History of Women and Revolution in the Modern World*. Vintage Books, New York, 1974.
9. Rowbotham, S. *Woman's Consciousness, Men's World*. Penguin Books, Harmondsworth, 1973, p.39.
10. Dworkin, A. *Pornography: Men Possessing Women*. Pedigree Books, New York, 1981.
11. Mamozai, M. *Herrenmenschen, Frauen im Deutschen Kolonialismus* rororo *aktuell*. Reinbek, Rentscher, R. u.a. Ware Liebe. Sextourismus. Prostitution. Frauenhandel. Peter Hammer Verlag, 1982.
12. Latza, B. 'Most Sex-Tourists have Psychological Problems', in *Bangkok Post*, 6 March 1986.
13. Ibid.
14. Than-dam Truong: *Sex, Money and Morality: Prostitution and Tourism in South-East Asia*. Zed Books, London, 1990; and P. Phongpaicit, *From Peasant Girls to Bangkok Masseuses*. International Labour Office, Geneva, 1982.
15. Garaudy, R. *Das schwache Geschlecht ist unsere Stärke: Für die Feminiserung der Gesellschaft*, dtv. Munich, 1986.
16. Klein, R.D. (ed.) *Infertility. Women Speak Out About Their Experiences of Reproductive Medicine*. Pandora Press, London, 1989.

17. Ibid.
18. Scherhorn. G., L. Reisch, G. Raab, *Kaufsucht*. *Bericht über eine empirische Untersuchung*. Institut fur Haushalts-und Konsumokonomik, Universität Hohenheim, Stuttgart, 1990.
19. Merchant, C. *The Death of Nature: Women, Ecology and the Scientific Revolution*. Harper & Row. San Francisco, 1983.
20. Sarkar, S. 'Die Bewegung und ihre Strategie', in *Kommune*, No. 5.
21. Eder, K. *Die Vergesellschaftung der Natur: Studien zur sozialen Evolution der Praktischen Vernunft*. Suhrkamp, Frankfurt, 1989, p. 254.
22. Ibid. p.232.
23. Bohme, H. and G. Bohme, *Dar Andere der Vernunft. Zur Entwicklung von Rationalitätsstrukturen am Beispiel Kants*. Suhrkamp. Frankfurt, 1985
24. Than-Dam Truong, 1990. op. cit.
25. Elias, N. (1978) *üben den Prozess der Zivilisation (The Civilizing Process)*, Vols. I & II, Suhrkamp, Frankfurt.
26. Bennholdt-Thomsen, V. (1985) 'Zivilisation, moderner Staat und Gewalt. Eine feministische Kritik an Norbert Erlias' Zivilisationstheorie, in: *Beitraege zur feministischen theorie und praxis*, Vol. 8, 1985, No. 13, pp. 23—36.
27. Merchant, 1983. op. cit; Mies, 1991, op. cit.
28. Steinbrugge, L. *Das moralische Geschlecht. Theorien und literarische Entwurfe uber due Natur der Frau in der französischen Aufklärung*. Beltz-Verlag, Weinheim, 1987.
29. Mies, 1991, op. cit., p.14.
30. Garaudy, 1985, op. cit.; F. Capra, *The Turning Point*, Flamingo, London, 1982.
31. Bodley, John F. *Victims of Progress*. The Benjamin Cummings Publishing Co. Inc., New York, 1982.
32. Ibid., p. 41.
33. Ibid., p. 42.
34. Ibid., p. 44.
35. Quoted in ibid., p. 76.
36. Quoted by Mamozai, 1982, op. cit. p. 58 (transl. M.M.)
37. Steinbrugge (1987), op. cit., p. 67.
38. Ibid., pp. 82 ff.
39. Quoted by v. Werlhof. C. *Männliche Natur und künstliches Geschlecht, Texte zur Erkenntniskrise der Moderne*. Wiener Frauenverlag, Vienna, 1991, p. 169.
40. Ibid.
41. Ibid., pp. 170 ff. See also V. Bennholdt Thomsen 'Zur Philosophie eines anderen Umgangs mit der Natur', in Die Grünen Saar (eds) *Naturschutz im Saarland*, Saarbrucken, 1989, pp. 1a-10a.
42. v. Werlhof (1991) op. cit., pp. 165-6.
43. I read today (21.7.1992) that the director of a zoo in Washington has 'recreated' a 2,200 sq.m. tropical rainforest in his animal park. Following the 'preservation' of animals in museums, now the rainforest, destroyed by patriarchal capitalism is also being put in a museum. *Die Tageszeitung*, 21 July 1992. See also *Frankfurter Rundschau*, 29 August 1989.
44. v. Werlhof, 1991, op. cit., p. 171.
45. Sieferle, R.P. *Fortschrittsfeinde. Opposition gegen Technik und Industrie. Von der Romantik bis zur Gegenwart*. C.H. Beck, Munich, 1986, p. 239.
46. Ibid., p. 256.
47. Neususs, Ch. *Die Kopfgeburten der Arbeiterbewegung, oder: Die Genossin Luzemburg bringt alles dirrcheinander*. Rasch and Rohring, Hamburg, 1985.

48. Sieferle, 1986, op. cit.
49. Pinl, C., 'Zum Muttermanifest', in *Die Tageszeitung,* 15 January 1990.
50. Mellor, M., 'Eco-Feminism and Eco-Socialism: Dilemmas of Essentialism and Materialism' in *Capitalism, Nature, Socialism* Vol. 3(2) Issue 10, June 1992, pp. 1 - 20.

11. Women's Indigenous Knowledge and Biodiversity Conservation

Vandana Shiva

Gender and diversity are linked in many ways. The construction of women as the 'second sex' is linked to the same inability to cope with difference as is the development paradigm that leads to the displacement and extinction of diversity in the biological world. The patriarchal world view sees man as the measure of all value, with no space for diversity, only for hierarchy. Woman, being different, is treated as unequal and inferior. Nature's diversity is seen as not intrinsically valuable in itself, its value is conferred only through economic exploitation for commercial gain. This criterion of commercial value thus reduces diversity to a problem, a deficiency. Destruction of diversity and the creation of monocultures becomes an imperative for capitalist patriarchy.

The marginalization of women and the destruction of biodiversity go hand in hand. Loss of diversity is the price paid in the patriarchal model of progress which pushes inexorably towards monocultures, uniformity and homogeneity. In this perverted logic of progress, even conservation suffers. Agricultural 'development' continues to work towards erasing diversity, while the same global interests that destroy biodiversity urge the Third World to conserve it. This separation of production and consumption, with 'production' based on uniformity and 'conservation' desperately attempting to preserve diversity militates against protecting biodiversity. It can be protected only by making diversity the basis, foundation and logic of the technology and economics of production.

The logic of diversity is best derived from biodiversity and from women's links to it. It helps look at dominant structures from below, from the ground of diversity, which reveal monocultures to be unproductive and the knowledge that produces them as primitive rather than sophisticated.

Diversity is, in many ways, the basis of women's politics and the politics of ecology; gender politics is largely a politics of difference. Eco-politics, too, is based on nature's variety and difference, as opposed to industrial commodities and processes which are uniform and homogeneous.

These two politics of diversity converge when women and biodiversity meet in fields and forest, in arid regions and wetlands.

Diversity as women's expertise

Diversity is the principle of women's work and knowledge. This is why they have been discounted in the patriarchal calculus. Yet it is also the matrix from which an alternative calculus of 'productivity' and 'skills' can be built that respects, not destroys, diversity.

The economies of many Third World communities depend on biological resources for their sustenance and well-being. In these societies, biodiversity is simultaneously a means of production, and an object of consumption. The survival and sustainability of livelihoods is ultimately connected to the conservation and sustainable use of biological resources in all their diversity. Tribal and peasant societies' biodiversity-based technologies, however, are seen as backward and primitive and are, therefore, displaced by 'progressive' technologies that destroy both diversity and people's livelihoods.

There is a general misconception that diversity-based production systems are low-productivity systems. However, the high productivity of uniform and homogenous systems is a contextual and theoretically constructed category, based on taking into account only one-dimensional yields and outputs. The alleged low productivity of the one against the alleged high productivity of the other is, therefore, not a neutral, scientific measure but biased towards commercial interests for whom maximizing the one-dimensional output is an economic imperative.

Crop uniformity, however, undermines the diversity of biological systems which form the production system as well as the livelihoods of people whose work is associated with diverse and multiple-use systems of forestry, agriculture and animal husbandry. For example, in the state of Kerala in India (its name derives from the coconut palm), coconut is cultivated in a multilayered, high-intensity cropping system, along with betel and pepper vines, bananas, tapioca, drumstick, papaya, jackfruit, mango and vegetables. The annual labour requirement in a mono-culture of coconut palm is 157 man-days per ha, while in a mixed cropping system, it is 960 man-days per ha. In the dry-land farm-ing systems of the Deccan, the shift from mixed cropping millets, pulses and oilseeds to eucalyptus monocultures led to an annual loss of employment of 250 man-days per ha.

When labour is scarce and costly, labour displacing technolo-gies are productive and efficient, but when labour is abundant, labour displacement is unproductive because it leads to poverty, dispossession and destruction of livelihoods. In Third World situ-ations, sustainability has therefore to be achieved at two levels simultaneously: sustainability of natural resources and sus-tainability of livelihoods. Consequently, biodiversity conservation must be linked to conservation of livelihoods derived from biodiversity.

Women's work and knowledge is central to biodiversity con-servation and utilization both because they work between 'sectors' and because they perform multiple tasks. Women, as farmers, have remained invisible despite their contribution. Econ-omists tend to discount women's work as 'production' because it falls outside the so-called 'production boundary'. These omissions arise not because too few women work, but too many women do too much work of too many different kinds.

Statisticians and researchers suffer a conceptual inability to define women's work inside and outside the house — and farm-ing is usually part of both. This recognition of what is and is not labour is exacerbated by the great volume and variety of work that women do. It is also related to the fact that although women work to sustain their families and communities, most of what they do is not measured in wages. Their work is also invisible because they are concentrated outside market-related or remunerated work, and they are normally engaged in multiple tasks.

Time allocation studies, which do not depend on an a priori definition of work, reflect more closely the multiplicity of tasks undertaken, and the seasonal, even daily movement in and out of the conventional labour force which characterize most rural women's livelihood strategy. Gender studies now being pub-lished, confirm that women in India are major producers of food in terms of value, volume and hours worked.

In the production and preparation of plant foods, women need skills and knowledge. To prepare seeds they need to know about seed preparation, germination requirements and soil choice. Seed preparation requires visual discrimination, fine motor co-ordination, sensitivity to humidity levels and weather conditions. To sow and strike seeds demands knowledge of seasons, climate, plant requirements, weather conditions, micro-climatic factors and soil-enrichment; sowing seeds requires physical dexterity and strength. To properly nurture plants calls for information about the nature of plant diseases, pruning, staking, water supplies, companion planting, predators, sequences, growing seasons and soil maintenance. Persistence and patience, physical strength and attention to plant needs are essential. Harvesting requires judgements in relation to weather, labour and grading; and knowledge of preserving, immediate use and propagation.

Women's knowledge has been the mainstay of the indigenous dairy industry. Dairying, as managed by women in rural India, embodies practices and logic rather different from those taught in dairy science at institutions of formal education in India, since the latter is essentially an import from Europe and North America. Women have been experts in the breeding and feeding of farm animals, including not only cows and buffaloes but also pigs, chickens, ducks and goats.

In forestry too, women's knowledge is crucial to the use of biomass for feed and fertilizer. Knowledge of the feed value of different fodder species, the fuel value of firewood types, and of food products and species is essential to agriculture-related forestry in which women are predominately active. In low input agriculture, fertility is transferred from forest and farm trees to the field by women's work either directly or via animals.

Women's work and knowledge in agriculture is uniquely found in the spaces 'in between' the interstices of 'sectors', the invisible ecological flows between sectors, and it is through these linkages that ecological stability, sustainability and productivity under resource-scarce conditions are maintained. The invisibility of women's work and knowledge arises from the gender bias which has a blind spot for realistic assessment of women's contributions. It is also rooted in the sectoral, fragmented and reductionist approach to development which treats forests, livestock and crops as independent of each other.

The focus of the 'green revolution' has been increasing grain yields of rice and wheat by techniques such as dwarfing, monocultures and multicropping. For an Indian woman farmer, rice is not only food, but also a source of cattle fodder and straw for thatch. High yield varieties (HYVs) can increase women's work; the shift from local varieties and indigenous crop-improvement strategies can also take away women's control over seeds and genetic resources. Women have been seed custodians since time immemorial, and their knowledge and skills should be the basis of all crop-improvement strategies.

Women: custodians of biodiversity

In most cultures women have been the custodians of biodiversity. They produce, reproduce, consume and conserve biodiversity in agriculture. However, in common with all other aspects of women's work and knowledge, their role in the development and conservation of biodiversity has been rendered as non-work and non-knowledge. Their labour and expertise has been defined into nature, even though it is based on sophisticated cultural and scientific practises. But women's biodiversity conservation differs from the dominant patriarchal notion of biodiversity conservation.

Recent concern with biodiversity at the global level has grown as a result of the erosion of diversity due to the expansion of large-scale monoculture-based agricultural production and its associated vulnerability. Nevertheless, the fragmentation of farming systems linked to the spread of monocultures continues to be the guiding paradigm for biodiversity conservation. Each element of the farm eco-system is viewed in isolation, and conservation of diversity is seen as an arithmetical exercise of collecting varieties.

In contrast, in the traditional Indian setting, biodiversity is a relational category in which each element acquires its characteristics and value through its relationships with other elements. Biodiversity is ecologically and culturally embedded. Diversity is reproduced and conserved through the reproduction and conservation of culture, in festivals and rituals which not only celebrate the renewal of life, but also provide a platform for subtle tests for seed selection and propagation. The dominant world view does not regard these tests as scientific because they do not emerge from the laboratory and the experimental plot, but are integral to the total world-view and lifestyle of people and are carried out, not by men in white coats, but by village woman. But because it is thus that the rich biological diversity in agriculture has been preserved they are systematically reliable.

When women conserve seed, they conserve diversity and

therefore conserve balance and harmony. *Navdanya* or nine seeds are the symbol of this renewal of diversity and balance, not only of the plant world, but of the planet and of the social world. This complex relationship web gives meaning to biodiversity in Indian culture and has been the basis of its conservation over millennia.

'Sacredness': a conservation category

In the indigenous setting, sacredness is a large part of conservation. Sacredness encompasses the intrinsic value of diversity; sacredness denotes a relationship of the part to the whole — a relationship that recognizes and preserves integrity. Profane seed violates the integrity of ecological cycles and linkages and fragments agricultural ecosystems and the relationships responsible for sustainable production at all the following levels:

1. Sacred seed is perceived as a microcosm of the macrocosm with *navdanya* symbolizing the Navagraha. The influences of planets and climate are seen as essential to plant productivity. In contrast, HYVs break links with all seasonal climatic and cosmic cycles. Multiple-cropping and photo-insensitivity are two important ways in which the HYV seeds are separated from planetary and climatic influences. But, 'freedom' from seasonal cycles is based on dependence on large dams and intensive irrigation.

2. Seed diversity and nutritional balance go hand in hand. Monocultures of HYV also cause nutritional deficiency and imbalance: pulses and oilseeds are sacrificed to increase the commodity-production of cereal crops.

3. Crop-diversity is essential for maintaining soil fertility. Monocultures fed on chemical fertilizers destroy the basis of soil fertility; biodiversity enhances it. Dwarf varieties yield no straw for recycling organic matter to the soil; chemicals kill soil fauna and flora.

4. Biodiversity is also essential to maintain the sustainability of self-provisioning farm units, where producers are also consumers. HYV monocultures mean that more farmers will become consumers of purchased seed, thereby creating dependency, increasing production costs and decreasing food entitlements at the local level.

6. Finally, purchased seeds displace women from decision-making and custodianship of seeds and transform them into unskilled labour. Main cereal crop associates are called *akadi* in Karnataka and women make all decisions relating to the *akadi* crop. In the words of a Lambani woman, 'What do (men) know

about the *akadi*, they only know how to *besaya* (plough).' Due to women's involvement in the *akadi* crop traditional seeds are preserved over generations. One woman said, 'they are the seeds grown by me, and my mother in my native family, and it is the seeds grown by the daughter.'

What insights can be derived from the everyday practice of women in agricultural communities in the conservation and renewal of biodiversity?

Firstly, the meaning of biodiversity, as epitomized in *navdanya* indicates that biodiversity is a relational not reductionist category — a contextual not atomized concept. Conserving biodiversity therefore implies conserving the relationship from which derive balance and harmony. Biodiversity cannot be conserved in fragments, except to serve raw materials requirements, as such it cannot serve as the basis of the vitality of living ecosystems and living cultures.

Secondly, the conservation of relatedness involves a notion of sacredness and inviolability. The concept of sacredness and diversity, of seed is located in an entirely different world view from that in which seed is only a commodity, with profit as its only value.

Thirdly, the self-provisioning nature of most sustainable agricultural systems implies a closed cycle of production and consumption. Dominant economics is unable to take such provision into account because it counts as production only that in which the producer and consumer are different, that means that only commodity production is production, and self-provisioning is non-productive work. This is the viewpoint that counts women's heavy work-load as non-work. Unfortunately, it also provides the framework that informs dominant strategies for the conservation of biodiversity.

Thus, while biological resources have social, ethical, cultural and economic values, it is the economic values that must be demonstrated to compete for the attention of government decision-makers. Three categories of the economic values of biological resources are named, as:

- 'consumptive value': value of products consumed directly without passing through a market, such as firewood, fodder and game meat;
- 'productive value': value of products commercially exploited; and
- 'non-consumptive use value': indirect value of eco-

system functions, such as watershed protection, photo-synthesis, regulation of climate and production of soil.

An interesting value framework has thus been constructed which predetermines analysis and opinions. If the Third World's poor, who derive their livelihoods directly from nature, only 'consume', while trading and commercial interests are the 'only' producers, it follows quite naturally that the Third World is responsible for the destruction of its biological wealth, and the North alone has the capacity to preserve it. The ideologically constructed divisions between consumption, production and conservation conceal the political economy of the processes which underlie the destruction of biological diversity.

In particular, it transforms women, the producers and conservers of biodiversity's value, into mere consumers. Instead of building conservation programmes based on their culture, values, skills, knowledge and wisdom, dominant conservation strategies erode them, and thereby create conditions for the erosion of biodiversity as the basis of sustainable livelihoods and production systems.

Diversity in the dominant world-view is seen as a numerical and arithmetical factor, not an ecological one. It relates to arithmetical variety not to relational symbiosis and complexity. Biodiversity is usually defined as the 'degree of nature's variety, including both the number and frequency of ecosystems, species and genes in a given assemblage'. In contrast, for cultures and economies which have practised diversity, biodiversity is a web of relationships which ensures balance and sustainability. On the grand scale this involves a relationship between planets and plants, between cosmic harmony and agricultural harmony captured in *navdanya*.

On the more earthly level, diversity and interrelationships are characteristic of all sustainable agricultural systems. Biodiversity in this context implies co-existence and interdependence of trees, crops and livestock, which maintains cycles of fertility through biomass flows. Women's work and knowledge is concentrated in these invisible 'spaces between'. In addition, there are ecological relationships between the diversity of crops in mixed and rotational cropping, relationships that maintain the ecological balance through multiple functions. Mixtures of cereals and pulses create nutrient balance in the nitrogen cycle; crop mixtures maintain pest-predator balance, controlling pests without chemical or genetic engineering. Diverse mixtures also maintain the water-cycle, and conserve the soil's moisture and fertility. This ecologically-rich meaning and practice of biodiversity has been conserved over millennia on India's small farms, and has provided food and nutrition on the basis of sustainability and justice.

Biotechnology and the destruction of biodiversity

There are a number of crucial ways in which the Third World women's relationship to biodiversity differs from corporate men's relationship to biodiversity. Women produce through biodiversity, whereas corporate scientists produce through uniformity.

For women farmers, biodiversity has intrinsic value — for global seed and agribusiness corporations, biodiversity derives its value only as 'raw material' for the biotechnology industry. For women farmers the essence of the seed is the continuity of life. For multinational corporations, the value of the seed lies in the discontinuity of its life. Seed corporations deliberately breed seeds that cannot give rise to future generations so that farmers are transformed from seed custodians into seed consumers. Hybrid seeds are 'biologically patented' in that the offspring cannot be used as seeds as farmers must go back to corporations to buy seed every year. Where hybrids do not force the farmers back to the market, legal patents and 'intellectual property rights' are used to prevent farmers from saving seed. Seed patents basically imply that corporations treat seed as their 'creation.' Patents prevent others from 'making' the patented product, hence patented seed cannot be used for making seed. Royalties have to be paid to the company that gets the patent.

The claim of 'creation' of life by corporate scientists is totally unjustified, it is in fact an interruption in the life flow of creation. It is also unjustified because nature and Third World farmers have made the seed that corporations are attempting to own as their innovation and their private property. Patents on seeds are thus a twenty-first century form of piracy, through which the shared heritage and custody of Third World women peasants is robbed and depleted by multinational corporations, helped by global institutions like GATT.

Patents and biotechnology contribute to a two-way theft. From Third World producers they steal biodiversity. From consumers everywhere they steal safe and healthy food.

Genetic engineering is being offered as a 'green' technology worldwide. President Bush ruled in May 1992 that genetically engineered foods should be treated as 'natural' and hence safe. However, genetic engineering is neither natural nor safe.

A number of risks associated with genetically engineered foods have been listed recently by the Food and Drug Administration of the US:

- New toxicants may be added to genetically engineered food.
- Nutritional quality of engineered food may be diminished.
- New substances may significantly alter the composition of food.
- New proteins that cause allergic reactions may enter the food supply.
- Antibiotic resistant genes may diminish the effectiveness of some antibiotics to human and domestic animal diseases.
- The deletion of genes may have harmful side effects.
- Genetic engineering may produce 'counterfeit freshness'.
- Engineered food may pose risks to domestic animals.
- Genetically engineered food crops may harm wildlife and change habitats.

When we are being asked to trust genetically engineered foods, we are being asked to trust the same companies that gave us pesticides in our food. Monsanto, which is now selling itself as Green was telling us that 'without chemicals, millions more would go hungry'. Today, when Bhopal has changed the image of these poisons, we are being told by the Monsantos, Ciba-Geigys, Duponts, ICIs and Dows that they will now give us Green products. However, as Jack Kloppenberg has recently said, 'Having been recognized as wolves, the industrial semoticians want to redefine themselves as sheep, and green sheep at that.'

12. New Reproductive Technologies: Sexist and Racist Implications*

Maria Mies

Introduction

Atomic technology having come under heavy attack, particularly after Chernobyl, its exalted place has been taken by biotechnology, mainly genetic engineering and reproduction technology, in company with computer technology. Together they are presented as the great hope in the so-called third technological revolution of 'high tech'. This chapter concentrates on the implications of the development of new reproductive technologies. But it should be borne in mind that in practice these technologies do not simply exist side by side; they are combined in a number of ways. Particularly the combination of genetic engineering and reproductive technology. It is precisely this combination that brings to light their destructive potential.

The discourse on these technologies usually follows the age-old principle of divide and rule: fundamental or 'pure' research is divided from applied research; genetic engineering is divided from reproductive technology; reproductive technology is divided into two — one intended for industrial societies and the other for underdeveloped societies. This separation of spheres and contexts, which essentially are linked, makes a critical assessment of this technological development very difficult.

In the following pages I therefore use the methodological principle of showing the connections and linkages between these technologies, spheres and contexts. Only by such a comprehensive and panoramic view is it possible to surmise whether or not these developments contribute to greater happiness for all peoples. First, a few basic theses:

(1) These technologies have been developed and produced on a mass scale, not to promote human happiness, but to overcome the difficulties faced by the present world system in continuing its

---

* This is a revised version of an article that first appeared in *Alternatives*, XII, 1987.

model of sustained growth, of a lifestyle based on material goods and the accumulation of capital. Since the markets for durable consumer goods are no longer expanding, new needs must be created for the new commodities developed by scientists and industry. The female body's generative capacity has now been discovered as a new 'area of investment' and profit-making for scientists, medical engineers and entrepreneurs in a situation where other areas of investment are no longer very promising.[1] Reproductive technologies have been developed not because *women* need them, but because *capital* and science need women for the continuation of their model of growth and progress.

(2) These technologies are introduced in a situation of social relations between men and women which, throughout the world, are based on exploitation and subordination. It is an historical fact that technological innovations within exploitative and unequal relationships lead to an intensification, not attenuation, of inequality, and to further exploitation of the groups concerned.

(3) These technologies are legitimized on humanitarian grounds by those who try to sell them, for example, to help infertile couples have a child of their own; to help women avoid bearing handicapped children, to minimize the hazards of pregnancy and child-bearing, and so on. The methodological principle is to highlight the plight and unhappiness of a single individual and appeal to the solidarity of all to help that individual. In this all kinds of psychological blackmail are used. The individual cases are only to introduce these technologies and to create the necessary acceptance among *all people;* the aim is total control of all women's reproductive capacity. In this the woman as a person with human dignity is ignored.

(4) It is often argued that these technologies as such are neither good nor bad, and that this can be determined only by their application. This argument is based on the widely-touted proposition that science and technology are value-free and have no bearing on social relations.

A closer analysis carried out by feminists in recent years has, however, revealed that the dominant social relations are also part and parcel of technology itself. We can no longer argue about whether reproductive technology or genetic technology as such are good or bad; the very basic principles of this technology have to be criticized no less than its methods.[2] These are based on exploitation and subordination alike of nature, women and other peoples (colonies).[3] In this context lies the inherent *sexist, racist and ultimately fascist* bias of the new reproductive technologies, a thesis that will be elaborated in the following pages.

Selection and elimination

Reproductive technology and genetic engineering are based on the same principles as physics and other sciences. Like other sciences, they involve the dissection of living organisms into ever smaller particles: molecules, cells, nuclei, genes, DNA and their various recombinations according to the plan of the (male) engineer. In this process *to select desirable* elements and *eliminate undesirable* ones is crucial. In fact, without the principle of selection and elimination, the whole technology of reproduction and genetics would make no sense. What purpose would a study of genetics serve if not to promote the propagation of what are considered to be desirable attributes and the elimination of those seen as undesirable? This applies as much to human genetics as to plant and animal genetics; and applies equally to reproductive technology, which is based on the selection of fertile elements (sperm, ova) and their combination outside the female body. This selection and elimination would not be possible if those living organisms were left intact and free to regulate their reproduction in accordance with their own desires, love and lust.

Carolyn Merchant finds a parallel to the dissection and invasion of nature in the torture of women in the witch pogroms, and shows that both types of violence are intrinsic to the method of modern science and technology.[4] Francis Bacon, founding father of the modern scientific method, perceived nature as a witch whose secrets had to be extracted by force. He wrote:

> For like as a man's disposition is never well known or proved till he be crossed, nor Proteus never changed shapes till he was *straitened* and *held fast,* so nature exhibits herself more clearly under the trials and vexations of art (mechanical devices) than when left to herself. [Emphases in original.][5]

Force and violence constitute the invisible foundation upon which modern science was built. Hence, violence against women in the witch pogroms, and violence against nature which was perceived as a woman.

This whole process of development of 'mechanical devices' and of modern science, however, would not have been possible without applying the same principles of violent subordination and exploitation against the colonies and their people. The people in America, Asia and Africa were treated, like women and nature in Europe, as 'savages'. Without the wealth robbed from the colonies, neither capitalism nor modern European science would have got off the ground between the sixteenth and nineteenth centuries.

It is well-known that at the beginning of the fifteenth century Europe was less developed than China or India. Modern European science owes much to China, India and Arabia, in the fields of medicine, mathematics, chemistry and biology. In India plastic surgery was used long before it was 'discovered' in Europe, and inoculation against smallpox was known and used long before it was 'introduced' by modern medicine men.[6] Similarly, the technologies in agriculture, iron smelting, smithing and in textile production were far in advance of those used in Europe around the fifteenth century.[7]

Not only technological practice but also theories about nature were more sophisticated in China and India than in Europe. Josef Needham has amply proved the excellence of ancient Chinese scientific thought. And about India he writes:

> Indian culture in all probability excelled in systematic thought about nature . . . When the balance comes to be made up, it will be found, I believe, that the Indian scientific history holds as many brilliant surprises as those which have emerged from the recent study of China — whether in mathematics, chemistry or biology and especially the theories which were framed about them.[8]

This shows that it was not, as is often claimed, European 'brain power' that was more advanced than Asian. There must, therefore, have been something else which, at the beginning of the development of modern European science, gave it an advantage over other civilizations. This something was the use of human (male) brain-power for *the arts of destruction and warfare*. Modern mechanics and physics would probably have taken a different course had they not, from their beginning, been closely associated with militarism and the development of arms. This is the secret of the European *Homo faber*, the European model of civilization and progress. European scientists were, from the fifteenth century onwards, 'Fathers of destruction'.[9] To legitimize the development of these arts of destruction, women, nature and the colonies had to be robbed of their 'human' quality, their soul. They became spiritless matter, raw material. The goal of these processes of subordinating nature, women and the colonies and treating them as spiritless and passive matter to be dissected and recombined as the male engineer wishes, was and is the optimization of human labour for the production of material wealth. This goal defines what is valuable and what is not, what should be selected and what eliminated. Thus, white people are considered more valuable than brown and yellow and black peoples; men are considered more valuable than women; owners of means of production are considered more valuable than those who work these means. Everything considered as less valuable was defined as 'nature'; everything that was valued higher was defined as 'human'. And *the* human being par excellence is the white man; he has the right to rule over all 'nature' and to promote his own creation — 'culture'.

Racism, sexism and the Enlightenment

Racism, sexism and fascism are neither ahistorical universal phenomena nor unique, recent developments, but are bound up with the colonial expansion of Europe and the rise of modern science. The distinction between white people as 'human' and blacks and browns as nearer to 'nature', along with the parallel distinction between men and women, found its clearest expression in the age of Enlightenment in the eighteenth and nineteenth centuries, not in the 'dark' Middle Ages. Many philosophers, scientists and politicians have contributed to the ideology of racism and sexism. The celebrated German philosopher Hegel wrote, around 1830, about the blacks:

> As we have said before, the Negro represents natural man in all his savagery and unruliness; if one wants to understand him correctly, one has to abstract from him all human respect and morality. In this character there is nothing that reminds one of the human. This is perfectly corroborated by the extensive reports of the missionaries. Therefore the Negroes get the total *contempt* of human beings. . . [emphasis added].

Hegel then argues that owing to this absence of human values the negro is destined to end up in slavery. Because, according to Hegel, 'it is the basis of slavery that man has not yet acquired an awareness of his freedom and hence is degraded to an object, a valueless thing'. For Hegel, the negro lives outside history and is incapable of development. He writes:

> From all these different features we can conclude that the

main characteristics of the Negro are his savagery and unbridledness. This character is not capable of development and education. As we see them today, so they have always been. The only connection the Negroes have ever had with Europeans and which they still have today is that of slavery.[10]

The distinction between civilized 'culture-peoples' *(Kultur-Volker)* and 'natives', or natural societies, ran like a dark thread through nineteenth-century discourse on colonies. But the Arabian traveller, Ibn Battuta, who, in 1352-53 travelled through Africa, described the natives in the following words:

The Negroes have some admirable qualities. They are hardly found to be unjust, because they abhor injustice more than any other people. Whosoever is found guilty of any small injustice finds no pardon with their Sultan. In their land there is perfect security. Neither travellers nor inhabitants have to be afraid of thieves or of violent men.[11]

As far back as 1352, Ibn Battuta counted the blacks among fellow human beings, whose high moral qualities he admired and respected. Five centuries later, the great modern German philosopher Hegel, regarded them as part and parcel of degraded, savage 'nature'. This is the core of modern racism, which developed with the rise of capitalism and science. The 'humanization' of some categories of people (the European males), their entry into the realm of reason, history and freedom is dialectically based on the 'naturalization' of other categories of people (brown and black races and women), who are now defined as 'savage', that is, purely biological, devoid of reason, ethics and history, and whose existence is bound by endless cycles of biological reproduction.

Not surprisingly, according to Hegel, women also belong to this 'prehistoric' realm, like the 'savage' people. They are bound up with the institution of family, which, for Hegel, constitutes the 'realm of death', that is, the realm of unconscious generative processes. But whereas the black has no ethos whatsoever, the white European woman can enter the realm of morality by being a mother who cares for her children. In her critique of Hegel's understanding of the dialectics of reproduction, Mary O'Brien writes: 'Female morality, like women themselves, remains particular and relates only to the individuals in the family, concentrating on biological life.'[12]

According to the dualistic and patriarchal logic, man, in the process of 'humanization' and 'civilization', emancipated himself from the realm of nature (the 'realm of necessity'), from woman and from savagery. This view was shared by many thinkers, including many socialists, in the nineteenth century. The emancipation and 'humanization' of the working class was also anticipated from the unlimited development of productive forces, which implies man's dominance over nature. Due to this theory also the European working-class movement accepted the division of the world's workers into those belonging to 'civilized nations' and those belonging to 'savage' or 'native' peoples. That was why the Social Democrats in imperial Germany were as little opposed to colonialism as were their British counterparts. For example, Bernstein, an SPD leader, wrote in 1896: 'We shall condemn certain *methods* of subjection of the savages, but not the fact that savages are to be subjected and that the claims of the higher civilizations are upheld against them.'[13] Even after World War I the German Social Democrats insisted on the right of Germany as a 'civilized nation' *(Kulturnation)* to own and exploit the territories of 'barbarian peoples' as colonies.[14]

The core of these arguments is the correct insight that the proletarian masses in the industrialized nations would not be able to rise to a higher standard of living or to a higher cultural level unless these nations could freely exploit the 'native people's' territories in search of raw material, cheap labour and promising markets.

Eugenics

Whereas in the first half of the nineteenth century sexist and racist ideology was encapsulated in the idealistic philosophical discourse on the dualism of 'nature' and 'culture', in the second half of the century it acquired a materialistic 'scientific' foundation. In this process Darwin's theory of evolution played a decisive role, particularly in the form of Social Darwinism developed by Spencer, which posited that 'survival of the fittest' was the selective mechanism by which 'superior' societies evolved from lower ones. The backwardness of the peoples in the colonies was now attributed to their being on a lower stage in the evolutionary process. At the pinnacle were the Anglo-Saxons or the Nordic race.

Such ideas gave rise to the *eugenic movement* started by Francis Galton, a cousin of Darwin, who coined the term 'eugenics' in 1883. Galton combined the ideas of Darwin with those of Malthus and advocated 'selective breeding' in order to prevent the deterioration of the race. The 'fit' were to be encouraged to breed more and the 'unfit' to breed less. Fitness and unfitness, however, were defined by the values of the English middle class. Galton was interested not only in the genetic *quality* of people, he was also a promoter of statistics in social research and introduced the grading system to measure people's genetic quality. By applying statistical methods to eugenics he gave 'scientific' legitimacy to his theories, because mathematical procedures and statistics were considered proof of scientific objectivity. Galton graded blacks two grades below whites in intelligence.

The eugenic movement had a great influence on social science, on psychology with its intelligence tests, on behaviourism and on politics. The movement gained momentum at the beginning of the twentieth century in Britain and the USA, particularly after the biological laws of heredity, first discovered by Gregor Mendel in 1865, were posthumously published in 1901. Charles B. Davenport, the main promoter of the eugenics movement in the USA, persuaded the powerful Carnegie Foundation and other wealthy families in the USA to support the eugenics movement. In 1904, the Laboratory for Experimental Evolution was founded at Cold Spring Harbor; in 1907, came the Eugenics Records Office. The aim of these institutions and the eugenicists who worked there was to make inventories of the racial qualities of peoples and to increase the reproduction of superior races as well as to reduce the breeding of inferior ones. In the climate prevailing in the USA before and after World War I positive eugenics meant faster reproduction of the white Anglo-Saxons or, at least, the Nordic race; negative eugenics meant a reduction in reproduction of the 'inferior' races, mainly of blacks and immigrants. These blatantly racist theories were supported by a host of scientists who demanded political action.

Eugenicists considered a whole range of human traits as hereditary, for example, intelligence, cleanliness, alcoholism, social behaviour, poverty. They demanded that the state should take action, like a good cattle breeder who selects those fit for reproduction and eliminates those he considers unfit. 'There are fig and thistles, grapes and thorns, wheat and tares in human society, and the state must practice family culture', wrote Whitney in 1934.[15]

The followers of the eugenics movement were to be found among ultra rightists as well as among socialists such as the Fabians. Even feminists, for example, Margaret Sanger, Stella

Browne and Eleanor Rathbone, supported the eugenics movement. Margaret Sanger advocated the combination of birth control with eugenic considerations. She wrote: 'More children from the fit, less from the unfit is the chief issue of birth control.'[16]

It was not surprising that eugenicists applauded Hitler when he passed a compulsory sterilization law in 1933, known as the Law on the Prevention of Hereditary Diseases in Future Generations. The British *Eugenics Review* hailed Hitler's Germany as a vast laboratory which was the scene of a 'gigantic eugenic experiment'. It observed that: 'It would be quite wrong and quite unscientific to decry everything that is going on in that country. . . In Germany the most advanced eugenics legislation is carried through without difficulty.'[17] Whitney praised Hitler's eugenic policy:

> Though not all of us, probably, will approve of the compulsory character of this law — as it applies, for instance to the sterilization of drunkards — we cannot but admire the foresight revealed by the plan in general, and realize that by this action Germany is going to make herself a stronger nation.[18]

The atrocities perpetrated by the Nazis on people who were considered 'unfit', particularly the Jews, but also the gypsies and the handicapped, brought the eugenics movement into disrepute after the collapse of the Third Reich. But many lieutenants of this movement entered the new field of population control and family planning after World War II. They now apply the eugenic principle of selection and elimination to the world population as a whole. The whites in Europe and the USA are encouraged to breed more, and the blacks and browns in the underdeveloped world are put under heavy pressure to diminish their population — if necessary, by compulsory sterilization campaigns. Professor Hans Harmsen, whose name has been associated with the compulsory sterilization of handicapped people in Nazi Germany, joined the population control establishment after the war and founded the German branch of the International Planned Parenthood Federation (IPPF), naming it 'Pro Familia'. He was president of this institution for a long time, and played an important role in shaping population control policies for the Third World.[19]

It was easy to denounce the genocide in Hitler's Germany as 'fascist', but few people can discern the genocide that stalks under the banner of eugenics; and fewer are prepared to decry it as fascist. There is, however, an historical continuity from the eugenics movement, via Nazi Germany, to the new reproductive technologies: prenatal diagnosis, genetic engineering, in vitro fertilization and suchlike. The promoters and practitioners of these technologies turn a blind eye to this historical heritage.

Sociobiology

The link between the old eugenics movement and the new genetic and reproduction technologies is provided by sociobiology. Its main spokesman, Edward Wilson, Harvard biologist, tries to combine biology with anthropology and behaviourism in order to prove that such human characteristics as, for instance, the sexual division of labour, the nuclear family, aggression and social inequality are hereditary because they have sprung from the genetic infrastructure of our primate ancestors.

Whereas the eugenics movement was aimed at the newly awakened workers and colonized peoples in the early twentieth century, sociobiology legitimizes modern wars as rooted in the 'genetically more aggressive male'. It is also directed against the new women's movement which wants to end male supremacy. Wilson projects the American nuclear family into the Stone Age cave, where, as Barbara Chasin observes, 'the man was the active, aggressive, subsistence-providing person, while the little woman cleaned the cave, cooked the mastodon and reared the kiddies'.[20]

Sociobiology arose in the USA when the government and the ruling classes were no longer willing to support welfare programmes and other ameliorative measures to help the disadvantaged. Social inequality was therefore explained as biologically determined, a matter of genes. Wilson and other sociobiologists have gone so far as to explain even socially and historically created institutions and customs (ethical rules, world-views, division of labour, form of government, marriage rules, religious convictions, and so on) in terms of inherited traits.[21] Sexual inequality was, of course, explained by biology.[22]

The amorality of biotechnology

Modern biological research, particularly genetic engineering and reproduction technology, has given rise to a new questioning of the ethical foundations of these technologies. These ethical questions, however, cannot be separated from the historical background noted above, from a concept of man and nature which implies that man's morality, his freedom and his subjectivity are based on his emancipation from nature. The human being is conceived of, not as part of nature, but as nature's master and lord. This lordship is justified by his rationality and his brainpower. Therefore the 'head' is considered superior to the 'lower' parts of the body, the man superior to the woman, culture superior to nature.

Rather than break with this model, biotechnology develops it further. Whereas formerly the 'head's' control over the body implied the control of a whole person, biotechnology now eliminates the human person as such. For biotechnologists, human beings are just heaps of organic matter, DNA, raw material, which can be dissected and reassembled into new bio-machines. Morality has no place in their laboratories. But, this absence of morality constitutes the innermost essence of modern science. Science is supposed to be value-free, motivated only by the 'pure' quest for knowledge, not by interest or ambition. Due to this concept of science, the question of ethics arises only outside the laboratory, when it comes to the question of whether or not the fabrications of the biotechnologists should be applied on a large scale. Ethics committees are set up only after the scientists have had ample time and money to experiment and publicize their results. Such reactive ethics, however, which can only try to prevent the most dangerous abuses of these inventions, is not only impotent, but is no ethics at all, since the main task of these committees is to promote the acceptability of these technologies.

As these 'ethical experts' usually accept the dominant scientific paradigm and its claim to value-freedom, they have no criteria for judging what is beneficial for humanity and what is not. As they have never dared to consider ethical aspects *before and within* the research process itself, they can no longer look at the scientific process as part of a comprehensive, all-embracing life process. Science is no longer seen as part of the human and natural universe, but as above it. Therefore, biotechnology as part of modern science and technology is amoral in its essence. This lack of ethics is most clearly manifested when we look more closely at the development of reproductive technology, because here women are the main source of 'organic matter', as well as the targets of man's control over nature.

Sexist and racist implications

Gena Corea gives abundant evidence of the absence of ethical considerations in, and the continuity between, the eugenics movement and today's genetic and reproductive technology. She quotes the Marxist geneticist Muller, who won a Nobel prize for his work on the effect of nuclear radiation on genes. Muller said that infertility, which seemed to be on the increase, provided an:

> excellent opportunity for the entering wedge of positive selection, since couples concerned are nearly always, under such circumstances, open to suggestion that they turn their exigency to their credit by having as well-endowed children as possible.[23]But the difference between Muller (who dreamt of breeding more men like Lenin, Newton, Leonardo da Vinci, Pasteur, Beethoven, Omar Khayyam, Pushkin, Sun Yat-Sen and Marx) and the old eugenicists is that for the former it is no longer necessary to have control over whole men and whole women and make them copulate in order to give birth to these supermen. Genetic research has advanced so far that it is possible now to use the donor sperm of geniuses to fertilize women, if the women also possess superior quality eggs.

A further step in the application of the principle of selection and elimination came with the perfection of the various methods of prenatal diagnosis and quality control and with the technology of in vitro fertilization (IVF). It is possible today not only to isolate and select ova and sperm according to certain quality standards, but also to isolate the genes, to cut up the DNA, to examine which of the chromosomes are defective, to recombine and manipulate pieces of the DNA, and thus to directly influence the genetic substance. Geneticists are busy everywhere mapping the genetic pool of humans, animals and plants in order to discover so-far-unknown genetic 'defects'. I should not be surprised if, in the near future, a whole new range of diseases were to be declared. The ideology of both eugenics and sociobiology will provide the criteria for what will be understood as 'healthy' and what as 'defective'. These new hereditary diseases will provide a large market for gene therapy and prenatal diagnosis. The aim of this whole enterprise is to adapt the human being to survive the destructions which *Homo faber* and technological progress have wrought on the environment.

Sexism

Sexist biases permeate the new reproductive technologies and genetic engineering at all levels. In general they imply that motherhood, the capacity of women to bring forth children, is transformed from a creative process, in which woman co-operated with her body as an active human being, to an industrial production process. In this process, not only is the symbiosis of mother and child disrupted, but the whole process is rationalized, objectified, planned and controlled by medical experts. More than ever before the woman is objectified and made passive. Under patriarchy she has always been an object for male subjects, but in the new reproductive technologies she is no longer one whole object but a series of objects which can be isolated, examined, recombined, sold, hired, or simply thrown away, like ova which are not used for experimentation or fertilization. This means that the integrity of the woman as a human person, an individual, as an integral indivisible being, is destroyed. It is the ideology of man's dominance over nature and woman, combined with the scientific method of analysis and synthesis that has led to the destruction of the woman as a human person and to her vivisection into a mass of reproductive matter. (See chapter 13).

For *women* these developments mean, above all, that their reproductive capacity will be placed under a rigid and constant quality control. Today the social pressure on pregnant women to produce perfect children is already enormous and will grow. In the industrialized countries women are already subjected to a whole series of pregnancy tests. If they are over 30 or 35 they are seen as 'risk-pregnancies', and pressured to undergo amniocentesis in order to avoid bearing a handicapped child.

In countries like India and China, amniocentesis, used as a sex-determination test, has led to large-scale abortions of female foetuses. Vimal Balasubrahmaniam has observed that this femicidal tendency, made possible by modern technology, was first propagated by some Western promoters of population control. 'Breeding male' was seen as the best remedy against the 'population explosion'.[24]

Apart from total quality control, the new reproductive technologies will mean for most women a loss of confidence in their own bodies and in their child-bearing competence. Already most young women are afraid to have babies without constant monitoring by a doctor. Most children are born in clinics. The new reproductive technologies, advertised as a means to widen women's choice, will greatly enhance women's fears. Women will eventually become totally passive, abandoning themselves to medical experts who know everything about them and the child inside them.

Reproduction engineers' propaganda clearly aims to devalue children born of women as 'inferior products'. Some French technodocs boasted of their IVF-babies being superior to *'les enfants banales'*, conceived and born 'wildly', that is, not produced scientifically under constant medical control. The difference between *'les enfants banales'* and the IVF-babies is seen as the difference between a creation of nature and an industrial product. It is not surprising that the new reproductive technologies are propagated in some countries, for example, in France, as a method of rationalizing reproduction, following rationalization of production through technological progress. The reproductive processes in women have therefore to be brought under the control of scientists and, eventually, of the state.[25]

The anti-women tendencies of the new reproductive technology are to be seen, not only in their potential for total social control of women, but also in their aggressive, invasive nature. The IVF programme starts with long-term fertility monitoring and hormonal treatment, the long-term effects of which are not known. Once the eggs are ripe, incisions are made into the woman's abdomen to remove them with the help of a laparoscope. This operation takes place under general anaesthesia while the woman's belly is blown-up by carbon dioxide. The transfer back of the fertilized egg into the woman's uterus is also invasive. She must again undergo hormonal treatment to prepare the uterus for the implantation and the growing of the embryo; subsequently she must undergo frequent ultrasound monitoring and amniocentesis.[26]

These physical invasions generate anxieties and traumas. Gena Corea describes the ups and downs of hope and despair of women at each stage of the IVF treatment.[27] The woman in these programmes is made a totally passive object, therefore the IVF procedures are not only painful and traumatic but also humiliating and degrading. In a study conducted among IVF patients in Australia, Barbara Burton found that many women complained that the whole process was very alienating. Doctors had no time to explain anything, particularly when there were failures. One woman said;

'The treatment is degrading. You have to give up your pride when you enter the hospital . . . You feel like a piece of flesh in a flesh factory. But when you want a child by all means you do it.'[28]

There is a rapid spread of IVF clinics in many countries. Research in this field is advancing by leaps and bounds; natural processes of giving birth are increasingly manipulated. It is reported that 60 per cent of deliveries in the clinics of Sao Paulo were by caesarean section; the doctors had persuaded the women that it was better for them because this would leave their vaginas 'attractive' for their men. If these women are later unable to have children the natural way, an IVF clinic is ready at hand. One of the IVF celebrities, Dr Nakamura of Sao Paulo, runs not only an IVF clinic, but also a family planning clinic. He has even conducted an IVF operation live on television. The patient unfortunately died, but Dr Nakamura did her the honour of naming his clinic after her.[29]

From fertility as a 'disease' to sterility as a 'disease'

To discover how medical experts obtained such sweeping control over women's reproductive capacities, we must recall the contraceptive movement of the past few decades. Long before sterility was so defined by the WHO, fertility had been treated as a disease, not only by the pharmaceutical firms which wanted to sell their contraceptives and by the medical establishment which had an obvious interest in defining women's fertility as a disease, but also by women themselves who had become 'sick of their fertility', as one woman put it at the 1985 Emergency Conference on Reproductive Technology in Sweden. Women's emancipation had for a long time been identified by many with women's control over their fertility. The invention of various contraceptives, particularly the pill, was hailed by many as the decisive technological innovation that would eventually liberate women from their unruly fertility. Yet, by looking at fertility as a disease, as a purely biological affair, women handed the responsibility for their generative powers to medical experts and scientists. Instead of changing the unequal sexual relationship between men and women, hopes of women's emancipation were pinned on technological innovation and medical treatment. This is also, basically, the approach of Shulamith Firestone, who considers woman's biology her greatest obstacle. She expects women's liberation to emerge from the artificial womb, the final rationalization of reproductive behaviour.

In the course of time many women actually became sick, but

not of their fertility; they fell sick by fighting fertility with contraceptives. It is well known that the sterility about which many women complain today is partly a result of invasive methods of contraception, for example, the Dalkon Shield and various other IUDs, and callous treatment by doctors.[30]

By perceiving fertility and sterility as 'diseases' it becomes impossible to see them as socially and historically influenced phenomena. They are defined as purely biological categories within the exclusive purview of medical experts. This precludes the possibility of women and men beginning to understand that they themselves have a responsibility for being fertile or sterile and that their generative power has something to do with the overall social and ecological climate in which they live. Any movement against the sexism inherent in the new reproductive technologies must start with the recognition that fertility or sterility are not just biological conditions and 'diseases' but socially determined. The definition of sterility and fertility as diseases is backed by the WHO. The WHO is thus persuading women worldwide to deliver themselves into the hands of powerful interests — the medical technologists and the pharmaceutical multinationals.

Racism: population control and reproductive technology in the Third World

The eugenic principle of selection and elimination manifests itself most clearly on a world scale, if we look not only at technologies aimed at sterility 'as a disease', but also at those which are meant to fight fertility 'on a war footing'. The target population for the latter are mainly the rural and urban poor in the underdeveloped countries. Whereas some women should produce children at any cost, others are prevented from so doing by all possible means. The myth of overpopulation in the poor countries serves as justification for the development of ever more anti-fertility technology.

The old Malthusian logic that development efforts are of no avail because the poor breed too many poor, today underpins the most widespread myth in the world. It had meanwhile been accepted as a fact not only by Western governments but also by Third World governments. Private corporate interests in the USA first convinced the US government, then the UN and the World Bank, and finally the dependent governments in the Third World countries to accept this myth,[31] and to legitimize intervention in the reproductive behaviour in virtually all countries in Africa, Asia and Latin America.[32] Fear of the 'population explosion' of black and brown people is so widespread today in the white world that population planners can disregard any ethical considerations when designing measures against the 'wild fertility' of the browns and blacks.The double-faced policy of selection and elimination is obvious if one looks into the fate of the 'basic right' to have a child of one's own (a 'right' so often highlighted to legitimize the use of new reproductive technology in the North) at the hands of population planners in such countries as Bangladesh, India, Thailand, Egypt, for example.

Farida Akhter has rightly pointed out that notions such as 'reproductive rights' for women, propagated by feminist groups in the West, have no meaning for the majority of women in Bangladesh who are covered by population control measures. Under relentless pressure of sheer survival needs, women in these countries may trade their fertility for some money and a sari, by joining a sterilization camp to undergo tubectomy. The contraceptive technology developed for these women increasingly reduces all elements of individual choice, and places more and more control over them in the hands of medical experts and health personnel; and the women are increasingly subjugated through political, economic and cultural coercion. 'Nowhere do the rights of women become any [one's] concern', says Farida Akhter.[33]

The blatant disregard for human rights and dignity inherent in population control technology can be demonstrated in a number of instances. Some of the more prominent ones are discussed below.

While in the 1960s and early 1970s the international population establishment still believed in educating and motivating people to accept contraceptives, from 1975 onwards coercive methods and a tendency towards such 'final solutions' as sterilization were increasingly accepted. India carried out a massive sterilization campaign during the Emergency from 1975-77, in the course of which millions of people were forcibly sterilized. This compulsory sterilization campaign aroused no resentment or protest in the West; nor does the Chinese population policy with its coercive methods, leading to female infanticide and foeticide, cause a stir. The attitude of many in the West today is the same as that of the US and British eugenicists towards Hitler's eugenic laws: they abhor compulsion, but see no alternative to arresting the 'reckless breeding' of 'those' people.

This double-faced stand with regard to human rights and dignity seeks justification on the grounds that the 'population explosion' has created a crisis situation and must be dealt with on a 'war footing' with crash programmes and methods of crisis management. This method is propagated today by USAID which thinks the multi-sectoral strategy of integrating family planning into development policies and health sectors is too time-consuming and does not yield direct results. In this strategy the fertility of — particularly poor — Asian, African and Latin American women is no longer seen as a 'disease', 'curable' by pills and IUDs, but as an *epidemic*, like cholera, malaria or smallpox.

The conceptualization of Third World women's fertility as an epidemic means that the *state* must intervene in people's reproductive behaviour. In most Third World countries population control — formerly called family planning — has become the state's concern. This state intervention began under the pressure of the 'international state' — the aid-giving agencies and credit-giving organizations such as the World Bank, which linked their economic measures and credits to population control. The state increasingly opted for final solutions; and increasingly women became the main targets of these solutions. While in India, in the years 1975-76, 75 per cent of the sterilizations were performed on men, in 1983-84, 85 per cent were performed on women.[34] In Bangladesh, among all contraceptive measures, the proportion of sterilizations went up from 19 per cent in 1979-80 to 39 per cent in 1983-84, and to 43 per cent in 1984-85.[35]

The trend towards enforcing final solutions is aimed particularly at women. This is borne out by the fact that, in Bangladesh, food-aid earmarked for distribution among the most distressed women is used to blackmail them into accepting sterilization in exchange for a few kilograms of wheat. Thus, the Vulnerable Group Feeding Programme (VGF) has been used to force the poorest women to be sterilized. The family planning authorities issue certificates to women who undergo sterilization, on which it is written: 'She can be given food under government relief.' Without such a certificate a woman gets none. Old women, women already sterilized, and widows are not entitled to food relief.[36]

Third World women as guinea-pigs

The strategy of fighting against poor Third World women's fertility 'on a war footing' ignores the long-term side-effects of contraceptive technology on women's health. Poor Third World women are treated not as persons but as numerical entities in demographic statistics. All that counts is a fall in the fertility rate,

irrespective of the effects on women. Many Third World governments are put under pressure by credit-giving agencies to perform
in the field of population control. The governments use the same
pressure tactics to get their functionaries to fulfil their 'targets' of
IUD-insertions, sterilizations, and so on. And for their part, the
functionaries often use direct coercion to bring people into the
family planning camps. Demographers like S. P. Jain admit that
the IUD programme in India was formulated under foreign pressure, that there was no consideration of the effects on women, and
that use of the loop was stopped only when it was found that a
large percentage of women suffered side-effects.[37]

Thus in this case, as in many others, Third World women
were used as guinea-pigs by multinational drug industries. It is
cheaper, faster and politically more convenient to use a crash
programme against fertility to discover long-term effects of a
contraceptive than it is to run clinical tests on samples of
women in the West. In this sense, a number of Third World
countries have been turned into human laboratories for transnational drug industries.

Moreover, contraceptives which are not yet licensed for use in
family planning programmes in the West, are being tested predominantly on Third World women; for example, the injectible
contraceptives (ICs). After Depoprovera was banned in the USA
because of its carcinogenic potential and other long-term effects,
the new IC which is now propagated is NET-OEN
(norethisterone-oenanthate), produced by German Remedies, a
subsidiary of the Schering Company of West Berlin. NET-OEN, a
synthetic hormone, is administered by intramuscular injection; its
contraceptive effect lasts for two to three months.[38]

NET-OEN is at present being tried out in India. The tests were
initiated in 1984 by family planning camps. Only after feminist
groups in India began to protest did the public become aware of
the methods used in these tests. These groups found that the
principle of informed consent was not followed when NET-OEN
was administered and the women were not informed that there
might be dangerous side-effects. A petition has been filed by
women's organizations in the Supreme Court of India pleading
that the tests of NET-OEN on several thousands of Indian women
are unethical and unsafe and should be stopped immediately.

Sponsored by the WHO, the test programme is administered by
the Indian Council of Medical Research, through the family planning and primary health centres. It was also found that the field

tests of NET-OEN were part of the national programme for research in human reproduction which is under way in a number of research centres in India and which uses a standardized uniform methodology in a multicentre clinical approach.[39] This gives the impression of a responsible and rigorously scientific approach. But it mystifies the health hazards for women and masks the racism inherent in these tests. The health hazards pointed out by the women's groups are: breast cancer; two types of uterine cancer; serious menstrual disturbances; and masculinization of female foetuses.[40]

Long-acting hormonal injectible contraceptives have been especially invented for illiterate Third World women, who, according to the understanding of the population planners, are incapable of exercising any rational control over their reproductive functions. This is clearly spelt out by the propagators of these ICs. They say that Third World women want injections, because they are accustomed to having injections whenever they are sick. Here, the method of treating Third World people as dumb creatures who need not be informed about their diseases but who only receive quick injections shows its results. Women now want injections against fertility as well. Injections are also seen as the most convenient means for the family planning personnel: with these, there is no need to educate, to persuade the people! Other methods, such as IUDs and the pill are regarded as 'more than underprivileged, undernourished, overworked women can handle'.[41] So ICs, like Depoprovera, NET-OEN, or the contraceptive Norplant (which is implanted under the skin and diffuses a steroid, levonorgestrel, over a period of five years), are specifically invented for this category of women.

Breeding male, or patriarchy as business

Sexist and racist aspects are most closely interwoven in prenatal diagnostic technology. As already mentioned, amniocentesis, first developed to discover genetic abnormalities in the foetus, is now widely used in India as a sex determination test. As female children are unwanted in India, particularly because of the high marriage /dowry demands this modern technology is used to strengthen patriarchal attitudes and institutions. When the amniocentesis test shows that the foetus is female, most women have it aborted. In spite of feminist groups' protest, this femicidal practice is spreading not only in absolute numbers but also geographically to the rural areas, and to the poorer classes; as the test costs only around Rs. 500, even working-class people can afford it.[42] It is often practised because the women, who may already have given birth to one or several daughters, are afraid to face their husbands and family with yet another one. Achin Vanaik writes:

> Almost 100% of the 51,914 abortions during 1984-85 carried out by a well-known abortion centre in Bombay were done after sex determination tests. There are now S.D. clinics in almost every medium-sized town in Maharashtra.[43]

The rapid spread of amniocentesis for sex determination and the abortion of female foetuses has given rise to a strong wave of protest by Indian feminists. Yet, while the feminist groups were still campaigning for a ban on sex determination tests, other more sophisticated methods to determine the sex of a child were already being practised in Bombay. Doctors in the private Citi Clinic in Bombay practice a pre-conception sex-selection technology, based on sperm, or rather chromosome separation by albumin filtration and artificial insemination. This technology, developed by the American, Dr Ericsson, in 1984 is used to select male-bearing sperm. By this filter method, the sperm containing Y-chromosomes, which are the male sex determinants is separated from the X-chromosome sperm, and concentrated. Doctors are able to select sperm containing 80 per cent of Y-chromosomes which is then injected into the woman, who must be prepared for this procedure in a similar way to women who undergo an IVF-programme. In an interview I was told that the success rate, that is, the birth of a boy, is about 80 per cent. The private clinic in Bombay is one of the 48 centres Dr Ericsson has meanwhile established all over the world as branches of the company GAMETRICS Ltd, which he founded and which sells the fluid albumin to these centres. Several of these centres are in Third World countries which have a strong preference for male offspring. The doctor who practises this technology in Bombay claims that it is more scientific and ethically more acceptable than amniocentesis and female foeticide. If one looks only at the technology as such, one can only agree with this doctor. All is very clean, very scientific, and it means business. But it will render women more than ever an 'endangered species', as Vibhuti Patel puts it, in countries with a strong patriarchal preference for boys. GAMETRICS can be sure of a bright future in such countries.

This example shows clearly that sexist and racist ideology is closely interwoven with capitalist profit motives, that the logic of selection and elimination has a definite economic base. Patriarchy and racism are not only ethically rejectable ideologies, they mean business indeed.

Conclusion

The development of reproductive technology, both for increasing and decreasing fertility, took place in an ideological climate which makes a sharp distinction between man and nature, culture and nature; and nature is something that must be conquered by White Man. The main method of conquest and control is predicated on the principle of selection and elimination, which principle permeates all reproductive technologies. Without selection and elimination, this technology would be quite different, hence, it cannot claim to be neutral; nor is it free from the sexist, racist and ultimately fascist biases in our societies. These biases are built into the technology itself, they are not merely a matter of its application. Apart from this, an historical continuity of these principles can be traced from the nineteenth century eugenics movement, to the fascist race politics of the Nazis, to the present day genetic, reproduction and population control technologies. It is a continuity which is not confined to ideas and research methods alone, but involves people also.

Notes

1. Mies, Maria 'Why Do We Need All This? A Call Against Genetic Engineering and Reproductive Technology', *Women's Studies International Forum*, Vol. 8, No. 6, 1985.
2. Ibid. See also Carolyn Merchant, *The Death of Nature: Women, Ecology and the Scientific Revolution*. San Francisco, Harper & Row, 1983.
3. Mies, Maria *Patriarchy and Accumulation on a World Scale: Women in the International Division of Labour*. London, Zed Books, 1986.
4. Merchant, op. cit.
5. Bacon, *Works*, Vol. 4, p. 263, quoted in Merchant op. cit., p. 169.
6. Alvares, Claude, *Homo Faber: Technology and Culture in India, China and the West 1500-1972*. New Delhi, Allied Publishers. 1979, Ch. 2. pp. 46-74.
7. Ibid.
8. Ibid., pp. 69-70.
9. Easlea, Brian *Fathering the Unthinkable: Masculinity, Scientists and the Nuclear Arms Race*. London, Pluto Press, 1986.
10. Hegel, Georg Wilhelm Friedrich *Vorlesungen uber die Philosophie der Geschichte*. Frankfurt, Suhrkamp, 1970, p. 122, trans. Maria Mies.

11. Quoted in: Bodo V. Borries, *Kolonialgeschichte und Weltwirtschaftssystem.* Dusseldorf, Schwaan Verlag, 1986, p. 83.
12. O'Brien, Mary *The Politics of Reproduction.* Boston, London, Henley-on-Thames, Routledge and Kegan Paul, 1983, p. 26.
13. Quoted in: Martha Mamozai, *Herrenmenschen, Frauen im deutschen Kolonialismus.* Rororo, Reinbek, 1982, p. 212, trans. Maria Mies.
14. Mandelbaum, Kurt 'Sozialdemokratie und Imperialismus', in: K. Mandelbaum (editor), *Sozialdemokratie und Leninismus, Zwei Aufsätze.* Berlin, Wagenbach, 1974.
15. Quoted in Gena Corea, *The Mother Machine: Reproductive Technologies from Artificial Insemination to Artificial Wombs.* New York, Harper and Row, 1985, p. 18.
16. Sanger, Margaret, *Birth Control Review,* May 1919.
17. Quoted in: Bonnie Mass, *Population Target: The Political Economy of Population Control in Latin America.* Toronto, Women's Press, 1976, p. 21.
18. Corea, Gena 'Was der Konig nicht sieht...', in: *Dokumentation Frauenfragen 1985.* Fachhochschule Koln, FB Sozialpädagogik, 1986.
19. Kaupen-Haas, Heidrun 'Eine Deutsche Biographie — Der Bevölkerungspolitiker Hans Harmsen', in: A. Ebbinghaus, H. Kaupen Haas, K. H. Roth (editors), *Heilen und Vernichten im Mustergau Hamburg.* Hamburg, Konkret Literatur Verlag, 1984.
20. Chasin, Barbara 'Sociobiology, a Pseudo-Scientific Synthesis', in: Arditti et al. (eds), *Science and Liberation.* Boston, South End Press, 1980, p. 35.
21. O. Wilson, Edward *On Human Nature.* Cambridge, London, Harvard University Press, 1978.
22. Chasin, op.cit., pp. 41-5.
23. Muller, H. J. 'The Guidance of Human Evolution', *Perspectives in Biology and Medicine,* Vol. III, No. 1, 1959.
24. Balasubrahmaniam, Vimal 'Medicine and the Male Utopia', *Economic and Political Weekly,* 23 October, 1982.
25. Gavarini, Laurence *'L'uterus sous influence ou la Mere Machine',* paper presented at the colloquium: Feminisme et Maternite, Paris, 7-8 January, 1984.
26. Duelli-Klein, Renate 'Könige, Königsklone und Prinzessinnen: Neuigkeiten aus der Retortenwelt', in: *Dokumentation Frauenfragen 1985.* Fachhochschule Koln, FB Sozialpädagogik, 1986.
27. Corea, op. cit.
28. Ibid, p. 26.
29. Regina, Ana Dos Gomes Reis, 'IVF in Brasil: The Story Told by the Newspapers', paper presented at FINRRAGE Emergency Conference on Reproductive Technology, Vallinge, Sweden, 3-5 July, 1985.
30. Klein, Renate, (ed.), *Infertility, Women Speak Out About their Experiences of Reproductive Medicine.* London, Pandora Press, 1989.
31. Mass, op. cit.
32. Akhter, Farida 'Depopulating Bangladesh: A Brief History of the External Intervention into the Reproductive Behaviour of a Society'. UBINIG, Dacca, 1986.
33. Ibid.
34. Daswanit, Mona 'Women and Reproductive Technology in India: The Injectable Menace', paper presented at the Congress of Women against Reproductive and Genetic Technology, Bonn, 19-21 April, 1985.
35. Akhter, op. cit., p. 21.

36. Akhter, Farida 'Wheat for Statistics: A Case Study of Use of VGF Wheat for Attaining Sterilization Target', unpublished paper, Dhaka, 1985.
37. Daswani op. cit.
38. *War on Want: Norethisterone Oenanthate, The OTHER Injectible Contraceptive*, Briefing Paper. London, War on Want, 1984.
39. *Eve's Weekly*, Bombay, 5 July 1986.
40. 'Ban Injectable Contraceptives', Leaflet, Bombay: Women's Centre Bombay, 1985. The case on NET-OEN is even now (1992) pending in court. According to Indian health activists it will never be brought to India, but meanwhile Norplant, another long-acting hormonal contraceptive has been introduced.
41. Kapil, Iris 'Case for Injectible Contraceptives', *Economic and Political Weekly*, 11 May 1985, p. 855.
42. Patel, Vibhuti 'Amniocentesis — An Abuse of Advanced Scientific Technique', paper presented at XI World Congress of Sociology, 18-22 August, 1986, New Delhi.
43. Achin Vanaik, *Times of India*, 20 June 1986.

13. From the Individual to the Dividual: the Supermarket of 'Reproductive Alternatives'*

Maria Mies

From 'Helping the infertile woman' to 'Reproductive alternatives'

Most discussions about 'benefits and risks' of the new Reproductive Technologies (nRTs) are based on the either tacit or explicit assumption that these technologies were developed in order to help individual infertile women and men to have a 'child from their own flesh and blood'. Yet, as far back as the 1985 congress in Bonn, 'Women against Reproductive and Genetic Engineering', the participants concluded that the objective of the nRTs was not to help infertile individuals but, rather, to promote a new reproduction industry with the aim of overcoming the 'growth' problems of industrial capitalism. As the old growth areas like steel, coal for example, are stagnating or declining, the female body with its generative power has been discovered as a new 'area of investment.'

This conclusion — perhaps speculative in 1985 — has already been confirmed by reality. This became clear to me after I read the papers from the project 'Reproductive Laws for the 1990s' (1987) carried out under the directorship of Nadine Taub and Carol Smith at Rutgers State University, New Jersey, USA. Lori B. Andrews' contribution: 'Feminist Perspectives on Reproductive Technologies' is part of this work. Lori B. Andrews is part of the Working Group for the Rutgers Project.[1] She is also associated with the American Bar Foundation and was the only woman on the Ethics Committee of the American Fertility Society, the professional association of about 10,000 American fertility 'specialists' and lay people. In 1986 this Committee had proposed a number of legal changes which would do away with most legal barriers

* First published in: ISSUES *Reproductive and Genetic Engineering*, Vol. 1, No. 3, 1988.

which still stand in the way of a fully-fledged 'free' reproduction industry (The Ethics Committee of the AFS, 1986).

In the following, my arguments are directed mainly at two works by Lori B. Andrews: (1) her paper 'Feminist Perspectives on New Reproductive Technologies' and (2) *The Hastings Center Report:* 'My Body, My Property.'[2] I also refer to some of the other papers presented in the Briefing Handbook *Reproductive Laws for the 1990s* of the Rutgers Project which was distributed in 1987.

Reading Andrews' papers, but also the Briefing Handbook Reproductive Laws in the 1990s I was immediately struck by the new terminology in which the discourse is conducted. The 'infertile woman' or 'couple' of earlier years, for whom reproductive technology was supposedly invented, is hardly mentioned in these texts. Instead, the new key terms — used particularly frequently by Andrews — are 'reproductive alternatives', 'reproductive options', 'reproductive choice', 'reproductive autonomy', and 'reproductive rights'. Andrews bases this 'free choice of reproductive alternatives' on the autonomy and privacy of reproductive decisions protected by the US Constitution, which according to her, constitute the 'right to abortion'.[3]

> . . . the constitutional underpinnings for reproductive choice regarding abortion and contraception also protect autonomy in the use of artificial insemination, embryo donation, surrogacy and so forth.

Put differently, the arguments by which some American feminists demanded a 'right to abortion' are now also used to legitimize 'alternative reproductive choices'. Andrews not only claims that there is a 'fundamental right' to a child from one's own flesh and blood, but now the various technologically produced reproductive options appear as part and parcel of the basic human rights, protected by the American Constitution. She quotes Norma Wikler who said that:

> The danger to the feminist program, of course, is that once the right to privacy in reproductive decision-making loses its status as a natural or constitutional right, women risk losing choices that they now have.[4]

This means that a new reproductive supermarket has opened up: Take your choice! Anything goes!

The concepts 'reproductive choice', 'reproductive alternatives' are also used by the other scholars in the Rutgers Project. These 'reproductive alternatives' not only comprise the various technologies necessary to produce a child *in vitro* for infertile couples, but they also include the 'right' to carry a 'normal' pregnancy to term. In other words, natural pregnancy and childbirth are put on an equal footing with a number of other 'reproductive alternatives'. What unites them is that they are all dependent on medical experts and on reproductive technology. Nancy Gertner — another member of the Rutgers Working Group — defines the concept 'reproductive choice' in the following way.

Reproductive choice shall be defined as:

1. an individual's choice to exercise her constitutional right to the performance of an abortion to the extent protected by state and federal constitutional law;

2. an individual's choice to exercise his/her constitutional right to be sterilized or to refuse sterilization to the extent protected by state and federal constitutional law;

3. an individual's choice to carry a pregnancy to term;[5]

4. an individual's choice to obtain and to use any lawful prescription for drugs or other substances designed to avoid pregnancy, whether by preventing implantation of a fertilized ovum or by any other method that operates before, at, or immediately after fertilisation;

5. an individual's choice to become pregnant through *in vitro* fertilisation, artificial insemination, or through any other procedure.

However, Lori B. Andrews does not stop at these general reproductive options. She extends the concept to include all possible technical and social alternatives. According to her, 'reproductive choice' and 'reproductive alternatives' comprise not only the use of IVF for infertile couples, but also the possibility for *anyone* to 'create' their own children without sexual intercourse. This includes 'rearing parents-to-be to contract for a child with no biological tie to them. They could use the combination of an egg donor a sperm donor, and a surrogate.'[6]

'Free choice of reproductive alternatives' means also, of course, the 'right' to enter into various types of contracts with 'surrogate mothers', and conversely, a woman's 'right' to become a so-called 'surrogate mother'. Furthermore, the technical methods of avoiding children with genetic 'defects' are part of this package of 'reproductive alternatives.' In Andrews' words: 'Alternative reproduction' may also be practised 'by a person who wants to rear a child, but does not wish to engage in sexual intercourse with a person of the opposite sex'.[7]

Such options would eventually lead to widespread genetic screening. Andrews is against compulsory genetic screening, but advocates both voluntary genetic and medical screening for women who (still?) procreate in the 'traditional manner'[8] and for those who use 'alternative reproduction'. This framework makes it possible for a woman whose uterus has been removed, but whose ovaries are intact to still become a 'genetic mother' by the help of a 'surrogate'. Similarly, Andrews recommends that women who undergo cancer treatment and who are afraid that this treatment 'might prove mutagenic to her eggs should be told about the possibility of freezing eggs or embryos in advance of treatment for subsequent use to create a child'.[9] 'Reproductive autonomy', according to Andrews, not only comprises the options to use techniques like cryoconservation of eggs, sperm or embryos, but also the possibility of selling 'body parts' to third parties, as she makes clear in her paper: 'My Body, My Property'.

Andrews not only discusses the technological possibilities among those 'reproductive alternatives' but also the new social relations created by reproductive technology. According to her, these technologies open up totally new family structures; hence, they fulfil, what the feminist movement — critical of repressive family structures, particularly of the nuclear type — has been demanding for many years. Thanks to the nRTs a child can now have several mothers and fathers — genetic ones, social ones, carrying mothers and rearing mothers, two mothers and no father, and so forth. Legal problems arising from such multiple parenthood arrangements for which there is no provision in the current family law (for example, the problem of custody), according to Andrews can be avoided: what is needed are contracts before conception that stipulate who will be the genetic mother/father, who will be the carrying mother, the social parents, and so on.[10] *This means that, by necessity, these new reproductive alternatives will lead to an invasion of these most intimate personal relationships by contract law.*

What surprised me most in this discussion of 'reproductive alternatives' was that there is no fundamental critique of the technologies. On the contrary, as I see it, both Andrews and the other members of the Rutgers Working Group consider them to be inventions with great potential to enhance women's 'reproductive autonomy'. Their main concern is that there should be no coercion and that all women, irrespective of class and race, should have equal access to these 'reproductive alternatives'.

The project's working group believes that ultimately one of the most pressing concerns is the trade-off between maximising individual reproductive autonomy and allocating societal resources in an equitable way . . . The group believes that a system of national health care insurance would help to allocate resources more equitably.[11]

The 'surrogate-mother' industry

The transition from 'helping the individual infertile woman or man' to a fully-fledged 'reproduction industry' can be traced clearly in Andrews' argument that all legal barriers should be removed which still stand in the way of hiring 'surrogate mothers', 'carrying mothers' or selling one's sperm, eggs or embryos. As we know, these legal debates — particularly about 'surrogacy' — have already begun. For the first time in history a lawyer, Judge Harvey Sorkow from New Jersey, has, in the case of Mary Beth Whitehead in 1987, put contract law over and above a woman's claim to a child born to her. While the New Jersey Supreme Court overturned Sorkow's ruling, if other states do not follow its lead the doors could still be open for the commercialization of reproduction.[12] The production of children can now become a new 'growth industry'. What was seen some years ago as a mere possibility has already become reality.[13]

The Sorkow judgement, however, did not fall from heaven. It has to be seen as a consequence of a discourse on 'reproductive alternatives' in which the question of human dignity, particularly of *women's dignity*, is not even asked. In Judge Sorkow's judgement, the so-called 'surrogate mother' becomes a mere 'factor of conception and for gestation' He says:

> If it is reproduction that is protected, then the means of reproduction are also to be protected. The value and interest underlying the creation of family are the same by whatever means obtained. This court holds that the protected means extend to the use of surrogates. The contract cannot fall because of the use of a third party. It is reasoned that the donor or surrogate aids the childless couple by contributing a *factor of conception and for gestation*. (My emphasis)[14]

I think that Andrews' arguments for the sanctity of surrogacy contracts are not far away from Judge Sorkow's. She discusses the different scruples which American feminists have forwarded against surrogacy, such as equating commercial surrogacy with baby selling, and the physical and mental risks for the surrogate mother.[15] (However, she does not discuss the real issue that many US feminists have critiqued surrogacy for; that is, the selling of women.) But she counters all these criticisms by stating that a signed contract based on informed consent has to be honoured.

She refutes the argument that payment of surrogate mothers amounts to the sale of children by quoting judgements of the Kentucky Supreme Court and a court in Nassau County, New York (both 1986) which held that paying a surrogate would not amount to baby selling — which is prohibited by American law.16 One of the reasons given by the two courts was that the decision to relinquish the child after birth was made prior to the pregnancy. As long as the surrogate was not coerced and had agreed to the contract with a cool head and fully informed about its consequences, one could not speak of selling children or of exploiting women. The exploitation of women, however, is precisely what worries feminist critics; specifically that poor women could be exploited by richer, white middle-class couples, and even, that a new class of 'breeder women' might arise, where women out of sheer necessity will be forced to become surrogates, or sell their gametes or eggs.

> . . . we can imagine circumstances in our own society in which a woman would feel compelled to be a surrogate to put food on her table, to pay for health care for a loved one or to buy some of the items or services that we legitimately feel that society has an obligation to provide.[17]

Andrews believes that in all these cases one cannot speak of exploitation. She quotes a potential surrogate who asked: 'Why is it exploitation to go through a surrogate pregnancy for someone else if I am paid, but not if I am *not* paid?'[18] Instead of banning surrogacy altogether, as some feminists demand, Andrews believes that surrogate mothers should be paid more.

In all her arguments Andrews claims to defend feminist principles and demands. This is also the case when she refutes the argument of some feminists that surrogacy is too 'risky'. According to her, the risks of a surrogate pregnancy are not higher than those of an 'ordinary' pregnancy. Moreover, she feels that people have traditionally been allowed to participate in risky activities (such as fire-fighting) if it is based on their voluntary informed consent. Thus, women should not be denied the possibility of being surrogate mothers.

Her strongest argument, however, is that women have to honour their surrogate contracts because they have to prove that they are capable of making responsible decisions: that they are not 'fickle', but mature citizens. She says:

> My personal opinion is that it would be a step backward for women to embrace any policy argument based on a presumed incapacity of women to make decisions. That after all was the rationale for so many legal principles oppressing women for so long, such as the rationale behind the laws not allowing women to hold property.[19]

It does not seem to occur to Andrews that both these legal principles and the rationale behind them — namely that women are incapable of rational decisions — have to be rejected as *sexist and patriarchal*. Instead, she feels that women have struggled hard to live up to these (nonsensical) principles; if we now allow women like Mary Beth Whitehead and others to keep their children, we jeopardize the 'gains' the women's movement has made. This point makes it clear what Andrews means by 'women's emancipation', namely the 'equal participation' of women in an overall patriarchal and capitalist economic and legal system. For this system to continue it is indeed necessary that contracts be honoured, that surrogacy contracts be honoured, and that all legal provisions that stem from an antiquated past when all the processes and relations around procreation were considered to be part of our natural existence, have to be scrapped and put under the rules of contract law, the law of the market. In the land of unlimited capital accumulation, contracts weigh more than the claim of a mother to the child carried and born of her.

Following from Andrews, it appears that surrogacy is not motherhood. It is not even a service, because the woman is not paid for the service she does for the contracting father. What she is paid for is the 'product', the child. Surrogacy is thus a new 'piece work industry' which functions analogously to the exploitation of women whose labour at home is contracted. The entrepreneur (the man) provides a part of the raw material (sperm, or a donor egg for which he pays) and advance payment for the 'carrier' woman. But the product has to be delivered. The delivery is essential. With respect to this demand, the surrogacy industry faces problems similar to those that the old home-based industries had to contend with in the beginning. It is to make sure that the producers deliver the products and do not keep them for themselves. This means that they have to be forced into accepting that what they produce is a *commodity*, not something of their own and that they are doing alienated labour.[20] Andrews takes great pains to draw women away from 'pre-capitalist' behaviour and makes them accept the law of the market for their reproductive behaviour.

In so doing, she consistently uses the concept of 'reproductive autonomy'. As I discussed earlier, this implies not only free access to all new reproductive technologies, but also to all kinds of new social arrangements. But looking at the discussion about surrogacy we discover the dilemma implicit in this argument. The concept of reproductive autonomy implies a total liberalization of the procreative process. Anything should be feasible, and what is technically and socially feasible should also be legally permitted. The state should, as far as possible, keep out of this sphere. So far so good. Yet, since reproductive behaviour has now been integrated into the market — thanks to the 'progress' of the nRTs — procreation has become a matter of selling and buying, of mine and thine. And for this, contracts are necessary. In other words reproductive autonomy — upheld so strongly by Andrews — ends at contract law. Let me repeat: reproductive autonomy ends at contract law! Women who enter such contracts, be it for surrogacy, the selling of embryos and other 'reproductive material' or for entering an IVF-programme can no longer interact with their own bodies and its procreative powers as a sovereign person.[21] Concepts like reproductive autonomy, reproductive choice, reproductive alternatives have a positive ring in the ears of feminists. But Andrews and her colleagues have turned these concepts around: they are used now to open up women's procreative power and bodies for total commercialization in the hands of profit- and fame-seeking industries and 'technodocs'.

My body — my property?

Apart from the problem that women might not show enough respect for surrogacy arrangements and other contracts related to reproductive transactions, there is yet another obstacle to overcome in order to free the way for total commercialization and industrialization of reproduction. According to Andrews, this is the fact that women, but also men, do not yet handle their bodies — or parts of their bodies — in a rational way, which, according to me means: appropriate for a capitalist market economy. They do not yet deal with their bodies as marketable, and hence profit-generating, property.

After her arguments in favour of liberalization of reproductive alternatives it is not surprising to learn that Andrews had already previously written an article in which she argues for establishing property relations to our own bodies. In her article 'My Body — My Property' she claims that not only the reproductive parts of our bodies, but all other body organs and substances such as blood, semen, tissue, body cells, etc. should be treated as the property of the owner of the body, too. She criticizes US legal practice according to which people can *donate* their body parts, but cannot *sell* them. On the other hand, she says, scientists and doctors who experiment with such body parts and substances — mainly taken for free from patients — are able to make a great sum of money from the product of these experiments. For instance, they patent and license cell lines and sell them. Andrews quotes the case of John Moore, a leukemia patient, whose blood was used by his physicians without his knowledge and consent to 'develop the patented and commercially valuable Mo cell line'.[22] As the demand for such body substances and body parts is on the increase — particularly through the growth of biotechnological research and experimentation — Andrews demands that all remaining legal obstacles should be removed which prevent the sale of body parts and substances. This, however, would imply that first and foremost the human body be defined as *property*. Only by treating the body and body parts as her or his property, the 'owner' of this property could legally prevent the misuse of these parts. S/he could also claim a share in the profits made by developing these into marketable commodities. The human body defined as property would also mean that s/he could demand compensation according to the tort law. Andrews quotes a case from a hospital in New York City where an attempt was made to fertilize a woman's egg with her husband's sperm. The chairman of the department removed the culture from the incubator and destroyed it. The couple sued him, charging conversion of personal property and infliction of emotional distress. Andrews is critical of the fact that the property claim was rejected whereas the emotional distress claim was accepted by the court. She is afraid that people who entrust their reproductive parts — embryos or gametes — to physicians will have no protection unless their body is declared property.

Advances in reproductive technology now frequently require people to entrust their gametes or embryos to the care of physician, laboratory worker, or health care facility. Yet if body parts are not considered property, there may be little protection for people who entrust their bodily materials to others.[23]

Andrews also discusses the possibilities of selling one's body parts and substances after one's death. This would mean that already in their life time people walk around as sold-out cadavers! However, as I see it, her main interest is clearly in the free commercialization of reproductive material, which is needed in large quantities by the rapidly expanding demands of the reproductive industry and research communities. In this she adopts the position of the American Fertility Society which argues that eggs, embryos, eggs cells and sperm are the property of the person from whom they are taken.[24] Apparently, the property argument is advanced also in support of feminists like Gena Corea who has objected that, without the women's knowledge, eggs are 'stolen' by physicians during operations, in order to be used for reproduction experiments.[25]

Andrews is of the opinion that the ethical problems are solved when these women are properly informed and consent to selling or donating their eggs or other reproductive matter without any coercion. She does not criticize the commercialization of these body parts as such, but only that today this happens without the owners' consent.

Consequences for 'sellers', 'buyers' and society

After introducing her main argument, Andrews also discusses various consequences which the introduction of the concept 'human-body-as-property' might have on the 'donors' — who, I think should now be called 'sellers': the prospective 'receivers' — or 'buyers' — and society at large. One argument which could be advanced against the definition of the human body as property is the fear that poor people could be forced to sell their kidneys and other body parts. This might even lead to a situation in which a poor woman or man could be considered an owner of 'capital' if s/he has two kidneys. One kidney costs about US$50,000. One could thus argue that this person has no right to claim social welfare. Andrews counters such arguments in a similar manner to the previously discussed case of the 'poor woman' who enters a surrogacy contract. For her, it is not ethically unacceptable if a poor person sells her or his body parts in order to feed their children, get medical treatment for a close friend or buy other necessary things. A ban on the sale of body parts, she says, would not do away with the poverty of this person. Instead, it would penalize her/him. Again, the 'poor woman' or man is being used to legitimize the introduction of the human body (or parts thereof) into the capitalist market. Andrews does not see ethical problems rising from the fact that body parts are sold and bought, she only discusses the possible health risks for the 'sellers' and 'buyers'. And she maintains that only the individual herself/himself can decide whether s/he will accept these risks. Her main concern is that there is no coercion and that people are properly informed. She feels that as long as the 'owners' sell their body parts, and not third parties — for instance relatives might sell the body parts of a deceased, or a hospital might sell those of a patient — there would be no ethical problem.[26] She does not say, however, how she will prevent others from treating my body as property if I myself consider it to be my property!

She also does not see an ethical problem in the fact that by defining the body as property the integrity of a human being is destroyed. Though she claims that the human person or the human body is more than the sum of its parts, she *de facto* treats the body as a reservoir of marketable materials. To justify this vivisection and commercialization of our various body parts and substances she argues that we have already been 'sold'. We sell our labour power and our brain power. Particularly the latter: the legal doctrine of copyright patents defines it and its products as 'intellectual property'. According to Andrews the selling of one's cognitive functions and properties is worse than selling only parts of our 'material' body. I believe that her idealistic view of the human person demonstrates that Andrews does not accept the feminist challenge to the division of ourselves into 'spirit' and 'matter'. She writes:

> I view my uniqueness as a person as more related to my intellectual products than my bodily products. (Definitions of personhood, for example, rarely revolve around the possession of body parts, but rather focus on sentience or other cognitive traits.) Arguably it commercialises me less as a person to sell my bone marrow than to sell my intellectual products. Thus I do not view payment of body parts as commercialising people.[27]

Has Andrews ever understood what the Boston Women's

Health Collective meant by saying: OUR BODIES OURSELVES?

She also refutes the argument that only well-to-do people could buy body parts and that the poor would be those who sell them. This would really be the most blatant form of commercial exploitation. She says that already today Third World people 'give' their body substances (for example blood plasma) to the rich in the industrialized countries.

> Even today, American drug companies undertake plasma collections in Third World countries throughout Latin America and Asia to meet the needs for plasma products here. People in poor countries are giving of their bodies to people in rich countries. Perhaps we should struggle to assure non-commercialisation of human body products in all countries. But if this reduced the blood supply, doctors might have to turn down some patients who needed surgery. Would proponents of total market bans support that outcome?[28]

Clearly, Andrews is not interested in a total market ban. On the contrary, her efforts are directed at opening up new areas for investment and commercialization and *not* at reducing these areas. In order to reach this aim, however, the human body, particularly its reproductive capacities and organs, have to be made 'freely' accessible to scientific and commercial interests. I believe that Andrews' analysis plays into the hands of these interest groups. Therefore, her remark about the 'poor *giving* of their bodies to the rich' (my emphasis) conceals the violence by which the poor are forced to 'give' to the rich.[29]

From liberalization to state control

In both her papers Andrews argues for total liberalization of laws which today still prevent the full commercialization of reproductive processes and body parts. Nevertheless, she is aware that this total liberalization and the breaking down of legal barriers will lead to malpractice and abuse of the new 'rights'. For instance, she acknowledges the danger that genetic or infectious diseases could be spread by the unrestricted commercialization of body parts.

While Andrews rejects screening for social and psychological fitness of potential users of reproductive technologies she is in a dilemma when it comes to screening sperm donors or surrogates for medical or genetic reasons. She regrets the lax handling of professional guidelines regarding sperm donors and surrogates and quotes studies which show that only 29 per cent of infertility specialists offering artificial insemination performed biochemical testing on the donors. But she also refers to several cases of state legislation which make the medical and/or genetic screening mandatory. It is clear that with the extension of the market of more and more 'factors of conception and gestation' and of other body parts the recipients' fears of genetic and infectious diseases will grow. Here the state has to step in to protect the potential buyers.

From the text it is not clear what Andrews' position is regarding state legislation on medical and genetic screening. She only refers rather vaguely to 'many feminists' who are in favour of medical screening of donors and surrogates.

> Many feminists would advocate infectious disease screen-ing of donors, for example, for AIDS, but have qualms about genetic disease screening since it seems to be a step toward an unpalatable eugenics.[30]

In spite of all the talk about 'autonomy' and 'individual choice,' when it comes to protecting the interests of individuals they have to call in the state and ask for its control. On the one hand, all legal barriers that prevent the commercialization of reproduction or body parts should be scrapped, but on the other hand, new legal controls have to be introduced to make sure that these new 'reproductive' and other alternatives are not misused. This means that the more the technological 'alternatives' advance and the more the existing moral and legal barriers are broken down which prevent the full commer-cialization of the human body and its reproductive capacities, the more state control is required. From this follows that more laws have to be made, and *more* bureaucracy and police are needed to sort out the conflicting interests of the various 'prop-erty owners'. This process of steady increase of state control is accelerated by the AIDS panic as well as by the fear of hospitals and medical staff of being sued for damages. For this increase in state control over reproductive processes it is irrelevant whether people live in a formal democracy or in states which are called 'totalitarian'. It also does not matter whether they have a socialized health care system like in Great Britain and, partly at least, in Germany, or a private system like in the USA. This increase in legal and state control over reproduction pro-cesses, particularly over women's bodies, is the logical and necessary consequence of the basic methodological principles of reproductive and genetic engineering. I want to formulate the followingthesis:

> *The technological feasibility to dissect reproductive and genetic processes and the human body, particularly the female body, which constitutes the holistic base of these processes into 'reproductive factors', 'reproductive components', 'reproductive and genetic material' and the possibility to recombine these 'components' etc. into new 'reproductive alternatives' is welcomed by some as an opportunity to enhance individual 'choice' and 'autonomy'. This increase of individual choice, however, will automatically lead to more state and legal control in the sphere of reproduction.*

The basic methodological principles of reproductive and genetic engineering are the same as in other 'hard' sciences. The dissection of organic or inorganic wholes into ever smaller particles and their recombination into new 'machines',[31] is based on the eugenic principle of selection and elimination. Desired particles are selected, undesired ones are eliminated. If these principles were not there, the whole dissection process and the recombination would not make sense. In the sphere of reproduction this dissection, this principle of 'divide-and-rule', begins by dividing the pregnant woman into 'the mother' and the 'embryo'. Within a system based on patriarchy and private interests this splitting up then automatically leads to a conflict of interests, an antagonism between mother and embryo. The foetus or embryo is now conceived as something separate from its mother, and in modern reproductive technology it is increasingly also *de facto* separated from the female body. In fact, more and more reproduction engineers are beginning to call the female uterus a 'dangerous environment' for the foetus.[32] In order to regulate this new antagonism between mother and foetus — an artificial antagonism invented by modern science and its makers — some (for example the right-to-life people) want to declare the foetus as a human person in the full legal sense of the term. They want to see it as a person whose 'foetal rights' have to be protected against its mother. For this they need 'Embryo-Protection Laws' as well as a state and legal machinery which enforce these laws.[33]

But there is not only the new antagonism between mother and foetus. The more reproductive technologies advance, the more embryo research is carried out in the laboratories, the more procedures of pre-natal diagnosis are developed, the more the foetus will not only be defined as a person, but also as a patient. In the concept 'foetus as patient' the eugenic principles mentioned above are fully realized. A 'defective' foetus has either to be eliminated or manipulated by gene therapy. In these processes and manipulations the antagonism between mother and embryo will be followed by antagonisms between doctor and child, and between doctor and mother/parents. There are already several cases in the USA where children born with a so-called genetic defect have sued the doctors and clinics for damage, because the defective foetus was not discovered and aborted in time. Mary Sue Henifin reports the case of the son of Rosemary Procanik who was born with birth defects. The doctors and the hospital were sued because they did not inform his mother in time about the dangers of measles during the first three months of pregnancy in time for her to have an abortion.[34] Sue Henifin is afraid that such 'wrongful life cases' and claims for damage will not only be directed against doctors and clinics, but also against the women who, during their pregnancy, may have refused to undergo certain pre-natal tests, may have taken drugs or have worked at dangerous jobs. That such fears are not without foundation is clearly expressed in the arguments of tort law specialist Margery Shaw (quoted by Henifin) who says that once a woman decides to carry the foetus to term she:

> incurs a 'conditional prospective liability' for negligent acts towards her foetus if it should be born alive. These acts could be considered negligent foetal abuse resulting in an injured child. A decision to carry a genetically defective foetus to term would be an example. Abuse of alcohol or drugs during pregnancy . . . withholding of necessary prenatal care, improper nutrition, exposure to mutagens and teratogens or even exposure to the mother's defective intrauterine environment caused by her genotype . . . could all result in an injured infant who might claim that his right to be born physically and mentally sound had been invaded.[35]

In other words, courts and legislatures should take action to make sure that foetuses will not be injured by others, particularly by their mothers. That these arguments are not just part of an academic discourse among lawyers is shown in the case of a woman in California who had given birth to a brain-dead child. She was jailed because she had ignored recommendations of the doctor during pregnancy. However, since no adequate laws for such a case existed, the accusation was withdrawn. To fill the gap a legislator immediately introduced a bill to deal with cases of 'maternal neglect' or 'wilful disregard' of doctors' orders.[36]

It is obvious that the enforcement and the extension of 'foetal rights' — be it of the 'foetus as person' or the 'foetus as patient' — can take place only at the expense of the women's individual rights. This will lead, as Janet Gallagher points out, to a system of:

> surveillance and coercion oppressive to all women of childbearing age. What are the options? Administration of pregnancy tests every month to all of us who aren't certifiably infertile and the issuance of cards that permit jogging, drinking or working? If hospitals become jails and doctors cops, the neediest pregnant women — the very poor, the very young, substance abusers — will be driven away from the prenatal care they need so badly.[37]

But not only those who want to expand the legal status of the foetus to full personhood — and hence consider the other as the enemy of the foetus — disrupt the life-preserving relationship between woman and embryo/foetus, but also those who consider the foetus as a 'thing', a piece of property that belongs to the woman. As I have stated earlier in this chapter, this group too, needs the state and its legal machinery to protect this 'property' from neglect and misuse and damage. With the expansion of the possibilities to dissect the reproductive processes and 'matter' into ever smaller parts, the possibility to harm and violate these parts, separated from the woman, increases. The chance of damaging deep-frozen embryos which are, according to Andrews, the property of the mother, is undoubtedly much greater than the possibility to harm an embryo inside the maternal womb! To protect the owner of such 'property' against damage, new laws have to be formulated, detailed contracts have to be drafted by which both the owners as well as the reproductive engineers try to protect their conflicting interests. And the state has to guarantee that these laws will be enforced and these contracts honoured.

Particularly, specialists in reproductive medicine and hospitals will increasingly insist on contracts — based on 'informed consent' — to protect themselves against claims for damages. The antagonism between doctor and patient is increasing. The state itself has a vital interest, too, in gaining more control over the whole sphere of reproduction. The nRTs do not only, as some of the feminists from the Rutgers Project seem to think, widen the 'reproductive choice' of the individual woman, but also the possibility for state intervention, particularly where there exists already a national health system. The state has an interest to have a sound population and to keep health expenditures low. AIDS and the fear of genetic diseases will doubtless lead to more state control. Eventually, the state will also have to decide what to do with surplus embryos and other 'reproductive material'.

I think it is an illusion to believe, as some of the women in the Rutgers Project do, that we could accept the nRTs as a means to widen the 'reproductive choice' of women and at the same time to keep the state out of this sphere of 'private decisions'. Those who allow 'technodocs' to dissect living processes and organisms into bits and pieces, have to accept the necessary antagonism arising from conflicts of interest between those divided parts. Notwithstanding their liberal rhetoric they will have to call in the state to regulate the conflicts over the so-called 'rights' of the respective parties. The atomized individuals demand that the state should respect the privacy and autonomy of the individual. At the same time they demand absolute safety for their own private decisions. More liberalism, therefore, will necessarily lead to more state control.

At this level of analysis, in my opinion, there are striking similarities between the liberal position articulated by Andrews and that of the Right-to-Life movement. Andrews, like many feminists, is strongly opposed to this movement because of its efforts to roll back the liberal legislation on abortion. In reality, however, the two positions are closer to each other than might appear if one only listens to the polemics of either side. Andrews is eager to establish that the human body, particularly its reproductive parts, is *property*, a thing. 'Reproductive autonomy', according to this concept, then means that the woman as proprietor has the right to sell, hire out, and so on this property in instalments. A pregnant woman hence, is the owner of the foetus, the foetus is a *thing*. The symbiosis between a pregnant woman — and her embryo and the living relationship by which the life of both is preserved — is disrupted, symbolically and also, due to the nRTs, in reality.

The Right-to-Life movement, on the other hand, wants to declare the foetus a full-fledged person in the legal sense, a person who has to be protected by law against the arbitrary interventions of the pregnant woman. In this case, too, the symbiotic relationship between the woman and the foetus is disrupted, at least symbolically, the woman is seen as the enemy of the child. In both cases, however, an antagonism in the woman's body between herself and her embryo is constructed. And in both cases, to solve this conflict, the state has to be called in; in other words, a further intrusion of the state into women's generative capacities becomes a necessity. Andrews needs the state to protect the woman's bodily *property*, the Right-to-Life movement needs the state to protect the *personhood* of the foetus.

As the person, however, as became clear in Andrews' arguments, is nothing more than an assembly of bodily parts and organs, governed by a brain, the difference between the human being as a *thing* and as a *person* disappears. The person, which the Right-to-Life movement wants to protect, is, in the last analysis, only a proprietor and seller of her or his own parts. It is this new type of economic and scientific cannibalism, based on the bourgeois property concept and the 'progress' of reproductive technology to which both positions, the liberal and the conservative, converge. As I see it, beneath the loud polemics of both camps there is the common base of a system, which since its beginning, has only one aim, namely to turn all things and living beings into commodities for the sake of capital accumulation.

From the individual to the dividual

Finally, I want to ask a question which kept intriguing me while reading the papers of the Rutgers Project, specifically those by Lori B. Andrews. Andrews makes a strong case for the human body and its parts and substances to be declared as property. In so doing, she grounds herself firmly within the foundations of bourgeois liberties and rights, namely within the institution of private property. These rights and liberties were meant only for those who were owners of property. People without property were not free or equal.

According to Andrews, as women are not yet owners of their own bodies, they cannot be free, equal and autonomous. Following from this logic it seems consistent to demand next that women *should* become the owners of their bodies so that they *can* buy and sell their body parts. But this freedom to sell and to buy depends on the dissection of their own bodies. Which again means that a 'whole' woman — an undissected one — cannot be free or autonomous. Here the question arises: who then is the person who sells and buys? If the *individual* — the undivided person — has been divided up into her/his saleable parts, the individual hasdisappeared. There is only the dividual which can be further divided up. But then we have to ask: how far can these divisions go? In how many parts can we be dissected and sold and continue to function as 'owner's and 'seller'? What is the essential part — the residual 'subject' which decides about the dissection and sale of other parts? Is it the brain? After all, without a designated subject, all talk of autonomy and self-determination remains empty. Even for the signing and honouring of contracts a subject is necessary. But this subject, this person, has been eliminated in theory and in practice. What is left is an assembly of parts. The bourgeois individual has eliminated itself. Hence, we can understand why there is no longer a place for ethical questions, neither within the individual body nor within the societal body. There are only unrelated parts which, moreover, fight against each other, as in Hobbes' Leviathan.38 No wonder that these atomized, antagonistic parts need a state which holds everything mechanistically together. But even this state is no longer a subject, in the true sense. What rules is the market mechanism of supply and demand. This mechanism determines the value of a human being: US $50,000 for a kidney, US $10,000 for a rented womb. Women — and men — as whole beings cease to exist.

Notes

1. Andrews, Lori B. (nd) distributed in 1987. 'Feminist Perspectives on New Reproductive Technologies.' In *Briefing Handbook: Reproductive Laws for the 1990s*. Women's Rights Litigation Clinic, and Institute for Research on Women, Rutgers Law School, Newark, NJ
2. Andrews, Lori B. 'My Body, My Property.' In *Hastings Center Report*, 1986, pp. 28-37.
3. Andrews, 1987, op. cit., p. 46.
4. Ibid. p. 46-7.
5. Gertner, Nancy (nd) distributed in 1987, 'Interference with Reproductive Rights,' In *Briefing Handbook: Reproductive Laws for the 1990s*, op.cit.
6. Andrews 1987, op. cit., Appendix A:3
7. Ibid. Appendix A:4.
8. Ibid. p. 27
9. Ibid. p. 4.
10. Ibid. p. 33.
11. *Reproductive Laws for the 1990s*, op. cit., p. 11.
12. Raymond, Janice, 'The Spermatic Market: Surrogate Stock and Liquid Assets.' In RAGE, No. 1, 1988, 65-75.
13. The lower New Jersey Court decision of Judge Harvey Sorkow was overturned by the New Jersey Supreme Court in February 1988. For a fuller discussion of this decision see *Reproductive and Genetic Engineering At Issue* 1(2): 175-181. (Also

see Rita Arditti, RAGE 1(1): 51-64 and Janice Raymond 1(1): 65-75.)
14. Superior Court of New Jersey 1987. In the Matter of Baby 'M'. Opinion 31 March pp. 1-121.
15. Andrews 1987, op. cit., p. 15-20.
16. Ibid. p. 19-20.
17. Ibid. p. 17.
18. Ibid. p. 16.
19. Ibid. p. 14.
20. The women in a tribal area in India, for instance, did not realize that the pottery they had made in the context of a development project aimed at establishing a piece-work industry, was to be sold in the marketplace. They wanted to keep the pots for themselves and did not understand that they had produced saleable commodities.
21. Klein, Renate, 'Where Choice Amounts to Coercion: The Experiences of Women in IVF Programmes'. Paper presented at 3rd International Interdisciplinary Congress on Women, Dublin, 5-11 July 1987.
22. Andrews, 1986, op. cit. p. 28.
23. Ibid. p. 30.
24. American Fertility Society. Ethical Statement on In Vitro Fertilization. In *Fertility and Sterility*, 1984, 41: 12.
25. Corea, Gena, *The Mother Machine* . Harper & Row, New York, 1985, p. 135.
26. Andrews 1986, pp. 32, 33.
27. Ibid. p. 35.
28. Ibid.
29. A news item in a German newspaper reported that 60 women and children from Bangladesh were kidnapped and brought across the Indian border. When the police interrogated the women it was found out that they were to be forced into prostitution. The children were to be killed and their kidneys to be removed and sold. I wonder if Lori B. Andrews would argue in a similar way in this case as she does with regard to plasma collected from the 'Third World'? How will she prevent poor Third World children being killed to save the life of some of the Western rich if the body and its parts are increasingly becoming marketable commodities? *Frankfurter Allgemeine Zeitung*, 27 February 1988.
30. Andrews, op. cit., 1987, p. 27.
31. Merchant, Carolyn, *The Death of Nature: Women, Ecology and the Scientific Revolution*. Harper & Row, San Francisco, 1983.
32. Henifin, Mary Sue, 'What's Wrong With 'Wrongful Life' Court Cases?' In *Gene Watch, A Bulletin of the Committee for Responsible Genetics*. 4(1), 1987, pp. 1-2, 11-15.
33. In Germany such an Embryo Protection Law came into force in 1991.
34. Henifin, op. cit., p. 2.
35. Ibid., p. 15.
36. Gallagher, Janet, J.D. (nd) distributed in 1987. 'Foetus as Patient.' Paper presented at A Forum on Reproductive Laws for the 1990s. In *Briefing Handbook: Reproductive Laws for the 1990s*. op.cit.
37. Gallagher, op. cit. pp. 2-3.
38. As Thomas Hobbes saw 'Man' as driven basically by egotistic motives, he needed a strong state to regulate the antagonistic interests of the atomized individuals in the 'social body'. Now, not only is the social body, society, made up of such selfish particles, but also the individual human body is thus dissected (see Hobbes, 1965).

14. Self-Determination: The End of a Utopia?*

Maria Mies

Introduction

The demand for self-determination, for autonomy with regard to
our bodies and our lives, is one of the fundamental demands of
the women's movement. It has been voiced during many campaigns: the campaign against violence against women; the campaign for autonomous and woman-sensitive health-care, and
above all in the context of the struggle against restrictive abortion
laws.

The political aim of self-determination for women, often designated as the *right* to self-determination, as autonomy and control
of one's body, has been consciously or unconsciously derived
from the fundamental right of self-determination, the right to
bodily intactness and integrity. This fundamental right stems, as
we know, from the catalogue of human rights put forward in the
course of the bourgeois revolutions. It was mainly upheld against
the state and its invasions into the private sphere of the individual.
What led the women of the old, and in part also of the new,
women's movement to the barricades, is the fact that this fundamental right, as written into all modern constitutions, does not
apply to women. For women were not granted this right of determination over the self, and especially not over our bodies, which
have been treated as the property of others, as a territory occupied
by men: medicine-men, statesmen, churchmen and of course men
in general. Female reproductive organs and female generative
power especially suffered from this occupation. Thus, for women,
self-determination meant first, the liberation from occupation, the
end of the determination-by-others, by men and by patriarchal

* Revised version of an article first published in *Resources for Feminist Research*, Vol.
18, No. 3, September 1989.

social powers. The demand for self-determination was, therefore, a defensive one, based on the right to resistance, the right to defend the self.

Yet this concept also include, and still includes an element of utopia, something that women saw as the goal of our struggles: the autonomous and self-determined woman.

Until recently this was my utopia also, but perhaps I did not reflect enough on its background and consequences. In the context of our struggle against the new genetic and reproductive technologies, however, I arrived at a different understanding, especially after having read papers by American feminists at Rutgers University, discussed in the last chapter. [1]

Before debating any further the dilemma concerning self-determination, revealed to us through new biomedical developments, I should like to name a second reason why we must reconsider the concept of self-determination.

In 1986, Farida Akhter in her article 'Depopulating Bangladesh' wrote that the most important strategy of Western radical feminists had been their distance, politically and intellectually, from the interventionists (the international establishment of population control). Yet this strategy had not been very successful in Bangladesh, where feminism was still considered a Western creed and also because Western women had not been the victims of such interventionist politics of reproduction. She continues:

> It is difficult for a feminist of the West to understand that a notion like the reproductive rights of women or the control of women over their own bodies has no meaning for the majority of women in Bangladesh. The processes of poverty and underdevelopment have reduced their lives to a margin narrowly above death by chronic starvation. The instinct of survival predominates over the urge for emancipation. In the sterilization camps and clinics of Bangladesh, when a woman undergoes surgery for ligation, she submits her body to mutilation not because she wants to emancipate herself from reproductive responsibilities, but in most cases for money and an apparel known as *sari*, which are received as incentives. They add to her ability to survive as they can be exchanged for food. Nowhere do the rights of women become of any concern. [2]

Farida Akhter insists that the question of emancipation is as important for Bangladeshi women as it is for Western feminists.

What she criticizes is that demands for 'control over one's own body' or for 'reproductive rights for women' are voiced by Western feminists in such countries as Bangladesh, without any regard for the economic, political, or cultural impositions of international capitalism.

When feminists in the West demand reproductive self-determination for all women, without at the same time attacking the exploitative economic world order from which they themselves profit, then this demand is on the same level as was Ronald Reagan's demand for human rights at a time when the US was supporting military dictatorships in the 'Third World'.

'Third World' women criticize the demand for self-determination for still another reason. The utopia of the independent, isolated and autonomous female individual is not attractive to them. They oppose patriarchal exploitation and oppression, which, in their world as in ours, is often perpetuated by the institution of the family. But their concept of women's liberation does not imply severing all communal relations, they cannot conceptualize the isolation of the individual woman as something positive. They know that for them there is no such safety net as the modern welfare state, and that they therefore need the net of relations provided by family, village and community. They do not wish to live free and alone in the anonymity of big cities, to die finally, as we shall, in a home for the old.

Thus, the demand for self-determination must be reconsidered from two perspectives. First, is self-determination of the individual woman still what we believe women's liberation essentially to be? Secondly, must we not take seriously the critique of this utopia, offered by our sisters of the 'Third World'?

Demands made by the 'Global Network on Reproductive Rights' for reproductive rights for women, for instance, not only transform questions of reproduction and sexuality into legal problems, but maintain the idea of individual self-determination of each woman as the essence of our emancipatory hopes. It is tacitly understood that these reproductive rights would be furthered by reproductive technologies of an anti-natalistic as well as a pro-natalistic character.[3]

The dilemma of self-determination

The dilemma concerning the right to self-determination which now confronts many of us, becomes evident in the following arguments: (a) if we oppose the new reproductive technologies, we should also oppose abortion. Thus we would come to the conservative position;[4] and (b) if we demand the right of abortion in the name of self-determination and reproductive autonomy, we must concede the same right to the woman who decides in favour of one or the other new 'reproductive alternatives'. Aside from coercion, any technology which enhances control over our bodies must be welcomed. This, for instance, is the argument of L.B. Andrews.[5]

What is wrong with this argument? Looking more closely, we notice that the original direction of the struggle for self-determination has changed. While we women strove originally for liberation from exploitative and oppressive male-female relations, we now deal with the question of 'emancipation' from the uncontrolled reproductive potential of the female body, of 'emancipation' from our female nature. This nature is more and more seen as a handicap from which bio-technical experts must liberate us, either through pro- or anti-natalist technology. Thus, women's liberation becomes the result of technical progress and no longer means the transformation of patriarchal man-woman relations.

Instead of steering our efforts toward changing gender relations between the sexes, including sexual relations, we are encouraged to accept fast 'technical fixes'. Male-female relations and their contextualizations remain unchanged; we can point to no major change in these relations in terms of greater autonomy for women. On the contrary, the quick 'technical fixes' have freed men more than ever from responsibility for the consequences of sexual intercourse and have imposed on women a new determination-by-others, a new *heteronomy*. This becomes domination by pharmaceutical concerns, medical experts, the state, as well as by men who now expect women to be always available to them.

The dilemma that women face with regard to self-determination is not at all recent. The old as well as the new women's movements have at least partially overworked themselves in their attempt to bring about the French Revolution *'aufeminin'*, demanding for women the freedom, equality and autonomy which, according to the bourgeois revolutions, would apply to all human beings. And in these efforts we come up against, now as then, the barrier which our female anatomy, our female body, seemingly constitutes. To overcome this barrier and to constitute woman as a self-determined *subject*, too, was the aim of the old women's liberation movement. As far as 'body politics' goes, the Movement for Birth Control, Sexual Reform, Self-determined Motherhood and

Protection of Mothers started at the end of the nineteenth century. This movement demanded, as Susan Zimmermann has shown, that women take conscious possession of their body and its needs. This was a central element in establishing the right over the self, the right to determine the self. And, further,

> the idea of such a right to self-determination over the body, a body which was analytically clearly seen as separated and apart from consciousness, has its roots, quite obviously, in the freedom of the individual from personal dependency and direct personal subjection. This freedom is a constitutive postulate of bourgeois society.[6]

Yet, it was already clear that this right of self-determination depends on whether or not a woman is the owner, the proprietor of her body. 'Woman must become the owner, the mistress of herself. . . Knowledge, humanity's only salvation, must empower woman to decide by herself whether she is to become a mother or not . . . That indeed will liberate woman.'[7] This movement strove to allow woman to rise from the position of 'object' to that of the intelligent individual, 'to being a self-steering subject, to rise from being a "thing" to being a person or personality — and thus, with the help of modern knowledge of the body, to acquire the ability to take possession of her materiality, to govern and steer it.'[8]

Susan Zimmermann points out that this attempt to become a self-determined subject meant not only that woman had to divide herself into an owning, governing, controlling part — the head — and controlled, possessed parts, but also that in the final analysis, this movement had to ask for the help of the state in guaranteeing the restructuring of woman as a civil subject. Thus, the state would gain control over the 'product and the production process'.[9] She concludes: 'Where bourgeois individuality emerges, every direct and spontaneous self-organization of the holistic living connectedness including that of the own person, broadly speaking — gets lost.'[10]

The questions we ask ourselves today in our struggle against the new reproductive technologies, are not in fact that new. But perhaps this is the first time we are looking critically at an idea which, since the Enlightenment, has become the fundamental concept of emancipation and freedom: the concept of self-determination.

Historical and philosophical foundations of the concept of self-determination

Why was the entire effort of the old women's movement focused upon finally giving woman the status of a citizen, of a subject? It was because this subject, this individual, this free, self-assured, autonomous person had been the goal of all attempts at emancipation, of all bourgeois revolutions. Yet when we look more closely at the history of these revolutions we notice that while freedom, equality, and autonomy were postulated as universal human rights for all, entire categories of human beings were *de facto* excluded from these human rights: the slaves who worked for European colonialists on the plantations in America; and workers without property. For only the *owners of property* could be subjects in the full societal sense.[11]

Thus, when we look at the totality of these processes, instead of narrowing our vision to an androcentric and eurocentric perspective, we can formulate the following thesis: the rise of man was based on the descent of woman. Europe's progress was based on the regression of colonies. The development of productive forces (science, technology) was based on robbery, warfare and violence, at home as well as in the colonies. And self-determination of the social individual, the subject, was — and is — based on the definition of the 'Other', the definition as object, of certain human beings. In other words: autonomy of the subject is based on heteronomy (being determined by others) of some Other (nature, other human beings, 'lower' parts of the self).

The relation between self-determination and determination-by-others is antagonistic, and necessarily so in this dualistic paradigm. We have been told that, since the eighteenth century, European citizenry had freed itself from being determined by others by its willingness for hard work — the protestant ethic, the progress of science and its new wealth. The fact is, however, that this new class, and civil society at large, would not have come into possession of these riches without the simultaneous colonization of the world, of nature, and of women.

The costs for the rise of the citizen, of the 'free' social subject, were borne by others. And these costs are usually justified — by liberals as well as Marxists — by reference to the teleology of history. They are said to have been necessary if humanity was to rise from barbarism to civilization, to culture, to freedom.[12]

Simone de Beauvoir's enlightenment heritage

If I said: self-determination cannot exist without determination-by-others, and put this within a larger historical context, it would become necessary to prove that my statement applies to the individual woman and to women in general. I do not only mean to say that white middle-class women in the North can gain more self-determination through further subjection of nature and of the Third World,[13] I mean this also with regard to the relation that the individual woman develops to herself, to her body. I have already mentioned that she had to learn, since the Age of Enlightenment, to perceive her own body — as well as nature — as something separate from the self, or even as her enemy. She had to split herself into this master-slave relationship or, to remind us of the supermarket of saleable body parts, to divide herself into several pieces, in order to become a social subject, the owner of her own person. This is the necessary consequence of the emancipatory utopia which began during the Enlightenment with the 'white man's' domination of nature, of women, of colonies.

As Evelyn Fox Keller[14] and others have argued, since the Enlightenment efforts have been made to erase from our concept of knowledge all that might remind us that humans are born from women and must die, that they have a body, senses, emotions, such as sympathy or antipathy, that furthermore they possess experience and, finally, that they are in a 'living relationship', with the environment: the earth, the water, the air, plants, animals, and other human beings.

The same process of self-alienation occurred with regard to the human body. Anatomy thus became the leading science that took power over the body and provided the methodological principles for the developing natural sciences: 'To render visible, to dissect, to discover' — the vivisection of the holistic, living interconnectedness and of the relationship between the human being and his/her body.[15]

Simone de Beauvoir's analysis of the 'woman question', as well as her utopia of women's emancipation, has its philosophical roots in the Hegelian master-slave dialectics, as mediated by Sartre.[16] According to Hegel, self-consciousness (the assuredness of the self) — and with it also self-determination, the so-called being-for-the-self — can develop only in opposition to life, in transcending the mere being immersed in life cycles. Yet this life, the organic world, the everyday world of particular experiences, is necessary because we are not purely mind. This being-immersed-in-life Sartre and de Beauvoir call *immanence*. Freedom, self-determination, higher values and culture can be reached only by transcending this immanence. According to Hegel, the self can only become conscious of itself in opposition to another consciousness, as external object. This object is at the same time the object of desire. The Ego (self-consciousness) tries to 'incorporate' the Other, the object, through overcoming its otherness. The satisfaction of desire implies overcoming the independent otherness. Through the destruction of the Other's independence, the Ego realizes its own self-consciousness as being in the world.

This is also how Simone de Beauvoir refers to the male-female relationship: man reaches his freedom and transcendence by separating himself from immanence and by making woman his Other, that is, by annihilating her autonomous being. De Beauvoir's problem then is: how can woman reach *transcendence?* For transcendence represents for de Beauvoir, as well as for Hegel and Sartre, freedom and self-determination. This cannot be attained through being immersed in everyday life. Women's emancipation means to achieve transcendence which is self-determination through freely chosen actions and projects, such as careers and social and cultural activity, rather than housework and childcare.

The dilemma of self-determination within the dualism of transcendence (self-determination/freedom, the universal) and immanence (life/nature, the organic/the animal, the particular) is clearly revealed. We as women must, according to de Beauvoir, face the problems of the conflict between our conscious being as autonomous subject and our physical being, our female body.

Even if we agree with de Beauvoir that it was men's doing to lock women into immanence (into life, into dailiness, kitchen, the mere life cycles, biology), we must ask how self-determination can be possible within this framework. According to de Beauvoir, what women 'demand today is to be recognized as existents by the same right as men and not to subordinate existence to life, the human being to its animality.'[17] She maintains the dualistic and hierarchical split between life and freedom/self-determination, between nature and culture, between spirit and matter. She maintains alienation from the body, especially from the female body which, according to her, hinders self-determination (transcendence). Our body is our enemy. Thus, she does not question this split, European man's project, particularly since the Enlightenment, as the prerequisite for freedom and emancipation. She wants to be like man, like the master, and sees no other possibility but to establish dominance of the head (master) within the female body (slave).

Although de Beauvoir states quite clearly that male self-determination is based on the subjection and determination-by-others of women and nature, she hopes to reach female self-determination by following exactly the same logic, which must however mean to subject some other Other. For, according to this paradigm, without object there is no subject, without immanence there is no transcendence, without slavery there is no freedom. Who then is the Other for women? That is de Beauvoir's question. It is, consequently, the female body perceived as enemy, particularly its 'wild' generative capacities.

In my view, here is the explanation of the fact that many feminists perceive the new reproductive technologies as a contribution to women's emancipation, for these technologies will seemingly make us more independent of this animal body. No wonder, then, that some French feminists declared that having rationalized production through technology, it is now logical to rationalize reproduction. Those who define autonomy, self-determination, transcendence, and freedom in Simone de Beauvoir's terms, cannot but agree to self-mutilation, or to the mutilation of others.

Re-creation of a 'living relation'[18]

As I said earlier, the position of so-called liberals and progressives, and of so-called conservatives, with regard to a pregnant woman's relation to the being growing within her, are not as different as loud polemics may infer.[19] In both cases the symbiosis between embryo and woman is analytically being dissected. The so-called liberals and progressives say that the embryo is nothing but a cluster of cells, a thing, a piece of property. The conservatives say that the embryo is a fully-fledged legal person who must above all be protected from the woman.

Both regard the embryo as something alien to and separate from the pregnant woman. As can be seen in this example as soon as this symbiosis, this living relation, is technically dissected, these parts enter into an antagonistic relation. One part will combat the other: there is a subject-object relationship. As the embryo does not yet have self-determination, the state, as the highest social subject, becomes a stand-in during the struggle against the mother. The same happens when the embryo is considered a thing, a piece of property, which then needs protection. Here also, in the final analysis, the state must guarantee that the interests of the given property-owners (of eggs, embryos, sperm, etc.) be respected against misuse and damages. In order to protect the interests of the concerned parties (as we must now call them) from damages and damage suits, detailed contracts must be concluded between clinic and woman, physician and woman, woman and man, and so forth. The state must guarantee the fulfilment of such contracts. More liberalization, therefore, leads necessarily to more state intervention. All demands for self-determination are addressed to the state: it should either provide more liberal laws or abolish limiting ones. What most women do not want to know, however, is that the state will do this only if we give it more control over all reproductive processes — pre-natal care, hospital births — and that it is technology that makes this increasing control possible.

Furthermore, women's demands for self-determination are directed to science and technology which are supposed to bring us either safer means of contraception or safe motherhood. In this many overlook that they put themselves more and more into the hands of multinational, profit-oriented pharmaceutical corporations that do worldwide business with fertility as well as with infertility. And what of 'self-determination' then? Women have the 'self-determined' choice between several pills, spirals, intrauterine devices, pessaries, abortions. They can choose between different firms that produce these means, as they can choose between 'Tide' and 'All'. The politics of population control within the 'Third World' is increasingly carried on according to methods of 'social marketing'. Here, women can maintain the illusion of 'self-determination' and 'freedom of choice' by having permission to choose between pink, green, and gold pills. Yet we women know that there is no contraceptive device that does not harm the female body. Self-determination has in fact been reduced to 'freedom of choice in the supermarket'. Self-determination still means then simultaneous determination-by-others of a part of ourselves, or else the harming of the symbioses we ourselves represent.

Since these connections have become clear to me, I cannot use the concept of self-determination in this naive way as an expression for a feminist utopia. Of course, that does not provide us with a different concept. But for me, the example of reproductive technologies has clarified one thing: we must oppose further vivisection by the techno-patriarchs in the name of our 'self-determination' of the living relations, the symbioses. For it is this technological split which renders possible the antagonism between parts, their marketing and use. The female body as provider of raw materials for the bio-future-industry of Mr All Powerful!

I am aware that the concept of symbiosis has negative connotations within the women's movement. In psychoanalysis, the separation of the individual from the symbiosis with the mother is considered the premise for adulthood, for autonomy. It is always implied that symbiosis, 'the living together' — for that is what symbiosis means — cannot but mean a parasitical, dominative relationship, supposedly glued to our female anatomy. Yet we know that this relationship of domination between mother and child is not simply 'nature', but rather the result of societal shaping of women within patriarchal societies, a result of violence. The problem does not lie with our anatomy which enables us to bring forth children, but rather with the destruction of living relations and patriarchal dominance. Technological strategies of contraception have not eliminated this dominance nor led to the preservation and rebuilding of these living connections, but rather to further degrade and atomize women.[20]

The re-creation of living relations does not only mean that we must refuse the technodocs further access to our bodies, but also that other human beings, women, men and children stand in a living social relation to the pregnant or to the infertile woman. The re-creation of living relations also means that the relation between the generations, above all between mothers and daughters, will be freed from patriarchal chains. Women's liberation cannot mean that each daughter-generation must first of all see itself in enmity to the mother-generation and that freedom must be exercised first as 'separation from the mothers'. From where should the support, knowledge, and, yes, love also, come, that a woman needs when she realizes that she is pregnant or that she is infertile? Without a supportive environment, a loving or living relation with, above all the mother-generation, the individual woman has nothing with which to oppose the technodocs, or the state.

Re-creating living relations also means that men, too, accept responsibility for life, including responsibility for the consequences of sexual intercourse, unlike the old saying: 'Lust for us, burden for women'. I see no prospect for the liberation of women in the removal, by technology, of the burden that our female corporality attaches to our lust, so that we, like men, could then enjoy 'pure lust'. In my opinion, women's liberation cannot mean separation from this corporality, a 'rise' into men's realm of transcendence; on the contrary, it must mean the attachment of men to these living connections, this dailiness, this burden, this immanence. For that, there is no need for new technologies but rather new relations between the sexes, where lust and burden will be shared equally. It is time that both women and men begin to understand that nature is not our enemy, that our body is not our enemy, that our mothers are not our enemies.

Notes

1. See Chapter 13.
2. Farida Akhter, *Depopulating Bangladesh.* Dhaka, UBINIG, 1986, pp. 2-3.
3. The position of the Global Network on Reproductive Rights is fundamentally the same as that of liberal feminism.
4. This argument was put forward after our first congress: 'Women Against Reproductive and Genetic Engineering' in Bonn, April 1985, by Arnim v. Gleich. (See Arnim v. Gleich, 'Gentechnologie und Feminismus.' *Kommune,* Vol. 3, No. 12, 1985, pp. 51-54.) This position was discussed in *Kommune* Vol. 3, No. 12, 1985, by Heidemarie Dann, Maria Mies and Regine Walch.
5. See Mies, Chapter 3. Several feminists have already addressed this argument which puts feminists and foetalists on an equal footing. Janice Raymond has pointed out that from a woman-centred position one could never say that feminists and foetalists are the same. (See Janice G. Raymond, 'Fetalists and Feminists: They are not the Same.' In *Made to Order: The Myth of Reproductive and Genetic Progress,* Patricia Spallone and Deborah L. Steinberg, (eds), London, Pergamon (1987). In West Germany, Renate Sadrozinski again discussed this point in the context of the debate on a new Embryo Protection Law proposed to the Parliament. (See Renate Sadrozinski, 'Kinder oder keine-entscheiden wir alleine' — On the Abolition of the Law Against Abortion and the Patriarchal Need to Protect Embryos. Reproductive and Genetic Engineering, Journal of International Feminist Analysis Vol. 2, No. 1 (1989), pp. 1-10.) I agree with Janice Raymond that the status of motherhood cannot be raised (as the foetalists would have it) until the status of women generally is raised (as the foetalists would not have it) (Raymond, p. 65), but I do not share her belief that an appeal to give women the same human rights as men will solve this dilemma.
6. Susan Zimmermann, 'Sexualreform und neue Konzepte von Mutterschaft und Mutterschutz Beginn des 20. Jahrhunderts.' Diploma dissertation, University of Vienna, 1985/86, p. 11.
7. Ibid., p. 12.
8. Ibid.
9. Ibid.
10. Ibid., p. 120.
11. Nevertheless this was not strictly observed for women. In the US and the UK, for instance, rich women property owners had the vote, but in the course of the nineteenth century the suffrage was taken away from them. Thus, woman, even if she owned property, could no longer be a political subject.

Obviously, this was the consequence of her being 'subject' to a man through marriage. We must note that women were not left behind, they were returned to a less developed stage. Slaves suffered the same fate when, in the British colonies for instance, they were forbidden to become Christians; slave status was considered incompatible with the (Protestant) freedom of the Christian. It was said, therefore, that 'negroes' were of a different species, were not full human beings. Hegel explained this demotion of 'negroes' to the level of sub-humans and therefore slavehood, by saying they had not risen above the natural state. (See G. Wilhelm Hegel, *Vorlesungen uber die Philosophie der Geschichte*. Frankfurt, Suhrkamp, 1970). Rhoda Reddock has shown that British settlers justified slavery by asserting, upon the findings of ethnologists, that 'negroes' belonged to another species. (See Rhoda Reddock, *A History of Women and Labour in Trinidad and Tobago*, Zed Books, London, 1993.) All these regressions from humanity to 'nature,' these 'naturizations' as I have called them, took place at the same time as bourgeois revolutions aimed at creating the free, self-determining individual.

12. Victims are being comforted by assurances that they also will at some time — through further development, and productive effort — reach the masters' level. What is good for the rulers, said Engels, is good for all. (See F. Engels, *The Family, Private Property and the State.*) But regardless of whether or not this is so, we must come to understand that the logic of a 'catching-up development' or the politics of the rise of the oppressed to the status of 'free and self-determining subjects' cannot succeed, either politically, economically, or culturally. For when the oppressed have climbed one step, the rulers will again be two steps ahead on the ladder of this unending process.

13. Irene Stoehr and Angelika Birk, 'Der Fortschritt entlasst seine Tochter.' In *Frauen und Ökologie, Gegen den Machbarkeitswahn*, Die GRÜNEN im Bundestag (Koln, Volksblattverlag, 1987). Maria Mies, *Patriarchy and Accumulation on a World Scale: Women in the International Division of Labour*. London, Zed Books, 1991.

14. Evelyn Fox Keller, *Reflections on Gender and Science*. New Haven, Yale University Press, 1985.

15. Hartmut Bohme and Gernot Bohme, *Das Andere der Vernunft, Zur Entwicklung von Rationalitatsstrukturen am Biespiel Kants*. Frankfurt, Suhrkamp, 1985, p. 52.

16. See also the discussion of Sartre and de Beauvoir in Mary O'Brien 'Sorry We Forgot Your Birthday,' in *The Politics of Reproduction*. London, Routledge and Kegan Paul, 1985. Genevieve Lloyd has also discussed and criticized de Beauvoir's conceptualization of women's emancipation. Genevieve Lloyd, *Male and Female in Western Philosophy*. University of Minnesota Press, 1985.

17. Simone de Beauvoir, *The Second Sex*. New York, Vintage Books, Random House, 1974, p. 73.

18. I am not sure if 'living relation' is the best translation of the German expression 'der lebendige Zusammenhang', which signifies the necessary living and life-sustaining interrelatedness of life on earth, at the personal as well as the social or communal level. It implies materiality and reciprocity.

19. Mies, see Chapter 4.

20. If a pregnant woman does not want to bring her pregnancy to term, this living symbiosis is also disrupted. But this is not, as Renate Sadrozinski has pointed out, an act of self-determination (see Sadrozinski, p. 4) but rather the choice to resist a situation which is basically determined by patriarchal structures.

15. GATT*, Agriculture and Third World Women

Vandana Shiva

Agriculture and related activities are the most important source of livelihood for Third World women. 'Free-trade' in agriculture as construed in GATT terms aims to create freedom for transnational corporations (TNCs) to invest, produce and trade in agricultural commodities without restriction, regulation or responsibility. This freedom for agribusiness is based on the denial of freedom to rural women to produce, process and consume food according to the local environmental, economic and cultural needs. What GATT aims to achieve is the replacement of women and other subsistence producers by TNCs as the main providers of food. Behind the obfuscation of such terms as 'market access', 'domestic support', 'sanitary and phytosanitary measures' and 'intellectual property rights' in the final draft of the GATT agreement, is a raw restructuring of power around food: taking it away from people and concentrating it in the hands of a handful of agro-industrial interests. The conflict is not between farmers of the North and those of the South, but between small farmers everywhere and multinationals. It is no surprise that the bulk of US, Japanese and European farmers are also opposed to the proposed GATT reforms, because these reforms are meant to drive the mass of small farmers out of business.

In the Third World, most small farmers are women, even though their role has remained invisible and has been neglected in official agriculture development programmes. By focusing on international trade in food, GATT policies are aimed at further marginalizing the household and domestic food economies in which women play a significant role. Further, since GATT is a self-executing treaty, it will automatically lead to the setting up of a Multilateral Trade Organization (MTO) which, with World Bank and IMF, will form the centre of world governance.

* General Agreement on Tariffs and Trade

Women and food production

The negative impact of GATT will be greater on Third World women because they play a major role in food production and processing, even though this fact has remained invisible and neglected.

In India, agriculture employs 70 per cent of the working population, and about 84 per cent of all economically active women.[1] For example, in the tribal economy of Orissa — shifting cultivation *(bogodo)* — women spend 105.4 days per year on agricultural operations compared to men's 59.11 days.[2]

According to Vir Singh's assessment in the Indian Himalaya, a pair of bullocks work for 1,064 hours, a man for 1,212 hours and a woman for 3,485 hours a year on a one hectare farm: a woman works longer than men and farm animals combined![3]

K. Saradamoni's study of women agricultural labourers and cultivators in three rice growing states — Kerala, Tamilnadu and West Bengal — shows that both groups of women make crucial contributions to production and processing.[4] Joan Mencher's studies in the Palghat region of Kerala reveal that outside ploughing, which is exclusively men's work, women have a predominant role in all other processes. On the basis of this study, it is estimated that more than two-thirds of the labour input is female.[5]

Bhati and Singh in a study of the gender division of labour in hill agriculture in Himachal Pradesh show that overall women contribute 61 per cent of the total labour on farms.[6] A detailed study by Jain and Chand in three villages each in Rajasthan and West Bengal, covering 127 households over 12 months, highlights the fact that women in the age group 19-70 spend longer hours than do men in a variety of activities.[7]

Women's work and livelihoods in subsistence agriculture, for example, are based on multiple use and management of biomass for fodder, fertilizer, food and fuel. The collection of fodder from the forest is part of the process of transferring fertility for crop production and managing soil and water stability. The work of the women engaged in such activity tends to be discounted and made invisible for all sectors.[8]

When these allied activities which are ecologically and economically critical are taken into account, agriculture is revealed as the major occupation of 'working' women in rural India. The majority of women in India are not simply 'housewives', but farmers.[9]

Displacing small farmers

GATT policies that encourage free export and import of agricultural products translate into policies for the destruction of small farmers' local food production capacities. By locating food in the domain of international trade, these policies dislocate its production in the household and community. Policies being imposed under 'market access' and 'domestic support' on the agriculture agreement are basically policies that allow TNCs to displace the small producer. Under 'market access'[10] countries are forced to allow free import of food grain and remove all restrictions on imports and exports. 'Market access' is thus an instrument for the conversion of the Third World's subsistence production of food into a 'market' for TNCs. Similarly, by relating domestic policy to international markets through clauses on domestic support, GATT facilitates the shifting of subsidies from poor producers and consumers to big agribusiness.

This has been India's experience under World Bank/IMF Structural Adjustment which forced the government to reduce domestic support and to import wheat. During 1992, as a result of the structural adjustment, there was a difference of Rs. 80 between market price and government procurement price of wheat. Enough wheat was produced in the country, but government policy, distorted by structural adjustment, failed to procure it. Using this artificially created scarcity, and under World Bank pressure for import liberalization of food grain, the Indian government bought 2.5 million tonnes of wheat in 1992 at the cost of Rs. 4,800 crore (one crore = one hundred million) in hard currency.

The structural adjustment programme prescribed that food subsidies which provided cheap food for public distribution, be removed; simultaneously, the Bank recommended liberalization of farm imports. The net result has been not the removal of food subsidies, but their redistribution; the beneficiaries are no longer India's poor but powerful transnational corporations in the US.

In 1991, India *exported* 672,000 tonnes of wheat at the cost of over Rs. 178 crore. Under the pressure of import liberalization and structural adjustment, however, India *imported* 2.5 million tonnes of wheat in 1992. Of this, one million tonnes was from the US, which gives a $30 per tonne subsidy to its exporters. Despite the US subsidy, the cost of imported wheat after adding transport and handling charges was higher than would have been the subsidy the government paid to Indian farmers — this amounted to

Rs. 260 per quintal (one quintal = 100 kg) of wheat, but imported wheat from North America costs Rs. 560 per quintal. Indian farmers' movements are therefore demanding that, rather than import wheat and subsidize multinational corporations (thereby draining foreign exchange and increasing debt), the government should raise the domestic support prices.

Neither fertilizer decontrol nor import liberalization have reduced the burden on the Indian exchequer. Public spending and foreign exchange expenditure have actually increased under the structural adjustment programme, although this is supposed to reduce both. The aim seems to be destabilization instead of stabilization of the economy, leaving India with no option but further dependence on the World Bank and TNCs. According to an ex-US Agricultural Secretary, 'the idea that developing countries should feed themselves is an anachronism from a bygone era. They could better ensure their food security by relying on US agricultural products which are available, in most cases, at a lower cost.'

However, US foodgrain is cheaper not because it is produced more efficiently at less cost but because despite high costs of production, US corporations and the US government can subsidize and fix prices.

In a letter to *Time* magazine, Senator Rudy Boschwitz, a spokesman of the Reagan farm policy, stated quite clearly that US farm policy was aimed at putting Third World food exporters out of business. He wrote: 'If we do not lower our farm prices to discourage these countries now, our worldwide competitive position will continue to slide and be much more difficult to regain. This discouragement should be one of the foremost goals of our agricultural policy.'[11]

Lowering food prices in the US is achieved by precisely those measures such as subsidies, which the World Bank, IMF and GATT want removed in Third World countries through their conditionalities. Thus in 1986, the US spent almost $10 billion to subsidize corn and wheat exports for which it received only $4.2 billion. While the World Bank uses arguments of cost effectiveness to dismantle public food distribution systems and remove food subsidies in the Third World, the US builds its food monopoly through totally subsidized and *cost ineffective* programmes.

Thus, the US lowered world prices of rice from around eight dollars to less than four dollars per hundredweight, not by reducing production costs, but by providing an export subsidy of $17 per hundredweight. This totally artificial price is nearly $80 per tonne below Third World costs of production, and approximately $140 per ton below the US production costs.[12]

The result is an overt attack on the survival of Third World farmers and Third World economies. The effect of the 50 per cent reduction in world rice prices by the US Farm Policy was so severely damaging to the four million Thai rice farmers that they were forced to demonstrate against the US Farm Bill at the US Embassy in Bangkok.

The dumping of subsidized surpluses brings business to food TNCs, but starvation to Third World peasants. During 1986, the US and the EC were selling wheat surpluses in West African countries, such as Mali and Burkina Faso, at prices as low as $60 per tonne — around one-third lower than equivalent production, transport and marketing costs for locally produced cereals such as sorghum. This was facilitated by direct and indirect subsidies and export prices.[13] Subsidized TNCs are thus pitted against Third World peasants who earn less from their produce as cheap imports depress the price of staples and are finally forced to leave agriculture when earnings fall below subsistence.

Food imports were forced upon Costa Rica through the World Bank's structural adjustment programme, which led to a ten per cent a year increase in imports and a sharp decline in the local production of staples. The Philippines has had a similar experience: from a position of near self-sufficiency in the mid-1980s, by 1990 the Philippines was importing some 600,000 tons of rice annually, equivalent to some 16 per cent of national consumption.[14]

The displacement of small farmers is a deliberate policy of GATT. The draft agreement has clauses for 'structural adjustment' for 'producer retirement' and 'resource retirement' which is merely a convoluted way of stating that farmers and their resources should be treated as surplus and dispensed with through 'programmes designed to remove land or other resources, including livestock, from marketable agricultural production.'[15] This includes violent mechanisms such as wasteful slaughter of livestock.

The models of agricultural production introduced by TNCs therefore necessitate the displacement of small farmers and their treatment as a 'surplus' population. The small peasants who produce for themselves will be threatened, because worldwide, World Bank structural adjustment loans have supported processes which are conducive to small farmers mortgaging their land and their consequent displacement. In addition, austerity measures and the liberalization of the banking sector mean that agricultural credit to small farmers is squeezed, and farm inputs and transport costs increase. Privatization of banks, and development of agribusiness also mean that land, the farmers' most important asset will pass into the hands of corporate agribusiness and banks. This process has already taken place in the US where farm debt rose from $120 billion in the early 1970s to $225 billion in the early 1980s. Farm population dropped by 30 per cent between 1950 and 1960 and a further 26 per cent between 1960 and 1970 as small farmers were thrown off their land. Since 1981, 600,000 small farmers have been driven off their land.[16] IMF/World Bank/GATT prescriptions aim at applying those same policies to Indian agriculture. Imagine the consequences if 50 per cent of Indian farmers and peasants were alienated from their land over the coming years! It cannot be argued that they can seek industrial employment because there, too, an 'exit' policy is under operation.

The displacement of women and other small peasants from agricultural production will also have a serious impact on food consumption since peasants' access to food is through participation in its production. As TNCs dump subsidized surpluses on the Third World, peasants are driven out of food production into famine.

A conservative assessment of the impact of so-called liberalization on food consumption indicates that in India, by the year 2000, there will be 5.6 per cent more hungry people than would have been the case if free trade in agriculture was not introduced. Free trade will lead to 26.2 per cent reduction in human consumption of agricultural produce.[17] The growth of free trade thus implies the growth of hunger.

The growth of TNC profits takes place at the cost of people's food needs being met. Since women have been responsible for food production and provisioning, the decline in food availability has direct impact on them. Control over food is thus increasingly taken out of the hands of Third World women and put in the hands of Northern TNCs. The concentration of markets, trade and power in the hands of a few TNCs makes competition by small farmers in the Third World impossible. US grain exports account for 76 per cent of world agricultural trade. In 1921, 36 firms accounted for 85 per cent of US wheat exports. By the end of the 1970s just six companies: Cargill, Continental Grain, Luis Dreyfus, Bunge, Andre & Co and Mitsui/Cook exported 85 per cent of all

US wheat, 95 per cent of its corn, 80 per cent of its sorghum. These same companies were handling 90 per cent of the EC's trade in wheat and corn, and 90 per cent of Australia's sorghum exports. Between them, Cargill, the largest private corporation in the US, and Continental Grain, the third largest, control 25 per cent of the market.[18]

When the corporate interest has been damaged the US government has retaliated politically. The threat posed to developing country food policy sovereignty in the Uruguay Round has been strengthened by the case of Nigeria — formerly sub-Sahara's largest wheat importer. In 1988, the Nigerian government imposed a ban on wheat imports; these had depressed domestic food prices and reduced the production of domestic staples such as cassava, yams and millet. The wheat campaign by Cargill Corporation (formerly Nigeria's main wheat supplier), has threatened trade sanctions against Nigerian textiles. It has also warned that a GATT settlement on agricultural trade liberalization will be applied to demand the restoration of free market access for US wheat. Clauses on cross retaliation in GATT are aimed at such disciplining. That this freedom will rob Nigerian farmers of freedom to produce their own staples is of little concern to Cargill or the US.[19] The recent import of wheat in India portends a similar vulnerability for that country. Cheap imports will not only push farmers out of agricultural production, they will also add to India's foreign debts and balance of payment position, because food is being imported instead of locally produced. Given the cosy relationship between government and corporations it is of little surprise that 'free trade' as interpreted on GATT platforms allows TNCs to regulate prices, again demonstrating that 'free trade' for corporations is based on the denial of freedom and autonomy to Third World governments and people.

Besides manipulating prices, TNCs also control exports and imports through the manipulation of food safety standards. The Dunkel draft clearly states that sanitary and phytosanitary measures will be 'harmonized' in order to minimize their negative effects on trade. The draft also states that standards will be set by international agencies such as Codex Alimentarius, Dupont, Chevron, Monsanto, Merck, American Gnanud, Mitsubishi, Shell or advisors to Codex, which are strongly influenced by TNCs. In addition, according to the draft, 'contracting parties shall ensure that sanitary and phytosanitary measures based on scientific principles are not maintained against available scientific evidence'.

Together, these principles mean that GATT can apply standards to regulate import and export for the convenience of TNCs. On such criteria, tailored to fit TNCs' interests, genetically-engineered organisms introduced by TNCs can be treated as 'safe', and organic food exported by the Third World can be treated as 'unsafe'.[20]

The removal of state controls over agriculture at the national level through GATT does not mean an absence of control over Third World farmers. But instead of being controlled by Third World governments, Third World farmers' fate is under the control of international bureaucracies (the IMF, World Bank and the MTO) which serve TNC interests. This does not imply any measure of freedom for farmers, but new and less accountable forms of control and regulation. Freedom at the small farmer level can be based only on freedom from state as well as transnational corporate sector control.

Intellectual Property Rights and ownership of seeds

Intellectual Property Rights (IPR) are another instrument in the GATT agreement which will dispossess rural women of their power, control, and knowledge. IPRs in GATT and other international platforms aim to take seed out of peasant women's custody and make it the private property of TNCs. By adding 'trade related' to IPRs, GATT has forced issues of the ownership of genetic resources and life forms on to the agenda of international trade through TRIPs.

At the conceptual level, Trade-Related Intellectual Property Rights (TRIPs) are restrictive, being by definition weighted in favour of transnational corporations, and against citizens in general, and particularly Third World peasants and forest-dwellers. People everywhere innovate and create. In fact, the poorest have to be the most innovative, since they have to create their means of survival while it is daily threatened. Women have been important innovators and protectors of seeds and genetic resources.

Limitations to the ownership of intellectual property rights, as construed in the trade negotiations, operate on a number of levels. The first is the shift from common to private rights: the preamble of the TRIPs agreement states that intellectual property rights are recognized only as private rights. This excludes all kinds of knowledge, ideas, and innovations that take place in the 'intellectual commons', in villages among farmers, in forests among tribals and even in universities among scientists. TRIPs is therefore a mechanism to privatize the intellectual commons and de-intelletualize civil society, so that in effect, the mind becomes a corporate monopoly.

The second limitation is that intellectual property rights are recognized only when knowledge and innovation generate profits, not when they meet social needs. According to Article 27.1,[21] to be recognized as an IPR, innovation must be capable of industrial application. Only profits and capital accumulation are recognized as viable uses of creativity. Under corporate control and the 'de-industrialization' of small-scale informal sector production, the social good is discounted.

The most significant limitation of IPRs is achieved by way of the prefix 'trade-related'. Most innovation by women is for domestic, local and public use, not for international trade; MNCs innovate for the sole purpose of increasing their share in global markets and international trade; and TRIPs in GATT will only enforce MNCs' rights to monopolize all production, distribution and profits at the cost of all citizens and small producers worldwide.

Article 27 on patentable matter is a clear indication that national decisions made on grounds of public interest are overruled. Article 27(1) states that 'patents shall be available for any inventions, whether products or processes, in all fields of technology, provided that they are new, involve an inventive step, and are capable of industrial application.' This nullifies the exclusions built into national patent laws for the protection of the public and the national interest. For example, in the Patent Act of India, 1970, methods of agriculture and horticulture were excluded, were not patentable, whereas the TRIPs text includes these as patentable. Under the Indian Patent Act, only process patents can be granted to food, medicines, drugs and chemical products, but under the MTO, the Third World will have to grant product patents also in this area. Article 27 calls for a review of the scope of patentability and subject matter of patents four years after signing the text. Within an MTO with no democratic structure, however, such a review will only be used by MNCs to expand the domain of their monopoly control. The worldwide movement against patents on life has rejected TRIPs in GATT, while Sustainable Agriculture Movements and biodiversity conservation movements have expressed concern about the universalization of patent regimes. Article 27(3) states that 'parties shall provide for the protection of plant varieties either by patents or by an effective *in generis* system or by any combination thereof.'[22]

Under the impact of this enforcement, farmers will not be allowed to save their own seed. The International Convention of the Union for the Protection of New Varieties of Plants (UPOV) had maintained farmers' rights to save seed, but in a March 1991 amendment this clause was removed. The new clause in UPOV (and TRIPs) can be used to enforce royalty payments on farmers if they save their own seed. With the stronger intellectual property rights regime being conceived under MTO, the transfer of extra funds as royalty payments from the poor to the rich countries would exacerbate the current Third World debt crisis tenfold. This is ironical, since most plant diversity originates in the Third World, and seeds and plant materials that today are under the control of the industrialized world, were originally taken freely from the farmers to whom they will now be sold back as patented material. As a result, seed companies will reap monopoly profits, while the genius of Third World farmers will go unrewarded and they will be banned from saving and using their own seeds.

IPRs in the area of seeds and plant material are in any case not easy to demarcate, since the genetic resources used by multinational corporations for claiming patents are the product of centuries of innovation and selection by Third World farmers, especially women. The UN Food and Agriculture Organization (FAO) has recognized these contributions in the form of 'Farmers' Rights'; and the Biodiversity Convention signed at the 1992 Earth Summit also recognizes them, and accepts the need to make IPRs subservient to the objectives of biodiversity conservation.

The TRIPs text, however, biased as it is in favour of acknowledging only MNC rights, goes against these agreements reached on other international platforms. The negative impact on farmers and other Third World citizens will be increased due to the extension of the working and the terms of the patent, and the reversal of the burden of proof. Article 34 of the draft text reverses the burden of proof in the area of process patents. In normal law, the accused is innocent unless proven guilty. Under the reversal in the MTO regime, however, it is the accused who must demonstrate their innocence; if they cannot do so, then they are deemed guilty of having infringed upon the right of the patent holder.[23]

In the area of agriculture this can have absurd and highly unjust consequences. MNCs are now taking out broad patents on plant varieties, covering ownership of traits and characteristics. With the reversal of the burden of proof clauses, it becomes legally possible for a corporation to accuse the farmers who originally contributed the seeds with a particular trait, of patent infringement. There is no clause in TRIPs to offer protection to farmers in such cases.

When this situation is combined with possibilities of cross-retaliation that the MTO will institutionalize, MNCs will have a very powerful tool to subsume all agriculture and all production under their monopoly control. This monopolization of the entire economy is the main motive for setting up an MTO with a TRIPs council.

The Third World has consistently maintained that IPRs have no place in international trade negotiations, furthermore, the relevance of applying IPRs to agriculture — biodiversity and biotechnology in particular — is a seriously contested issue. These are debates that need to evolve and be resolved democratically in order to protect people's health, and their environmental rights. To set up an MTO with the central issue of IPRs still unresolved, implies that only MNCs have rights, citizens have none. This regime is based not on free trade but corporations' freedom to engage in restrictive business practices thus providing a scenario for a global command economy based on coercion and non-accountable power.

Seeds will be at the centre of this conflict. Patented seed varieties linked to agrochemicals and agroprocessing are central to the creation of new dependencies. The New Seed Policy has already allowed the entry of multinationals in the seed sector; Trade Related Investments Measures (TRIMs) in GATT will make such investment even freer. TNCs, as we have noted, will thus take farmers' seeds, process them, and sell them back as patented varieties.

In India, the pharmaceutical giant, Sandoz (India), has entered into an agreement with Northup King of the US, subsidiary of its multinational parent company, and with the Dutch vegetable king, Zaaduine. ITC is tying up with Pacific Seeds, a subsidiary of Australia's Continental Grains; the US seed giant Cargill has tied up with Gill and Company, retaining a controlling interest in the company. Two other US companies, Seedtec International and Dehlgien, have entered into agreements with Maharashtra Hybrid and Nath Seed Company, respectively. Pioneer Hibred has started an Indian subsidiary Pioneer Seed Company. Apart from these, Hindustan Lever is negotiating with a Belgian firm, while Hoechst, Ciba-Geigy are reportedly moving in with other tie-ups.[24]

In addition to loss of control over genetic resources is a new threat of loss of control over ownership of land. As banks become privatized and contract farming is introduced, the farmer will risk losing his/her land. Protection of rights to land, water and genetic resources are central to the freedom of farmers. GATT, however, defines legal protection only in terms of the interests of the corporate sector and freedom of TNCs. Whose rights to resources need protection from the viewpoint of sustainability and justice? This question will move centre stage as farmers' and environmental movements begin to address the emerging control over natural resources by global interests for global profits.

Local control over natural resources is an essential precondition for farmers' freedom. But free trade which, as we have seen, implies a relocation of control over natural resources for farmers and Third World governments to global institutions has serious environmental consequences.

Corporations use land, water and genetic resources in non-renewable, non-sustainable ways, being mainly concerned to maximize profits rather than to conserve local resources. Local laws and regulations for limiting environmental degradation will be treated as barriers to free trade. Local communities' democratic decisions on resource conservation are thus excluded by GATT. The GATT draft by Dunkel requires that central governments adopt measures to ensure that state governments comply with GATT rules, which further reduces farmers' influence in decision-making. Thus farmers' organizations will be weakened, as will state legislators and parliament: all power will be concentrated in the hands of GATT and TNCs.

TNCs *vs* freedom for subsistence producers

The freedom that transnational corporations are claiming through intellectual property rights protection in the GATT agreement on TRIPs is the freedom that European colonizers have claimed since 1492 when Columbus set precedence in treating the licence to conquer non-European peoples as a *natural right* of European men. The land titles issued by the Pope through European kings and queens were the first patents. Charters and patents issued to merchant adventurers were authorizations to 'discover, find, search out and view such remote heathen and barbarous lands, countries and territories not actually possessed of any Christian prince or people.'[25] The colonizers' freedom was built on the slavery and subjugation of the people with original rights to the land.

This violent take-over was rendered 'natural' by defining the colonized people into nature, thus denying them their humanity and freedom.

Locke's treatise on property[26] effectually legitimized this same process of theft and robbery during the enclosure movement in Europe. Locke clearly articulates capitalism's freedom to build on the freedom to steal; he states that property is created by removing resources from nature through mixing with labour. But this 'labour' is not physical labour, but labour in its 'spiritual' form as manifested in the control of capital. According to Locke, only capital can add value to appropriated nature, and hence only those who own capital have the natural right to own natural resources; a right that supersedes the common rights of others with prior claims. Capital is thus defined as a source of freedom, but this freedom is based on the denial of freedom to the land, forests, rivers and biodiversity that capital claims as its own. Because property obtained through privatization of commons is equated with freedom, those commoners laying claim to it are perceived to be depriving the owner of capital of freedom. Thus peasants and tribals who demand the return of their rights and access to resources are regarded as thieves.

Within the ambit of IPRs, the Lockean concept of property merges with the Cartesian concept of knowledge, to give shape to a perverted world which appears 'natural' in the eyes of capitalist patriarchy. During the scientific revolution, Descartes fashioned a new intellectual world order in which mind and body were deemed to be totally separate, and only the male, European mind was considered capable of complete intellectual transcendence of the body. Intellectual and manual labour were thus pronounced to be 'unrelated', even though all human labour, however simple, requires a degree of unity of 'head and hand'. But capitalist patriarchy denies the 'head', the mind, to women and Third World peoples. The application of IPRs to agriculture is the ultimate denial of the intellectual creativity and contribution of Third World peasants, women and men who have saved and used seed over millennia.

The implication of a world-view that assumes the possession of an intellect to be limited to only one class of human beings is that they are entitled to claim all products of intellectual labour as their private property, even when they have appropriated it from others — the Third World. Intellectual property rights and patents on life are the ultimate expression of capitalist patriarchy's impulse to control all that is living and free.

GATT is the platform where capitalist patriarchy's notion of freedom as the unrestrained right of men with economic power to own, control and destroy life is articulated as 'free-trade'. But for the Third World, and for women, freedom has different meanings. In what seems the remote domain of international trade, these different meanings of freedom are a focus of contest and conflict. Free trade in food and agriculture is the concrete location of the most fundamental ethical and economic issues of human existence of the present times. It is here that Third World women have a unique contribution to make, because in their daily lives they embody the three colonizations on which modern patriarchy is based; the colonization of nature, of women and of the Third World.

Notes

1. National Sample Survey, 38th Round, Report No. 341.
2. Fernandes, Walter, and Geeta Menon, 'Tribal Women and Forest Economy', Indian Social Institute, New Delhi, 1987.
3. Singh, Vir, 'Hills of Hardship', *The Hindustan Times Weekly*, 18 January 1987.
4. Saradamoni, K., 'Labour, Land and Rice Production: Women's Involvement in their States', *Economic and Political Weekly*, 22 (17) 1987.
5. Mencher, Joan, 'Women's Work and Poverty: Women's Contribution to Household Maintenance in Two Regions of South India', in Droyer, D. and J. Bruce (eds) *A Home Divided: Women and Income Control in the Third World*, Stanford University Press, Stanford, 1987.
6. Bhati, J. B. and D. V. Singh, 'Women's Contribution to Agricultural Economy in Hill Regions of North West India', *Economic and Political Weekly*, Vol. 22, No. 17, 1987.
7. Jain, Devaki and Malini Chand Seth, 'Domestic Work: Its Implication for Enumeration of Workers', in Saradamoni (ed.) *Women, Work and Society*, Indian Statistical Institute, Delhi 1985.
8. Shiva, Vandana, *Staying Alive.Women, Ecology and Survival*. Kali, New Delhi, 1988 and Zed Books, 1990, London.
9. Shiva, Vandana, 'Women's Knowledge and Work in Mountain Agriculture'. Paper presented at Conference on Women in Mountain Development, ICIMOD, Kathmandu, 1988.
10. Draft Final Agreement on GATT, GATT Secretariat, Geneva, December 1991.
11. Shiva, Vandana, 'Structural Reforms and Agriculture', *Observer*, November 1992.
12. Ritchie, Mark and Kevin Ristau, 'Crisis by Design: A Brief Review of U.S. Farm Policy', League of Rural Voters Education Project, Minneapolis, 1987.
13. Watkins, Kevin, 'GATT and the Third World' in *Race and Class*, 'The New Conquistadors', Vol. 34, No. 1, July-September 1992.
14. Ibid.
15. GATT Draft Agreement

16. Ritchie, Mark and Kevin Ristau, op. cit.
17. Frohberg, K., G. Fischer and K. Parikh, 'Would Developing Countries Benefit from Agricultural Trade Liberalisation in OECD Countries' in Goldin, I. and Knudsen Odin (eds) *Agricultural Trade Liberalisation — Implications for Developing Countries.* OECD, Paris, 1990.
18. Morgan, Dan *Merchants of Grain.* New York, Viking, 1979.
19. Ritchie, Mark, 'GATT, Agriculture and the Environment, the US Double Zero Plan,' *Ecologist* Vol. 20, No. 6, November-December 1990.
20. Lang, Tim, 'Food Fit for the World? How the GATT Food Trade Talks Challenge Public Health, the Environment and the Citizen', Sustainable Agriculture, Food and the Environment (SAFE) Alliance, London, March 1992.
21. Draft Agreement, GATT.
22. Ibid.
23. Ibid.
24. 'Seeds — A Hard Row to Hoe', *India Today,* 15 February 1989.
25. Kadir, Djelal, *Columbus and the Ends of the Earth.* University of California Press, 1992, p. 90.
26. Locke, John, Peter Caslett (ed) *Two Treatises of Government.* Cambridge University Press, 1967.

16. The Chipko Women's Concept of Freedom

Vandana Shiva

On 30 November 1986, Chamundeyi, a woman of Nahi-Kala village in Doon Valley, was collecting fodder in the forest when she heard trucks climbing up the mountain toward the limestone quarry in the area. But since September 1986 there had been a Chipko camp on the road to the quarry set up by the village communities of Thano region, to stop the mining operations which have created ecological havoc in the region; the trucks should not, therefore, have been there. The quarry workers had attacked the protesters, removed them from the blockade, and driven the trucks through. Chamundeyi threw down her sickle, raced down the slope and stood in front of the climbing trucks, telling the drivers that they could go only over her dead body. After dragging her for a distance, they stopped and reversed.

In April 1987 the people of Nahi-Kala were still protesting because the government had been tardy in taking action to close the mine although the lease had expired in 1982. The mining operations were also in total violation of the 1980 Forest Conservation Act. People's direct action to stop the mining was an outcome of the government's failure to implement its own laws. The quarry contractor meantime tried to take the law into his own hands. On 20 March 1987, he brought about 200 hired thugs to the area who attacked the peaceful protesters with stones and iron rods. But the children, women and men did not withdraw from the blockade. They are their own leaders, their own decision-makers, their own source of strength.

The myth that movements are created and sustained by charismatic leaders from outside is shattered by the non-violent struggle in Nahi-Kala in which ordinary women like Itwari Devi and Chamundeyi have provided local leadership through extraordinary strength. It is the invisible strength of women like them that is the source of the staying power of Chipko — a movement whose activities in its two decades of evolution have been extended from embracing trees to embracing living mountains and living waters. Each new phase of Chipko is created by invisible women. In 1977, Bachni Devi of Advani created Chipko's ecological slogan: 'What do the forests bear? Soil, water and pure air.'

A decade later, in Doon Valley, Chamundeyi inspired the Chipko poet Ghanshyam 'Shailani' to write a new song:

> A fight for truth has begun
> At Sinsyaru Khala
> A fight for rights has begun
> In Malkot Thano
> Sister, it is a fight to protect
> Our mountains and forests.
> They give us life
> Embrace the life of the living trees
> And streams to your hearts
> Resist the digging of mountains
> Which kills our forests and streams
> A fight for life has begun at
> Sinsyaru Khala

On 29 March during a meeting of friends of Chipko, I spent a day with Chamundeyi and Itwari Devi — to learn about their hidden strengths, to learn from them about the hidden strengths of nature. Here are some extracts from our exchange of experiences:

Vandana: *What destruction has been caused by limestone mining in Nahi-Kala?*

Chamundeyi: When I came to Nahi 17 years ago, the forests were rich and dense with ringal, tun, sinsyaru, gald, chir, and banj. Gujral's mine has destroyed the ringal, the oak, the sinsyaru. Our water sources which are nourished by the forests have also dried up. Twelve springs have gone dry. Two years ago, the perennial waterfall, Mande-ka-Chara which originates in Patali-ka-Dhar and feeds Sinsyaru Khala went dry. Mining is killing our forests and streams, our sources of life. That is why we are ready to give up our lives to save our forests and rivers.

Itwari: Sinsyaru-ka-Khala was a narrow perennial stream full of lush sinsyaru bushes. Today it is a wide barren bed of limestone boulders. With the destruction caused by mining our water, mills, forests and paddy fields have been washed away. When Gujral first came he was in rags. I remember I had come to the water mill to get flour ground. Gujral had come with a dilapidated truck, and his lunch was a dry chappati, with raw onion. Today, after having robbed our mountain for 26 years, Gujral is a rich man with 12 trucks who can hire armies of thugs to trouble and attack us, as he hired armies of labour to dig our mountain. We have been camping on the road for seven months now to stop his mine, and his efforts to hurt us and threats to kill us keep increasing.

First he started picking limestone boulders from the river bed. Then he climbed the mountain. He has done ten years of very intensive mining and turned our rich and productive mountain into a desert. The source of Sinsyaru has become a desert. We decided then that the mine must be closed if our children were to survive.

The young boys of the Yuvak Mandal who are working with our Mahila Mandal to get the mine closed, were six months or one year old when Gujral first came to our village. They have spent a lifetime watching him treat our land and resources as his private property. The Chipko protest was precipitated when the boys went to demand royalty payment for the mining in Gram Sabha land. Gujral said to them, 'You have grown on crumbs I have thrown to you — how dare you demand royalty from me.' The boys said, 'We have grown with the nurturance of our mothers — and the mountains and forests and streams which are like our mothers — and we will no longer let you destroy our sources of sustenance. We will not let your trucks go to the mine.

C: On 20 March we saw Gujral's truck come. They pushed out the five people who were at the Satyagraha camp — meantime the women rushed down to the camp. We held on to the trucks and said, 'Please stop, listen to us.' They had hired women from the Dehra Dun slums to assault us — they pushed us aside and went to the line. Eight thugs stayed with us and said, 'Listen, mothers and sisters, you have been sitting on a Chipko protest for six months now with the Chipko activists. What facilities have they created for you in six months?' I said, 'Listen brothers, Gujral has been digging our mountain for 26 years, what has he done for us? The Chipko people have been with us for only six months of struggle — come back in 26 years and find out what they helped us create.' Gujral's people said, 'Ask for whatever you need — we will provide it.' We replied, 'We have only one need and one demand, that the mine be closed.' They said they would stop mining and only take what has already been mined. We told them, 'No, those stones came from the mountain and we will put them back to stabilize it. We will make check-dams with them. We will protect our forests and mountain with the boulders. These boulders are the flesh of *Dharti Ma* (Mother Earth). We will return them to where they belong, and heal her wounds.' Then they said, 'For each trip we make, we will give you earnings from our truckload of limestone.' We continued to insist that we wanted the mine closed, that nothing could tempt us. They said 'We will give you a truck for transport. Bahuguna cannot give you that.' We answered 'We are our own transport, our feet are our most dependable transport. We do not need your trucks. We only want the mine closed.'

V: *This is the third time they have attacked you; what happened in the November [1986] incident?*

C: I had just fed my children and was going to the forest for fodder with my sons Suraj Singh and Bharat Singh. I saw a truck coming. I sent Suraj Singh to inform the Satyagrahis at the Camp, but they had already been attacked and removed from the road. I met the trucks half way up the mine and put myself in front of them and said, 'The trucks can go only over my dead body.' They finally turned back.

V: *What are the three most important things in life you want to conserve?*

C: Our freedom and forests and food. Without these, we are nothing, we are impoverished. With our own food production we are prosperous — we do not need jobs from businessmen and governments — we make our own livelihood — we even produce crops for sale like rajma and ginger; two quintals of ginger can take care of all our needs. Forests are central as sources of fertilizer and fodder. Our freedom to work in the forests and to farm is very important. Gujral's mine is destroying our work and our prosperity while they talk of mining and 'creating' work and prosperity.

V: *Do you feel tempted by his bribes?*

I: Gujral offered my son Rs.500,000 if he would remove me from the Chipko protest. My son replied, 'Money I can get anywhere, but my mother's dignity and respect comes from the village community, and we can never sacrifice that.'

C: They went to my brother and said, 'Get your sister away.' Gujral himself came and said he would make a school and hospital for us. We asked him why it had taken him 26 years to think of all this? Now it was too late. We are determined to close his mine and protect ourselves.

V: *What is your source of strength (shakti)? What is Chipko's strength?*

I: *Shakti* comes to us from these forests and grasslands, we watch them grow, year in and year out through their internal *shakti* and we derive our strength from it. We watch our streams renew themselves and we drink their clear, sparkling water, that gives us shakti. We drink fresh milk, we eat ghee, we eat food from our own fields. All this gives us not just nourishment for the body but a moral strength, that we are our own masters, we control and produce our own wealth. That is why it is 'primitive', 'backward' women who do not buy their needs from the market but produce for themselves, who are leading Chipko. Our power is nature's power. Our power against Gujral comes from these inner sources and is strengthened by his attempts to oppress and bully us with his false power of money. We have offered ourselves, even at the cost of our lives, for a peaceful protest to close this mine, to challenge and oppose the power that Gujral represents. Each attempt to violate us has strengthened our integrity. They stoned us on 20 March when they returned from the mine. They stoned our children and hit them with iron rods, but they could not destroy our *shakti*.

17. Liberating the Consumer*

Maria Mies

Since the publication of the Club of Rome's *Limits to Growth*[1] and of the *Global 2000* Report to the President[2] it has become clear that the resource base of our planet is limited and that to pursue the economic philosophy of unlimited growth of goods and services, and hence money revenue, will necessarily outreach the planet's ecological limits. It is also clear that the 'good life' model, the living standard or consumer-oriented model prevailing in the rich countries of the industrialized North cannot be generalized to the rest of the world. (See Chapter 4.) Nevertheless, virtually all conceptions and strategies of development, both national and international, are explicitly or implicitly based on the assumption that this is possible in the long term. Even the strategy of sustainable development does not question the paradigm of permanent growth.

Without the past and present exploitation of the colonized South the indulgent living standards in the rich countries of the North could not be maintained. If all labour incorporated in the imported commodities sold in the rich countries was paid for at the rates of a skilled (male) European worker most of them could be afforded by only a small minority. So-called development (Vandana Shiva calls it maldevelopment) is not an evolutionary process from a lower to a higher stage but a polarizing process in which some get richer and richer because they make others poorer and poorer. Two hundred years ago the Western world was only five times richer than today's poor countries; in 1960 the ratio was 20:1, and in 1983 it was 46:1.[3] The ever-increasing wealth of the rich countries within a limited world is at the expense of what I continue to call the colonies: nature, women, the (so-called) 'Third World', or the 'South'.

*This is an extensively revised version of a paper presented at the Symposium 'Women and Children First', Geneva, 27-30 May, 1991.

This continuous economic growth in the rich countries is also reflected in their populations' consumption patterns. In West Germany, for example, between 1950 and 1980 private consumption grew five-fold, an increase accompanied by a change in consumption patterns. Whereas around 1950 almost half of household expenses were spent on food this proportion was only 23 per cent in 1987. A much greater part of private households' income was now spent on leisure activities and luxury items. Consumption patterns differ between lower and higher income groups, but compared to the poor countries in the world even the lower income groups were relatively better off, spending 10.2 per cent of their income on leisure goods and activities.[4]

Apart from exhausting scarce resources and exploiting colonies, the industrial growth model also produces ever-increasing mountains of waste, of toxic garbage, it destroys the ozone-layer and is responsible for the greenhouse effect. Not only does one-quarter of the world's population consume 75 per cent of the world's energy but also produces 80 per cent of the CO_2 emissions.[5] Adding to the proliferation of industrial — often toxic — waste are increasing quantities of domestic wastes. In West Germany, for example, between 1971 and 1982, private, domestic waste increased from 350 kg per person to 775 kg per person per year.[6] The resultant problem is that the rich, industrialized countries need places to dump their garbage, and it seems inevitable that their solution is to use the poor countries of the South as garbage colonies, even, or especially, for toxic waste.

Indisputably, a growth-oriented industrial world market system is non-sustainable and non-generalizable worldwide. Someone said that to extend the rich countries' living standard and consumption patterns worldwide two more planet earths would be needed; one for the raw materials and the other as a waste-dump.

The continuation of the industrial growth model can only lead to further ecological destruction and to greater inequality, deeper poverty. And the first to be affected will be women and children. If this is to be avoided, and the aim is to put 'women and children first' in a different, benevolent sense, then the industrial, world-market- and profit-oriented growth model must be transcended. This transcendence, as Vandana Shiva has convincingly shown,[7] is a matter of survival for women and children in the poor countries and regions. They explicitly oppose 'development' and 'modernization', which they know will destroy their survival base

— their access to the commons: land, water, air, forests, their communities, their culture.

As Chapter 4 shows, this catching-up development and consumerism model that prevails in the North and the affluent classes of the South, is not generalizable for all people living on this planet. Furthermore, in view of the increasing ecological catastrophies and the deterioration of even material life in the affluent countries, it can also be said that neither is such generalization even desirable. This means that new visions and ways are essential in order to solve the ecological problems as well as the problem of increasing poverty and starvation in the South. The strategy of catching-up development is not the solution, it is the problem.

Emerging from all recent analyses of the interrelation between ecological deterioration, increased poverty in the South and increasing wealth in the North is a demand for the North and the affluent classes of the South to relinquish their extravagant life-style. This solution, given the present global situation, is precisely one that all politicians and most citizens of the affluent industrial nations are unwilling to accept. The Earth Summit in Rio de Janeiro in June 1992, for example, showed the reluctance of the North's politicians to draw the obvious conclusions from analyses that demonstrated that the North consumes most energy and causes most environmental pollution, including depletion of the ozone layer and global warming. Most people living in the North too, including women, are loath to translate their insights into action.

Increasingly, however, particularly after the UNCED in Rio, more and more people understand that shifting over and shrugging off responsibilities cannot go on, and they are beginning to look for viable alternatives.

Voluntary simplicity and consumer liberation

The transcendence of this consumerist model must start in the rich, industrial countries; and one possible way to achieve this is by a voluntary reduction in the living standards and a change of consumer patterns by the rich countries and classes. If sustainability and self-sufficiency is good for people in poor countries then it must also be good for those in the rich countries; a double standard is not acceptable. We cannot demand that the Brazilians do not destroy their rainforest while we in the industrial North continue to destroy the world's climate by, for example, an ever-growing car industry and private transport systems.

Many people understand the need to change their life-style, but usually they leave the responsibility for change to the politicians, the governments or scientists and entrepreneurs. Without laws to change production — or even consumption — patterns, such as introducing speed limits etc. the individual consumer continues in his/her usual way of life. In democratic societies, however, politicians are unwilling to introduce unpopular measures unless they are convinced that people will accept them. Therefore a consumer liberation movement must start from the consumers themselves. Only when such a movement becomes strong and widespread will the politicians and entrepreneurs follow them.

But before this can happen people must begin to realize that *less is more*, by defining what constitutes an alternative 'good life'. This new definition of a 'good life' will emphasize different values such as: self-sufficiency, co-operation instead of competitiveness with others and with nature, respect for all creatures on the earth and their diversity, belief in the subjectivity of not only human beings but also non-human beings, communality instead of aggressive self-interest, creativity instead of the 'catching-up-with-the-Joneses' factor that is responsible for much superfluous consumption in our societies and to find satisfaction and joy in one's work and life. But it is essential that consumer *liberation* is understood as a liberation and not perceived as deprivation or an ascetic exercise. The aim of consumer liberation is to *improve the quality of life*. Many people in the affluent societies are aware of the need for such improvements but perhaps unaware of — or unwilling to acknowledge — the connection between consumerism and deterioration of the quality of life. Investigations in Europe and elsewhere, however, show that many people are prepared to do more to protect the environment.[8]

Different ways to satisfy fundamental needs

A definition of the 'good life' implies different ways of satisfying *fundamental human needs*. Max-Neef and his colleagues, who developed this concept of fundamental human needs in the workshop of Human Scale Development for Latin America, stress that fundamental human needs are universal, but that their *satisfiers*, the ways and means to satisfy these needs, may vary according to culture, region, historical conditions. In industrial capitalism the production of economic goods along with the system of allocating them has conditioned the type of satisfiers that predominate.[9] The distinction between needs and satisfiers is useful for this discussion on consumer liberation, because it enables us to see that there are different ways to satisfy the same fundamental human needs. Max-Neef and his colleagues have identified nine fundamental human needs, namely: *subsistence* (for example, health, food, shelter, clothing); *protection* (care, solidarity, work etc.); *affection* (self-esteem, love, care, solidarity and so on); *understanding* (among others: study, learning, analysis); *participation* (responsibilities, sharing of rights and duties); *leisure/idleness* (curiosity, imagination, games, relaxation, fun); *creation* (including intuition, imagination, work, curiosity); *identity* (sense of belonging, differentiation, self-esteem and so on); *freedom* (autonomy, self-esteem, self-determination, equality).[10]

These fundamental human needs are universal and apply to rich and poor, to 'overdeveloped' and 'underdeveloped' countries. In overdeveloped or industrial societies these needs are almost exclusively catered for by satisfiers which must be bought in the market, produced industrially. These are often only pseudo-satisfiers, which ultimately provide no real satisfaction.

For example, cars bought to enhance status, cosmetics to answer the need for love and admiration. Others, such as arms manufacture and purchase, legitimized by the alleged need to provide protection, subsistence and freedom, are simply destructive.

Consumer liberation and a changed life-style would mean choosing different satisfiers which are neither pseudo nor destructive, which eschew further deterioration of the relationship between human beings and the ecology, which do not exacerbate existing patriarchal relations between men and women, and neither endanger future generations' living conditions, nor enhance dependency but promote self-reliance.

If we try to break out of the mentality created by industrial society and exported to all poor countries, we can discover many different ways, many not dependent on the market, to satisfy fundamental needs. For example, for many women in the affluent societies, a 'shopping spree' is an attempt to satisfy their need for affection and recognition. Many buy clothes to satisfy this need, hoping that by following the latest fashion they will win admiration, and their partner's affection. Women's self-esteem in industrialized societies is closely linked to their outward appearance, but in spite of these efforts at compensatory consumption, this need can never be met by buying new clothes; they are pseudo-satisfiers. A deep human need cannot be fulfilled by buying a commodity. Within a consumer liberation movement new ways must be found or created, particularly non-commoditized ways, to satisfy this need for affection. This could mean, for example, spending more time with children, playing with them instead of buying ever more toys. Many non-commoditized satisfiers have the advantage of being synergetic: satisfying several needs simultaneously. Taking time to play with children answers various needs: for affection, for protection, for understanding, for leisure, freedom, identity. And this applies both to the children and to the adults. If fundamental human needs are satisfied in non-commercial ways (I call them 'subsistence ways') then these satisfactions are often reciprocal: the one who gives also receives. For example, a mother who breastfeeds her baby both gives and receives something. Such a change of life-style on a large scale in the rich countries would not only end destruction of the ecology and exploitation of the 'Third World', but would also change the consumption model which the North's middle classes provide for their own country's lower classes and for people of the South. A practical critique of this model, coming from the affluent societies themselves is essential to dispel the fascination of 'catching-up development' and imitative consumption. The North's consumption patterns are imported into the South as desirable means to the ultimate 'good life' by political and economic power groups. These consumption patterns then lead to increased dependency, indebtedness, internal imbalances and a loss of cultural identity.[11] Max-Neef and his colleagues stress the need for 'Third World' countries to abandon these imitative consumption patterns in order to free themselves from economic and cultural dependence and to make more efficient use of their own resources for their own well-being; this would be a step towards self-reliance. It is my opinion that abandoning the imposed consumption patterns would also be a step towards self-reliance of hitherto overdeveloped, affluent countries. Most of these countries, as we saw, depend very largely on exploiting the 'Third World' countries and their resources. If aiming for sustainability and self-reliance is considered prudent and appropriate for countries of the South, then it must also be prudent and appropriate for the North.

Different economies

Economies based on the aims of self-reliance and ecological sustainability would be quite different from the present growth- and profit-oriented economies. I have written elsewhere on such a 'moral economy'[12] — an economy based on ethical principles rather than on cost-benefit calculations of the market — and will mention only the most prominent features here.

Ecological sustainability, self-reliance and prioritization of the needs of women and children, cannot be maintained in vast economic units. These would need to be much smaller, decentralized units. Production and consumption could then be co-ordinated — and synchronizing production with consumption needs would also enable genuine participation of people in production decisions. Smaller economic units would facilitate co-operation among communities and also be a necessary step towards self-reliance and engender the operation of such as mutual help and reciprocity.

The present sexual division of labour would also have to change. Men and women alike would have to share responsibility for the production and maintenance of life in its broadest sense: to care for children, the aged, the sick, to look after the household, to provide emotional support would not be the task of women alone but that of men too. And since under such an economy these fundamental human needs could not be commoditized, then men would have less time for destructive activities, such as war games and so on. If men had to share full responsibility for maintaining life they would eventually also have to change their identity. The present upsurge of an aggressive, militarized, Rambo-image of masculinity would become obsolete, and this would be of the greatest benefit to women and children. Because as long as maleness is identified with Ramboism and machoism, women and children will be the first — but only the first — victims of men's wars against women, nature and other peoples. As a Russian woman put it after the Chernobyl disaster: 'Men do not feel responsible for life. They are only interested in conquering nature and the enemy.'[13]

The industrial system cannot function unless it is able to create and expand the markets for its ever-growing quantity of material and non-material commodities. This market is mainly provided by those, especially in the North, who have the purchasing power due to the exploitative international and sexual division of labour. To a lesser extent, it is also provided by the urban middle classes in the South. The market function is also facilitated by the states' monopolies over, for example, education, health, the postal system and, above all, defence.

Women: subjects and objects of consumption patterns

Historically, the problem of the expansion of growth-oriented industrial system's markets could only be solved by mobilizing women to act as agents of consumption. It was in the 1920s that the private household as market for industrially produced consumer goods was discovered. Until World War I many things to satisfy daily needs were produced in the household; the period after the war is characterized by the expansion of such consumer goods as detergents, soaps, washing machines, clothes, food items.

Feminist historians have analysed this process of the creation of the modern household and the modern housewife — a process which I call housewifization[14] — as necessary for the market needs of industrial capitalism.[15] They describe how women were mobilized by the Home Science Movement, but also, how, in spite of all efforts to professionalize housework, housewives, isolated in their domestic sphere, suffered from what was called the domestic void — a void that was filled with ever-more, ever-newer consumer goods.Basically this situation has not changed. Modern consumer industries produce endless labour-saving gadgets, fast foods, ready made clothes, cosmetics, and so on for women to buy. But these foods fail to fill the void many women feel at their work place or in their household. The satisfaction a woman derives from buying such items rapidly degenerates into boredom, consequently yesterday's purchase is thrown out today to be replaced by a new item tomorrow. This throw-away society has created a new addiction: 'shopaholicism'. Recent analyses show that shopaholics are mostly women who experience an inner urge to buy and buy, irrespective of need. Many of them are seriously indebted, but continue to buy. As Scherhorn et al show in their study on shopaholics in Germany, the majority of addicted women buy clothes and cosmetics. This addiction is, they analyse, closely related to these women's lack of self-respect and self-confidence. Buying new clothes is an attempt to compensate for the lack of value generally experienced by women in our society.[16] There may be cause for this addiction in early childhood experiences, but it is undeniable that the consumption patterns propagated by industry and to which these women respond strongly influence women in general. They correspond to the image of womanhood that modern industrial society has created.

Consumer liberation, therefore, would not only benefit the poor countries in the South, but would also liberate women and people generally from these addictions. It would mean a restoration of truly need-based consumption patterns.There are different attempts to change our wasteful lifestyle, ranging from individual efforts to large consumer boycotts. I want to point out two particular initiatives here. The Global Action Plan (GAP)[17] developed in the USA, which aims to bring together groups of friends who commit themselves to specific ecological changes in their everyday life. And another initiative is that of the magazine: *The Ethical Consumer*,[18] which tries to reintroduce ethical considerations and motives into people's purchasing decisions. Similar approaches are also pursued by Hazel Henderson's efforts to bring about a change in our economic behaviour.[19]

One of the most impressive movements towards consumer liberation is that of the Japanese women who started the Seikatsu Club (SC) in the early 1970s. Following is a brief account of that movement.

The Seikatsu Club

When I first wrote about the need for a consumer liberation movement in industrialized societies, a movement that could contribute to the liberation of women, nature and the 'Third World', many reservations were expressed about such a strategy. Critics of this approach usually emphasized the same point; namely: reduction of consumption would result in individualistic, isolated action which would make no impact on the producers, the MNCs; it would hit the poor and women, who are already at the receiving end of the North's exploitative economy. This strategy was inoperable, because it was based purely on ethical, moralistic appeals, not on interests people would not follow such a strategy. Moreover, it would deny each person's individual right to consume as much as they are able. And it would lead to a process of de-politicization, because the appeal to change would not come from politicians. Another often-voiced argument was that a process of consumer liberation was too slow, that the situation had already gone too far to be remedied by such a strategy.

I do not think that arguments will convince the North's people of the need to change their life-style and to liberate themselves from consumerism. Criticism of the North's over-consumption was loudly and clearly voiced by representatives of the South at the UNCED conference in Rio de Janeiro, but it did not result in political action on the part of the North's representatives. It may, therefore, be more encouraging to present examples of women and men who have already gone a long way to put this strategy into practice.

The Seikatsu Club in Japan is one of the earliest examples of a consumer liberation movement. This consumer-producer-cooperative was founded by women, particularly mothers, in the early 1970s in a reaction to the Minamata disease, and who were concerned about food pollution — PCB, food additives, AF2 and so on. They realized that they were no longer able to feed their families safely; that the use of atomic energy was poisoning the environment; and that agricultural chemicals were polluting mothers' milk. The women started to buy milk from cattle farmers whom they knew practised ecological farming. Through this movement women and other consumers began to take a direct interest in agricultural methods, in agricultural policy in general, and to realize the dangers inherent in official policy, which was prepared to sacrifice self-sufficiency in food to preserve the interests of, among others, their car industry. They began to consider what an agricultural policy should be, one which would take women's and children's interests seriously. The Seikatsu Club used the purchasing power of consumers, particularly of women, to promote the development of organic and ecological farming and, in general, promote Japan's self-sufficiency in food. They understood that what farmers do to the earth and to animals will eventually also affect the consumers. Based on this understanding, co-operation between 'producers and the consumers' in order to promote organic agriculture became active as a life reform movement.[20]

The consumers promise to buy all the products of the farmers with whom they have a direct relationship. At first they had to search for organic farmers, but the Club has since witnessed an exponential growth. Its membership in 1989 was 170,000 households, organized in 27,000 hans (basic local groups of about eight members each). 'In the Seikatsu Club we are seeking to empower each and every member with a voice and a role in participatory politics'.[21] Women comprise 80 per cent of the Club's Board of Directors. The SC has not only influenced Japan's agricultural policy and changed many people's life-style, but has also empowered women, in particular, to assume an active role in shaping their country's politics and social life.

> We stand by the belief that housewives can begin to create
> a society that is harmonious with nature by taking action
> from the home. And through our purchases and con-
> sumption we are attempting to change the ways Japanese
> agriculture and fisheries are operated.[22]

But the concern of SC members is not limited to unpolluted
food and other products for themselves, their aim is to steer the
whole society in the direction which we call a self-reliant, ecological subsistence society.

> SC is calling on the public to create a self-managed life-
> style in order to change the present wasteful lifestyle,
> which is a fall-out of the present capitalist-controlled soci-
> ety. We believe that the way to improve the quality of life
> is to create a simple but meaningful existence, refusing to
> fall under the having-it-all illusion created by commercial
> products. To control and manage your own life is a signif-
> icant factor in realizing a higher quality of life . . . The
> objective of SC is to learn how to self-govern society
> through self-management of our lives. Our visions to re-
> build local societies derive from this principle. One of our
> directions is to create locally based economies.[23]

Apart from these activities the SC has also participated in a
number of campaigns; after Chernobyl, for example, they started
the Radiation Disaster Alert Network. The Club created women
workers' collectives to help working women with child-care,
health education, food preparation and so on. The first SC member was elected to the Tokyo City Council in 1979, by 1922 there
were SC members, all women, in Chiba, Tokyo and Yokohama.
Local groups have formed networks all over the country; their
slogan is 'Woman Democracy: Peace. Life. Future. Nature. Earth'.
The SC has set ambitious aims for itself. In its campaign: 'From
Collective Buying to All Life' the Club aims to contact all households in Japan and recruit 10-30 per cent of them.

> Through such a cooperative community based on the ide-
> als of the SC in various branches of life, welfare, health,
> education, culture, environment, etc. the present day
> urban and rural societies can be regenerated and
> humanised.[24]

The example of the Seikatsu Club shows that consumer action
or, as I prefer to put it, consumer liberation, particularly if started

from women's concerns and experiences, is quite different from the petty NIMBYism (not in my backyard) of self-interested, atomized individuals. It can develop a dynamic which really can transform the 'All Life'. Chizuko Ueno, who has written about women's networking in Japan, is even of the opinion that these women's consumer-producer-cooperatives and networks can change the world. These networks extend beyond the Seikatsu Club, and according to Ueno can indeed create a total circulation of production and consumption, based not on capitalist principles, but on principles of moral economy: mutual help, trust, care, community, respect of humans and of nature.

> . . . they have an ambition to substitute capitalist circulation of goods and services by creating alternative routes that connect producers and consumers directly. After all, producers are consumers and there is no need to make it profitable for capitalists.[25]

Notes

1. Meadows, Dennis, Donella Meadows, E. Zahn and P. Milling, *The Limits to Growth*. Universe Books, New York, 1972.
2 *Global 2000*. Report to the President, Council of Environmental Quality (ed) US Foreign Department, Washington, 1972.
3 Trainer, F. E. *Developed to Death: Rethinking Third World Development*. Green Print, London, 1989, p. 14.
4 Dorr G. and K. Prinz 'Entwicklungstendenzen des Konsums privater Haushalte,' in E. Hildebrand (ed) *Okologischer Konsum*. Schriftenreihe des O.O.W. 25/89. Berlin, 1990, p. 46-8.
5 Muller, M. 'SPD-Experten orten Krise des Kapitalismus in naher Zukunft', in *Frankfurter Rundschau*, 25 March 1991.
6 *Der Fischer Öko-Almanach* 1984/85. Fischer, Frankfurt, p. 245.
7 Shiva, V. *Staying Alive: Women, Ecology and Survival*. New Delhi and London, Kali for Women, 1988 and Zed Books, 1990.
8 Strumpel, B., 'Die Eiderspruche zwischen Umweltbewtsein und Massenkonsum', in *Frankfurter Rundschau*, 26 March 1991.
9 Max-Neef, M. et al, 'Human Scale Development: An Option for the Future,' *Development Dialogue*. CEPAUR Dag Hammarskjold Foundation, Santiago, Chile, 1989, p. 27. English edition, Zed Books, London, 1992.
10. Ibid., p. 49.
11. Ibid., p. 47.
12. Mies, M., 'Moral Economy. A Concept and a Perspective'. Paper presented at the congress, 'Challenges', Science and Peace in a Rapidly Changing Environment, Berlin, 29 November, 1991.

13. See chapter 6 in this book.
14. Mies, op. cit., 1991.
15. Ehrenreich, B. and D. English, 'The Manufacture of Housework', in *Socialist Revolution*, No. 26, 1975.
16. Scherhorn, G., L. Reisch and G. Raab, *Kaufsucht, Bericht uber eine empirische Untersuchung*. Institut fur Haushants- und Konsumokonomik, Universitat Hohenheim, Stuttgart, 1990.
17. Gershon, D. and R. Gilman (n.d.) *Global Action Plan for the Earth*. 57 A Krumville Road, Olivebridge, New York 12461.
18. *The Ethical Consumer* (various), London.
19. Henderson, H. *Creating Alternative Futures*. Pedigree Books, New York, 1979; and 'Reframing the Global Debate Over Development From 'Economism' to Systems Theory.' Papers presented at International Meeting of Experts, Die Grünen im Bundestag, Bonn, Germany.
20. *Consumer Currents in Japan*, Katsuko Nomura, Hideki Nakahara and Meiko Katsube (eds). The Information Centre for the Public Citizens, c/o Ohdake Foundation, Tokyo, April 1983, p. 35.
21. Quoted by Paul Ekins, *A New World Order, Grassroots Movements for Global Change, Seikatsu Club Consumers Cooperative* (Japan). Routledge, London, 1992, p. 131.
22. Ibid., p. 132.
23. Ibid., pp. 131-2.
24. Ibid., p. 133.
25. Ueno, Chizuko, *Women's Networking Is Changing the World*. Nikon Keizei Shinbunscha, Tokyo, 1988. (English summary of this book, unpublished paper).

18. Decolonizing the North*

Vandana Shiva

The White Man's Burden is becoming increasingly heavy for the earth and especially for the South. The past 500 years of history reveal that each time a relationship of colonization has been established between the North and nature and people outside the North, the colonizing men and society have assumed a position of superiority, and thus of responsibility for the future of the earth and for other peoples and cultures. Out of the assumption of superiority flows the notion of the white man's burden. Out of the *idea* of the white man's burden flows the *reality* of the burdens imposed by the white man on nature, women and others. Therefore, decolonizing the South is intimately linked to the issue of decolonizing the North.

Gandhi clearly formulated the individuality of freedom, not only in the sense that the oppressed of the world are one, but also in the wider sense that the oppressor too, is caught in the culture of oppression. Decolonization is therefore as relevant in the context of the colonizer as in that of the colonized. Decolonization in the North is also essential because processes of wealth creation simultaneously create poverty, processes of knowledge creation simultaneously generate ignorance, and processes for the creation of freedom simultaneously generate unfreedom.

In the early phases of colonization, the white man's burden consisted of the need to 'civilize' the non-white peoples of the world — this meant, above all, depriving them of their resources and rights. In the later phase of colonization, the white man's burden consisted of the need to 'develop' the Third World, and this again involved depriving local communities of their resources and rights. We are now on the threshold of the third phase of colonization, in which the white man's burden is to protect the environment, especially the Third World's environment — and this, too, involves taking control of rights and resources.

* This is a revised version of a paper first prepared for the Festival of India in Germany, 1992.

It seems that each time the North has claimed new control over the lives of people in the South, it has been legitimized on the basis of some form of the white man's 'burden' arising from notions of superiority. The paradoxical consequence of the white man's burden is that the earth and other peoples carry new burdens in the form of environmental destruction and the creation of poverty and dispossession. Decolonization in the North becomes essential if what is called the 'environment and development' crisis in the South is to be overcome. The North's prescription for the South's salvation has always created new burdens and new bondages, and the salvation of the environment cannot be achieved through the old colonial order based on the white man's burden. The two are ethically, economically and epistemologically incongruent.

Ethical decolonization

From the democracy of all life to man's empire over nature. Most non-Western cultures have been based on the democracy of all life. As a schoolgirl, one lesson I learnt in the Hindi class was that human beings are part of *Vasudhaiva Kutumkam* or the earth family. As a part of the earth family, one participates in the democracy of all life. Rabindranath Tagore, our national poet, writing in *Tapovan* at the peak of the independence movement, stated that the distinctiveness of Indian culture consists in its having defined the principles of life in nature as the highest form of cultural evolution.

> The culture of the forest has fuelled the culture of Indian society. The culture that has arisen from the forest has been influenced by the diverse processes of renewal of life which are always at play in the forest, varying from species to species, from season to season, in sight and sound and smell. The unifying principle of life in diversity, of democratic pluralism, thus became the principle of Indian civilization.[1]

As a source of life, nature was venerated as sacred, and human evolution was measured in terms of the human capacity to interact in harmony with her rhythms and patterns, intellectually and emotionally. In the final analysis, the ecological crisis is rooted in the mistaken belief that human beings are not part of the democracy of nature's life, that they stand *apart* from and *above* nature. For example, Robert Boyle, the famous scientist who was also the Governor of the New England Company, saw the rise of mechanical philosophy as an instrument of power not just over nature but also over the original inhabitants of America. He explicitly declared his intention of ridding the New England Indians of their absurd notions about the workings of nature. He attacked their perception of nature 'as a kind of goddess', and argued that 'the veneration, wherewith men are imbued for what they call nature, has been a discouraging impediment to the empire of man over the inferior creatures of God'.[2] 'Man's empire over the inferior creatures of God' was thus substituted for the 'earth family'.

This conceptual diminution was essential to the project of colonization and capitalism. The concept of an earth family excluded the possibilities of exploitation and domination, therefore a denial of the rights of nature and nature-based societies was essential in order to facilitate an uncontrolled right to exploitation and profits.

As Crosby observes: 'Again and again, during the centuries of European imperialism, the Christian view that all men are brothers was to lead to persecution of non-Europeans — he who is my brother sins to the extent that he is unlike me.'[3] Whenever Europeans 'discovered' the native peoples of America, Africa or Asia, they projected upon them the identity of savages in need of redemption by a superior race. Even slavery was justified on these grounds, in so far as to carry Africans into slavery was seen as an act of benevolence, because at the same time they were carried out of an 'endless night of savage barbarism' into the embrace of a 'superior civilization'. All brutality was sanctioned on the basis of this assumed superiority and European men's exclusive status as fully human. The decimation of indigenous peoples everywhere was morally justified on the grounds that they were not really human; they were part of the fauna. As Pilger has observed for Australia, the *Encyclopaedia Britannica*[4] appeared to be in no doubt about this. 'Man in Australia is an animal of prey. More ferocious than the lynx, the leopard, or the hyena, he devours his own people'. In an Australian textbook *Triumph in the Tropics*,[5] Australian aborigines were equated with their half-wild dogs. As animals, the indigenous Australians, Americans, Africans and Asians had no rights as humans. As Basil Davidson observes, the moral justification for invading and expropriating the territory and possessions of other peoples was the assumed 'natural' superiority of Europeans to the 'tribes without law' the 'fluttered folk and wild'.[6]

Scientific missions combined with religious missions to deny rights to nature. The rise of the mechanical philosophy with the emergence of the scientific revolution was based on the destruction of concepts of a self-regenerative, self-organizing nature which sustained all life. For Bacon, who is called the father of modern science, nature was no longer Mother Nature, but a female nature, to be conquered by an aggressive masculine mind. As Carolyn Merchant points out,[7] this transformation of nature from a living, nurturing mother to inert and manipulable matter was eminently suited to the exploitation imperative of growing capitalism.

> The removal of animistic, organic assumptions about the cosmos constituted the death of nature — the most far-reaching effect of the scientific revolution. Because nature was now viewed as a system of dead, inert particles moved by external, rather than inherent forces, the mechanical framework itself could legitimate the manipulation of nature. Moreover, as a conceptual framework, the mechanical order had associated with it a framework of values based on power, fully compatible with the directions taken by commercial capitalism.[8]

While the ethical aspect of the ecological crisis can be traced to the white man's self-perceived burden as the only species with rights, the white man's burden is again seen as instrumental in solving the problems of the ecological crisis linked to the idea that the North's ethical discourse is generously expanding to concede rights to other peoples and other species.Most importantly, simultaneous with a pervasive Eurocentric assumption that an ethical expansion of rights to include nature in all its manifestations is taking place, is a blindness to the diminution and alienation of nature's rights at deeper levels than ever before, and a shrinkage of poor people's right to survival. This split is best exemplified in the area of biodiversity. While on the one hand biodiversity conservation is ethically justified on the grounds of the intrinsic value and rights of all species to exist, developments in biotechnology are predicated on the assumption that species have no intrinsic worth. Species are being robbed of their rights. And since the ethics based on the democracy of all life makes no distinction between rights of nature and rights of human communities, this new violation of the rights of nature is intimately linked to the violation of rights of farmers, tribals and women as knowers and users of biodiversity.

The population problem

Population 'explosions' have always emerged as images created by modern patriarchy in periods of increasing social and economic polarization. The latest concern with overpopulation is related to concern for the environment. Popularized through disquiet about degradation of the ecology of the earth the picture of the world's hungry hoards have made population control appear acceptable and even imperative.

This focus on numbers disguises people's unequal access to resources and the unequal environmental burden they place on the earth. In global terms, as we saw elsewhere in this book, a drastic decrease of population in the poorest areas of Asia, Africa and Latin America would make an environmental impact immeasurably less than a decrease of only five per cent in present consumption levels of the ten richest countries.[9] The dominant economic and political processes, however, are concerned to protect the North's wasteful 'way of life' whatever the cost, and the poor are considered only when it comes to accusing them of overburdening the planet's resources and whose fertility must therefore be stringently controlled.

These strategies of triage create an artificial conflict of interest between women, children and the earth. Through population control programmes, women's bodies must be brutally invaded in order to protect the earth from the threat of overpopulation.

Economic colonization: The growth of affluence, the growth of poverty

Two economic myths facilitate a separation between two intimately linked processes: the growth of affluence and the growth of poverty. Firstly, growth is viewed only as growth of capital. What goes unperceived is the destruction in nature and in people's subsistence economy that this growth creates. The two simultaneously created 'externalities' of growth — environmental destruction and poverty creation — are then causally linked, not to the processes of growth, but to each other. Poverty, it is stated, *causes* environmental destruction. The disease is then offered as a cure: growth will solve the problems of poverty and the environmental crisis it has given rise to in the first place. This is the message of World Bank development reports, of the Bruntland report, *Our Common Future*[10] and of the UNCED process.

The second myth that separates affluence from poverty, as we have noted earlier, is the assumption that if you produce what you consume, you do not produce. This is the basis on which the production boundary is drawn for national accounting that measures economic growth. Both myths contribute to the mystification of growth and consumerism, but they also hide the real processes that create poverty. First, the market economy dominated by capital is not the only economy; development has, however, been based on the growth of the market economy. The invisible costs of development have been the destruction of two other economies: nature's processes and people's survival. The ignorance or neglect of these two vital economies is the reason why development has posed a threat of ecological destruction and a threat to human survival, both of which, however, have remained 'hidden negative externalities' of the development process.

Trade and exchange of goods and services have always existed in human societies, but these were subjected to nature's and people's economies. The elevation of the domain of the market and man-made capital to the position of the highest organizing principle for societies has led to the neglect and destruction of the other two organizing principles — ecology and survival — which maintain and sustain life in nature and society.

Modern economics and concepts of development cover only a negligible part of the history of human interaction with nature. For centuries, principles of sustenance have given human societies the material basis of survival by deriving livelihoods directly from nature through self-provisioning mechanisms. Limits in nature have been respected and have guided the limits of human consumption. In most countries of the South large numbers of people continue to derive their sustenance in the survival economy which remains invisible to market-oriented development. All people in all societies depend on nature's economy for survival. When the organizing principle for society's relationship with nature is sustenance, nature exists as a commons. It becomes a resource when profits and accumulation become the organizing principles and create an imperative for the exploitation of resources for the market. Without clean water, fertile soils and crop and plant genetic diversity, human survival is not possible. These commons have been destroyed by economic development, resulting in the creation of a new contradiction between the economy of natural processes and the survival economy, because those people deprived of their traditional land and means of survival by development are forced to survive on an increasingly eroded nature.

While development as economic growth, and commercialization are now recognized as the root of the ecological crisis in the South, they are, paradoxically, offered as a cure for the ecological crisis in the form of 'sustainable development'. The result is that the very meaning of sustainability is lost. The ideology of sustainable development is, however, contained within the limits of the market economy. It views the natural resource conflicts and ecological destruction as separate from the economic crisis, and proposes a solution to that crisis in the expansion of the market system. As a result, instead of programmes of gradual ecological regeneration of nature's and the survival economy, the solution prescribed is the immediate and augmented exploitation of natural resources with higher capital investment. Clausen, as the President of the World Bank, recommended that 'a better environment, more often than not, depends on continued growth'.[11] Later, Chandler[12] further renewed the argument in favour of a market-oriented solution to ecological problems, believing that viable steps toward conservation can come only through the market.

Economic growth is facilitated through overexploiting natural resources, and in turn this creates a scarcity of those resources. Further economic growth cannot help in the regeneration of the very spheres which must be destroyed to enable economic growth to take place; nature shrinks as capital grows. The growth of the market cannot solve the crisis it creates. Further, while natural resources can be transformed into cash, cash cannot be transformed into nature's ecological processes. But in nature's economy, the currency is not money, it is life. The neglect of people's economy and nature's economy is also linked to the failure to recognize production in these domains. In the self-provisioning economies of the South, producers are simultaneously consumers and conservers, but their production capacity is negated, and they are reduced to mere consumers. An illustration of this approach is the World Bank, World Resources Institute (WRI), International Union for the Conservation of Nature (IUCN), World Wildlife Fund (WWF) programme on biodiversity conservation.[13] In this proposal, economic value is divided into the following categories:

- consumptive value: value of products consumed directly without passing through a market, such as firewood, fodder and game meat;
- productive use value: value of products commercially exploited; and
- non-consumptive use value: indirect value of ecosystem functions, such as watershed protection, photosynthesis, regulation of climate and production of soil.

An interesting value framework has thus been constructed which predetermines analysis and options. If the South's poor, who derive their livelihoods directly from nature, are only 'consumers', and the trading and commercial interests are the only 'producers' it follows quite naturally that the South is responsible for the destruction of its biological wealth, and the North alone has the capacity to conserve it. This ideologically constructed divide between consumption, production and conservation hides the political economy of the processes which underlie the destruction of biological diversity. Above all, it denies the South's role as the real donors to North, in terms of biological resources, most primary commodities, and even in terms of financial resources.The first myth that needs to be abandoned in the decolonization of the North is that goods and finances flow only from the industrial economies to the South. In fact, in the 1980s, the South's poor countries have been massive exporters of capital. The net transfer of resources from South to North is US$50 billion per year.[14] If the plants, germ plasm, cheap cassava, soya beans, fish and forest products that the South 'donates' to the North — in so far as the low commodity prices for these items reflect neither their environmental nor social value — are added, the reverse flow of resources is much greater. The South's poverty is generated through the very processes that generate the North's affluence.

Intellectual colonization: the growth of knowledge, the spread of ignorance

Never before has human knowledge increased exponentially at such a high rate — never before has our ignorance about our world been deeper. And the ignorance has largely been created by the explosion of scientific knowledge. As Ravetz states,

> We can no longer maintain the traditional view of science as rolling back the boundary with ignorance ... Ignorance

will always be with us, and indeed man-made ignorance constitutes a great and ever-increasing threat to our survival . . . The system maintains its plausibility by enforcing a sort of 'ignorance of ignorance'.[15]

When we consider the complexity and inter-relatedness of the cycles by which Gaia maintains her balances, the massiveness of the disruptions which we now impose on her, the primitive quality of the scientific materials by which we attempt to decipher her clues, then truly we can speak of a man-made ignorance, criminal or pitiful, depending on your point of view, in our relations with Gaia. A system of knowledge which enforces the 'ignorance of ignorance' has been assigned the prime place in creating the modern world. Science has been called the engine of growth and progress. On the one hand contemporary society perceives itself as a science-based civilization, with science providing both the logic and the impulse for social transformation. In this aspect science is self-consciously embedded in society. On the other hand, unlike all other forms of social organization and social production, science is assumed to be value neutral and universal and thus is placed *above* society. It can neither be judged, questioned, nor evaluated in the public domain. As Harding has observed:

Neither God not tradition is privileged with the same credibility as scientific rationality in modern cultures . . . The project that science's sacredness makes taboo is the examination of science in just the ways any other institution or set of social practices can be examined.[16]

While science itself is a product of social forces and has a social agenda determined by those who can mobilize scientific production, in contemporary times scientific activity has been assigned a privileged epistemological position of being socially and politically neutral. Thus science takes on a dual character: it offers technological fixes for social and political problems, but absolves and distances itself from the new social and political problems it creates. Reflecting the priorities and perceptions of particular class, gender, or cultural interests, scientific thought organizes and transforms the natural and social order. However, since both nature and society have their own organization, the superimposition of a new order does not necessarily take place in a faultless and orderly fashion. There is often resistance from people and nature, a resistance which is externalized as 'unanticipated side effects'.

Science remains immune from social assessment, and insulated from its own impacts. Through this split identity the 'sacredness' of science is created.

The issue of making visible the hidden links between science, technology and society and making manifest and vocal the kind of issues that are kept concealed and unspoken is linked with the relationship between the North and the South. Unless and until there can be social accountability of the science and technology structures and the systems to whose needs they respond, there can be no balance and no accountability in terms of relationships between North and South. This need for accountability will be extremely critical, more so than ever before, in the biotechnology revolution. In the absence of binding international conventions that create ethical and political boundaries, the biotechnology revolution will increase the polarization between the North and the South and the rich and poor.The asymmetrical relationship between science, technology and society will become further skewed as one part of society has a monopoly of the knowledge and profits linked to the biorevolution, and the rest of society is excluded from the knowledge and benefits but forced to bear the ecological, political and economic costs. Without the creation of institutions of social accountability and social control, the South will become the laboratory, providing the guinea pigs, the dump yards for all the risks that are to come while the benefits flow to the industrialized North. In fact, this has already started to happen; it is not a fear of the future, we are facing it already.

The UNCED process, instead of challenging the sanctity of science and technology and rendering these structures more transparent, actually makes technology more opaque, more mystical and magical. The environmental crisis was precipitated by the view that nature was inadequate, and that technology could improve on it. Now it seems that the dominant view is to propose the disease as the medicine, and 'technology transfer' has become the magical cure for every ecological illness. As Angus Wright has pointed out: 'Historically, science and technology made their first advances by rejecting the idea of miracles in the natural world. Perhaps it would be best to return to that position.'[17]

To question the omnipotence of science and technology's ability to solve ecological problems is an important step in the decolonization of the North. The second step is linked to a refusal to acquiesce to the growing, the pervasive power of 'intellectual property rights.' Even while the South still labours under the

burden of older colonization processes, new burdens of recolonization are added. The General Agreement on Tariffs and Trade
functions similarly to the old East India Company in demanding
freedom for the North's financial and industrial interests and
denying the South's citizens the freedom of their rights to survival
— rights which are to be treated as 'non-tariff' trade barriers that
interfere in global trade. As in the earlier phases of colonization,
the South's original inhabitants are to be robbed of their rights as
citizens to make way for the stateless corporations' rights as
super-citizens in every state. Trade and plunder merge once again,
especially in Trade-Related Intellectual Property Rights. The land,
forests, rivers, oceans, having all been colonized, it becomes necessary to find new spaces to colonize because capital accumulation
would otherwise stop. The only remaining spaces are those within
— within plants, animals and women's bodies.

There seems to be an abandonment of the 'human' aspect. The
dimensions that comprise human-ness and dynamic life have
been subsumed by an assumption that the cerebral is superior and
that the human aspect can only adulterate the purity of the cerebral; and because the North has lost touch with the bases of
life-in-nature it has become intoxicated with what it sees as possibilities of recreating nature closer to its own perceived — arid —
desires; playing God in fact. The horror of this is that the final
outcome can only be a dead planet — and, if anything at all, a
truly sub-human world, possibly within a totally artificial man-
made atmosphere, submerged beneath the wastes of nature. Not
so much *1984*, as Aldous Huxley's earlier, satirical novel, *Brave
New World*.

The construction of 'intellectual property' is linked to multiple
levels of dispossession. At the first level, the creation of the disem-
bodied knowing mind is linked to the destruction of knowledge as
a commons. The Latin root of *private* property, *privare*, means 'to
deprive'. The laws of private property which rose during the
fifteenth and sixteenth centuries simultaneously eroded people's
common right to the use of forests and pastures, while creating the
social conditions for capital accumulation through industrialization. The new laws of private property were aimed at protecting
individual rights to property as a commodity, while destroying
collective rights to commons as a basis of sustenance.

Trade negotiations are a strange place for products of the mind
to be discussed. Yet that is precisely what has happened with the
rich countries of the North having forced the so-called TRIPs onto

the agenda of the Uruguay Round of multilateral trade negotiations being held under the auspices of GATT. The multinationals of the North are sending their representatives to each country to ask for stricter intellectual property protection for everything that can be made in their laboratories. And with the new technologies, that includes life. From the MNCs' perspective intellectual property rights are essential for progress and development. Those countries which do not have them are accused of putting national interest above 'internationally' accepted principles of fair trade. They insist that the assertion of intellectual property rights is essential in order to stimulate investment and research.

On the other hand, countries in the South, such as India, have adapted their patent laws to promote technology transfer and defend themselves against subjugation. They have modified patent terms, excluded vital sectors such as food and health from monopoly control and strengthened compulsory licensing by stipulating that patents must be used in local production processes or the patent rights will be forfeited.[18]

During the 1960s and 1970s these discussions took place through the United Nations system. But in the 1980s the rich countries decided that the intellectual property discussions should be transferred from the UN, where the world's majority rules, to GATT, where the minority from the industrialized North effectively rules. The South's patent laws, designed to protect the public interest against monopolies, are no longer seen as a tool for development, but as a cover-up for economic embezzlement. The US international trade commissions estimate that US industry is losing anything between US$100 and 300 million due to 'weak' patent laws. If the stricter intellectual property rights regime demanded by the US takes shape, the transfer of these extra funds from poor to rich countries would exacerbate the current debt crises of the South ten times over. The MNCs, from which citizens need protection, are to have new power to monitor markets. The industrialized countries want border controls, seizure and destruction of infringing goods, imprisonment, forfeiture, criminal sanctions, fines, compensation and the like.

While market power is the apparent motivation for this drive to privatize and own life itself, the social acceptability of the changes derives from a worldview that continues to see the white man as a privileged species upon whom other species (including other peoples) depend for survival and value.

The earth and the South have paid heavily for 500 years for the white man's burden. Probably the most significant step in striving towards re-establishing an earth community is the recognition that the democracy of all life is inconsistent with the idea that this beautiful planet is the white man's burden. Unlike the mythical Atlas, we do not carry the earth; the earth carries us.

Notes

1. Rabindranath Tagore, *Tapovan*, (Hindi). Gandhi Bhavan, Tikamgarh, undated.
2. Quoted in Brian Easlea, *Science and Sexual Oppression: Patriarchy's Confrontation with Woman and Nature*. London, Weidenfeld and Nicholson, 1981, p. 64.
3. Alfred Cosby, *The Columbian Exchange*, Greenwood Press, Westport, Connecticut, 1972, p. 36.
4. John Pilger, *A Secret Country*. Vintage, London, 1989, p. 26.
5. Ibid.
6. Basil Davidson, *Africa in History*, Collier Books, New York, 1974, p. 262.
7. Carolyn Merchant, *The Death of Nature: Women, Ecology and the Scientific Revolution*. New York, Harper & Row, 1980, p. 182.
8. Ibid., p. 193.
9. 'Consumption', paper contributed by the Indira Gandhi Institute, Bombay, to UNCED, 1991.
10. WCED, *Our Common Future*, Geneva, 1987.
11. Edward Goldsmith, 'The World Bank: Global Financing of Impoverishment and Famine', *The Ecologist*, Vol. 15, No. 1/2, 1985.
12. W.D. Chandler, World Watch Paper 72. Washington, DC World Watch Institute.
13. WRI, IUCN, WWF, *Biodiversity Conservation*. Geneva, 1991.
14. NGLS, UNDP, NGO *Guide to Trade and Aid*, 1990.
15. J. Ravetz, 'Gaia and the Philosophy of Science', in Peter Bunyard and Edward Goldsmith, (ed) GAIA, *The Thesis, the Mechanisms and the Implications*. Cornwall, Wadebridge Ecological Centre, 1988, p. 133.
16. Sandra Harding, *The Science Question in Feminism*, Ithaca, Cornell University Press, 1986, p. 30.
17. Angus Wright, 'Innocents Abroad: American Agricultural Research in Mexico,' in Wes Jackson et. al, (ed), *Meeting the Expectations of the Land*. San Francisco, North Point Press, 1984.
18. Pocket book on Indian Patent Law, National Working Group on Patents, New York.

19. People or Population: Towards a New Ecology of Reproduction

Maria Mies and Vandana Shiva

Population, environment and people

Some years ago the continuing and increasing poverty in the countries of the South was attributed to the population explosion. Since the appearance of *The Limits to Growth*[1] population growth is seen increasingly as the main cause of environmental deterioration on a global scale. This assumed causal connection between the rising numbers of people and the destruction of the earth's ecological foundations was strongly emphasized in the political discourse around the June 1992 Earth Summit (UNCED) in Rio de Janeiro. Arguments supporting this view were propagated worldwide by the media, and more and more outright cynical and inhuman population control policies were proposed, including coercive contraceptive technologies for women and denial of basic health care for children, for example in a proposal by Maurice King in 1990.[2]

That industrialization, technological progress and the affluent life-style of the developed nations have precipitated the acceleration of environmental degradation worldwide can no longer be ignored. The main threats are: 1) degradation of land (for example, desertification, salination, loss of arable land); 2) deforestation, mainly of tropical forests; 3) climate change, due to the destruction of the ozone layer; and 4) global warming, due mainly to increasing rates of carbon dioxide and other gaseous emissions. But instead of looking into the root causes of these threats which it is feared are approaching catastrophic thresholds, they are today almost universally attributed to a single cause: population growth. Not only the affluent North and dominant political and economic interests but UN organizations also subscribe to this view. Thus the United Nations Fund for Population Action (UNFPA), in its latest report, The State of World Population 1990 states:

> For any given type of technology, for any given level of consumption or waste, for any given level of poverty or

inequality, the more people there are the greater the impact on the environment.[3]

In the affluent North there is a decline in the birth-rate, but this is balanced by immigrations; the culprits are seen as people living in the poor countries of the South. No less than 95 per cent of global population growth over the next thirty-five years will be in the developing countries of Africa, Asia and Latin America.

World population is growing at a rate of three people per second — or a quarter of a million people per day. This is faster than at any time in history. The most rapid growth is in developing countries. But will the earth's damaged environment be able to sustain such numbers in the 1990s and beyond?No account is taken of the exploitative and colonial world system, of the prevailing development paradigm or of the wasteful production and consumption patterns of the industrialized societies which are responsible for most of the environmental destruction, as, in fact, is admitted in the UNFPA report:

> By far the largest share of the resources used, and waste created, is currently the responsibility of the 'top billion' people, those in the industrialized countries. These are the countries overwhelmingly responsible for the damage to the ozone layer and acidification, as well as for roughly two-thirds of global warming.[4]

Despite these insights, however, the main policy to stem these threatening trends is to halt population growth. This means that it is not the rich, who have caused the problems, who must take action, but the poor, in the exploited countries of the South.

Arguments to support this Malthusian logic are usually based on statistical projections, which in turn are based on the assumption that the social and economic model of the industrialized North, the growth model, will eventually be followed by all people living in the South. Such arguments are always introduced by such phrases as: If present trends continue ... If the pattern of the past is repeated ... one example is the projection with regard to the growth of car production:

> As incomes grow, lifestyles and technologies will come to resemble those of Europe, North America or Japan . . . There will be an increase in car ownership. Since 1950 the human population has doubled, but the car population [sic] has increased seven times. The world car fleet is

projected to grow from present 400 million to 700 million over the next twenty years — twice as fast as the human population.

After such a statement it might be expected that a reduction in the North's rate of car production would follow, but instead we read: 'If past trends continue, developing countries will be emitting 16.6 billion tonnes of carbon annually by 2025, over four times as much as the developed countries today.'[5]

The real threat, therefore, is considered to be that a growing world population would emulate the life-style of the average person in the North, with as many cars, TVs, refrigerators, and so on. While it is recognized that the generalization of this life-style would be catastrophic for nature, the North's industry, economy and its consumers and politicians know of no other way to support this life-style than that of the permanent proliferation of cars and so on. The 'car population' must grow, but in order to curb the environmental damage this causes, the South's human population (those who will not buy cars) must decrease. This is the industrial system's real dilemma. It does not want to abandon its growth therefore it lays the blame for the damage it causes on its victims: the South's poor, particularly the women who produce too many children. This becomes clear from a reading of UNFPA's 1990 report which targets these women as in need of family planning techniques and as mainly responsible for degrading the environment.

In patriarchal society women are responsible for the production and maintenance of everyday life, of subsistence, for water, fuel, food and fodder as well as for land preservation. But with more 'development' and more modernization propagated by the North they are pushed ever-closer to the margins of their life-sustaining systems. They are accused of destroying the forests in search of fuel, polluting and exhausting water sources in search of drinking water, and exhausting the land resources by producing too many additional mouths to feed.

All the methods proposed in the UNFPA Report to curb over-population are directed towards women. The responsibility of men, and their cult of machismo, for the large number of births is mentioned only en passant. It is stated that most women in the South want fewer children, but the men are not addressed when it comes to contraceptive methods. It seems to be feared that to directly attack and attempt to change patriarchal culture would probably be interpreted as interference and the imposition of cultural imperialism by the North: if any UN organization attacked patriarchal culture in respect of sexual relations this would probably lead to political reactions. Instead, a policy of raising women's status is propounded.

This policy consists mainly of demanding the promotion of women's education, health, and income-earning capacities. Better-educated women, it is assumed, will practise family planning, as various examples show. But education is usually seen in isolation and its relations to class, to rural or urban backgrounds and other circumstances are ignored. Education alone has not solved the problem of poverty for many women, nor the problem of an insurance in old age, which is one reason why people in the South continue to have large families. In the absence of a social security system children are the only old-age insurance. The policy of family planning is always propagated by the argument that a small family is a happy family. But the UNFPA or other population control agencies have never asked whether in fact reducing the number of children in a family has made them happier or more prosperous. We can read only that the gap between the South's rich and poor is widening. As the world's political leaders dare not openly oppose the system based on permanent growth and demand drastically reduced consumption patterns in the North, the solution is increasingly seen in kind of lifeboat or triage philosophy. This philosophy is even promulgated by local family-planning workers in Bangladesh.

> You see, there are only nine cabins in the steamer launch which comes from Dhaka to Pathuakhali [a Bangladeshi village]. In the nine cabins only 18 people can travel. The ticket is expensive, so only the rich people travel in the cabins. The rest of the common passengers travel in the deck. The latrine facility is only provided for the cabin passengers. But sometimes cabin passengers allow them to use the latrine because they are afraid that if the poor deck passengers get angry then they might go down and make a hole in the launch. Then the launch will sink: they will die no doubt but the rich cabin passengers will not survive either. So, my dear sisters, do not give birth to more children as they cause a problem for the cabin passengers.[6]

The North's 'cabin passengers' fear of the South's population explosion is shared by the South's affluent middle-classes. Population control policy mobilizes these imperialist and class fears.

Discourses on population and poverty and on population and environment are permeated by several fundamental anomalies inherent in capitalist industrial society. These are the assumed contradictions between people and the environment, the individual and society, production and reproduction, and sexuality and procreation. For capitalist philosophy the basic economic unit is the isolated individual with his/her egotistic and aggressive self-interest, which is perceived as fundamentally antagonistic to that of other such self-interested individuals. Therefore, there is a conflict of interests between the individual and the community which, according to the Hobbesian concept of man and society, can only be solved by an all-powerful state. Adam Smith tried to solve this dilemma by his famous 'invisible hand', which means allowing aggressive competition between these self-interested egotistic individuals for their economic gains, which eventually would result in optimal wealth for all.

Already underlying this concept of the human being and society is a statistical view or a 'political arithmetic', first developed by William Petty in 1690. Quantifying society, people and their relationship to nature (today one would say resources), became necessary for rising capitalism. Following Bacon, Petty saw a parallel between the 'body natural' and the 'body politic' and he tried to demonstrate that the wealth and power of the state depends on the number and character of its subjects.[7]

According to Barbara Duden, however, it was not before 1800 that statistics became the new language of all modern science, particularly economics, and that the term 'population' lost its tie to actual people.[8]

Meanwhile, actual living persons, real people, real communities, their history, culture and diversity have vanished behind the abstraction of aggregate numbers, expressed in population figures, growth rates, pressures and policies. The term population can refer, as Barbara Duden writes, as much to 'mosquitoes as to humans'.[9] This concept of population that transforms living people into mere numbers makes possible, as we have noted, even for a UN document to compare the growth of the 'car population' with that of the 'human population'.

But not only did people disappear when populations were identified as mainly responsible for underdevelopment, poverty and environmental destruction, but other, different anomalies emerged with the new capitalist population policies, namely: in the relationship between the sexual and reproductive behaviour of individuals and the well-being of the community; and between production and reproduction. In capitalist patriarchy's liberal philosophy the sexual behaviour of individuals is assumed to be determined by natural laws expressed as biological drives, whereby, as in the case of economic self-interest, people simply follow their egotistic pleasure-seeking, careless of the well-being of others or the community, and of the consequences of sexual activity for women. It is assumed that eventually this individual sexual self-interest, unless checked by external forces, technologies, the state and new contraceptive devices, will result in 'overpopulation'.

The same liberal philosophy is applied to justify not only the separation between sexuality and procreation but also to conceptualize an individual's sexual and reproductive activity as a purely individual affair, rather than as the expression of a social relation, interconnected with other social, economic and cultural spheres and relations. This is why many women put emphases only on women's individual reproductive rights, without demanding changes in the overall political and economic structures of the present world (dis)order. They see only the individual woman and the need to protect her reproductive freedom or 'choice'.[10] The population controllers, however, see women only as aggregated uteruses and prospective perpetrators of over-population. Both views stem from the same philosophy and both are based on abstractions which ignore the real social relations through which people — real men and women — interact with themselves, with each other and with nature as producers and reproducers. The separation between production and reproduction facilitated by capitalist patriarchy is such that producers conceive of themselves as separate from and superior to the nature around and within them, and women as reproducers experience themselves as passive and alienated from their own bodies, their procreative capacities and from any subjectivity.

Feminists in the North subscribe to the people and population anomaly by their demand for 'control over our own body' and safe contraceptives, without asking who controls the production of contraceptives, for what purposes and within which political and economic framework. Women of the South, however, experience this anomaly in the fact that they are increasingly reduced to numbers, targets, wombs, tubes and other reproductive parts by the population controllers.

The aim in this chapter is to show that these apparent anomalies are not only based on false assumptions but also on a viewpoint that blames the planet's ills on victims, mainly poor women.

Who carries whom?

Maurice King, in his analysis of the 'Demographic Trap',[11] assumes that local population pressure is the only pressure on ecosystems, that there is a straightforward carrying capacity calculus for human societies as there is for non-human communities.

Most ecosystems in the Third World, however, do not merely carry local populations; they also carry the North's demands for industrial raw material and consumption. This demand on Third World resources means that the threshold for the support of local populations is lowered. In other words, what would be a sustainable population size on the basis of local production, consumption and life-style patterns becomes non-sustainable due to external resource-exploitation. The theoretical and conceptual challenge is to find the roots of non-sustainable use not only in visible local demand but also in the invisible, non-local resource demand; otherwise, the search for sustainable population will become an ideological war declared against the victims of environmental degradation in the Third World, without removing the real pressures on the environment inflicted by global economic systems.

The 'carrying capacity' in the case of human societies is not simply a matter of local population size and local biological support systems. It is a more complex relationship of populations in the North to populations and ecosystems in the South. The South's ecosystems (E) carry a double burden: supplying commodities and raw materials to the global market (G); and supporting the survival of local communities (L).

Reducing L, and ignoring G, cannot protect E. Moreover, most analyses of the relationship between population and the environment ignore non-local demand for resources, as does Garett Hardin in his seminal essay, 'Tragedy of the Commons'. What he failed to notice about the degradation of the commons is that it is accelerated when the commons are enclosed, that is, when they stop being commons and become privatized.

Enclosure of the Commons separates people from resources; people are displaced and resources exploited for private profit. In England, enclosure of the commons forced peasants off the land in order to pasture sheep. 'Enclosures make fat beasts and lean people', 'Sheep eat men' were some of the sayings that character-ized the consequences of the enclosure. 'Carrying capacity' had been problematized because the land was no longer available to support people but sheep, largely to provide wool for Britain's emerging textile industry. The disenfranchized people were turned into a resource, worth only the market price of their labour power. Displacement from land makes a necessity of growth in numbers.

But not all these poor peasants and craftsmen, driven from their land and robbed of the commons, were absorbed by the rising industry as free wage labourers. Many had to migrate to the new colonies in America and Canada or, for petty thefts and the like, were deported to Australia. After the violent clearing of peo-ple from the Scottish Highlands to make room for sheep, many Highlanders were forced to migrate to Canada to work as lumber-jacks or were recruited into the British army to fight in the new colonies.

Similar processes — privatization of the commons, eviction of the rural poor — took place in the other industrializing countries of Europe, and its pauperized masses were exported to the colonies. After the mid-19th century there was a wave of mass migration of poor Europeans to North America, and to other colonies, such as Brazil and South Africa. A wave of out-migration after World War II was not, however, confined to the poor. It was this out-migration of Europe's poor (and the ambitious) rather than advances in medicine, the rise of general living standards and the invention of new contraceptives, which led to a demographic decline in Europe.The conse-quences of colonization and development projects in the Third World have been the same as the enclosure of commons in Britain and Europe.

Population growth is not a cause of the environmental crisis but one aspect of it, and both are related to resource alienation and destruction of livelihoods, first by colonialism and then continued by Northern-imposed models of maldevelopment. Until 1600 India's population was between 100 and 125 million: in 1880 it remained stable. Then it began to rise: 130 million in 1845; 175 million in 1855; 194 million in 1867; 255 million in 1871. The beginning of the 'population explosion' dove-tailed neatly with the expansion of British rule in India, when the people's resources, rights and livelihoods were confiscated.

What is also ignored in this 'carrying capacity' discourse is the history of colonial intervention into people's reproductive behaviour. This intervention was initially motivated, as in Europe, by the need for more disposable labour, labour freed from subsistence activities and forced to work productively on plantations, farms, roads, in mines and so on for the benefit of foreign capital. This policy vacillated between a largely anti-natalist regime for slaves in most of the Caribbean, who were cheaper to purchase than to breed,[12] and a pro-natalist approach later implemented in South Africa — when the white farmers needed more labour. After the Herero rebellion South African women were punished if they aborted or used contraceptives. This pro-natalist policy was supported throughout the colonial period by Christian missionaries who everywhere campaigned against indigenous institutions, family forms and methods and sexual practices which, women in particular, had used for centuries to regulate their procreative potential to maintain a balance with the ecological limits of their region that provided their livelihood.

The focus on population as the cause of environmental destruction is erroneous at two levels: 1) it blames the victims — mainly women; and 2) by failing to address economic insecurity and by denying rights to survival, the current policy prescriptions avoid the real problem. False perceptions lead to false solutions. As a result, environmental degradation, poverty creation, and population growth continue unabated, despite the billions of dollars spent on population control programmes.

It might then well be more fruitful to directly address the roots of the problem: the exploitative world market syste which *produces* poverty. Giving people rights and access to resources so that they can generate sustainable livelihoods is the only solution to environmental destruction and the population growth that accompanies it.

False assumptions, false conclusions

The discourse on the prime responsibility of the 'population explosion' for environmental destruction is also erroneous in so far as it is based on a number of patriarchal and eurocentric assumptions and theories which, in the light of careful socio-historical analysis, are untenable.

The first of these is the well-known Malthusian 'population law', according to which population grows geometrically, while food production proceeds arithmetically. This 'law' is based on what demographers have later called the concept of 'natural fertility'; that is, unchecked, uncontrolled human fertility, with no recourse to contraception or birth control, implying a purely unconscious, biological process.

Such a concept can only mean that, after a certain stage, there will be neither enough space nor food to 'carry' the people. The discourse on the ecological carrying capacity of earth is based on this Malthusian logic. But it is also based on what we have called the myth of catching-up development. This means population growth is seen not only as a biological and statistical process, but implies that all people worldwide, now and in future, will aspire to and eventually attain the level of consumption now prevailing in the North and in the rich classes of the South.

The Malthusian logic underpinning most demographic analyses and population policies of such UN organizations as the UNFPA, and of the World Bank, the Population Council and other national and international agencies, is augmented by the concept of 'natural fertility' employed by some demographers in regard to pre-modern, pre-industrial, traditional societies. When these demographers characterize the reproductive behaviour of modern, industrial society in Europe, USA and Japan they apply the concept of 'controlled fertility behaviour'. They assume that 'natural fertility behaviour' prevailed in all pre-industrial societies before the end of the 18th century, meaning that contraception was unknown in these societies, in and outside Europe. 'Natural fertility' was assumed to always have been high and generally stable, checked only by biological factors: diseases; epidemics; wars; low standards of living; and institutional constraints such as sex taboos.

In Europe, however, after what the demographers have called the period of transition in the 18th and 19th centuries, natural fertility is said to have been replaced by controlled fertility; mid-19th century high fertility rates gave way to lower ones in the 20th century. Increased population in 19th-century Europe is usually attributed to industrial progress: better medicines; improved hygiene and standards of living; lower mortality rates. Similar modernization technology, particularly in the field of medicine, has supposedly led to the South's population explosion, because it said to have checked epidemics and diseases, the so-called 'natural' controls on population growth. But whereas this sudden population growth in Europe was supposedly checked by the invention of modern contraceptives, and by education, particularly of women, with gainful employment and more consumer goods bought by the masses, the same did not happen in the South. (The fact that Europe exported its poor to the colonies is usually disregarded.) Since the mid-1970s, feminists and other scholars have challenged the assumptions of overall natural fertility in pre-modern societies and convincingly demonstrated that women, in particular, knew and practised methods of contraception and birth control before the invention of the pill.

In her history of birth control in America, Linda Gordon showed that as early as 1877, it existed long before modern contraceptives were invented:

> There is a prevalent myth in our technological society that birth control technology came to us with modern medicine. This is far from the truth, as modern medicine did almost nothing until the last twenty years to improve on birth control devices that were literally more than a millenium old.[13]

From ancient times, women almost everywhere have known of methods and techniques of birth control; men, too, were aware of practices that precluded conception. As Wacjman argues, modern contraceptives were developed with a view to population control rather than motivated by a desire to further women's self-determination.[14] Feminist historians have provided ample evidence that the so-called witches, who for several centuries were persecuted and brutally murdered in Europe, were in fact the wise-women, well-versed in medicine and midwifery, who knew many methods whereby women were enabled to balance the number of their children. Since the Renaissance and the rise of mercantile capitalism, however, more people were needed as labourers. Therefore, theoreticians of the modern absolutist state, for example, Jean Bodin in France or Francis Bacon in Britain, were among those who accused these 'wise-women' of witchcraft because their contraceptive knowledge was an obstacle to their pro-natalist population policy. With the annihilation of these women went the disappearance of their birth-control and other knowledge [15] According to Heinsohn and Steiger, it was the systematic destruction of these women and their knowledge together with the modern capitalist states' deliberate pro-natalist population policy, which led to rapid population growth in 19th-century Europe, and not advances in medicine, hygiene and nutrition.[16]

This critical historical research has been barely noticed by modern demographers and the population control establishment. They continue to cling to their theory of natural fertility for so-called pre-modern societies and project their interpretation of European history on to these. There is scant effort to study these societies' actual social history relating to sexuality and procreative behaviour.

To give one example: B.F. Mussalam has shown that the theory that pre-modern societies were ignorant of methods of contraception is false even for medieval Islam, a society which supposedly is more strongly traditional and patriarchal than European society. In a detailed socio-historical analysis, Mussalam shows that birth control, particularly the method of *coitus interruptus* was not only permitted by the Koran and Islamic law but also widely practised in Islamic society. In addition, techniques, mainly barrier methods, were employed by women. The concept of natural fertility cannot, therefore, be upheld, even for medieval Islamic society,[17] any more that it can be upheld for pre-industrial Europe or for other traditional societies in the South.

Many more social historical studies on sexual and generative behaviour in different cultures are needed. What has to be explained is how and why, in many societies, colonial intervention led to the knowledge of traditional birth control methods falling into disuse, or destroyed in order to produce more labourers for the Empire. And why, after World War II, were modern contraceptives developed by transnational pharmaceutical corporations in order to fight overpopulation in the South. Unlike traditional methods, modern contraceptive technology is totally controlled by scientists, the profit interests of pharmaceutical corporations, and the state. These technologies are based on a perception of women as an assemblage of reproductive components, uteruses, ovaries, tubes.

Women as wombs and targets

The process whereby people become populations is to be understood not only as a mere epistemological change. In practice it meant and means a direct and usually coercive intervention into people's lives — particularly women's, because they have been identified as responsible for population growth.

Following the quantitative and divisive logic of modern reductionist science and capitalist patriarchy, population controllers and developmentalists both conceptualize people as separated from their resource base and women as separated from their reproductive organs. The population control establishment, including the producers of contraceptive devices, the multinational pharmaceutical corporations, are not concerned with real women, but only with the control of some of their reproductive parts: their wombs, tubes, their hormones and so on.

In the process of developing ever-more effective technical fixes to depopulate the South,[18] women's dignity and integrity, their health and that of their children are of little concern. This accounts for the fact that most of the contraceptives produced for and introduced into the South have, and continue to have negative side-effects on women. Moreover, hormonal contraceptives (Depo-provera, Net-OEN, and the latest Norplant or RU 486) increasingly take away from women control over reproduction processes and put it into the hands of doctors and the pharmaceutical industry. The latest in this process of alienating women from their reproductive capacities is the research into anti-fertility vaccines.[19] Apart from these, sterilization, mainly of women, is seen as the most efficient method of population control.

Since the early 1970s, population control policies have been criticized as racist, sexist, imperialist and anti the poor. These critics are equally concerned about the health of nations and their people and raise some uncomfortable questions for which there are no easy answers. Why are population policies and research into fertility control supported by certain countries' defence wings and why do they see population growth as 'a security threat,' evoking their intervention through subtle coercion of national governments and through them of their people, which almost invariably happens to be women? If stringent population policy is truly an anti-poverty measure, why have those Latin American countries who have had 80 per cent of their women sterilized become poorer and more deprived than before? If the intention was a qualitatively better life, then fewer poor street children should have been killed in Brazil to supply the richer countries with a thriving organ trade, especially as Brazil's birth rate declined by 50 per cent in two decades, a feat that the North took several centuries to achieve.

Development at whose cost?

Structural adjustment programmes forced on country after debt-ridden country in the South will serve only to increase disparities and indebtedness in the long term. Horrifying statisticsbearevidence of rising infant and maternal mortality, an increase in the number of street children and uncontrolled urbanization. Throughout history, African, Asian or Latin American countries have suffered a brutal plunder of their peoples and natural resources in order to further the North's economies. Today, while an increase in population is held responsible for environmental degradation, the Sarawak forests are being cleared and their peoples made homeless in their own land, in order that Japan can have its supply of disposable chopsticks; Indonesian forests are being felled to make toilet paper and tissues; and Amazon forests are burnt down to create cattle ranches to provide beefburgers. The plunder of such countries continues under unjustifiable world trade practices, loan servicing terms, and unrealistic interest rates on debts. As poverty increases and concomitantly, social insecurity, the poor and the illiterate will tend to look for security in numbers, and national governments will have to apply increasingly coercive measures in order to comply with the population control conditions linked to foreign aid.

In 1951, with its first Five Year Plan, India was the first country to formulate a National Population Policy. Typically 'top down', it was centrally planned, financed and monitored, to be applied at state and local levels. Guided, formulated and designed by external agencies it was to be implemented by India's government and its employees. It did not need the Planning Commission's midterm evaluation report to assess the population policy a failure, as it became evident through statistics that it had not met people's needs. After the failure of the coercive sterilization campaign during the Emergency (1975-77) the programme's title changed from 'family planning' to 'family welfare', but the strategies and approaches in respect of women remained unchanged. Women were seen as ignorant, illiterate and stupid beings who wanted only to produce children — curbing their fertility was obviously needed. For those involved in health-care, Indian population control policies were a double tragedy: first, because they failed to understand and cater to women's contraceptive needs; and second, because they marginalized and eclipsed all other health-care work.

The current population control policy in the South has been criticized not only by people concerned about the exploitative and imperialist world order, but also by health workers and feminists, particularly in the South. Thus, regarding India's population which treats women not as human beings but as 'tubes, wombs and targets', Mira Shiva draws attention to the total lack of accountability that characterized the drive for women to undergo tubectomies, for which financial incentives are on offer not only for those who accept sterilization 'but also for the family planning workers'. In a social context where little change was attempted in other areas, coercion was the one stick seen as a means to beat the population growth rate. The costs borne by women were all too apparent in a violation of their dignity and a denial of their right to unbiased information, to safe and effective contraceptive care and to follow-up services to make the whole process accountable to those involved.'The deterioration of the health status of women in several regions and a [skewed] sex ratio call for intervention in several areas, contraceptive needs being only one among several components of human welfare.' Mira Shiva, a health activist, writes about the side effects of the various contraceptive devices tried out on Indian women, all advertised as safe and 100 per cent effective:

> Lippes Loop was first introduced into India following a strong advertising blitz announcing it as the wonder contraceptive for women. Again, when Dalkon Shield was introduced in the '60s, it was pronounced 'safe' until litigation in the U.S., following the death of seven women users, brought to light the intrauterine infections that had developed in thousands of women users across the world. In India, the problem is inevitably compounded by the fact that due to a lack of access to their own medical records, no compensation is possible even when women develop serious complications. Even if access was possible, the almost non-existent follow up would have nullified any gains made through a control over their own medical records.

The method of female sterilization by means of the costly imported laparoscope was seen as a revolutionary step in the Indian family planning programme. Yet, Indian doctors' callous use of this technology, citing with pride the number of sterilizations performed within the hour, caused it to fall into grave disrepute.

Curiously, long-acting injectable contraceptives are considered safe and effective for anaemic, malnourished and underweight Third World women, while in the North, recognition of the hazards of hormonal doses have led to minimizing their use in the contraceptive pill. Western women who use a hormonal contraceptive, do so on the basis of an 'informed' choice, adequate nutritional status and with access to follow-up, diagnosis and treatment. The average Indian or Bangladeshi woman would be denied all these advantages, and the significant menstrual blood loss recognized as a side-effect of long-acting hormonal contraceptives would be especially damaging for an already severely anaemic woman. Also, no assurances or 'pep' talks by health workers can camouflage the fact that prolonged menstruation is as culturally unacceptable as amenorrhea or an absence of menses. And there are other questions: what effect would hormones have on the foetus if they were administered to a woman who was unaware of her pregnancy? It is widely recognized that introduced hormones can negatively influence the growth of the foetus (teratogenic effect), therefore can this effect be non-existent or insignificant in the case of long-acting hormonal contraceptives? Fears have been raised on this score by health, women's and consumer groups of target chasing once again dominating the programme without adequate warning of side effects being made available to users. In the West, Thalidomide and Diethylstilbaestrol were considered safe for pregnant women. There was no realization that infants would be born without limbs as an effect of the former: or that the long-term effects of the latter would result in the development of breast and cervical cancer, and that even the next generation was found to be affected as young adult daughters developed vaginal cancers, and sons abnormalities in their testes.[20]

Population control and coercion

The population-environment discourse gave rise to panic in some quarters and nullified any ethical, humanistic opposition to an open policy of coercive interventions into people's reproductive behaviour. Such interventions, of course, are not new — India, during the (1975-77) Emergency, and Bangladesh have been subjected to them. Farida Akhter from Bangladesh is one of the most outspoken critics of this 'coercive depopulation policy'. In numerous speeches and articles she has shown convincingly that population control programmes were devised to serve the commercial interests of the multinational pharmaceutical companies; forced on the Bangladeshi people as a pre-condition for aid and credit; and that, increasingly, coercion is applied in the implementation of these programmes. Additionally, in Bangladesh, sterilization is performed without prior examination of the women; even pregnant women are sterilized. But the government, which is responsible for enforcing these programmes, has no programme to treat the resultant health problems that women experience. In India and in Bangladesh, women are used as guinea-pigs to test new hormonal contraceptives: Norplant was administered to 1,000 women in Bangladesh, none of whom were told that they were participating in a test sponsored by the Bangladesh Fertility Research Programme.[21]

Farida Akhter has also pointed out the contradiction between this coercive policy vis-a-vis the South and the marketing rhetoric of 'free-choice', and 'reproductive freedom' in respect of new contraceptives and reproductive technologies in the North. She shows how the population control establishment increasingly co-opts the slogans of the North's Reproductive Rights Movement to legitimize depopulating strategies in the South. She also criticizes those feminists of the North who emphasize individualistic 'rights' and seemingly forget that reproduction as well as production is integral to social relations. To isolate the individual sexual and reproductive behaviour from the social fabric can only be harmful to women, in the South and the North.[22]

A new ecology of reproduction

Our critique of an anti-human, anti-woman, anti-poor, racist, imperialist and coercive population control policy, however, does not imply that no one, particularly women, should have access to birth control and contraceptive methods. From an ecofeminist perspective it is essential that women be asked what they themselves want. In target-oriented, coercive population control programmes, poor women's views on family size are not sought.

Most poor women of the South are the objects of two forces which try to control their sexuality and procreative activity: 1) the patriarchal institutions, ideologies, norms, attitudes, which deny a woman's sovereignty over her own body: and 2) the international population control establishment, for whom the women are only potential breeders whose reproductive capacities must be controlled. But in neither the North nor the South do these population control agencies dare openly criticize patriarchal institutions and attitudes.

An ecofeminist perspective, however, is not to look at reproduction in isolation, but to see it in the light of men-women relations, the sexual division of labour, sexual relations, and the overall economic, political and social situation, all of which, at present, are influenced by patriarchal and capitalist ideology and practice. Therefore a primary demand is that women regain greater autonomy with regard to their sexuality and procreative capacities.

This implies first, that women must begin to overcome the alienation from, and learn again to be one with, their bodies. This alienation, brought about by capitalist, patriarchal reproduction relations and technologies has affected women in the North more than poor women in the South. Poor, rural women in the South may still be knowledgeable in respect of their bodily cycles and evidence of fertility and infertility, but women in the North have virtually lost this intimate knowledge and instead increasingly depend on medical experts to tell them what is happening in their bodies. A new ecology of reproduction would mean that women reappropriate this 'fertility awareness', as Mira Sadgopal calls it,[23] and realize that traditional as well as modern sources can show them the way. Secondly, men too, must begin to be educated in women's fertility awareness and to respect it, which implies a new, creative interaction of the procreative potential of women and men.

It is essential to bear in mind that the sexual relationship must also be understood as an ecological one, embedded in overall production relations. Unless these relationships are freed from exploitation and dominance, the oppressors, as well as the oppressed, will face ruinous consequences. Liberating sexual relationships from patriarchal dominance and exploitation is not solely a matter of contraceptive technology, but demands a change in attitudes/life-style, institutions, and the everyday conduct of men and women. Clearly the introduction of new contraceptive devices has not resulted in the expected fundamental change in sexual relationships, even in the North. Social change cannot be facilitated by technological fixes; neither can production relations, or the earth, be freed from exploitation and dominance by technology alone.

If men and women begin to understand sexual intercourse as a caring and loving interaction with nature, their own and their partners, then they will also be able to find birth control methods which do not harm women. Such a loving and caring relationship would lead to a new understanding of sexuality — not as a selfish, aggressive 'drive' but as the human capacity for relatedness to ourselves, to each other and, by implication, the earth and all its inhabitants.

Development of this new sexual and reproductive ecology is essential if women are to be enabled to maintain their human dignity; it is even more important for men who, in militaristic, patriarchal society are taught to identify their sexuality with aggression. This aggression, however, is directed not only against their sexual partners, but also against themselves. To conquer the 'enemy', 'nature', women, other people, they must first learn to conquer themselves, which means they must reject and destroy in themselves the caring, loving, nurturing characteristics that are generally attributed to women, and for which they are devalued.

This new understanding of non-patriarchal sexuality can develop only together with changes in the sexual division of labour, the economy and politics. Only when men begin seriously to share in caring for children, the old, the weak, and for nature, when they recognize that this life-preserving subsistence work is more important than work for cash, will they be able to develop a caring, responsible, erotic relationship to their partners, be they men or women.

Such relationships will enable the opposition between 'people' and 'population' to be resolved, thus: individuals' sexual and procreative activity need not be opposed to a community's need for a 'sustainable' number of children. We have shown that the concept of 'natural fertility' is a eurocentric, patriarchal myth propagated since the 18th century. Women, in particular, have always known methods and techniques of birth control and contraception. A new ecology of reproduction within the context of economic and political eco-regions will lead to new and/or rediscovered ways to ensure a balanced ratio of people to the environment, without coercive national or international intervention. From an ecofeminist perspective we demand the exclusion of state interference in the sphere of reproduction.

Notes

1. Meadows, et al, *The Limits to Growth*. Universe Books, New York, 1972.
2. King, Maurice: 'Health is a Sustainable State,' in *Lancet*, 15 September, 1990, abridged version in *Third World Resurgence* No. 16, pp. 31-32.
3. Nafis Sadik (ed.) *The State of World Population* 1990. United Nations Population Fund (UNFPA), New York 1990, p. 10.
4. Ibid. pp. 1-2.

5. Ibid. p. 12.
6. Akhter, F., 'New Reasons to Depopulate the Third World,' in *Third World Resurgence*, No 16, pp. 21-23.
7. Duden, Barbara, 'Population,' in W. Sachs (ed), *Development Dictionary*. Zed Books, London 1992 p. 147.
8. Ibid.
9. Ibid., p. 148.
10. For a critique of this narrow and individualistic concept of 'reproductive rights' see F. Akhter: 'On the Question of Reproductive Right,' in Akhter, F. *Depopulating Bangladesh, Essays on the Politics of Fertility*. Narigrantha Prabartana, Dhaka, 1992, p. 33.
11. King, Maurice, *The Demographic Trap*.
12. Reddock, Rhoda, *A History of Women and Labour in Trinidad and Tobago*. Zed Books, London (forthcoming).
13. Gordon, Linda *Woman's Body, Woman's Right: A Social History of Birth Control in America*. Harmondsworth, Penguin, 1977 p. 25.
14. Wajcman, J. *Feminism Confronts Technology*. The Pennsylvania State University Press. Pennsylvania 1991, p. 76.
15. For a discussion of the witch-hunt and its impact on women see Mies, M. *Patriarchy and Accumulation on a World Scale: Women in the International Division of Labour*. Zed Books, London 1991.
16. Heinsohn G. and Steiger O. *Die Vernichtung der Weisen Frauen, Hexenverfolgung, Bevolkerungspolitik*. Marz-Verlag, Herbstein 1984.
17. Mussalam, B.F. *Sex and Society in Islam*, Cambridge University Press, Cambridge 1986.
18. Akhter, Farida, op. cit.
19. Dr Talwar in Bombay is one of the researchers who is working on the development of an anti-fertility vaccine. (See Video Documentary 'Something like a War' by Deepa Dhanraj and Abha Bhaiya.)
20. Vandana Shiva and Mira Shiva, 'Population and Environment: An Indian Perspective' in *Power, Population and the Environment: Women Speak*. WEED Foundation, Toronto 1992 (compiled by Gillian Philipps) pp. 43-51.
21. Akhter, F. op. cit. pp. 26-32.
22. Ibid., pp. 41-56.
23. Sadgopal, Mira, 'Fertility Awareness Education in the Context of Development Issues.' Paper presented at a Seminar on Women and Development, Pune University, 6 February 1992.

20. The Need for a New Vision: the Subsistence Perspective

Maria Mies

The Earth Summit in Rio de Janeiro (UNCED, June 1992) again made clear that solutions to the present worldwide ecological, economic and social problems cannot be expected from the ruling elites of the North or the South. As Vandana Shiva points out in this book, a new vision — a new life for present and future generations, and for our fellow creatures on earth — in which praxis and theory are respected and preserved can be found only in the survival struggles of grassroots movements. The men and women who actively participate in such movements radically reject the industrialized countries' prevailing model of capitalist-patriarchal development. They do not want to be developed according to this blueprint, but rather want to preserve their subsistence base intact, under their own control.

This quest for a new vision, however, is to be found not only among people in the South, who cannot ever expect to reap the fruits of 'development'; the search for an ecologically sound, non-exploitative, just, non-patriarchal, self-sustaining society can also be found among some groups in the North. Here, too, this search for a new perspective involves not only middle-class people, disenchanted and despairing about the end-result of the modernization process, but even by some at the bottom of the social pyramid.

We have called this new vision the *subsistence perspective,* or the *survival perspective.*

This concept was first developed to analyse the hidden, unpaid or poorly paid work of housewives, subsistence peasants and small producers in the so-called informal sector, particularly in the South, as the underpinning and foundation of capitalist patriarchy's model of unlimited growth of goods and money. Subsistence work as life-producing and life-preserving work in all these production relations was and is a necessary precondition for survival; and the bulk of this work is done by women.[1]

With increasing ecological destruction in recent decades, howver, it becomes obvious that this subsistence — or life production — was and is not only a kind of hidden underground of the capitalist market economy, it can also show the way out of the many impasses of this destructive system called industrial society, market economy or capitalist patriarchy.

This has become particularly clear since the alternative to capitalist industrialism, which the socialist version of catching-up development had provided, collapsed in Eastern Europe and what was the USSR. The socialist alternative had been a guiding star for many countries in the South. But it is now evident that the path of development pursued in these ex-socialist countries can no longer be seen as a blueprint for a better society. In their efforts to emulate the capitalist model of industrial society these systems caused greater environmental destruction than have their capitalist counterparts; their relationship to nature was based on the same exploitative principles as in the West. Furthermore, as Kurz points out, they were based on the same economic model of alienated, generalized commodity production first developed by capitalism[2] which, as we have shown elsewhere,[3] is based on the colonization of women, nature and other peoples. It is due to this inherent colonialism that this model of commodity-producing society is neither sustainable nor generalizable worldwide.

Kurz does not identify the inherent need for colonies in the capitalist or socialist versions of commodity-producing systems; rather he sees the reason for the breakdown of erstwhile 'Actually Existing Socialism' (AES) in the dilemma of generalized commodity production as such. Before trying to delineate the contours of a subsistence perspective as an alternative to generalized commodity production it may be useful to look again at the contradictions of this strange economic system which is now propagated as the only possible way of satisfying human needs.

The schizophrenia of commodity-producing societies

The logic of commodity-producing systems consists in the principle of surplus value production and the impetus for permanent growth. This logic is / was the same in both capitalist and AES-states, differing only in so far as in capitalist societies the surplus is accumulated privately and in the AES-countries it was accumulated by the state. In both systems people are in principle *subjects*, both as producers and as consumers. As producers they exchange their labour power for a wage (money); as consumers they exchange this money for commodities to satisfy their needs. In both systems there is a fundamental contradiction between production and consumption, because the sphere of production of commodities is principally separated from that of consumption by the sphere of circulation or the market.

But also the individuals, the economic subjects, are dichotomized into producers and consumers with contradictory interests. 'As producer the commodity-subject or exchange subject is not interested in the use-value of his products, irrespective of whether he is "worker" or "capitalist", capitalist manager or production-director in a "real" socialist unit. They do not produce for their own consumption but for an anonymous market. The objective of the whole enterprise is not the sensuous, direct satisfaction of needs but the transformation of work into money (wages, profit).'[4]

For the producer his own products are de-sensualized, have become abstract 'work-amalgams [gallerts]. . . because they are nothing but potential money.'[5] It makes no difference to them whether they produce Sachertortes or neutron bombs, writes Kurz. But as consumer, the same person has a quite opposite interest in the sensuous, concrete use-value of the things bought '. . . as individuals who eat, drink, need a house, wear clothes, people have to be sensuous . . .'[6]

It is this contradiction between production and consumption, between exchange and use-values, which is ultimately responsible for the destruction of nature in industrial, commodity-producing society. The exclusive concern of people as producers is maximizing the money output of their production and they will therefore continue to produce poisonous substances, nuclear power, weapons, more and more cars. But as consumers they want clean air, unpolluted food, and a safe place for their waste, far away from their home.

As long as production and consumption are structured in this contradictory way, inherent in generalized commodity production, no solution of the various economic, ecological and political/ethical/spiritual crises can be expected.

Some people think that the solution lies in substituting environmentally noxious substances, technologies and commodities with nature-friendly, life-preserving ones. They propose harnessing commodity production and market forces to the service of sustainable development, replacing the production and marketing of destructive goods by 'eco-marketing'. They want to mobilize funds from the corporate sector, even from those firms known for ruthless environmental pollution, to sponsor the activities of environmental organizations. But industry uses this eco-sponsoring more to improve its image than as a move to change their overall policy. The latest development in this Greening of Capitalism strategy is the initiative taken by Stephan Schmidtheiny, Swiss industrialist and billionaire, who founded and leads the Business Council for Sustainable Development — a group of 48 leading international industrialists — and who was advisor to Maurice Strong, the secretary of the 1992 UNCED in Rio. Schmidtheiny and this Business Council developed a strategy showing how industry should, in future, combine growth with ecologically sound production.[7] But the fundamentally contradictory relationships inherent in commodity production and consumption are not criticized. Nor is there a critique of the basic principles of capitalist production: individual self-interest, generalized competition and the system's need for permanent growth. On the contrary, eco-marketing and eco-sponsoring are seen as a new area of investment, a new opportunity to extend commodity production and marketing. Green capitalism will serve only to transform ever more parts of nature into private property and commodities.

A way out of this destructive and irrational system of commodity production cannot be found in catching-up development and technological fixes, even if technological alternatives could be quickly found to end and to repair some of the environmental damage caused by industrialism. Nowhere is this more clearly demonstrated than in East Germany, whose citizens had hoped to catch-up with West Germany when the Deutschemark (DM) was introduced and they became equal citizens in a unified Germany. Now even West German industry realizes it would take at least 20 years for the living standard of East Germany to equal that of West Germany.

But, as we argued in chapter 4 catching-up development is not even desirable. Nevertheless, this utopia of the modern industrial society is not fundamentally criticized even in those countries where it has already collapsed and a de-industrialization process has begun. This is the case in, for example, Peru, Argentina, Mexico, Brazil and many other countries of the South which tried to catch-up with the North through credit-based industrialization. These countries are now caught in the debt trap, victims of the structural adjustment policy of the World Bank and the IMF.

But this de-industrialization process has also begun in Eastern Europe, in the erstwhile Soviet Union and in Cuba whose economy and modernization policy was totally dependent on imports from and exports to the Soviet Union. Since the collapse of the USSR these imports, particularly of oil and machinery, stopped. Cuba now faces the dilemma either of becoming a neo-colony of the USA or of trying to survive economically and politically as an independent entity by reviving subsistence technologies and production.

To make up for the lack of oil, Fidel Castro imported 100,000 bicycles from China and replaced the tractors in agriculture by 100,000 oxen as draught animals. Some years ago, such 'going back' to pre-industrial methods of production would have been derided as impossible, particularly by so-called progressives. The survival of Cuba as an independent society will depend on whether the people can see this compulsory return to subsistence production as a chance rather than a defeat. But this would entail the people's acceptance of a different concept of socialism or of a 'good society', based on regional self-sufficiency, ecological sustainability and social equality.

While Cuba can still expect some international solidarity, this will hardly come forward for all those new nation states proclaiming their independence from the erstwhile Soviet Union: the Baltic States, the Ukraine, Georgia and others. Some of these, with the collapse of the socialist system of commodity production and distribution, are also forced to re-introduce self-provisioning, subsistence production and technology in agriculture, like using horses instead of tractors, producing for their own community instead of for an anonymous market.

Such survival strategies are also the only way out of the de-industrialization crisis in Africa. But unlike the post-socialist societies in Eastern Europe most sub-Saharan African societies cannot assume that de-industrialization and enforced de-modernization is only a temporary affair and that the 'world community' — 20 per cent of the world's rich nations — will come to their rescue. Countries such as Ethiopia, Somalia, Mozambique are already facing mass starvation. Some African leaders have apparently understood that they can no longer expect anything from the catching-up development strategy, particularly after the East-West detente. They see that money will now flow towards the East rather than to starving Africa.

At a conference at the University of Dar es Salaam in December

1989, representatives of the academic community, churches, trade unions, women's organizations, NGOs, students and government officials across the African continent discussed alternative development strategies, particularly after the new East-West detente which leads to an 'involuntary de-linking' of Africa from the aid and trade flows of the world-market. At the end of the conference the participants adopted the Dar es Salaam Declaration: Alternative Development Strategies for Africa.[8]

After condemning the IMF and World Bank strategy of enforcing harsh conditionalities on African debtor countries in pursuance of Structural Adjustment Programmes and after calling for the cancellation of all debts, the Conference stressed that African governments should adopt Alternative Development Strategies, based on:

> People-centred development, popular democracy and so-
> cial justice on the basis of effective African integration at
> sub-regional and regional levels as well as South-South
> Cooperation. This re-orientation of African development
> should focus on planned disengagement from interna-
> tional capitalism, regional food self-sufficiency, satisfac-
> tion of basic needs for all, development from below
> through the termination of anti-rural bias as well as con-
> centration on relevant small and medium scale enter-
> prises.[9]

Conference participants were able, it seems, to transform the 'involuntary delinking from the capitalist world market' into a voluntary new social, economic and political/cultural strategy in which self-reliance, self-provisioning, food self-sufficiency, regionality, the need for re-ruralization, participatory democracy, inter-regional co-operation are the key concepts.

This Declaration contains many of the structural elements which I would consider necessary for a subsistence perspective. Conference participants understood that for Africa, catching-up development or industrialization according to the World Bank model is neither possible nor desirable. Conversely, a subsistence perspective, which would not be based on the colonization of women, nature and other peoples, can show a way forward for Africa and other countries of the South, as well as for the North.

As mentioned earlier, the new vision of a non-exploitative, non-colonial, non-patriarchal society which respects, not destroys nature, did not emanate from research institutes, UN-organizations or governments, but from grassroots movements, in both the South and the North, who fought and fight for survival. And in these movements it is women who more than men understand that a subsistence perspective is the only guarantee of the survival of all, even of the poorest, and not integration into and continuation of the industrial growth system.

Many recent studies on the impact of ecological deterioration on women, particularly the poorest women in the South, have highlighted not only the fact that women and children are the main victims of this war against nature but also that women are the most active, most creative, and most concerned and committed in movements for conservation and protection of nature and for healing the damage done to her.[10] While women's role as 'saviours of the environment' may be welcomed by many, including those who want to combine sustainability of eco-systems with permanent economic growth, few voices emphasize that these grassroots women's movements also implicitly and explicitly criticize the prevailing capitalist, profit and growth-oriented, patriarchal development paradigm and that they advocate a new alternative; a subsistence alternative.

This perspective was most clearly spelt out by the women of the Chipko Movement, who in Vandana Shiva's interview with some of its leaders in Garwhal (chapter 16) clearly said that they expect nothing from 'development' or from the money economy. They want only to preserve their autonomous control over their subsistence base, their common property resources: the land, water, forests, hills. From history and their own experience they know that their survival (their bread) as well as their freedom and dignity — all essentials for survival — can be maintained only as long as they have control over these resources. They do not need the money offered by the government or the industrialists to survive. Their concept of freedom and the good life differs from that offered by the global supermarket of the capitalist patriarchal industrial system. Remarkably, even their sons are not fascinated by this supermarket model unlike many young men in the South who are the first to be lured by the promises of the market and money economy. Few men today are ready to say: my mother's dignity cannot be bought with money.

The conflict between a subsistence and survival, and a market and money perspective is frequently a source of conflict between men and women, even in some of the Chipko struggles. Whereas the women participated in hugging the trees and wanted to preserve their subsistence base, their men wanted modernization and waged work. They also objected to their women having become leaders in this movement. Gopal Joshi reports about one Chipko struggle in Dungari Paitoali, where the women opposed a development project to establish a potato seed farm that would entail felling 50 ha of the village's common forest. The leading men of the village, however, favoured the project and the money it would bring. They spread ill-natured rumours about the women activists, and were particularly angry that the women challenged their role as village leaders. But the women claimed their right to leadership because of their responsibility for daily survival. They said:

> As the men do not collect fuel or fodder they are not concerned about the maintenance of the forests. They are more interested to earn money, even if they have to cut trees for that. But the forests are the women's wealth.[11]

Elsewhere in the world too, women are more concerned about a survival subsistence perspective than are men, most of whom continue to believe that more growth, technology, science and 'progress' will simultaneously solve the ecological and economic crises; they place money and power above life. At a conference on women and ecology in Sweden in February 1992 a Samo woman, reporting on tribal people's efforts to create global networks and groups, said that at such global gatherings the men were mainly interested in competing for political power in the organization, whereas the women's concern centred on preserving their cultural and survival base, independent of governmental or NGO development programmes. Vandana Shiva also observed this women/men opposition at the conference: 'What it Means to be Green in South Africa' (September 1992), organized by the ANC. While the male leaders and speakers seemed to expect South Africa's economic and ecological problems to be solved through full integration into the growth-oriented world economy, the women, who had so far borne the burden of modernization and development, were much more sceptical. One 60-year-old woman said that, 'The (government's) betterment scheme has been the best strategy to push us into the depth of poverty. It accelerated the migratory system.'

The men were forced to migrate to the cities in search of jobs, whereas the women, together with the old and the children, had to try to survive in the rural areas. Meanwhile, the white government destroyed all assets and possessions by which the women tried to maintain their subsistence: 'We were dispossessed of our goats, donkeys and other animals. They were taken away by force and we got only 20 cents as compensation per head.'

This woman had experienced the contradictory impact of 'betterment' or development as the government understood it. She knew that some must always pay the price for this development and that usually its victims are the women. Therefore she was not enthusiastic about further integration of the new non-racist, democratic South Africa into the world market. Rather she demanded land and the security of independent subsistence. (*Source:* Vandana Shiva.)

One reason why women are becoming increasingly critical of modern development and integration into the world market is the recognition that this has led to more and more violence against women, particularly in areas where it was successful. For example, in India's Green Revolution areas, like the Punjab, women's deaths due to dowry-killings increased together with the new affluence; female foeticide after amniocentesis also increases with the new wealth in these regions.[12]

In the industrialized North too, many women's projects and initiatives implicitly or explicitly seek to develop an alternative to the destructive patriarchal and capitalist system. These groups sprang up in the course of the women's, peace, and ecology movements, which found campaigns and protests not enough but wanted to put their beliefs into practice. We have already mentioned the Seikatsu Club in Japan, started by housewives after the Minamata disaster. There are many such producer-consumer cooperatives in the North, started or led by women. Several feminist groups have gone to the countryside and sought to build up a self-sufficient subsistence base as gardeners, sheep farmers, or handicraft workers. A group of unemployed women in Cologne initiated a scheme to exchange things with each other rather than to buy new ones. Feminist architects and city planners are devising plans to make cities livable again for women and children, and that means bringing nature back into the cities. They experiment with permaculture and food production, while others are thinking of reclaiming the commons, also in the cities, not only for recreation but for food production for the poor. There are also more comprehensive and global initiatives actively opposed to the growth and profit oriented system. For example, the efforts of Hazel Henderson[13] to establish an alternative economy, Marilyn

Waring's[14] critique of the concept of work, prevalent in capitalist industrial society, or Margrit Kennedy's[15] proposal, following Gsell, to strip money of its 'productive' capacity to produce ever more money, namely through interest.

To subsume all these practical and theoretical efforts to find an alternative to the existing destructive system under the rubic 'subsistence perspective' would be incorrect; many differences exist, in detail and perhaps also in perspective. But there is a commonality in these initiatives: the need for a qualitative, not simply a quantitative change in what we are accustomed to call the economy. Men, increasingly, also begin to understand that an ecologically sound, just, women-and-children friendly, peaceful society cannot be built up by a continuation of the growth oriented industrial society.

Rather than developing an abstract model (some of whose main principles and features I have spelt out earlier)[16] I shall present two accounts of how people have tried to put this subsistence perspective into practice. One, in the South, is the case of a people's movement towards water preservation and subsistence in India. The other is an account of a commune in Germany which tries to solve the ecological problem of waste disposal within the framework of a subsistence perspective. These are particular cases, but they encapsulate the main elements of a society which is no longer based on industrialism and generalized commodity production for profit, permanent growth and consumerism.

Peoples' dams: the Baliraja Dam, India. Projects for the construction of mega-dams in many Southern countries is one strategy designed to harness nature's resources in the service of modern industrial development. These projects have been opposed almost everywhere by strong, peoples' movements, particularly of peasants, tribals and others whose ancestral lands and livelihood bases will be flooded or submerged by these dams. Ecologically concerned people also oppose the construction of these dams because, in most cases, primeval forests, ancient temples, ecologically and culturally unique areas will be destroyed forever by these 'temples of modernity' as Nehru called the big dams. One of the better-known resistance movements is that against the Narmada Valley Project (NVP) in India, a mega-project financed by the World Bank. It is the biggest of its kind in the world, with two very large and 28 major dams to be constructed on the river Narmada. The benefits projected are: the irrigation of more than

2.2 million ha of land; the production of electric power, particularly for Gujarat's industrial cities; and the supply of drinking water. All the benefits would accrue to people and interest groups outside the flood area, but the costs would be borne by the environment and the 200,000 tribal people who will be displaced by the flooding of their ancestral land. The campaign against the NVP, the Narmada Bachao Andolan, stresses that these victims of the NVP cannot expect any adequate compensation or resettlement and will only increase the masses of migrants and beggars who eventually end up in the slums of the big cities. Moreover, damage to the forests, wildlife, species diversity and risks due to waterlogging, siltation and salination cannot be calculated even now.[17]

This movement against the NVP is supported by middle-class social activists like Medha Patkar and Baba Amte and many urban-based concerned people. Apart from such movements there have for several years been initiatives seeking an alternative solution to the water and energy problems of drought-prone areas in India, solutions which would restore both the ecological and social balance without sacrificing the future for short-term present gains.

The Peoples' Dams movement in Khanapur in Sangli district in Maharashtra is an outcome of this search for alternative water management, stemming from an alternative concept of development; this movement started during the prolonged textile workers' strike in Bombay. Many who returned to their villages in search of support for the strike, found that for several years the people of Khanapur had been suffering from severe drought, crop failures and water shortage. Before the strike these workers had tried to help their villages by sending money home to build or repair temples. But, as Bharat Patankar points out, they showed scant solidarity with the poor peasants, the class from which they originated. The simultaneous strike and drought situation changed this. In order to survive, returned textile workers tried to get work on the government's Employment Guarantee Scheme (EGS). Trade unions in India, as in other countries of the South, have no big strike funds to support workers during long strikes. Nevertheless, the Bombay textile workers continued their strike against the introduction of technology to replace labour for more than a year.

An organization of the workers and poor, landless peasants — the Mukti Sangarsh — was formed which successfully agitated for proper wages and against corruption on the EGS schemes. Whereas other trade unions and political parties demanded that EGS workers be given the same status as other regular permanent workers, they argued that drought had become almost a regular feature in their area and that EGS-work should be seen as regular work. The Mukti Sangarsh and the people, in the belief that droughts should be eradicated, then began to study the reasons for their recurrence. They asked older people what had been the situation in their time and found that the three rivers through Khanapur Taluka had flowed perennially until the 1970s; there were also sufficient wells and enough water. Today these rivers, particularly the biggest, are dry sand-beds with occasional flows during the monsoon. What had happened? Since the 1980s private contractors had excavated sand from the dried-up river-beds and sold it to construction firms in the cities. Consequently, water percolation was further reduced and the wells dried up.

Moreover, since the mid-1970s this area had been transformed from more or less subsistence-oriented agriculture to Green Revolution capitalist farming. Old subsistence crops like *bajra* and *jowar* (millets) were replaced by commercial crops like sugar-cane, which not only need chemical fertilizers and pesticides, but also vast quantities of water. In this process the old farming methods disappeared. The peasants became dependent on seed, fertilizer and chemical companies, on banks and market fluctuations. Due to the compulsions to produce for the market, small peasants became increasingly indebted and many had to migrate to the city in search of work. The big farmers survived and used up most of the water. This agro-industrial development was supported by the Maharashtra government because it had a stable vote base in the area.

The Mukti Sangarsh and the Peoples' Science Organization of Maharashtra organized science fairs and discussions in the villages during which people studied water management from an historical perspective. The old cropping methods, the geological conditions and the vegetation of the area were also examined and viable schemes for an alternative agriculture were proposed.

It was decided that the people would refuse to do the stone-breaking, road-building and such like tasks the government's Food for Work programmes provided in times of drought, which also provided cheap labour for road extensions and other similar infrastructural projects. The EGS workers insisted that their labour be used productively towards eradicating drought in their area.

After a conference on drought organized in 1985 peasants of two villages produced a plan to build a peoples' dam, the Baliraja dam. They also demonstrated at Kolhapur University, demanding that scientists and students should help the drought-affected peasants. As a result a Drought Eradication Committee was formed, and professors and students helped with surveys.

Controlling their own resources: To finance construction of the dam the people decided that they themselves would sell a small quantity of sand from the Yerala river bed; according to law, the sand in the rivers belongs to the government. They also wanted to stop all commercial sand excavation by outside contractors. In November 1986, the construction of the dam began. College students made a 40 days' camp and offered their voluntary labour together with the free labour of the peasant. Sympathizers in Bombay and Pune collected about Rs 100,000 as interest-free loans.

The government opposed construction of the dam, arguing that the peoples' estimate of Rs 700,000 was insufficient to cover the costs and that at least Rs 2,800,000 would be needed; moreover, their water estimates were incorrect. The people, however, persisted, emphasizing the ecological advantages of a small dam like theirs; the need for water preservation; the prevention of wells drying up, and so on. They demanded no help from the government, except its permission to build the dam and stop commercial excavation of their sand.

They received the government sanction in 1988 and in 1990 the dam was completed. The Baliraja Dam is an example of how people can use their own resources and at the same time conserve the ecological balance. They take from nature but they also give back to nature.

A new water distribution system: In discussing their water problems the people had identified that one reason for recurring droughts was the unequal water distribution system that prevailed so far: those who possessed most land also got most water to irrigate their commercial crops. Water collected in the Baliraja Dam, however was, from the beginning, to be distributed equitably, based on the following principles:

- Water as a resource belongs to everybody and must be distributed on a per capita basis, not on a land-holding basis.
- Every person, including landless people and women, to receive the same share.

- Landless people can either lease land on a share-cropping basis and use their water share or lease it out or sell it.
- Each water share costs Rs 10, or is equivalent to one day's *shramdan* (free labour) on the dam site.

Consequently, no sugar-cane may be grown on the fields irrigated by the Baliraja Dam water, because it needs too much.[18]

Thus, the people not only wanted to regain control over their own resources and restore the ecological balance in their area, they also began to change the unequal social relationships between the classes and genders. For the first time women received a share in a resource which actually belongs to everyone and to nature.

A new cropping system — and an alternative agriculture: The Mukti Sangarsh Movement also wanted to change the socially and ecologically disastrous capitalist farming system. A new cropping system was proposed in which the various resources — land, water, different species — should be used to facilitate an ecologically, socially and economically sustainable system. The crops, the land and the water should be divided in an alternative way: a family of five would possess an average of three acres of land (which is the average in Maharashtra).

K.J. Joy, one of the Mukti Sangarsh activists explained this new cropping pattern, particularly the cultivation of bio-mass:

It is now a well-established fact that if bio-mass production is integrated with subsistence crop production and with judicious use of water, the productivity of the marginal farmers could be increased substantially, sustainable over a period of time, could give security in meeting subsistence needs and can also reduce cash inputs needed for agriculture. Surpluses of fuelwood, timber and fodder could be created over and above the production and consumption needs, thus bringing in some non-agricultural income. Nearly 20-40 per cent of the bio-mass (leaf, brush-wood etc) has an important role to play as input in the agro-subsystem. It serves as fodder and/or fertilizer. . . produce from the agro-subsystem and tree crops would (also) serve as a base for decentralized and agro-based industrial development.[19]

In the course of the movement for people's dams, people not only re-evaluated their old subsistence knowledge and skills, but also began to question the role of science and technology in the 'development' of apparently backward areas, and when the people are treated as passive and ignorant. In this movement the people participated fully in developing an alternative technology, and scientists and engineers who supported the movement were able to use the peoples' knowledge creatively as well as combine it with modern science. The project of a new, decentralized agro-based industry (see quote above) is inspired by the new insights for an ecological use of biomass, not only as fertilizer or pesticide or in new agricultural methods like those of Fukuoka, Jean Paine or Bill Mollison, but also as raw material for manufacturing items for which so far non-renewable energy sources and raw material have been used. Thus, for example, bio-mass, fly-ash and small timber could be used to create a concrete substitute, called geocrete. Another new category of synthetic materials is biomass-based filter-fabrics called geofabrics, which can be used for drainage and seepage control.

The development of new biomass-based materials and technologies is intended not only to provide substitutes for imported, energy intensive and non-renewable resources but also to facilitate the integration of social organization, of people's active participation in the development of knowledge and community work, and in the re-creation of an ecologically and economically sustainable livelihood. Even engineers who supported the Peoples' Dams movement clearly saw the need for such an integrated approach.[20]

The Baliraja Dam in Khanapur is evidence of the fruitfulness of such a subsistence-oriented, integrated, synergic approach in which the key elements are:

- social organization of the people;
- recovery of their subsistence knowledge and skills;
- active participation in the development process;
- a serious attempt to change structures of social inequality and exploitation, including sexual inequality and exploitation;
- a critique of mainstream science and technology and the development of locally based, ecologically sustainable alternatives;
- an effort to end further privatization of the commons, and instead, a move to recreate community control over common resources like water, sand, and so on.

These component parts of an integrative strategy are all centred around the main goal of this approach: to regain self-reliance and subsistence security, that is, to become ecologically, socially and economically more independent from external market forces.

From garbage to subsistence

Phase 1: From students' movement to squatter movement: The Sozialistische Selbsthilfe Köln (SSK) is one of the oldest self-help initiatives in Cologne (Germany); its beginning dates back to the Students Movement in the early 1970s. Inspired by Herbert Marcuse's argument that the 'revolution', the alternative to capitalist, industrial society, could no longer be expected from the working class in industrialized, affluent societies, but rather from drop-outs, marginalized groups and the colonized in the Third World, a group of students in Cologne initiated a scheme whose objective was to give shelter to youngsters who had run away from authoritarian homes, remand homes or even prisons. They claimed that they could offer a better education and better prospects for life to these young people than could the establishment institutions. Their initiative was originally called *Sozialpädagogische Sondermassnahme Köln* (Special Social-Pedagogical Measures, Cologne) and they laid down a set of principles according to which anybody would be accepted in their commune. Initially, the project was supported by the Social Welfare Department of the Municipality of Cologne, who not only gave a house to the SSK but also agreed to pay the same amount for a boy or a girl, which they would have paid to a remand home. Eventually however, it became evident that this project was too expensive for the municipality. Moreover, neighbours began to protest against the SSK, which accepted everybody, including alcoholics and drug addicts.

When, in 1974, the Social Welfare Department decided to close down the SSK, the group, which then consisted of about 100 people, found temporary political asylum in the *Fachhochschule Köln* in the Department of Social Pedagogy and Social Work.

The question then arose of whether the SSK could survive without the municipality's financial support. About 30 people decided to continue the SSK and to depend only on their own work and the help of friends and sympathizers. They henceforth changed the name to: Sozialistische Selbsthilfe Köln (Socialist Self-Help, Cologne, SSK) and laid down a series of strict rules for all who wished to become members. The most important of these were:

- No money is accepted from the state, not even social welfare money. Self-reliance is the main principle.
- Everybody, men and women must work for the livelihood of all. Every morning this work is distributed by the whole commune.
- All income is pooled and distributed equally.
- No violence (beating, harassing etc.) is allowed within the SSK.
- No drugs and alcohol are allowed.
- Everybody must participate in political work and actions.
- The SSK has no leadership. All problems are discussed in plenary sessions and decisions are taken according to the consensus principle

The SSK-commune saw these rules and principles not only as necessary for their own survival but also as the beginning of a truly socialist society in which both the capitalist and the centralist and bureaucratic socialist models of society, then prevailing in Eastern Europe, were to be transcended. They saw their own commune as a model of such a society.

For their livelihood the SSK did various odd jobs, such as: transporting coal; collecting and re-selling old furniture, clothes or household equipment; repair jobs; cleaning houses; gardening, and so on. They virtually lived off the garbage of our rich society.

The SSK's political activities centred around the problems created by the modernization strategy of the commercial community and the city planners, which penalized mainly the poor, the elderly, and foreign workers. Due to this policy of transforming the city centre of Cologne into a complex of banks, insurance and business centres, older and cheaper housing areas were destroyed and their inhabitants pushed to the (more expensive) city periphery. For many years the SSK-commune was in the forefront of the squatter movement in Cologne, which fought against the destruction of old, cheap neighbourhoods.

Another important political struggle centred around the inhuman conditions which prevailed in many state-run psychiatric clinics. By publicly exposing these conditions and offering shelter in their commune to patients who had run away from these institutions, they initiated a wide critical debate on Germany's psychiatric system, forced the authorities to close one of the more notorious clinics and start reforming the others.

In these and many other political struggles the SSK's strength lay in its potential for quick, direct, non-bureaucratic action, innovative publicity by means of wall-newspapers, a direct link between action and reflection, and their commitment to live by their own strength and be open to all the downtrodden, the social 'garbage' of our industrial society. Over the years the SSK became well-known and through its struggles gained considerable power. The bureaucrats in CologneTown Hall feared SSK exposures and often gave in to their demands. Five new SSK centres, which followed the same principles, were eventually created in the region around Cologne.

Phase 2: From Chernobyl to the ecology question and the discovery of subsistence: About 1986, after the meltdown at Chernobyl, the SSK-commune became aware of the ecology problem. They began to question their model of socialism and asked themselves what was its use in an environment poisoned and polluted by radioactivity and other toxic wastes of industrial society. They held many discussions on how to change the SSK in order to contribute to a more ecologically sound society. But they failed to arrive at a consensus, and the organization faced a grave crisis, while several members left the commune.

Around this time my friend Claudia v. Werlhof and I organized a conference at the Evangelische Akademie, Bad Boll — Die Subsistenzperspektive, ein Weg ins Freie (The Subsistence Perspective — a Path into the Open). The conference's objective was to bring together activists and theoreticians from the women's movement, the alternative and ecology movements and the Third World in order to clarify our ideas about a possible common strategy or perspective: the Subsistence Perspective. Three members of the SSK were also invited because I felt that they had practised this perspective for years. This conference later proved to have indeed opened a 'path into the open' for the SSK, because not only did the three activists discover the global interconnections between their own work and ideals and such diverse movements as a peasants' movement in Venezuela, the peoples' struggles against modernization and industrialization in Ladakh, the Chipko movement in India, but they also discovered the richness encapsulated in the concept subsistence. They realized that it encompassed what they had been aspiring to during all those years. In an SSK brochure called 'Land in Sight' Lothar Gothe (one of SSK's founders) and Maggie Lucke defined the concept as follows:

The word (subsistence) is derived from the Latin word *subsistere*, which has several meanings: "to stand still, to make a halt, to persist, to resist, to stay back, to remain backward." Today the word means: "to be able to live on (by) the basic (minimum) necessities of life" or: "to exist and sustain oneself by one's own strength".

Today we include all these meanings and connotations when we talk of the Subsistence Perspective as the way out, the emergency exit out of our blockaded, overgrown, industrial society.

To live according to the guiding star of subsistence means no longer to live off the exploitation of the environment or of foreign peoples. For human life it means a new balance between talking and giving, between each one of us and other people, our people and other peoples, our species and the other species in nature. . .[21]

Phase 3: From garbage to compost: The Subsistence Conference at Bad Boll not only meant the discovery of a new guiding concept but also the beginning of a new process in which their old utopia could be re-created within a new ecological framework. Through a friend present at this conference, the three SSK activists came into contact with a biologist, Peter van Dohlen who had developed a method to make compost out of organic kitchen waste in closed containers. He had tried in vain to persuade the Green Party of Cologne to propagate this compost-technology, which was particularly appropriate for cities. When the three activists met Peter it was a meeting of people who, left to themselves, had begun to despair and saw no way out of their crisis. But by coming together and exchanging ideas a new and creative process started which is still on-going. To make a long story short: the technology developed by Peter provided the SSK with a new type of meaningful, self-sustaining ecological work, while for him, here at last were people who grasped the significance of his compost-making technology and, as a collective, were ready to work to make it function. Having adapted an old oil container for compost-making, the SSK people collected kitchen garbage from their neighbourhood in Gummersbach and experimented with it. The result was excellent: within three weeks kitchen garbage could be transformed into compost. In addition they also learned Jean Paine's method, whereby biomass from tree branches, shrubs and hedges is used not only to generate heat in a bio-generator but can also be used to restore soil fertility.

At the same time, in accordance with their principles of combining practical, manual subsistence work with political work, the SSK approached the municipal authorities in cities and towns where they had branches, and demanded contracts for SSK groups to make compost out of household organic waste. They demanded to be paid a sum equal to that paid by citizens for the dumping of their household garbage — at present this is almost 300DM per ton. The struggle for contracts lasted several years, but the SSK had already begun work and their compost project gained more and more support from the people.

The political significance of this project is that a new, cheap, people-controlled ecological technology was developed to return the bio-mass (kitchen garbage) back to the soil as compost, instead of simply dumping or burning it, and thus further polluting the environment. From the beginning, Lothar Gothe clearly saw the strategic importance of the waste problem to which industrial society has no solution. What consumerist society calls waste to be rid of as soon as possible, is raw material for a newly emerging waste disposal industry; the more waste produced the better for this industry. The main waste-disposal industrialist in the area who holds a monopoly of this industry, Edelhoff, had contracts with all the municipalities to collect all household waste, including organic waste. The SSK, by claiming this waste which constitutes about 40 per cent of the household garbage, effectively resisted the privatization and the destruction of valuable bio-mass, a common resource, for the sake of profit-making.

Today the SSK has composting contracts in Cologne and four other towns and municipalities. It is noteworthy that the municipal council of Gummersbach has agreed to change its contract with Edelhoff and to extend the SSK's contract to 400 more households. The municipal authorities have apparently begun to understand that the industrial disposal of waste and kitchen garbage cannot be a solution. Despite their initial resistance they are now in favour of such groups as the SSK.

Phase 4: From compost to subsistence agriculture: From the beginning the SSK had stressed the interconnections between the various problems with which they dealt: joblessness; the ecology problem; the inanity of most work; a sense of futility; loneliness; health problems; lack of dignity and recognition; overconsumption and addictions, and so on. Therefore also in their practical, political work similar also synergetic solutions should be sought.

A logical continuation of the composting process was that some SSK-groups began to look around for land, for compost belongs to the land, as Lothar Gothe said. At first the SSK sold the compost in Green shops, to gardeners and others, but it became clear that not enough city- or townspeople needed or wanted it. What then to do with the compost?

A piece of waste land in a valley called 'Duster Grundchen' was therefore acquired — privately purchased but used communely. For the first time some SSK members who, so far, knew only an urban existence began to work on the land; cleaning; laying out an experimental plot; looking after the bio-generator and so on. For the first time these urbanites began to experience the joy of doing hard, manual but ecologically meaningful work on the land, in co-operation with nature. Some of the SSK Gummersbach's younger members were so enthusiastic that they would walk 15 km from Gummersbach to work in this valley.

For Lothar Gothe the question was, could this ecological subsistence work be accepted not only by the SSK members but eventually provide a solution for society at large? Because only if people began to *understand* the significance and the need for this work on the land and to *enjoy doing it* could this approach have a future. *The combination of work as a burden and work as pleasure* is a necessary precondition for healing both the earth and society.

Work in the Duster Grundchen, the logical continuation of the strategy of consumption critique, the use of organic garbage for compost-making, began to reveal the interconnected character of the holistic social and ecological approach we called 'subsistence perspective'.

It not only sparked off a new sense of enthusiasm, enjoyment, meaningfulness, political and personal purpose in SSK members and others, particularly some younger people, but also a new wave of reflection, theorizing and political creativity. In a paper produced in this process of action and reflection sent to the chairman of the local authority (Regierungspräsident), Lothar Gothe pointed out that neither the government nor any official party had succeeded in solving so many interrelated problems in one single project, namely: combining ecological with social problem-solving; healing the earth as well as people and communities by creating meaningful work, giving a new sense of purpose to socially marginalized women and men; developing a new, appropriate technology out of discarded, obsolete objects; recultivating wasteland; re-establishing a new community-sense among people who are concerned and feel responsible for the future of life on this planet; and finally, creating new hope not only for those directly involved in the project but for many who have lost a sense of orientation.

It is this project's *synergic* character which was not planned but which developed out of necessity and which guarantees its survival. Had it been developed as a monocultural one-issue project, planned by experts, it could not have survived.

Guided by the subsistence perspective and the need to get enough hay for the animals, the next step was to buy an old farmhouse and repair the old equipment for subsistence production. At the same time the group secured a contract for composting the kitchen garbage for a series of villages. This compost is used as fertilizer in the new fields and gardens where experimental organic farming is carried out to produce vegetables for the SSK workers on the farm. Chickens, pigs, ducks, goats, sheep and a horse which pulls a cart to collect garbage, are kept on the farm. At present about six to eight people can live by this subsistence work.

Conclusion

In summarizing the main features of the subsistence perspective which has informed and inspired the initiatives described above, as well as many ecological and feminist grassroots movements referred to in this book, we can see that these struggles for survival are a practical critique not only of an aggressive, exploitative, ecologically destructive technology, but of commodity-producing, growth-oriented capitalist, or socialist industrial systems. Although none of these movements, initiatives, communities have spelt out a full-fledged explicit new utopia for an ecologically sound, feminist, non-colonial, non-exploitative society there is enough evidence in their practice and theory to show that their concept of a 'good society' differs from the classical Marxian utopia. While Marx and his followers saw capitalism as the 'midwife' of the 'material base' upon which a socialist society could be built, these movements and initiatives demonstrate their rejection of the universal supermarket as a model of a better society, even if it was equally accessible to all. Neither do they accept Engel's statement that what is good for the ruling class should be good for everybody.[22] These women's and men's concept of what constitutes a 'good life', of 'freedom' is different, as is their concept of economics, politics and culture. Their utopia may not yet be spelt out explicitly, but its components are already being tested in everyday practice, it is a potentially *concrete utopia*. What are the main characteristics of this subsistence perspective?

1. The aim of *economic activity* is not to produce an ever-growing mountain of commodities and money (wages or profit) for an anonymous market but the creation and re-creation of *life,* that means, the satisfaction of fundamental human needs mainly by the production of use-values not by the purchase of commodities. Self-provisioning, self-sufficiency, particularly in food and other basic needs; regionality; and decentralization from a state bureaucracy are the main economic principles. The local and regional resources are used but not exploited; the market plays a subordinate role.

2. These economic activities are based on new *relationships:* a) to *nature:* nature is respected in her richness and diversity, both for her own sake and as a precondition for the survival of all creatures on this planet. Hence, nature is not exploited for the sake of profit, instead, wherever possible, the damage done to nature by capitalism is being healed. Human interaction with nature is based on respect, co-operation and reciprocity. Man's domination over nature — the principle that has guided Northern society since the Renaissance — is replaced by the recognition that humans are part of nature, that nature has her own subjectivity.

b) *Among people.* As man's domination over nature is related to man's domination over women and other human beings[23] a different, non-exploitative relationship to nature cannot be established without a change in human relationships, particularly between *women and men.* This means not only a change in the various *divisions of labour* (sexual division; manual/mental and urban/rural labour, and so on) but mainly the substitution of money or commodity relationships by such principles as reciprocity, mutuality, solidarity, reliability, sharing and caring, respect for the individual and responsibility for the 'whole'. The need for *subsistence security* is satisfied not by trust in one's bank account or a social welfare state, but by trust in the reliability of one's community. A subsistence perspective can be realized only within such a network of reliable, stable human relations, it cannot be based on the atomized, self-centred individuality of the market economy.

3. A subsistence perspective is based on and promotes participatory or grassroots' democracy — not only in so far as political decisions per se are concerned, but also with regard to all economic, social and technological decisions. Divisions between politics and economics, or public and private spheres are largely abolished. The personal is the political. Not only the parliament

but also everyday life and life-style are battlefields of politics. Political responsibility and action is no longer expected solely from elected representatives but assumed by all in a communal and practical way.

4. A subsistence perspective necessarily requires a multidimensional or synergic problem-solving approach. It is based on the recognition that not only the different dominance systems and problems are interconnected, but also that they cannot be solved in isolation or by a mere technological fix. Thus social problems (patriarchal relations, inequality, alienation, poverty) must be solved together with ecological problems. This interconnectedness of all life on earth, of problems and solutions is one of the main insights of ecofeminism.[24]

5. A subsistence perspective demands a new paradigm of science, technology and knowledge. Instead of the prevailing instrumentalist, reductionist science and technology — based on dualistic dichotomies which have constituted and maintain man's domination over nature, women and other people — ecologically sound, feminist, subsistence science and technology will be developed in participatory action with the people. Such a grass-roots, women and people-based knowledge and science will lead to a re-evaluation of older survival wisdom and traditions and also utilize modern knowledge in such a way that people maintain control over their technology and survival base. Social relations are not external to technology but rather incorporated in the artefacts as such. Such science and technology will therefore not reinforce unequal social relationships but will be such as to make possible greater social justice.

6. A subsistence perspective leads to a reintegration of culture and work, of work as both burden and pleasure. It does not promise bread without sweat nor imply a life of toil and tears. On the contrary, the main aim is happiness and a fulfilled life. Culture is wider than specialized activity exclusive to a professional elite — it imbues everyday life.

This also necessitates a reintegration of spirit and matter, a rejection of both mechanical materialism and of airy spirituality. This perspective cannot be realized within a dualistic worldview.

7. A subsistence perspective resists all efforts to further privatize, and/or commercialize the commons: water, air, waste, soil, resources. Instead it fosters common responsibility for these gifts of nature and demands their preservation and regeneration.

8. Most of the characteristics in the foregoing would also be

appropriate to the conception of an ecofeminist society. In particular, the practical and theoretical insistence on the interconnectedness of all life, on a concept of politics that puts everyday practice and experiential ethics, the consistency of means and ends, in the forefront. And yet, the two examples previously documented are not feminist projects in the narrow sense in which this term is often understood, namely, all-women initiatives in which men have no role to play. In fact, the initiators of these projects were men. In the ecofeminist movement there are many examples of women-only projects and initiatives. But the question is: can we conceive of a perspective for a better future society by concentrating only on women, or by building all-women islands within a capitalist-patriarchal ocean? As ecofeminists emphasize overcoming established dualisms and false dichotomies, as they want to put the interdependence of all life at the centre of a new ethic and politics,[25] it would be quite inconsistent to exclude men from this network of responsibility for the creation and continuation of life. Ecofeminism does not mean, as some argue, that women will clean up the ecological mess which capitalist-patriarchal men have caused; women will not eternally be the *Trummerfrauen* (the women who clear up the ruins after the patriarchal wars). Therefore, a subsistence perspective necessarily means men begin to share, *in practice,* the responsibility for the creation and preservation of life on this planet. Therefore, men must start a movement to redefine their identity. They must give up their involvement in destructive commodity production for the sake of accumulation and begin to share women's work for the preservation of life. In practical terms this means they have to share unpaid subsistence work: in the household, with children, with the old and sick, in ecological work to heal the earth, in new forms of subsistence production.

In this respect it is essential that the old sexist division of labour criticized by the feminists in the 1970s — that is, men become the theoreticians of the subsistence perspective while women do the practical work — is abolished. This division between mental and manual labour is contrary to the principles of a subsistence perspective. The two examples documented above are significant in this respect, in so far as they demonstrate that men have begun to see the importance of the need to overcome this dichotomy.

9. Moreover, if the dichotomy between life-producing and preserving and commodity-producing activities is abolished, if men acquire caring and nurturing qualities which have so far been

considered women's domain, and if, in an economy based on self-reliance, mutuality, self-provisioning, not women alone but men too are involved in subsistence production they will have neither time nor the inclination to pursue their destructive war games. A subsistence perspective will be the most significant contribution to the de-militarization of men and society. Only a society based on a subsistence perspective can afford to live in peace with nature, and uphold peace between nations, generations and men and women, because it does not base its concept of a good life on the exploitation and domination of nature and other people.

Finally, it must be pointed out that we are not the first to spell out a subsistence perspective as a vision for a better society. Wherever women and men have envisaged a society in which all — women and men, old and young, all races and cultures — could share the 'good life', where social justice, equality, human dignity, beauty and joy in life were not just utopian dreams never to be realized (except for a small elite or postponed to an after-life), there has been close to what we call a subsistence perspective. Kamla Bhasin, an Indian feminist who tried to spell out what 'sustainable development' could mean for all women in the world lists a number of principles of sustainability similar to the features of a subsistence perspective.[26] It is clear to her, as it is to many women and men who are not blind to the reality that we live in a limited world, that sustainability is not compatible with the existing profit- and growth-oriented development paradigm. And this means that the standard of living of the North's affluent societies cannot be generalized. This was already clear to Mahatma Gandhi 60 years ago, who, when asked by a British journalist whether he would like India to have the same standard of living as Britain, replied: 'To have its standard of living a tiny country like Britain had to exploit half the globe. How many globes will India need to exploit to have the same standard of living?'[27] From an ecological and feminist perspective, moreover, even if there were more globes to be exploited, it is not even desirable that this development paradigm and standard of living was generalized, because it has failed to fulfil its promises of happiness, freedom, dignity and peace, even for those who have profited from it.

Notes

1. Mies, Maria, et al, *Women: the Last Colony*, Zed Books, London, 1988; Mies, M. (1991) *Patriarchy and Accumulation on a World Scale: Women in the International Division of Labour*, Zed Books, London, 1991.
2. Kurz, R. *Der Kollaps der Modernisierung*, Vom Zusammenbruch des Kasernensozialismus zur Krise der Weltökonomie. Eichborn Verlag, Frankfurt, 1991.
3. Mies, et al, (1988) op. cit.
4. Kurz, op. cit. p.101.
5. Ibid.
6. Ibid., p.102.
7. Schmidtheiny, Stephan, *Changing Course — A Global Perspective on Development and Environment*. Massachusetts Institute of Technology, 1992.
8. Dar es Salaam Declaration: Alternative Development Strategies for Africa. Institute for African Alternatives (IFAA), London, 1989.
9. Ibid.
10. Dankelman I. and J. Davidson, *Women and Environment in the Third World. Alliance for the Future*. Earthscan Publications, London, 1988. Women's Feature Service (ed) *The Power to Change: Women in the Third World Redefine their Environment*. Kali for Women, New Delhi, 1992; Zed Books, London, 1993.
11. Joshi, Gopal (1988) Alltag im Himalya, in: Tüting, Ludmilla (ed), *Menschen, Bäume, Erosionen, Kahlschlag im Himalya; Wege aus der Zerstörung*. Der Grune Zweig, Lohrbach, pp.38-41.
12. Chhaya Datar reported the increase of violence against women in areas where development had led to more affluence among some sections of the rural people, at a seminar 'Challenges before Agriculture', University of Pune, 1-2 August, 1992.
13. Henderson, Hazel, *Creating Alternative Futures*. Pedigree Books, New York, 1978.
14. Waring, Marilyn, *If Women Counted*. Macmillan, London, 1989. See also: Mary Mellor, *Breaking the Boundaries: Towards a Feminist Green Socialism*. Virago Press, London, 1992.
15. Kennedy, Margrit, *Geld ohne Zinsen*. Goldmann, Munchen, 1992.
16. Mies, 1989, op cit.
17. Ekins, Paul, *A New World Order: Grassroots Movements for Global Change*. Routledge & Kegan Paul, London, 1992.
18. Joy, K. J. 'Baliraja Smruthi Dharan: The People's Dam. An Alternative Path to Development.' Unpublished paper, October, 1990. Patankar, Bharat,' Alternative Water Management: The Case of Baliraja Dam,' in: *Our Indivisible Environment. A Report of Perspectives*, Bangalore 1-7 October, 1990, pp.51-52. Personal communication, from K.R. Datye, Gail Omvedt and Bharat Patankar.
19. Joy, op. cit. p.7.
20. Datye, K.R. 'Opportunities for Sustainable Livelihoods in Semi-Arid Environment.' Paper presented at Expert Meeting on Vulnerability Generated by Water Scarcity in Semi-Arid Regions, Vadstena, Sweden, February, 1989.
21. Gothe, 'Lothar and Meggie Lucke, *Land in Sight*, Cologne, 1990.
22. Engels, Friedrich, 'Origin of the Family, Private Property and the State' in: Marx/Engels *Selected Works*, Vol 3, Progress Publishers, Moscow 1976.

23. Bookchin, Murray, *Toward an Ecological Society.* Black Rose Books, Montreal, Buffalo, 1986. Mies, 1991, op. cit. Ackelsberg, Martha and Irene Diamond, 'Is Ecofeminism a New Phase of Anarchism?' Paper presented at Eighth Berkshire Conference on the History of Women, Douglass College, New Brunswick, New Jersey, 8-10 June, 1990.
24. Ackelsberg and Diamond. op. cit.
25. Diamond, Irene and Gloria Feman-Orenstein, *Reweaving the World: The Emergence of Ecofeminism.* Sierra Club Books, San Francisco, 1990.
26. Bhasin, Kamla, 'Environment, Daily Life and Health: Women's Strategies for Our Common Future.' Speech at Fifth International Congress on Women's Health. Copenhagen, 25 August 1992.
27. Quoted by Kamla Bhasin, op. cit. p.11.

Index